A TRAILS BOOKS GUIDE

GREAT
WISCONSIN
WINTER WEEKENDS

CANDICE GAUKEL ANDREWS

D1237330

TRAILS BOOKS
Madison, Wisconsin

Library of Congress Control Number: 2006926045
ISBN-13: 978-1-931599-71-9
ISBN-10: 1-931599-71-8

Editor: Mark Knickelbine
Designer: Kathie Campbell
Cover Photo: John T. Andrews

Printed in the United States of America by Versa Press, Inc.
11 10 09 08 07 06   6 5 4 3 2 1

Trails Books, a division of Big Earth Publishing
923 Williamson Street • Madison, WI 53703
(800) 258-5830 • www.trailsbooks.com

DEDICATION

To Travis and Shane, my heart and soul;
to John, my solid footing in each new territory;
and to Dad, always my horizon.

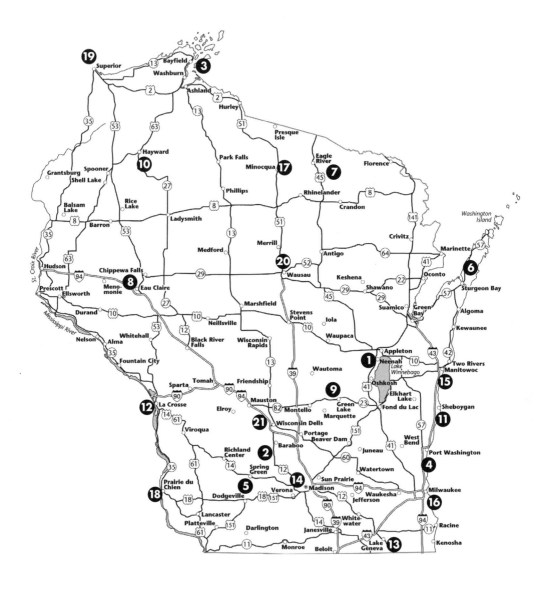

CONTENTS

PREFACE

WINTER IS an inward season; its quietness and reflectiveness have always appealed to me as a writer. People, when you do see them, are more apt to linger for a bit more conversation and talk about topics that go a degree or two deeper. Those things alone have always made me long for the last season of the year.

It often seems to me today that we try to erase weather if its extremes should fall just outside our comfort zone. We'd rather stay inside in a climatically controlled, year-round 70 degrees than go outside and experience real weather head on—never catching that first snowflake on our tongues or seeing the last of the ice break up on the river. These are things that should not be missed, but I fear sometimes we'll all miss them once global warming hits us hard. We should enjoy winter while we still have it.

As much as I have enjoyed winter over the years in my own backyard, while writing this book in the past year I have had the opportunity to get to know winter in ways I had never imagined. Traveling all over the state of Wisconsin on numerous great weekends, I discovered amazing new places where winter thrives and inspiring Wisconsinites who find innovative ways to celebrate and embrace the season.

I snowshoed Rib Mountain, the fourth highest peak in the state, on a beautiful, cold, and calm January Saturday in -20 degree weather and needed to take my jacket off in the effort. I saw no one else the whole time I was there, as if the whole state park were my very own. I hiked past quartzite rocks, glazed in ice, that sparkled so my sunglasses weren't enough protection to face them. The trees in the forest were close and tight, all legs. I heard them popping and cracking and making noises up in their heads high above me; I didn't know until then that trees had a language all their own and often talked among themselves. Two deer came out to see just what I was up to.

I toed the sidelines at the start of the largest cross-country ski race in the nation, the American Birkebeiner in Cable. Thousands of avid Nordic skiers and I sang "Wild Thing" as we waited for 10 "waves" to push off.

I stood on the shores of the mighty Mississippi River in Prairie du Chien in the last hour of December 31. I counted down the seconds with the happy people around me as a huge carp was lowered to ring in the New Year. The bonfire was so warm, I had to move away from the heat on a –5 degree night. Who could have guessed that kissing carp was a surefire way to bring you good luck all year?

I walked to the shore of Lake Michigan on another winter weekend and watched as Santa Claus arrived in the port town of Manitowoc on a "Christmas Tree Ship" that delivered trees just as it had 100 years ago. On another—but frozen—lake in Merrill, I watched dragsters race on the ice in an exciting show of speed. On another great lake, Lake Superior, I took a wild ride on a "windsled" on the state's only officially recognized road made of ice to an island at the other end.

I've stood in the sugar bush in Appleton and tasted 100 percent maple syrup next to the tree that gave it. At Mirror Lake, I fell asleep watching the stars in the only Frank Lloyd Wright–designed home in the world where you can lay your head down for the night.

I saw artists from all over the country sculpt intricate masterpieces from snow at the National Snow Sculpting Competition in Lake Geneva and the state competition in Wisconsin Dells. I saw the hands of nature, with the same artistic flair, sculpt fantastic ice caves in Bayfield. There, too, I cheered for the teams taking on the challenge of the Apostle Islands Sled Dog Race, the dogs' enthusiasm for the snow infecting all who could hear them.

I've been surprised by bald eagles in Wyalusing State Park who rose up from a cliff below me without a single sound of warning to fish where the Wisconsin and Mississippi rivers meet. For such large birds, they are amazingly quiet and inspired the same respectful silence in me.

For five months, I traveled through Wisconsin, looking to find winter. Not the season, but the spirit of it. I did. I hope you will, too.

C. G. A.
Sun Prairie, Wisconsin
January 1, 2006

ACKNOWLEDGMENTS

A NY GUIDEBOOK such as this one is a collaborative effort. It wouldn't have been possible without the guidance of a large network of kind people all over the state—and country—and my family and friends.

Thanks to John, Shane, and Travis Andrews, the men I have been privileged to share my heart, home, and life with. John, you are artist, photographer, critic, and driver extraordinaire. The vast majority of photos in this book are his. Travis, this project wouldn't have been possible without your generous gift of dog-sitting services. Shane, your sound advice and confidence have been of invaluable help.

Thanks to my mom, Gladys, who first taught me a love of nature, and my dad, Howard, who gave me more than he will ever know, including a love for books and an appreciation for the power of written words. Thank you to my brother, John, for his sense of humor and knowledge of the outdoors, and to my sister, Judy, for her loving support of me in all I write and her graciousness as a host when I need to crash "somewhere else." A big thank-you to Jeff Kaplan, who recently took me on my first upside-down roller coaster. I still don't know how you talked me into it, but the bragging rights have made my life richer ever since. Cherrie, my sister: I can't wait to dance and share a laugh with you again. I owe a debt of gratitude to all of the dogs and cats who have shared their lives—and secrets—with me over the years.

Thank you to Matt Kareus, for first believing in me as a nature and travel writer, and to Eric Rock, for teaching me what adventure truly is. Matt, you gave me the chance; Eric, you gave me the dream. Thank you to Ben Bressler, who does the best phone impersonations I have ever heard. My sincere love and thanks go to the best traveling companions a woman could ever have, who I now am proud to call my friends: Kit, Helen, Dorothy, Mareda, Jennifer, Frieda, Carlyn and Ed, Dean and Sandy, Win and Newell, Kay, and, of course, Muriel. When we travel together, the fun and laughter just never stop.

Thanks to all of the wonderful people throughout the state—many of whose voices you'll hear in this book and who are far too numerous to list—who shared their knowledge of Wisconsin, their homes and generosity of time with me. You showed me a Wisconsin I didn't know existed. Thank you to Larry J. Schweiger, president and chief executive officer of the National Wildlife Federation, who allowed me to reprint his article "The Tree in Your Front Yard." My heartfelt thanks go to the staff at Trails Books for their enthusiasm for this book project and for all their help in making it a reality.

I hope readers will be as pleasantly surprised as I am by the gifts a Wisconsin winter brings and warmly reminded of what a great state Wisconsin is. — C. G. A.

Chapter One
WINTER WALKS
Appleton/Fox Cities

THE FOX CITIES OF Appleton, Neenah, Menasha, and Kaukauna together make up the third-largest metropolitan area in the state. The common thread stitched through them and the core they share is the Fox River, one of the few rivers in North America to flow northward. The river and its beautiful valley in east-central Wisconsin have seen groups of Native Americans, then French explorers, and finally Europeans set up communities along its shores.

Appleton is the largest of the Fox Cities. It is the location of the world's first home lighted by a central hydroelectric station, now the Hearthstone Historic House Museum. It was also the home of the young magician, Harry Houdini. On the north end of Wisconsin's largest lake, Lake Winnebago, the "twin cities" of Neenah and Menasha sit where the Fox River flows out of the lake. The two are characterized by graceful, early 1900s waterfront mansions built by paper-manufacturing barons. In Kaukauna, just a few miles north of Appleton, the Fox River has played a huge role in a city full of railroad, canal, and paper-industry history.

Kaukauna has done even more to earn a chapter in Wisconsin history books. In 1793, Wisconsin's first recorded land deed was granted to the city's first permanent white settler, Dominique Ducharme. Ducharme received several hundred acres of land for the initial payment of two barrels of rum. In 1818, Augustin Grignon set up a home on a government grant of 1,000 acres of land, where later his son, Charles, built his "Mansion in the Woods" in 1837. The Charles A. Grignon Home is the oldest home in Outagamie County and is listed on the National Register of Historic Places.

As urban as this region is, there are plenty of places to enjoy the outdoors in winter. In fact, the Fox Cities have gone out of their way to accommodate walkers and hikers by constructing boardwalks through many of their beautiful, natural areas. At Appleton's Gordon Bubolz Nature Preserve, you can hike or snowshoe through Wisconsin meadows and cedar swamps. In Heckrodt Wetland Reserve in Menasha, elevated boardwalks carry you to cattail marshes and forested wetlands. At High Cliff State Park, on the northeast shore of the only state-owned recreational area on Lake Winnebago, you can walk atop the Niagara Escarpment, past cliff environments, through an undisturbed, mesic forest, and around 1,000-year-old effigy mounds. In Kaukauna, the 1000 Islands Environmental Center and Conservancy Zone invites you to travel the boardwalk trails to the forest homes of white-tailed deer.

Whether it's on a plank-and-rope boardwalk, an escarpment formed millions of years ago or a path blazed by deer, the Fox Cities are great places for walking in a winter wonderland.

Day One
MORNING AND AFTERNOON

Upon arriving in Appleton, stop for an early lunch at **Good Company.** Pondering the extensive menu of focaccia sandwiches and wraps, burgers, soups, pastas, pizzas, and seafood will give you time to get your bearings. That itself, though, may be difficult since Good Company is composed of several very different themed rooms, such as the "Library" or the "French Quarter."

This will be a weekend of winter walks, and your first one will be on one of the most beautiful boardwalks in the state. The **Heckrodt Wetland Reserve** in Menasha is a 62-acre nature reserve on the north shore of Lake Winnebago. Despite the urbanization growing up all around it, the reserve is an enclave of forested wetlands, cattail marshes, open water, open fields, and upland forests. Several species of reptiles, amphibians, and mammals call it home. Migrating songbirds and waterfowl nest and feed in its protection. Two miles of elevated boardwalk trails provide access to the wetlands. Not only do these boardwalks provide a clearly marked trail for **winter hikers** and **snowshoers,** they also help animals in their winter travels by assisting them in deep snow and by providing a roofed freeway for smaller creatures that are able to travel underneath. Snowshoes can be rented here for a small fee.

Stop inside the 4,000-square-foot nature center to get warm. This impressive educational facility features a "Living Waters" exhibit with a live indoor wetland and aquariums full of local fish, turtles, and snakes. The center strives to show visitors the great diversity found in the natural world, teach ecological lessons, and provide a moment of wilderness.

Central Appleton will be your base for this Fox Cities visit. However, before checking into the downtown **Wingate Inn** at 300 Mall Drive—a convenient, central location for your explorations of all the Fox Cities—plan to spend an hour or two at the **Appleton Family Ice Center**. (It's a good idea to call ahead for open skate times, since they change.) The ice arena is located inside the 139-acre **Memorial Park,** which also has a **sledding hill** and an **outdoor ice rink**. In nearby Neenah, the **Tri-County Ice Arena** offers public skating times on its **indoor ice-skating rink** (call for times), and the city's **Washington Park** has an **outdoor ice-skating rink** with separate hockey and figure skating areas, a warming house, and lights.

EVENING

Tonight's dinner is a one-of-a-kind experience among former Green Bay Packers football coach Vince Lombardi's personal memorabilia. **Vince Lombardi's Steakhouse** in Appleton's Paper Valley Hotel serves awesome food: Be sure to bring your full appetite. Winter specials include stuffed bison tenderloin, sea-salt-baked sea bass, and volcano orange-spiced lamb chops. Lombardi's serves only USDA prime steaks, the highest quality, most expensive grade of beef available. The strawberry shortcake (actually, a sweetened biscuit) resembles a mountain—you'll be sorry if you don't share it with your dinner partner!

A replica Vince Lombardi trophy dominates the dining room, and Frank Sinatra tunes gently reverberate off the serene green walls and dark wood.

After dinner, catch a **men's basketball game** at the University of Wisconsin–Fox Valley, at 1478 Midway Road in Menasha, or go back to your lodging and rest your feet.

Day Two
MORNING

Start your morning with a good breakfast at your bed and breakfast, or get that first sniff of fresh coffee at **Brewed Awakenings** in downtown Appleton. You'll find a variety of omelets, oatmeal, and an old-fashioned breakfast of three eggs, bacon or sausage, and toast.

Today, you'll have the chance to take another wonderful winter walk in a great venue. North of Appleton is the 775-acre **Gordon Bubolz Nature Preserve**. The preserve was established in 1974 to protect a lowland white cedar forest and its diverse ecosystem. Today, eight

---

READING WINTER TREES
By Joann Engel

Joann Engel grew up on a hobby farm in Waupaca, Wisconsin. After graduating from the University of Wisconsin–Stevens Point, she followed her passion for the outdoors. She worked for the Wisconsin Department of Natural Resources and then became the outdoor–environmental educator for the Gordon Bubolz Nature Preserve in Appleton. She now resides in rural Waupaca County and enjoys hiking, biking, cross-country skiing, geocaching, and reading.

Cross-country skiers often find good reading out in the woods—right in the trees they pass. Here are a few reading tips:

Squirrel and bird nests from the previous seasons often adorn the branches. A tightly packed twig-and-leaf mass about the size of a bicycle tire is usually the summer home of a squirrel. During the winter months, squirrels will line hollow limbs with leaves and moss to stay cozy and warm.

Discarded pine cones at the base of the tree that are picked clean of their seeds indicate that squirrels are living nearby.

Wood chips found at the base of a tree and a gaping hole in the trunk means a woodpecker has either been looking for insect larvae or building a nest for the upcoming spring.

Twigs that branch out from the base of a tree may have buds and branches nibbled off. Cottontail rabbits use these buds during the winter as a source of energy, and buds nipped off straight across or at a V-angle are a sign of rabbits foraging. White-tailed deer will tear the buds off, leaving shards sticking out.

Furry bundles about the size of your thumb at the base of the tree could mean you're under an owl's roosting site. Owls eat small rodents and birds whole, then regurgitate the indigestible feathers, bones, and fur.

---

miles of tracked **cross-country ski trails** *[See "Reading Winter Trees" sidebar]* and three miles of **winter hiking** and **snowshoe trails** wind through the 200-acre Northern white cedar swamp—one of the southernmost in the nation—lowland hardwood forest, meadows, and prairies. Skis and snowshoes are available for rent, and there is a warming shelter. However, with hawks, pheasants, ruffed grouse, Canada geese, beavers, otters, foxes, coyotes, and deer, you may be too preoccupied to rest. Admission is free, and trails are open in daylight hours.

A nature center that is built into the earth features natural history exhibits and offers several programs and ski clinics throughout the year. A real treat is **Maple Syrup Saturday** *[See "Making Maple Syrup" sidebar]* in March, where you can tour the sugar bush, watch how trees are tapped, see the syrup being boiled down, and taste it on an ice cream sundae.

MAKING MAPLE SYRUP

If you have trees in your yard, you can make your own syrup in late winter or early spring. Any tree can make syrup, but syrup from maple trees will have more sugar, especially sugar maple trees, making sweeter syrup.

Tap your tree. Sap in a tree runs up in the morning and down in the evening. Inserting a tap in the tree will collect sap at both times. Using a hand-operated drill with a 7/16-inch drill bit, drill a hole in the tree that is slightly smaller than your sap spile (spigot). The hole should be 1.5–2 inches deep, at an upward angle of 10–20 degrees. When a tree is 20 inches in diameter, it can handle two taps without damage to the tree. A spile needs to stay about 12 inches away from the previous year's taps.

Once the hole has been drilled, gently tap in the spile for a snug fit. Hang a bucket from the spile and cover as much of the bucket as you can to keep rain, leaves, and insects out of the sap collection.

Collect the sap. As the bucket becomes full, transfer the contents into a holding bin (a large, clean bucket). The sap can stay in the holding bin for up to three days, if the weather stays cool.

Evaporate the sap. Over a hot outdoor fire, begin boiling the sap. Skim the froth off the top with a strainer. Add more sap as the boiling-pan sap diminishes; the sap should be kept at least 1.5 inches deep in the pan. The syrup is ready to be moved to the finishing pot when it reaches 7.1 degrees Fahrenheit above the boiling point of water (or 219.1 degrees). Forty gallons of sap will equal about one gallon of syrup.

JOHN T. ANDREWS

Bob Brodhagen describes the making of maple syrup during Maple Syrup Saturday in Gordon Bubolz Nature Preserve.

Finish the syrup. To "finish" syrup, you filter it. Pour the syrup through a fabric such as felt or paper towels. The filtering will remove "sugar sand," the calcium compounds common in sap.

Cool it. Let the syrup cool on its own. It can be stored in the refrigerator for up to three months. Homemade maple syrup served on ice cream is a delicious treat for family and friends. While most store-bought syrups are only 4 to 7 percent syrup, your homemade version will be 100 percent pure.

On selected weekends in February, you can take a **sleigh ride,** courtesy of Belgian draft horses, through the snow-covered prairies and forests.

AFTERNOON

There's only one place to get Fox River crab cakes and butternut squash ravioli, all served with a view of the Fox River from floor-to-ceiling windows: **Fratello's Riverfront Restaurant** in Appleton. The building sits on the site of the 1909 Vulcan hydroelectric plant. Watch for soaring eagles.

This afternoon is a photographer's dream and one of the best places in the state to explore on foot. The 1,147-acre **High Cliff State Park**, on the northeast shore of Lake Winnebago, was founded where the Western Lime and Cement quarry and kiln company operated from 1895 to 1956. The kilns, which separated the lime from the stone, were heated to 2,200 degrees Fahrenheit, first by wood fire and later by coal. Once the kilns were fired up, they'd stay in continual operation from six months to a year, producing about a thousand pounds of lime per hour. The limekilns still stand in beautiful isolation—don't miss this opportunity for some artistic winter shots.

JOHN T. ANDREWS

The remnants of limekilns stand as silent sentinels at the base of High Cliff State Park.

The other great highlights of the park are the 500- to 1,000-year-old effigy mounds, constructed by nomadic woodland Native Americans. Four mounds have been identified as panthers, one of which is 285 feet long. Another is called Twin Buffaloes. As always, remember to respect effigy mounds as you walk near them.

High Cliff gets its name from the long limestone ledge rising more than 200 feet above the Lake Winnebago shore, with vertical cliffs as high as 25 feet. The ledge is on the western side of the Niagara Escarpment, which stretches almost a thousand miles east, through

Door County, across Michigan and Canada, and creates Niagara Falls at the other end. From the top of the escarpment, you can see all of the Fox River Valley: Appleton, Neenah, Menasha, and Kaukauna. It is said that Winnebago (Ho-Chunk) Chief Red Bird liked to stand on this cliff in the early 1800s, "listening" to the lake and telling children about the good life beyond the calm waters. A 12-foot-tall bronze statue of Chief Red Bird still stands there today.

Cross-country skiing through High Cliff State Park will take you to the heights or to history. The two-mile **Lime-Kiln Trail** runs from the limekilns to the lake and up the east side of the escarpment. The longer **Red Bird Trail**, mostly level and wooded, loops for 4.2 miles through the quarry and around the campground. The southern section of the trail lies along the top of the ledge and offers excellent views of the valley. You'll meet sugar maples, cottonwood, shagbark hickory, and hop-hornbeam (ironwood) trees. If you're lucky, you may meet a 13-striped ground squirrel or a red fox.

Ice fishers looking for northerns and pan fish can set up their shanties on the pond by the park office or on the lake. On Lake Winnebago, anglers may catch walleyes. Winter visitors also have an unusual opportunity to spear lake sturgeon through the ice during special spearing seasons. Sturgeons, Wisconsin's largest fish, can range in weight from 50 to 100 pounds.

Snowshoeing and winter hiking are permitted anywhere in High Cliff, except on ski trails when snow covered. If you've never snowshoed or winter hiked before, High Cliff is a good place to begin. It's peaceful and photogenic, and there are plenty of woods, ledges, lakes, and lime quarries to explore. **Snowmobilers** will find six trails through the park that connect to the county's extensive trail system.

If you can break away from High Cliff State Park by 4:30 p.m., you may want to catch the show at the world-class **Barlow Planetarium** on the campus of the University of Wisconsin–Fox Valley. A 48-foot projection dome uses 3-D special effects and surround

JOHN T. ANDREWS

Cross-country skiing in Wisconsin's state parks, such as here in High Cliff, affords a solitude rarely found in warmer seasons.

sound to create a replica of Wisconsin's night skies. You'll learn just what you should be looking for tonight in the season's clear upper reaches.

EVENING

If you'd like to stay in Appleton for dinner, go to **The Seasons: An American Bistro**. The atmosphere is urban, and dishes are described as "classic, with a twist." There's a martini bar and live jazz every Friday and Saturday night. If you prefer Asian food, **Cy's Asian Bistro** in downtown Neenah is the place to be. *Fox Cities Magazine* readers often select Cy's as having the "Best Asian Food" in annual surveys. The service is excellent, say local residents.

On the north side of Appleton is **Erb Park**, a community park where the **sledding hill** is lighted for nighttime snow fun. Or for a thrilling evening on ice, take in a fast-paced **Fox Cities Ice Dogs hockey game** at the Appleton Family Ice Center. This U.S. Amateur Elite Hockey team is a member of the Great Lakes Hockey League.

Day Three
MORNING AND AFTERNOON

Take in a breakfast diner experience this morning at **The Queen Bee** in downtown Appleton. Skillet breakfasts are big here, and their homemade hash browns are a specialty.

After breakfast, get in some last Appleton winter fun by trying the **ice-skating** or **sledding** at **Erb Park** during the daylight hours or **cross-country skiing** at **Reid Municipal Golf Course**.

The weekend will end as it began—with another great walk. The **1000 Islands Environmental Center and Conservancy Zone** in Kaukauna is a 350-acre reminder of the great role Wisconsin plays in the lives of bird communities. Wisconsin is on the Mississippi Flyway for waterfowl and predatory birds. Birds have used this corridor twice annually for thousands of years. 1000 Islands also sits in the midst of another significant natural spot called the "tension zone." The zone is an irregular, 10- to 20-mile-wide band across the north-central tier of states in which northern and more southerly species of plants and animals *[See "How*

HOW COLD WILL IT GET THIS WINTER?

By Joann Engel

Humans have been predicting the severity of winter for centuries. Some people say they can forecast winter weather by observing wildlife in the fall. Here are a few signs one might see during fall that may mean a cold, long, and severe winter is approaching:

✸ Deer grow extra thick fur, and a squirrel's tail is bushier.
✸ Muskrats build new houses.
✸ The hair of wooly bear caterpillars grows so the black stripes are wider than the brown ones.
✸ Onion skins grow unusually thick.
✸ Rose bushes bend over, heavy with rosehips.
✸ Squirrels and chipmunks are extra busy storing their piles of nuts and seeds.
✸ The tops of spruce and pine trees have a lot of cones.
✸ Beavers build their winter lodges unusually early in the fall.

Cold Will It Get This Winter?" sidebar] can comingle and reach their normal limits of existence. The acreage here supports a stand of chinquapin oaks, which are rare in the state.

JOHN T. ANDREWS

A hike along the 1000 Islands Environmental Center boardwalks will reveal magical winter sights and sounds.

Miles of boardwalks will take you between the rushing Fox River on one side of you and babbling rivulets on the other. Rarely can you hear such sounds together. Whether you are in **winter hiking** boots, strapped onto **snowshoes** or clipped to **cross-country skis**, an outing here will be one of the most wondrous winter walks you've ever taken.

FOR MORE INFORMATION
**FOX CITIES CONVENTION &
VISITORS BUREAU**
3433 W. College Ave., Appleton, WI 54914
(920) 734-3358 or (800) 236-6673, www.foxcities.org

WINTER ATTRACTIONS
APPLETON FAMILY ICE CENTER
1717 E. Witzke Blvd., Appleton, WI 54911
(920) 830-7679

BARLOW PLANETARIUM
(public shows every Friday, Saturday, and Sunday)
University of Wisconsin–Fox Valley
1478 Midway Rd., Menasha, WI 54952
(920) 832-2848, www.fox.uwc.edu/barlow

ERB PARK
1800 N. Morrison St., Appleton, WI 54912
(920) 832-5917

FOX CITIES ICE DOGS HOCKEY TEAM
P.O. Box 1941, Appleton, WI 54912
(920) 209-0405, www.icedogshockey.net

GORDON BUBOLZ NATURE PRESERVE
(nature center open Friday 8:00 a.m.– 4:30 p.m.;
Saturday 11:00 a.m.–4:30 p.m.,
Sunday noon–4:30 p.m.)
4815 N. Lynndale Dr., Appleton, WI 54913
(920) 731-6041, http://my.athenet.net/~bubolz

HECKRODT WETLAND RESERVE
(reserve open daily 6:00 a.m.–9:00 p.m; nature cen-
ter open Friday 8:00 a.m.–4:30 p.m., Saturday and
Sunday 11:00 a.m.–4:00 p.m.)
1305 Plank Rd., Menasha, WI 54952
(920) 720-9349, www.heckrodtwetland.com

HIGH CLIFF STATE PARK
N7630 State Park Rd., Sherwood, WI 54169
(920) 989-1106, www.wiparks.net

MEMORIAL PARK
1313 Witzke Blvd., Appleton, WI 54911
(920) 993-1900, www.memorialparkarb.org

**1000 ISLANDS ENVIRONMENTAL CENTER
AND CONSERVANCY ZONE**
(environmental center open weekdays 8:00 a.m.–
4:00 p.m; weekends 10:00 a.m.–3:30 p.m.)
1000 Beaulieu Ct., Kaukauna, WI 54130
(414) 766-4733
http://home.new.rr.com/thousandisland

REID MUNICIPAL GOLF COURSE
1100 E. Fremont St., Appleton, WI 54915
(920) 832-5926

TRI-COUNTY ICE ARENA
700 E. Shady Ln., Neenah, WI 54956
(920) 731-9731

UNIVERSITY OF WISCONSIN–FOX VALLEY
1478 Midway Rd., Menasha, WI 54952
(920) 832-2848, www.fox.uwc.edu/athletics

WASHINGTON PARK
631 W. Winneconne Ave., Neenah, WI 54956
(920) 886-6060, www.ci.neenah.wi.us

WINTER FESTIVALS
**ANNUAL CHRISTMAS PARADE—late No-
vember.** Downtown Appleton. 6:30 p.m. The
largest nighttime Christmas parade in Wisconsin with more than 100 floats and bands. Prior
to the parade is the one-mile Santa Scamper
Run. (920) 954-9112 or www. appletondown
town.org.

**PARADE OF ORNAMENTS AT HEARTH-
STONE—late November to mid-January.**
Decked out for the holidays in "The Many Faces
of Santa," the Parade of Ornaments at the
world's first home lit by a central hydroelectric
power station offers a spectacular display. The
fireplaces, stained glass windows and ornate
woodwork are surrounded by early-settler decorations, images, and ornaments. During the first
three Thursdays in December, visitors can tour
the holiday mansion by candlelight and see the
original light switches, in operation since 1882.
(920) 730-8204.

**ADOPT A BUCKET/BUBOLZ NATURE PRE-
SERVE—early February.** 11:00 a.m.–3:00 p.m.
Participants will decorate a pail with their
favorite designs. A picture will be taken of the
family and decorated bucket. Demonstrations
on how to tap a maple tree in the preserve's
sugar bushes will be followed by the hanging of
the decorated buckets to catch the sap. (920)
731-6041 or www.athenet.net/~bubolz.

MOONLIGHT SKI & HIKE—mid-February.
Gordon Bubolz Nature Preserve. 5:00–8:00 p.m.
Enjoy the preserve's cross-country ski trails and
winter hiking trails at night. Trails are lit by the
rising moon, built a flashlight or headlamp is recommended. Ski rental available at $5 per person.
Trail fees $3. Hot beverages available in the
building. (920) 731-6041 or www.athenet.net/~
bubolz.

ARTFUL EMPTY BOWLS—mid-March. Appleton Art Center. 5:00 p.m. and 7:00 p.m. In part-
nership with America's Second Harvest of Wisconsin, the Appleton Art Center, 111 W. College
Ave., Appleton, WI 54911, presents this anti-
hunger event. Enjoy soups served in handcrafted
ceramic bowls that you get to take home with
you, breads, and desserts. Silent auction. (920)
733-4089 or www.appletonartcenter.org.

MAPLE SYRUP SATURDAY—mid-March. Gordon Bubolz Nature Preserve. 10:00 a.m.–3:00 p.m. Tours of the preserve's syrup-producing process begin with a hike through the woods for a look at the sugar bush. Last stop will be to see the final processing of the syrup for bottling. After the tours, taste fresh maple syrup on an ice cream sundae. (920) 731-6041 or www.athenet.net/~bubolz.

RESTAURANTS
BREWED AWAKENINGS
(breakfast and lunch)
107 E. College Ave., Appleton, WI 54911
(920) 882-9336, www.brewedawake.com

CY'S ASIAN BISTRO
(lunch and dinner)
208 W. Wisconsin Ave., Neenah, WI 54956
(920) 969-9549

FRATELLO'S RIVERFRONT RESTAURANT
(lunch and dinner)
504 W. Water St., Appleton, WI 54911
(920) 993-9087
www.supplerestaurantgroup.com/fratellos-appleton

GOOD COMPANY
(lunch and dinner)
110 N. Richmond St., Appleton, WI 54911
(920) 735-9500

THE QUEEN BEE *(breakfast and lunch)*
216 E. College Ave., Appleton, WI 54911
(920) 739-8207

THE SEASONS: AN AMERICAN BISTRO
(lunch and dinner)
213 S. Nicolet Rd., Appleton, WI 54914
(920) 993-9860, www.theseasonsrestaurant.com

TRIM B'S RESTAURANT & PUB
(lunch and dinner)
201 S. Walnut St., Appleton, WI 54911
(920) 734-9204

VINCE LOMBARDI'S STEAKHOUSE
(dinner)
333 W. College Ave., Appleton, WI 54911
(920) 380-9390

LODGING
FRANKLIN STREET INN BED AND BREAKFAST
318 E. Franklin St., Appleton, WI 54911
(920) 993-1711 or (888) 993-1711
www.franklinstreetinn.com

QUILT-N-BE BED & BREAKFAST
300 W. Prospect Ave., Appleton, WI 54911
(920) 954-0754, www.quiltingbb.com

RADISSON PAPER VALLEY HOTEL
333 W. College Ave., Appleton, WI 54911
(920) 733-8000 or (800) 242-3499
www.radissonpapervalley.com

THE ROOST BED AND BREAKFAST
1900 S. Lee St., Appleton, WI 54914
(920) 882-8427 or (866) 803-7814
www.theroostbandb.com

SOLIE HOME BED AND BREAKFAST
914 E. Hancock St., Appleton, WI 54911
(920) 733-0863

WINGATE INN
300 Mall Dr., Appleton, WI 54913
(920) 993-1200 or (800) 228-1000
www.wingateinnappleton.com

Chapter Two

A NATURAL WINTER
Baraboo/Prairie du Sac

WISCONSIN HAS MORE than 60 state parks, forests, and recreation areas, and each one has its own personality. By spending just three days in the Baraboo vicinity, you can experience Wisconsin's most popular state park, enjoy one of its lesser known and quieter ones, visit its oldest natural area, and walk or ski down its oldest trail.

In Baraboo, the billion-and-a-half-year-old quartzite bluffs of the heather-hued Baraboo Range rise above the icy waters of a deep lake. The 8,000 acres surrounding them, known as Devil's Lake State Park, draw more visitors annually than Yellowstone National Park. Scientists, too, are called to the park, one of the most topographically diverse areas of Wisconsin. More than a hundred colleges and universities conduct field trips to Devil's Lake every year to study the bluffs, fields, and river valleys.

Mirror Lake State Park, on the other hand, is a quiet cousin. The narrow eastern half of the park features golden sandstone bluffs that rise up to 50 feet in the air. These bluffs keep Mirror Lake calm, allowing smooth reflections, as if you were looking into a mirror. Forest covers almost all of the park's 2,179 acres, although wetlands surround the western end of the lake, and meadows and prairies are scattered throughout.

Only four miles from Devil's Lake is Parfrey's Glen. For the price of a quarter-mile trek through a cool and dripping canyon, you can access the state's oldest natural area. Walk or snowshoe past giant walls studded with quartzite boulders embedded by glacial wash. Between hushed silence and gurgling waters, take dramatic photos of mossy ridge walls and snow-covered boardwalks. There are plant communities here left over from the Ice Age and birds not commonly found in the southern half of the state. There is a world of microclimates in the glen and more than a billion years of geology.

On a trail called Ice Age, part of which winds through Devil's Lake State Park, travelers gain lofty vistas and sweeping panoramas of the Baraboo Valley and extinct glacial lakes. The glacier quit its gouging and depositing here, stopped by the hardy Baraboo Bluffs.

The Baraboo Hills are among the oldest visible physical features on Earth. The Nature

Conservancy has designated the hills as a Last Great Place, identifying them as one of the western hemisphere's most significant ecosystems. They have also been named a National Natural Landmark.

Be prepared to be awed by nature this weekend—and by the gifts of wintry glaciers.

COURTESY OF CASCADE MOUNTAIN SKI & SNOWBOARD AREA

Cascade Mountain's state-of-the-art snowmaking techniques extend the season for downhill-skiing enthusiasts.

Day One
MORNING

In the mid-1800s, a man named August Ringling operated his harness shops in Baraboo. His sons, Albert (1852–1916), Otto (1858–1911), Alfred (1861–1919), Charles (1864–1926), and John (1866–1936) developed a love for the entertainment life and began their "Greatest Show on Earth" here in 1884. Brothers Henry and August joined the circus in the 1880s. The company winter-quartered along the Baraboo River; in fact, some people claim that at least one elephant is buried along its banks. The Ringling cousins, the Gollmars, also operated a circus out of Baraboo, and numerous city residents were employed in wagon and harness making for the shows. Performers had homes in town, with practice barns in their back-yards. Historic downtown Baraboo still resonates with this colorful history.

Get your Baraboo winter weekend started with an early lunch at the **Log Cabin Restaurant** on Highway 33. "You are in cabin country," claims a wooden plaque in one booth. With carved wooden bears outside, snowshoes on the walls inside, beam ceilings, and fall leaves under the glass-topped tables, it couldn't feel truer. The Log Cabin Restaurant was given a People's Choice Award by local residents for best dessert, breakfast, and atmosphere. Try the "Taste of Fall" pumpkin waffle, and you'll immediately know how you'd cast your vote.

One of Wisconsin's lesser known gems is **Mirror Lake State Park** [See "*Reflections on Mirror Lake*" sidebar], off Fern Dell Road. Covered mostly by forests, the park is home to unique birds, including the pileated woodpecker, the second largest woodpecker in the United States. **Snowshoe, winter hike, cross-country ski, ice fish**, or **winter camp** in the peaceful and private environs.

REFLECTIONS ON MIRROR LAKE

By Mark Blakeslee

Mark Blakeslee was born and grew up in Middleton, Wisconsin. In 1962, his father bought a cottage on Mirror Lake, and that changed his summers and the family's lives forever. He is now president of the Mirror Lake Association.

I consider Mirror Lake and the surrounding area the best natural area in all of Wisconsin. It has one of the most diverse landscapes, and there's certainly no better place to canoe or kayak than down its narrow and winding channels past towering pines and tall, steep sandstone cliffs. Mirror Lake is the oldest manmade lake in Wisconsin. It was built in 1857 by the LaBar family to provide power for their feed mill. They dammed up Dell Creek with logs, which are still under the concrete dam today. The lake is approximately four miles long.

I was five years old when my father bought our cottage, which was built in the 1800s. I thought we were living like pioneers, even though many people, who had all the modern conveniences, lived around us. We had to hand pump our water, and the only plumbing was an outhouse. Every evening we would head down to the lake to a swimming hole to take our baths. We would meet similar cottage dwellers doing the same thing and have what you might call a neighborhood get-together. Our days would be filled with fishing, boating, or running through the woods barefoot, exploring and pretending to be Davy Crockett or Daniel Boone.

Forty years later, I find myself doing the same things, only at a slower pace. We did install running water in our cottage, but other than that everything else is much the same as it was back then. We now wake up to the sounds of sandhill cranes at the crack of dawn, and we know it's time to wrap up the day when they call us at dusk and tell the frogs that it's their turn to make their nightly music.

Ten years ago, I was elected to be on the board of the Mirror Lake Association. This association was formed to watch the lake and make sure that it is treated with respect and stays the natural treasure that it is. The dedicated work and support of the association and other people have kept Mirror Lake unspoiled and very slightly developed.

There are nearly 20 miles of **hiking trails** in the park. The most popular is the 0.6-mile **Echo Rock Trail**, which features fantastic lake views. The trail is generally level with a set of steps leading down to some especially scenic bluffs. There are 1.2 miles of easy to intermediate **snowshoe trails**.

The **Winnebago** and **Blue Water Bay Trails**, more than 19 miles, are groomed for **cross-country skiing**. The **Fern Dell** and **Turtleville Loops** accommodate skate-skiers. Through woods, open fields, and prairies, the trails twist and roll enough for a bit of a challenge without being too difficult.

Ice fishing on Mirror Lake yields pan fish and occasional catches of northerns, and there are 13 **winter campsites** in Sandstone Campground.

AFTERNOON

Just as the early afternoon hours are coming on, visit **Parfrey's Glen State Natural Area**. At the far east end of Devil's Lake State Park (on County Road DL, four miles east of the lake), the 480-acre gorge is one of the most beautiful spots in the state. The glen was designated the first state natural area because of its many rare plants and ferns, and innate beauty. With minimal sunlight and cold air that settles at the bottom of the ravines, the plants in the glen are more typical of northern Wisconsin than of southern.

Only .25 mile long, the **Parfrey's Glen Scientific Area Trail** takes you deeper and deeper into the ever-narrowing gorge, where each new corner reveals another photogenic scene. The sense of unfolding wonder is even more pronounced in winter, when reedlike plants called scouring rush, an ancient variety that predates leafy, flowering plants, pushes up through pristine mounds of snow.

Trees with great character manage to cling to crevices in the glen's sheer walls. Green moss and multicolored lichens paint a natural mural. Layers of sandstone in the massive rocks are separated by bands of purple quartzite stones, evidence of ancient seas that created beaches at different levels as they gradually filled the gorge.

The natural way to follow up your visit to such a natural area is to check into the **Seth Peterson Cottage** in Mirror Lake State Park. Overlooking the west end of the lake, the cottage is the only Frank Lloyd Wright–designed house available for vacation rentals, although reservations must be made as much as a year in advance. The cottage sits on the edge of a steep, wooded slope that plunges down to Mirror Lake. Watch dazzling sunsets over the lake from either the stone terrace or through the bank of windows that frame the living area on three sides. The house, designed in 1958 of local sandstone, wood, and glass, has a combined living, dining, and kitchen area; a low-ceilinged bedroom; an adjoining bathroom with a stone-floored shower; and a huge, sandstone fireplace. Be sure to bring along

The Seth Peterson Cottage exhibits the signature style of Frank Lloyd Wright by blending into its natural surroundings.

a few breakfast food items so you can leisurely enjoy tomorrow's dawn and early morning hours in one of the most lovely and naturally integrated homes in the state.

Only 880 square feet, the cottage was Wright's last Wisconsin commission. It is listed on the National Register of Historic Places and has been described as having "more architecture" per square foot than any other building Wright designed. Named for the man who commissioned it [see "Who Was Seth Peterson?" sidebar], the cottage was acquired by the state in 1966 when the park opened. In 1989, a local citizens group refurbished the cottage and built the furniture that Wright had originally designed for it.

WHO WAS SETH PETERSON?

As a boy growing up in the 1940s in Black Earth, Wisconsin, Seth Peterson was fascinated by architecture and soon became a fan of Frank Lloyd Wright, a fellow Wisconsinite. He spent many weekends taking the train to Oak Park, Illinois, just to view Wright's buildings.

After a tour in the army, Peterson returned to Black Earth and took a job with the state of Wisconsin. On several occasions, he asked Wright to design a home for him. Wright continually said no, until Peterson finally presented him with a retainer—which the designer soon spent. To make good, Wright was finally forced to design the dream house for Peterson's property on Mirror Lake.

Construction began in 1959, just months before Wright died. In 1960, Peterson also passed away, shortly before the house was finished.

The house was bought and completed by a Milwaukee family. One of the family members—and his Afghan hounds—lived in the house for five years. In 1966, Wisconsin purchased the house and land for inclusion in Mirror Lake State Park. Not knowing how the cottage could be used, park managers boarded it up. The cottage sat empty and deteriorating for the next 20 years.

In 1989, the nonprofit Seth Peterson Cottage Conservancy was formed to restore the house for use as an overnight rental. After a $300,000 restoration, the cottage was opened to travelers for overnight stays in July 1992.

The cottage has garnered awards for excellence in historic preservation from the Wisconsin Association of Historic Preservation Commissions, the State Historical Society of Wisconsin, the Wisconsin Trust for Historical Preservation, and the American Institute of Architects. It is on the national and Wisconsin State Register of Historic Places.

The Seth Peterson Cottage is now living up to Peterson's hopeful designation of "dream house." If you're lucky enough to be able to spend a winter evening or two in its embrace, you'll know what he meant.

EVENING

Tonight, enjoy leek crepes or mushroom stroganoff at **The Cheese Factory Restaurant**, a vegetarian restaurant in nearby Wisconsin Dells.

Back at the cottage, bring in some wood from the shed and start a fire. Let your bare feet feel the warm, smooth stones of the floor as you get ready for bed. Watch the sky darken and the stars grow brighter from the rectangular, low windows in the bedroom. Let the sight of the best of the outdoors soothe you to sleep, while being warmed by the fire inside.

Day Two
MORNING

Have breakfast at your inn or bed and breakfast, or, if you were lucky enough to have booked the Seth Peterson Cottage, make some warm oatmeal and sit on the stone patio overlooking Mirror Lake. If a light snow starts to fall, eat inside the cottage and drink your coffee in front of the floor-to-ceiling windows.

Today is the day to enjoy Wisconsin's largest and arguably most popular state park—**Devil's Lake State Park**. These 9,360 acres of spectacular scenery have long been a sacred site for Native Americans, including the Winnebagos (Ho-Chunk), who built effigy and burial mounds along the lake. There are several theories about the name "Devil's Lake." A Winnebago myth tells us that giant thunderbirds battled with spirits who lived in the watery depths. They fought with thunderbolts against the water gods' boulders. Eons later, the thunderbirds eventually won, but the rocks and bluffs were left with scars. Thus the Winnebagos dubbed it Spirit Lake. Settlers in the 1840s may have slightly mistranslated the name.

Another myth that white settlers passed along describes a great meteor that crashed into the earth, throwing up rocks on all sides. Heat radiated from the hole for days, after which it rained. When people were finally able to go near the spot, they discovered a beautiful lake had filled the gap. It may have made them think of evil spirits. Or it could be that the name Devil's Lake was applied since no one knew just how deep the lake was. Today, we measure it at 45 feet deep and covering 360 acres.

The fact that the park can be called the state's most popular makes it even more appealing to visit in winter. Without the crowds, you truly have the space to take in the natural beauty. Below the three 500-foot bluffs, where cold air accumulates, northern plant species, such as white pine, are prevalent. Southern plants, including prairie remnants, are found on the bluffs and in the rest of the park.

Devil's Lake State Park has majestic **cross-country ski trails**, great **ice fishing**, **sledding**, and comfortable **winter camping**. Twenty-nine campsites stay open in winter. Park rangers say they have even seen some winter campers build igloos! There are 27 **winter hiking trails**.

Devil's Lake is one of the best parks in southern Wisconsin to explore by **snowshoe**. If you prefer to snowshoe on trails, the .5-mile **Group Camp Trail** and the .7-mile **Grottos Trail** are rated easy. A warming shelter is available, and a **sledding hill** is located near the nature center.

There are 17 **cross-country ski trails** (22.4 miles). The **East Bluff Woods Trail, Ice Age Trail Loop, Steinke Basin Loop, Johnson Moraine Loop**, and the 1.5-mile road through the **Ice Age Campground** are groomed for cross-country skiing. The north half of the Johnson Moraine Loop and the path through the Ice Age Campground accommodate skate-skiing.

The cross-country ski trails include uphill climbs, downhill runs, passes over snowy ridges, and rock-lined valleys. Glide down the gently curving East Bluff Woods Trail and watch the forest swoosh by and bald eagles soar overhead.

Devil's Lake is under the auspices of the Wisconsin Department of Natural Resources, but the park is also one of nine official segments of the **Ice Age National Scientific Reserve**. The **Ice Age National Scenic Trail** is a 1,000-mile journey that winds across forests, parks, and private lands. Stretching from the Door County Peninsula in the east and looping down and up until reaching the St. Croix River in the west, the Ice Age National Scenic Trail is a magical landscape of gorgeous natural features and glacial ghosts.

Wisconsin's section of the Ice Age National Scenic Trail is one of the most exciting treks in the Midwest. Edging the terminal moraine (rock, boulders, and stone-laden soil) of an ice sheet that melted before humans took a step on the planet, the trail's geologic features include bowl-shaped depressions, snakelike ridges, rounded hills, and old lakes.

The **Devil's Lake State Park Ice Age Trail** (7.1 miles) loops through and runs into the **Parfrey's Glen Ice Age Trail**. The start/finish is at the north end beach. Other than four very steep, short sections, the climb is fairly gradual. Most of the trail is in a hardwood and pine forest. As you get near the 400-foot, mile-long downhill—the only one in the state—you'll see caution signs. The initial drop is 100 feet in 500 feet of distance!

JOHN T. ANDREWS

The billion-year-old walls of Parfrey's Glen create a dramatic frame for your winter explorations.

17

MAKING SNOW ON CASCADE MOUNTAIN

Each year, Cascade Mountain makes less and less snow—not because Mother Nature has been helping out, but because the ski area is one of the most efficient snowmakers in the country. Rob Walz, mountain manager and snowmaking expert, has been running Cascade's outside operations for more than 10 years. Here is Rob's shorthand version of how you go about making snow:

1. Water is supplied either from a river or water well.

2. The water is stored in a settling pond and cooled to 36 to 38 degrees. From the settling pond, the water is directed to a pump house. The pump house is similar to a city's pump station which pumps water to a water main. The pump forces the water into a pipe, then pushes it up the mountain at high pressure to the snow guns. Snowmaking will only work at a pressure of 200 pounds or more.

3. At the snow guns, half of the water is used for nucleation and half for bulk water. Nucleation is the process of combining air and water at cold temperatures to force a snow crystal to be made.

4. Once a snow crystal or nucleus is created, bulk water can be added to the outside of it. Snow production comes from the bulk water. Depending on the temperature, more or less bulk water is added. If it's a marginal snowmaking day, not much bulk water will be added. If it's a very cold day, more water will be needed to produce snow.

Even though today most snow guns are automatic, there is still a fair amount of training required. "A typical snowmaker needs one or two seasons under his belt before he can go out and have his own crew," says Walz.

At Cascade, snow guns are situated all along the mountain. "The latest trend is to have more tower-mounted snow guns so you don't need to move them around," explains Walz. "We have about 50 percent of our fleet tower-mounted and 50 percent mobile. We set them back off the trail in the trees for low visibility. The last thing you want to see when you're skiing on a beautiful run is a big, steel tower."

Recently, Cascade installed the first fully automated snowmaking system—with 120 automated snow guns—in the Midwest, saving natural resources and money. According to Walz, "Four years ago, we used 100 million gallons of water to make snow. Last year, we used 76 million gallons. Before, we might have had one or two thermometers on the hill; now we have 14 weather stations. There can be five or six different temperatures on the mountain within two to five degrees. When we see an optimum snowmaking temperature at a certain location, we'll fire up that area's snow gun," he says.

Since installing the new system, the cost of an acre-foot of snow has dropped from $152 to $92. At the local power plant, 1.1 million pounds of coal have been saved.

If you'd like to get in some **downhill skiing**, **snowboarding**, or **snow tubing**, you have two nearby options. **Devil's Head Resort and Convention Center** in Merrimac has 28 **downhill ski** runs, with panoramic views of Lake Wisconsin and miles of forest and farmlands. There are three quad chairlifts, one triple chairlift, six double chairlifts, and five rope tows. **Cross-country skiing** in daylight hours and **snowboarding** are also available.

Cascade Mountain Ski & Snowboard Area near Portage has 34 **downhill ski** runs and 10 lifts—including a high-speed, quad chairlift that gets you to the top in two and a half minutes *[see "Making Snow on Cascade Mountain" sidebar]*. For **snowboarders,** each of the four terrain parks features different jumps and rails that change daily. Cascade's Superpark contains the Midwest's only superpipe and a school bus that was converted into the world's biggest rail. The **snow-tubing** park has four long chutes and a tube tow.

A lone skier takes on the challenge of the mogul field.

AFTERNOON

Back in Baraboo's historic town square, stop for lunch at **Garden Party Café**. Choose from a variety of fresh salads and warm sandwiches in this cheery eatery.

Just six miles west of Baraboo is North Freedom and the **Mid-Continent Railway and Museum.** The volunteers of the 300-member Mid-Continent Railway Historical Society operate a **Santa Claus Express** (late November) and **Snow Train** (mid-February) on a few select winter weekends. Chugging through the Baraboo Hills in winter is a photographer's dream. Dress warmly and wear boots because snow along the tracks can be quite deep as you get off the train for an extra-special photo. The conductor happily accommodates you by backing up the train and then running it past you just so you can catch a steam locomotive in action. For an unforgettable experience, consider taking the Snow Train dinner departure.

For locomotion by your own power, lace up your ice skates and practice your camels and cross-overs on the outdoor **ice-skating rinks** at **Langer Park** at Fourth and Remington Streets and **Weber Park Pleasure Rink** on Elm Street *[see "Peggy Fleming Had It All: Ice-Skating Tips" in the Milwaukee chapter]*.

EVENING

Treat yourself to dinner at **Little Village Café** in Baraboo. The restaurant has an extensive wine list with more than 50 wines by the glass and a large micro beer selection. Well known for its burritos, salads, and seafood, the café also caters to vegetarians. Stay to enjoy the maple pecan chocolate torte or peanut butter pie.

If you're in town during early January or early February, close out the evening with **Mirror Lake's Candlelight Ski and Hike**.

Day Three

MORNING

Begin your last day with a "Weekend Breakfast" at the **Java Café** in downtown Baraboo. From 9:00 a.m. to 1:00 p.m., the menu includes items such as baked French toast, granola, lox and bagels, a fresh spinach omelet, and a variety of egg scrambles. Of course, as the name suggests, there are cappuccinos, lattes, and hot chocolates to accompany the meal.

AFTERNOON

Once you've checked out of your accommodations, consider taking the 100-mile **Baraboo Range Snowmobile Tour** (contact the Baraboo Chamber of Commerce for details) or plan to spend the rest of your weekend in **Prairie du Sac**.

On Water Street in downtown Prairie du Sac, city spotting scopes are set up for **watching the bald eagles** along the Wisconsin River. If you visit in mid-January, you'll be able to participate in the city's **Bald Eagle Watching Days**. During the festival, there are guided bus tours to three prime eagle-gathering locations along the Wisconsin River, naturalist-led raptor seminars, wine tasting, and children's activities.

A visit to Prairie du Sac wouldn't be complete without a wine tour and tasting at **Wollersheim Winery**. Located on 23 hilly acres above the Wisconsin River, the golden-colored limestone winery was built by a German immigrant, Peter Kehl, in the 1860s and used until the turn of the century. It lay dormant until 1972 when the Wollersheims replanted the vineyards. Sample the award-winning white Prairie Fumé, the red Domaine du Sac, or a new winter wine released in November of each year.

Chances are you'll choose to take a few bottles of wine home as a remembrance of your state parks weekend. Later, as you pop the cork on the first one, remember to toast a long-gone glacier that made your enjoyment of this weekend's natural beauty possible.

FOR MORE INFORMATION

BARABOO CHAMBER OF COMMERCE
660 W. Chestnut St., Baraboo, WI 53913
(608) 356-8333 or (800) 227-2266
www.baraboo.com/chamber

SAUK-PRAIRIE CHAMBER OF COMMERCE
PO Box 7, Sauk City, WI 53583, (608) 634-4168

WINTER ATTRACTIONS

CASCADE MOUNTAIN SKI & SNOWBOARD AREA
W10441 Cascade Mountain Rd.,
Portage, WI 53901, (608) 742-5588 or
(800) 992-2754
www.cascademountain.com

DEVIL'S HEAD RESORT AND CONVENTION CENTER
S6330 Bluff Rd., Merrimac, WI 53561
(608) 493-2251 or (800) 472-6670
www.devils-head.com

DEVIL'S LAKE STATE PARK
S5975 Park Rd., Baraboo, WI 53913
(608) 356-8301, www.wiparks.net

ICE AGE PARK & TRAIL FOUNDATION
207 E. Buffalo St., Suite 515
Milwaukee, WI 53202
(414) 278-8518 or (800) 227-0046
www.iceagetrail.org

LANGER PARK ICE RINK
Fourth St. and Remington St.
Baraboo, WI 53913
(608) 355-2760

MID-CONTINENT RAILWAY AND MUSEUM
E8948 Diamond Hill Rd.
North Freedom, WI 53951
(608) 522-4261 or (800) 930-1385
www.midcontinent.org

MIRROR LAKE STATE PARK
E10320 Fern Dell Rd., Baraboo, WI 53913
(608) 254-2333, www.wiparks.net

PARFREY'S GLEN STATE NATURAL AREA
Devil's Lake State Park (Administrator)
S5975 Park Rd., Baraboo, WI 53913
(608) 356-8301
www.dnr.state.wi.us/org/land/er/sna/sna1.htm

WEBER PARK PLEASURE RINK
300 Block of Elm St., Baraboo, WI 53913
(608) 355-2760

WOLLERSHEIM WINERY
7876 Highway 188, Prairie du Sac, WI 53578
(608) 643-6515 or (800) 847-9463
www.wollersheim.com

WINTER FESTIVALS

WOLLERSHEIM WINERY NOUVEAU WINE TASTING—mid-November (Saturday before Thanksgiving). Taste the first release of a new wine in the winery's Great Room along with Wisconsin cheeses. 10:00 a.m.–5:00 p.m. (800) 847-9463 or www.wollersheim.com.

HOLIDAY LIGHT PARADE—late November. Downtown Baraboo, www.downtownbaraboo.com.

MID-CONTINENT RAILWAY MUSEUM SANTA CLAUS EXPRESS—late November/early December. Santa greets children of all ages aboard the turn-of-the-century passenger train. (800) 930-1385 or www.santatrain.org.

CANDLELIGHT SKI AND HIKE, MIRROR LAKE STATE PARK—early January and early February. Two separate trails will be lit by torches from 6:00 to 8:00 p.m.; one for skiers, the other for hikers, snowshoers, and leashed pets. Afterwards, join the Friends of Mirror Lake State Park around the fire for hot beverages and snacks. (608) 254-2333 or www.dnr.state.wi.us/org/caer/ce/news/candlelight.htm.

BALD EAGLE WATCHING DAYS—mid-January. Activities along the Wisconsin River and guided bus tours to three prime eagle-gathering sites. (608) 643-2417 or www.ferrybluffeaglecouncil.org/index.html.

MIRROR LAKE OPEN HOUSE AND DELTON SPORTSMEN'S CLUB FISHEREE—mid-January. Fishermen of all levels take part in this annual ice fishing competition with several winter contests and games. (608) 254-2333.

WOLLERSHEIM WINERY PORT RELEASE CELEBRATION—late January. Taste the first release of the year's port wine, the perfect sipping wine for a cold winter day. Light food and live jazz. (608) 643-6515 or www.wollersheim.com.

MID-CONTINENT RAILWAY MUSEUM SNOW TRAIN—third weekend in February. Enjoy views of forests in winter aboard a historic train. Ride through the Sauk County countryside into the Baraboo bluffs. Passenger trains offer coach, first-class, and dinner excursions. (608) 522-4261 or (800) 930-1385 or www.midcontinent.org.

WOLLERSHEIM WINERY OPEN HOUSE— first full weekend of March. (608) 643-6515 or www.wollersheim.com.

RESTAURANTS

THE CHEESE FACTORY RESTAURANT
(lunch and dinner; Sunday breakfast, lunch, and dinner)
521 Wisconsin Dells Pkwy. *(Highway 12)*
Wisconsin Dells, WI 53965
(608) 253-6065
www.cookingvegetarian.com

GARDEN PARTY CAFÉ *(lunch; closed Sunday)*
528 Oak St., Baraboo, WI 53913
(608) 355-0355

JAVA CAFÉ *(breakfast and lunch)*
106 Fourth Ave., Baraboo, WI 53913
(608) 355-1053, www.baraboo.com/javacafe

LITTLE VILLAGE CAFÉ
(lunch and dinner; closed Sunday)
146 Fourth Ave., Baraboo, WI 53913
(608) 356-2800, www.littlevillagecafe.com

LOG CABIN RESTAURANT
(breakfast, lunch, and dinner)
1215 Eighth St. (Highway 33), Baraboo, WI 53913
(608) 356-8034, www.baraboo-logcabin.com

MONK'S BAR & GRILL *(lunch and dinner)*
116 Fourth Ave., Baraboo, WI 53913
(608) 355-0977
www.monksbarandgrill.com

LODGING
THE GOLLMAR GUEST HOUSE BED & BREAKFAST
422 Third St., Baraboo, WI 53913, (608) 356-9432
www.gollmar.com

MOON VALLEY RESORT & MARINA
E13105 Highway 78, Merrimac, WI 53561
(608) 493-2226, www.moon-valley.com

PINEHAVEN BED & BREAKFAST
E13083 Highway 33, Baraboo, WI 53913
(608) 356-3489, www.pinehavenbnb.com

RUSTIC RIDGE LOG CABIN RENTALS
E13981 Highway DL, Merrimac, WI 53561,
(608) 493-2440, www.rusticridgecabins.com

SETH PETERSON COTTAGE
Mirror Lake State Park, (608) 254-6551
www.sethpeterson.org

VICTORIAN ROSE BED & BREAKFAST
423 Third Ave., Baraboo, WI 53913
(608) 356-7828

Chapter Three

TRUE NORTH
Bayfield

IF BOOKS SUCH AS Jack London's *The Call of the Wild* and Benedict and Nancy Freedman's *Mrs. Mike* captured your heart as a youngster, you'll find Bayfield a place that satisfies your longing for adventure. In this quaint village, you can have a true experience of the North—complete with mushing, exploring caves created by frozen waters, and traveling on roads made of ice.

The Apostle Islands Sled Dog Race is a close relative of the more famous Iditarod and Yukon Quest annual events in Alaska. The Bayfield race has all the excitement of those far-off challenges but with the added benefit of easy accessibility. On Friday night, you can mingle with the mushers at the pre-race Meet the Mushers dinner; and on Saturday and Sunday, you can post yourself at the start/finish line to cheer the teams off and then back in. You can watch as the mushers ready the dogs in the early morning hours before the race and listen as more than 600 canine voices express a readiness to start their own Bayfield adventures. At first surging against their harnesses and barking with an urge to dash, a team of eight dogs soon hits a rhythm on the soft snow and begins to run silently as one. It's a transformation that fires your own adrenaline.

Bayfield points the way to the Apostle Islands National Lakeshore, 22 islands in the white-and-dark-blue expanse of Lake Superior in winter. And *only* in winter can you travel from Bayfield to Madeline Island on the frozen, Christmas-tree-marked "Ice Road." For even more adventure, catch the "windsled" that runs between Bayfield and La Pointe on the island. The sled is operational before complete freezing in the winter and during first thaw in the spring. And when Lake Superior waters rise up against the rocks, crash along the shore, and freeze, intricate ice caves appear, making a landscape that is far more North Pole than northern Wisconsin.

Bayfield has a population of approximately 600. In summer, that number often swells to more than 3,000. To have room to breathe in Bayfield, to truly take in its hardwood forests, marshes, and shoreline habitats without feeling the squeeze and press of humanity, it is best to visit in winter.

In the May/June 2003 issue of *Orion* magazine, author William Cronon called the Apostle Islands "a storied wilderness." In the tradition of Jack London and the Freedmans, follow your younger heart on this Bayfield winter weekend and write your own true Northern adventure.

The dogs start arriving in the early morning hours for the Apostle Islands Sled Dog Race.

Day One
LATE MORNING AND AFTERNOON

The first impression Bayfield makes on you is that of a charming village that the last 100 years forgot. Fifty-two buildings here are on the National Historic Register, and at least 80 of the picturesque Victorian-era homes standing in the hilly streets above the Lake Superior shoreline have been turned into gracious bed and breakfasts or welcoming inns. Upon arriving in Bayfield, take your camera out of its bag and leave it out. A brief walk on Rittenhouse Avenue and its cross streets will reward you with shots of what looks like a miniature Victorian village on a Christmas buffet table. Stop at **Maggie's** on Manypenny Avenue for an early lunch. Known for its sandwiches, burgers, Lake Superior whitefish livers, and unusual decorations—lots of pink flamingos—Maggie's is a local favorite.

MADELINE ISLAND'S WINTER HIGHWAY

by Charles R. Nelson
(parts taken from On Thin Ice*)*

Windsled and aviation historian Charles R. Nelson is the author of On Thin Ice: Windsleds at Madeline Island. *A native and year-round resident of Madeline Island, Charles has served as an EMS ice rescue instructor and windsled operator and is currently pursuing his dream of becoming a pilot. His love of exploring the Apostle Islands by water and air has made a life on Madeline an easy decision. Contact him at windavmu@cheqnet.net.*

Ice highway, lifeline, artery, winter road. By any name, Madeline Island's beloved ice road is by far the greatest factor in maintaining a year-round island population. For some, the lack of a winter highway would certainly tip the scales in favor of departing on the last ferry.

Mother Nature's annual gift of two to three months of weather to maintain the ice road is as dear to most islanders as Madeline herself. The ice road is also a big part of what being an islander is all about.

"You drive a car on ice? You drive when there is 10 inches of water on it? Are you nuts?"

For me, one of the best things about being an islander is being questioned by summer visitors about how we get across the lake after the ferryboats quit for the season. Seeing the astonished look on their faces when we start to tell them about the windsled and ice road really makes it all worthwhile. You can't help but feel a bit special.

The ice road is a gift—it isn't owed to us. There is no guarantee or accurate way of predicting the size of the gift that we will receive each year or that we will even get it. Presently, meteorologists are capable of predicting a three- to five-day weather forecast, but there are far too many factors involved to ever predict when an ice road will appear. This could only be done if they not only knew the daily temps, snow, and wind we would be getting each winter, but also knew the precise time they would each happen. The timing is very important. As an example, if a storm were to deposit 16 inches of fresh snow onto newly formed ice that was four to six inches thick, the snow would not only insulate the ice—preventing it from continuing to form—but the thin ice would most likely sink and flood under the added weight. This is the scenario that islanders fear the most: the ice is too thin to support a snowplow, and if we don't clear the snow exposing the ice to the elements, we will not have an ice road—at least not with that ice.

If you want to go out onto the ice road for the first time and decide to ask an islander how the road is, you might get an answer you won't quite understand: "Sure, the road is O.K. But before you go out there, open your windows, unlock your door and for God's sake, take off your seatbelt. As soon as you get on the ice at the Bayfield approach, next to the 'No life guard on duty' sign, turn hard to the left so you don't put your car through the shove-crack like that guy did an hour ago. Once you get out there, follow the road along the trees until you see trees in the road. Then, you get out of the road because the trees are marking the spot where someone put their back tires through yesterday. The ice is starting to candle, so keep moving; don't stop out there. If someone needs a ride, open your door and let them jump in while you're moving—don't stop on the ice! Out in the middle, there is an expansion-crack that buckled the road last week. Arnie and Ronnie placed timbers over it, so you need to drive on them. When you get to the island, follow the yellow ribbons until you get to the truck sticking out of the ice that belonged to the guy that didn't ask for directions—I think his insurance company owns it now. Stay to the right of that. Go slow over the shove-crack, but then speed up so you are going fast enough to get up the approach. Yeah, it's no problem."

The two-mile crossing between Madeline and Bayfield is a very exciting and rare experience that is well worth the trip.

Jump right into your real wilderness adventure by planning to spend the rest of the day at the largest of the 22 Apostle Islands, **Madeline Island**, and **Big Bay State Park**. It's a good idea to carry a backpack with some snacks and extra clothing, such as socks, hats, and gloves. Weather around Lake Superior can be unpredictable, and while the **Mission Hill Coffee House** on Madeline Island in La Pointe serves muffins and sandwiches, it's about seven miles from the park.

Your adventure starts before you even get to Madeline Island, however, down by the city dock. You'll be taking the state's only public **"Ice Road."** When the five-mile passage between Bayfield and La Pointe on the island is completely frozen, an ice highway is created by marking a lane on both sides with discarded Christmas trees. Visitors can simply drive over to the island—a distinct winter advantage! If you happen to visit Bayfield before a complete freeze or during spring thaw, you may be able to catch a ride on the **windsled** [see "Madeline Island's Winter Highway" sidebar]. Be prepared for an afternoon of exploring on foot if you take the windsled, however, since you won't have your vehicle on the island.

Once on Madeline Island, the 2,418-acre **Big Bay State Park** offers opportunities for

The two-mile crossing between Madeline Island and Bayfield is always an exciting experience, but it is made even more rare and special on the windsled.

cross-country skiing, snowshoeing, winter hiking, and **winter camping.** In Wisconsin's northernmost state park, you can cross-country ski on 5.2 miles of groomed trails and snowshoe throughout the park. There are nine miles of trails for winter hikers. More than 240 bird species live on or visit the Apostle Islands, and deer, beavers, and bears occupy the park. If you're feeling very hardy, you can **winter camp** at designated park sites.

If you happen to visit the island—or the mainland—after a long stretch of cold weather, you may be able to ski or walk on the Lake Superior ice to visit some of the dazzling **ice caves.** Most winters, the lake builds the caves along the jagged shoreline cliffs of the island and the mainland near Meyers Road. Frozen waterfalls and crashing waves create thousands of delicate icicles in the rock chambers.

Return to the mainland by late afternoon and check into your accommodations. Bayfield has many bed and breakfasts, and one is sure to fit your tastes. If you'd like a roomy, real home away from home, consider the **Sailor's Solace Suites**. This two-apartment building sits on a quiet, wooded hill just a bit above the city. The full apartment on the upper level has a view of Lake Superior from the front porch.

JOHN T. ANDREWS

The Bayfield city dock takes on an otherworldly beauty in winter.

EVENING

If you've scheduled your Bayfield weekend during the **Apostle Islands Sled Dog Race** in early February, go to the **Meet the Mushers dinner** at the **Bayfield Lakeside Pavilion**. Rub elbows with mushers from all over the country and world, learn about the next day's trail conditions and the rules for the race. Sitting at the tables covered with plates of spaghetti and surrounded by race and dog talk, you could easily think you were at the Iditarod or Yukon Quest preparations in Fairbanks, Alaska.

If tonight you'd prefer something on the more elegant end of the dining scale, make reservations at the **Old Rittenhouse Inn**, the best-known bed and breakfast in the village.

A restored Victorian mansion dating from the 1890s, the inn serves five-course, candlelight dinners, with entrées such as hazelnut-encrusted breast of pheasant or fresh lake trout drizzled with hollandaise sauce.

Day Two

MORNING AND AFTERNOON

Today, you'll have the quintessential Northern experience—whether you're in Bayfield for the **Apostle Islands Sled Dog Race** or not.

Start your morning with a hot breakfast and a great cup of coffee at the **Blue Horizons Café & Catering** on Rittenhouse Avenue before heading out to the gravel pit, the staging, starting, and finishing area for the race.

The race starts at 10:00 a.m., but the real show begins early in the morning around seven o'clock when the mushers and their dogs start to arrive. Get there early to take photos of beautiful, blue-eyed Siberian Huskies, hundreds of excited dogs, and the close relationships between the human and canine members of the teams *[see "Happy Feet: Maintaining Sled Dog Toes in the Cold" sidebar]*.

The Apostle Islands Sled Dog Race is the biggest in northern Wisconsin; 100 teams were registered in 2005. The competitions include an eight-dog, 88-mile race (44 miles per day);

MICHAEL C. YATES/WWW.TRAVELWISCONSIN.COM

The Apostle Islands Sled Dog Race is the biggest in northern Wisconsin and embodies the spirit of the True North.

HAPPY FEET: MAINTAINING SLED DOG TOES IN THE COLD

by Margaret Eastman, DVM

Dr. Eastman grew up in Green Bay. After graduating from the University of Wisconsin School of Veterinary Medicine, she began volunteering as a trail veterinarian for long-distance sled dog races in Michigan, Minnesota, and, eventually, Alaska. She worked as a veterinarian for the Iditarod and the Yukon Quest International Sled Dog Race, and Alaska "stuck." She now resides in North Pole, Alaska, with her husband, baby, four dogs, and four cats.

One of the greatest thrills I've ever experienced in life has been the start of a sled dog race. Sled dogs are amazing athletes, and the enthusiasm with which they move down the trail is unmatched. A unique combination of genetics, nutrition, dog care, and training results in a dog that can easily cover 100 miles per day over the course of a 1,000-mile race.

There is an old saying in mushing, "No feet, no dog." Sled dog feet are vulnerable to a unique condition that involves small fissures or "splits" in the webbing between the toes. Snow wedges itself in the warm interdigital spaces, melts a bit, and forms ice, which can cause discomfort and the splits. Cold conditions and granular snow are particularly problematic for husky feet.

The introduction of booties has made keeping dog feet healthy much easier. The original dog booties were made of polar fleece and held in place with electric tape, lasting 25 miles at the most. The booties you see at sled dog races today are much more durable. They're made of a supple but hearty nylon with Velcro to hold them in place.

Mushers use a combination of booties and foot ointments to prevent and treat splits as the dogs run. The foot ointments usually have a zinc oxide base, with antibiotic added. A mix of hydrogenated peanut oil and rosemary has also gained favor.

Sled dogs aren't the only canines that can have sore feet after moving through the snow. Pet dogs can be equally susceptible to web injuries. Booties come in different sizes, so if your Labrador or terrier has trouble with snow between the toes, look into a set of booties. Your dog can have happy feet in the cold, too.

---

a six-dog, 66-mile race (33 miles per day); a 15-mile Sportsmen's Race; and a 5-mile Madeline Island Sprint Race.

At the start/finish line, you can comfortably enjoy the race activities in a warming tent with hot food and beverages, retail booths, and restrooms. Outside, a huge bonfire roars. Apple brats cook on the grill all day long (that's something even the Iditarod doesn't have!).

If you'd prefer to do the mushing yourself or you're not in Bayfield during the Apostle Islands Sled Dog Race, contact **Wolfsong Adventures in Mushing**. Owners John and Mary Thiel have thousands of miles of mushing experience and offer you a daylong mushing outing where you'll learn to handle and harness the dogs, and either drive your own sled or ride with one of the guides. You'll even get a hot meal on the trail. The Thiels live with 38 Siberian Huskies, and Mary says she'll match your personality with those of the dogs.

Bayfield is proud of its cooperative community spirit, and there is an excellent partnering between sled dog enthusiasts and snowmobilers. Both groups work together to maintain trails for all users *[see "Working Together" sidebar]*. There are 599 miles of **snowmobile** trails in the Bayfield area. Corridor 31 goes through the **Chequamegon–Nicolet National Forest.** Call (715) 373-6125 for snowmobile trail conditions.

If you're not grabbing lunch with the dogs of Wolfsong out on the trail, stop at **Captain's Deli & Spirits** on North Street for a bowl of homemade soup or a deli sandwich made to your order with fresh meats and cheeses. Captain's also has a wide selection of wines, along with beer and local coffee brews.

If **cross-country skiing, winter hiking,** or **ATVing** are on your agenda, visit the **Mt. Valhalla Recreational Area** nestled in the Chequamegon side of the **Chequamegon–Nicolet National Forest.** There are 18.6 miles of groomed and tracked trails in this land sculpted by glaciers for classic and skate-skiing. Once used to train the U.S. Olympic Ski Team, the three **Valkyrie Loops** run 10.3 miles through magnificent red and jack pine forests. The eight-mile **Teuton Ski Trail** also features three loops, but these are in a mixed birch and maple forest—with a roller coaster hill near the end of Loop B. The entire Teuton Trail is groomed for skate-skiing. County Road C runs between the Valkyrie and Teuton Trails, with a parking area and chalet on the Teuton side of C.

EVENING

You'll appreciate a hearty, warm meal at the end of the day, and **Fore 'N Aft** can accommodate. Located a half mile south of Bayfield, the restaurant's menu includes fish, chicken, steaks, pasta, sandwiches, pizza, and a Saturday prime rib special.

Day Three
MORNING

For a breakfast you'll never forget, call for a reservation at the **Old Rittenhouse Inn.** A typical Sunday breakfast here includes a choice of juices, an entrée choice of wild rice pancakes, Belgian waffles, or an egg scramble—such as the Lake Superior trout, wild leeks, and cheddar cheese—and a side choice of potatoes, bacon, or smoked turkey sausage with apples and Gouda—all exceptionally prepared. A basket of home-baked breads delivered to your table allows you to sample the Rittenhouse's own gourmet jams and jellies.

AFTERNOON

Spend the last hours of your northern adventure in Bayfield enjoying your favorite outdoor winter sport. Take up temporary residence in the **ice fishing** shantytown located off the city dock. Or go to **Mt. Ashwabay,** three miles south of Bayfield, where you can **downhill ski, snowboard, cross-country ski,** or **snowshoe.** The emphasis at Mt. Ashwabay is on incredible scenery rather than high-tech amenities. Fourteen **downhill runs** range from beginner to expert and are accessed from a T-bar and four rope tows. **Snowboarders** can have fun on a quarter-pipe.

The 25 miles of wilderness **cross-country trails** at Mt. Ashwabay will lead you to stunning views of the Apostle Islands National Lakeshore and the Chequamegon National Forest. With ratings from beginner to expert, the trails are groomed and tracked weekly.

Snowshoers are welcome on the sides of the cross-country trails, as well as on the snow-shoe-specific trails.

If you prefer to forge your own path, follow the shore of Lake Superior. Look for the nearest frozen spot, strap on a pair of **ice skates**, and answer your own call of the wild.

WORKING TOGETHER

by John Thiel

Born in Fond du Lac, Wisconsin, John Thiel moved "up north" to Manitowish Waters in 1991. He married Mary Weikie in 1993, the same year he bought his first sled dogs. In Bayfield in 1995, the Thiels founded Dreamcatcher Sailing Charters and their two winter businesses: Wolfsong Adventures in Mushing and Wolfsong Wear Outerwear of Bayfield.

The Apostle Islands Sled Dog Race brings hundreds of mushers and spectators to the Bayfield area every year. The Bayfield County Snowmobile Alliance helps groom the 30 miles of race trails. The mushers say that with so many dog teams doing the course, the groomed portion is by far the best surface for running. Many of the visiting mushers comment that they are happy to see how well mushers and snowmobilers get along here. But it isn't just a coincidence.

Several years ago, there was a controversy between snowmobilers and mushers over trail use. At a Bayfield County Forestry Committee meeting, many argued over whether or not the snowmobile trails on county forestland should be closed to all other users. Tempers flared. The county board sided with the snowmobile clubs but instructed both sides to work together to provide a transition for the mushers until a new trail system could be developed.

In the following year, the two groups sat down face to face in an effort to resolve the problem. Right away we realized that both sides had overblown the issue. As we were all outdoor enthusiasts, we found that we had a lot in common.

For the first year, the snowmobile alliance agreed that mushers could use the trails midweek until they could develop a trail system of their own. The Northern Wisconsin Dog Mushers Association was formed to develop the trails. Because of the support of the Bayfield County Forestry Department, Bayfield County Tourism and Recreation Department, and the Wisconsin Conservation Corps, there now exists about 80 miles of marked trails that are used by local and regional mushers.

Both mushers and snowmobilers now appreciate not worrying about conflicts and potential accidents. For the most part, the mushing trails are open to all users in the winter—including snowmobilers, who help to keep the trails packed. Encounters between dog mushers and snowmobilers usually result in friendly waves, mutual courtesy, and often snowmobilers taking photos. I have met snowmobilers on the trail who came to the area specifically in hopes of seeing a dog team.

In the past four years, a small section of the Apostle Islands Sled Dog Race trail has shared a town road with snowmobile trail 5C. Many snowmobilers have volunteered to help in the race. Some park at the trail crossings to warn snowmobilers of the race and help mushers through these sometimes confusing intersections.

Friendships between former opponents have developed. Working together has been much more fun than fighting. Bayfield is a model for other adversarial groups, and the town is now a better place for us all.

www.travelwisconsin.com

Lake Superior fashions spectacular ice caves only for winter visitors.

FOR MORE INFORMATION
BAYFIELD CHAMBER OF COMMERCE
42 S. Broad St., Bayfield, WI 54814
(715) 779-3335 or (800) 447-4094
www.bayfield.org

BAYFIELD COUNTY TOURISM & RECREATION
PO Box 832SM, Washburn, WI 54891
(800) 472-6338, www.travelbayfieldcounty.com

WINTER ATTRACTIONS
BAYFIELD LAKESIDE PAVILION
1 North Front St., Bayfield, WI 54814
(715) 779-3335

BIG BAY STATE PARK
141 S. Third St., Box 589
Bayfield, WI 54814-0589, (715) 747-6425
www.dnr.state.wi.us/org/land/parks/specific/bigbay

MT. ASHWABAY
32525 Ski Hill Rd., Bayfield, WI 54814

(715) 779-3227
www.ski-guide.com/stats.cfm/wi13.htm

MT. VALHALLA RECREATIONAL AREA
Chequamegon–Nicolet National Forest
County Road C (10 miles west of Washburn)
Washburn Ranger District
113 Bayfield St. East, Washburn, WI 54891
(715) 373-2667, www.fs.fed.us/r9/cnnf

WOLFSONG ADVENTURES IN MUSHING
88265 Happy Hollow Rd.
Bayfield, WI 54814
(715) 779-5561 or (800) 262-4176
www.wolfsongadventures.com

WINTER FESTIVALS
HOLIDAY WEEKEND MAGIC I—last weekend in November. City tree lighting and community social. (800) 447-4094 or www.bayfield.org.

HOLIDAY WEEKEND MAGIC II—first weekend in December. Held at the Bayfield Lakeside

Pavilion. Santa visits on a ferry. (800) 447-4094 or www.bayfield.org.

HOLIDAY WEEKEND MAGIC III—second weekend in December. Held at the Bayfield Lakeside Pavilion. Arts and crafts sale, and Bayfield Holiday Art Gallery Tour. (800) 447-4094 or www.bayfield.org.

SLEIGH AND CUTTER PARADE—mid-January. Experience a narrated parade of horses and sleighs in the Northwoods Harness Club Sleigh and Cutter Rally. Hook-up is at 11:00 a.m., followed by the parade at 1:00 p.m. (715) 682-2256 or www.bayfield.org.

APOSTLE ISLANDS SLED DOG RACE—early February. Nearly 100 teams of six to eight dogs each compete for a $5,000 purse. Professional and recreational classes compete in four different two-day races. (800) 447-4094 or www.bayfield.org/visitor/dogsled.asp.

BLUE MOON BALL—mid-February. Held at the Bayfield Lakeside Pavilion, this black-tie and vintage-dress prom for adults includes a 15-piece orchestra. (715) 779-3335 or www.bayfield.org.

RUN ON WATER—mid-February. A family fun run takes runners on the ice road from Bayfield to Madeline Island and back. Participants may run, walk, ski, or snowshoe the five-mile course. (800) 447-4094 or www.bayfield.org.

BOOK ACROSS THE BAY—late February. A 6.2-mile race on a groomed course crossing the frozen Chequamegon Bay of Lake Superior. The race begins at 6:00 p.m. in Ashland and ends in Washburn. The entire course is lit by hundreds of candles in ice luminaries. (800) 284-9484 or www.batb.org.

RESTAURANTS
BLUE HORIZONS CAFÉ & CATERING
(breakfast and lunch)
117 Rittenhouse Ave., Bayfield, WI 54814
(715) 779-9619

CAPTAIN'S DELI & SPIRITS
(breakfast and lunch)
33 N. First St., Bayfield, WI 54814
(715) 779-5313, www.captainsbayfield.com

FORE 'N AFT *(dinner)*
84810 Highway 13, Bayfield, WI 54814
(877) 235-4675, www.forenaft.com

MAGGIE'S *(lunch and dinner)*
257 Manypenny Ave., Bayfield, WI 54814
(715) 779-5641, www.maggies-bayfield.com

MISSION HILL COFFEE HOUSE
(limited winter hours)
105–106 Lake View Place, La Pointe, WI 54850
(715) 747-3100

OLD RITTENHOUSE INN
(breakfast and dinner)
301 Rittenhouse Ave., Bayfield, WI 54814
(715) 779-5111 or (800) 779-2129
www.rittenhouseinn.com

LODGING
Here is just a sampling of the many Bayfield bed and breakfasts which welcome winter visitors:
BAY FRONT INN
15 Front St., Bayfield, WI 54814
(715) 779-3880 or (888) 243-4191
www.explorewisconsin.com/pierplazarestaurantandbayfrontinn

THE BAYFIELD INN
20 Rittenhouse Ave., Bayfield, WI 54814
(715) 779-3363 or (800) 382-0995
www.bayfieldinn.com

OLD RITTENHOUSE INN
301 Rittenhouse Ave., Bayfield, WI 54814
(715) 779-5111 or (800) 779-2129
www.rittenhouseinn.com

SAILOR'S SOLACE SUITES
85640 Woodland Trail, Bayfield, WI 54814
(715) 779-3320, www.sailorssolace.com

SEAGULL BAY MOTEL
325 S. Seventh St., Bayfield, WI 54814
(715) 779-5558, www.seagullbay.com

Chapter Four

SEASONAL CHARM
Cedarburg/Port Washington

CEDARBURG IS A HISTORIC WONDER at any time of year, but in winter it is at its best. During its many winter festivals, the 19th-century streets take on an added glow of gaiety and old-fashioned charm. The downtown area stretches a mere six blocks, but it is six blocks of buildings that are all listed on the National Register of Historic Places.

Just a half hour north of Milwaukee, Cedarburg' original settlers were primarily German immigrants, who built numerous mills along Cedar Creek. Cedar Creek Settlement, once the village's hub, made material for the blue uniforms of Union troops during the Civil War. That building, and more than 100 other original brick buildings, have been restored and now comprise the state's most concentrated area of bed and breakfasts, restaurants, boutique shops, and galleries.

But Cedarburg is far more than stores and dining establishments. The village is also a place for winter recreation and festivals. The Ozaukee Interurban Trail runs through the center of town, and events such as Christmas in the Country, the Winter Festival, and the Cedar Creek Winery & Settlement Open House keep the downtown area alive with music, fun, and good company all season long.

In Port Washington, just 10 miles away, you can experience another historic town and novel winter festival—Christmas on the Corners. At this special winter weekend celebration, you almost lose yourself in time walking through downtown next to horse-drawn wagons and real reindeer. Port Washington is on the National Register of Historic Downtowns and brags of Wisconsin's largest collection of pre-Civil War buildings.

Two sentries watch over Port Washington. Sitting on a hill overlooking the city is St. Mary's Church, with its tall spire. An 1860 lighthouse is the second set of eyes. This coastal community is a quintessential Great Lakes fishing town. On Grand Avenue, the tourist center is in a building known as the Pebble House, which was made of stones scavenged from the beaches along the lake.

Called the City of the Seven Hills, Port Washington is as visually picturesque as

Black Peter and St. Nicholas are just some of the charming characters at Port Washington's Christmas on the Corners festival.

Cedarburg, but a world apart in tranquility. While Cedarburg has all the hustle and bustle that comes with excited holiday shoppers, Port Washington feels unhurried in winter. Together, these two nostalgic towns give you both sides of an Old World winter. But ghost towns they certainly are not. They are vibrant communities of working artists, busy innkeepers, and joyful festival-goers. They are the pictures of how Wisconsinites once took pleasure in the year's fourth season— and still do.

Day One
MØRNING

If you can choose only one winter weekend to visit Cedarburg, make it the weekend of **Christmas in the Country**. The village decks itself out with fresh green wreaths, bright red bows, twinkling lights, and strolling carolers, and it holds special events in its historic, stone buildings.

Get a feel for the old Cedarburg by first stopping at the **Cedarburg General Store Museum** at the top of the downtown strip. The 1860 building houses the town's visitor center and a collection of vintage advertising art, such as apothecary jars and dry goods items. Grab yourself a cup of steaming coffee and a raspberry scone at the **Dancing Goat Espresso Bar & Café** on the downtown strip and get started on your explorations.

The Christmas in the Country arts-and-crafts festival is held in **Cedar Creek Settlement** on the corner of Washington and Bridge Streets. This 1864 former woolen mill on Cedar Creek now is the home to more than 30 specialty shops, artists' studios, and restaurants. Held in the lower level of the settlement, the holiday boutique features more than 50 artisans. From carved wooden reindeer to wreaths to sweaters, the fair has it all. At least a third of all the items are newly created by the artists each year, and their first showing is exclusive to the Cedarburg show.

While at the settlement, make sure to stop at the **Cedar Creek Winery**. Sample the Christmas wines and pick up a boxed set to savor by the fireplace for the rest of the winter.

AFTERNOON

Stop for lunch at **Tomaso's Italian American Restaurant**, just south of the Washington and Bridge Roads intersection. *Milwaukee Magazine* and Ozaukee County survey results have named Tomaso's the number one choice for pizza. A variety of lunch sandwiches and specials round out the menu.

As a complement to this morning's Cedarburg shopping, this afternoon will be reserved for Cedarburg's recreational offerings. The **Ozaukee Ice Center** on Pioneer Road holds a **public skate** on Fridays from 11:00 a.m. to 1:00 p.m. and Saturdays from 1:00 p.m. to 3:00 p.m. Skates can be rented for a nominal fee. If you prefer to stay outdoors, you'll find a picture-perfect, cleared **ice-skating rink** behind the **Cedar Creek Settlement**.

Wearing **cross-country skis**—or **winter hiking** boots if there is a lack snow—is fashionable in downtown Cedarburg, so feel free to lace on your boots. That's because the 30-mile **Ozaukee Interurban Trail** passes right through downtown Cedarburg as it traverses Ozaukee County, north to south. Opened in 2002, this free trail goes through eight of the county's communities, including not only Cedarburg, but also Belgium, Port Washington, Grafton, Mequon, and Thiensville. The trail's route is based on the interurban railway that connected Ozaukee County to Milwaukee. Birdwatchers should note that the Wisconsin Department of Natural Resources has designated the Ozaukee trail a Great Wisconsin Birding and Nature Trail.

Before leaving the Cedarburg festival, ice-skating rinks, and trails, stop by the **Cedarburg Coffee Roastery** for a hot drink and bakery goods. Even if you don't partake in any treats, seeing the roastery in the center of the store is worth a look. The philosophy of the company is that coffee is best when it is fresh, and the best way to get fresh coffee is to roast it often and close to the people. In fact, they say, 30 hours after roasting, coffee beans reach their peak flavor. The roastery's coffees are all marked with the date of the roast, so you get the best-tasting cup possible. They offer an extensive variety of coffees from around the world, from Guatemala to Kenya to Hawaii.

JOHN T. ANDREWS

Christmas in the Country's holiday craft show is held in the 1864 Cedar Creek Settlement, a former woolen mill.

On your way out of Cedarburg, visit a piece of Wisconsin's heritage by stopping at **Covered Bridge County Park**, five minutes northwest of town at Covered Bridge Road (the junction of Highways 60 and 143).

Here you'll find what is believed to be the last covered bridge of what had been 40 in the state. Built in 1876 and retired in 1962, the bridge's pine logs were cut and milled near Baraboo, then hauled to the site and fitted in place. Interlacing, 3 x 10-inch planks were secured with 2-inch hardwood pins—there are no nails or bolts. This construction is known as "lattice truss" and is now very rare. This pedestrian-only bridge measures about 120 feet long and 12 feet wide. During the winter, when the trees are bare, an unobstructed view of the bridge affords great photo opportunities. The grounds surrounding the bridge provide a quiet place to walk.

Your home for this weekend will be in Port Washington, just 10 miles northeast of Cedarburg. Check into the 1903 **Port Washington Inn** and immerse yourself in a second dose of rich Wisconsin history.

Cedarburg decks itself out with bright-red bows and twinkling lights for Christmas in the Country weekend.

Appointed with dark woodwork, hardwood floors, stained glass windows, and coved ceilings, the Port Washington Inn features four-poster, carved beds and lace-trimmed quilts. From Dorothy's Room, you'll enjoy a view of Lake Michigan. Make sure to borrow the book from the inn's library on Port Washington's history, published by the Homecoming Committee of 1908 (the cost of the book at that time was 25 cents). It describes Port Washington as the "Little City of Seven Hills" and claims that the Port Washington brewing company is the "brewer and bottler of Premo, the beer that made Milwaukee furious."

In fact, it was George and Eva Blessing, the owners of Old Port Brewing Corp., who built the Port Washington Inn in 1903 as the house of their dreams. They chose one of the highest points in town, Sweetcake Hill, as the location.

EVENING

Enjoy a relaxing dinner at Port Washington's **The Farmstead.** Order the restaurant's signature garlic mashed potatoes and garlic steak. Then head back to your inn and open one of the Cedar Creek Winery's Christmas wines, while watching the stars come out over Lake Michigan from your room's window *[see "Mulling Over a Winter Evening" sidebar].*

MORNING

Today will be your chance to really get to know the great little town of Port Washington and its environs. You can expect your breakfast at the Port Washington Inn to be something like this: fresh spinach omelet, blueberries and bananas with yogurt, toast, homemade granola, poached pears, ham, coffee, and juices. You'll be well fueled for the day.

Take a brief tour of downtown Port Washington by first stopping for a photograph at the **Pebble House Visitor Center.** On the National Register of Historic Places, this building,

MULLING OVER A WINTER EVENING

Mulled wine—or wine that is heated and spiced—has been comforting cold-weather residents since at least the Middle Ages. Originally called *Ypocras* or *Hipocris* after the physician Hippocrates, mulled wines were thought to be heath drinks. With the unsanitary water conditions in medieval times, those who drank mulled wines in favor of water probably were healthier than their water-only drinking brethren. Mulled wine later became a favorite drink in Victorian England.

Today's mulled wine recipes run the gamut of ingredients, but most require heating with various citrus fruits and spices such as cinnamon, cloves, allspice, or nutmeg. Mulled wine is generally sweetened with sugar and fortified with a spirit, such as brandy. Red or white wine can be mulled. Here's a simple mulled wine recipe to try at home:

Mulled Wine

1 bottle of moderately priced wine (such as merlot, zinfandel, or burgundy)

1 cup of brandy, sweet vermouth, or cognac

1/2 cup sugar

3 cinnamon sticks

6 whole cloves

6 whole allspice

2 oranges, sliced

1 lemon, sliced

Add the bottle of wine to a slow cooker or large saucepan and begin heating over low heat. As the wine warms, add the sugar and spices. You can either make a pouch from cheesecloth to insert the cinnamon, cloves, and allspice and then tie the opening closed, or put the spices in the pot loose and strain the mixture later. Stir until the sugar is dissolved.

Add the brandy and continue heating thoroughly, but do not allow the wine to reach the boiling point. Add the lemon and orange. Simmer over low heat; about 1 hour. Serve in napkin-wrapped goblets or tumblers.

However, if an hour seems like too long to wait for your winter health drink, simply go to the Cedar Creek Winery located in the Cedar Creek Settlement. Purchase a bottle of Cedarburg Spice—a sweet red infused with mulling spices—pop the cork, and feel the warmth inside.

---

a Greek revival-style home, has stone walls 20 inches thick. The foundation of the 1848 building is constructed of rocks collected along the Michigan shoreline by its original owners, Elizabeth and Henry Dodge. In 1985, the house was moved to its current location.

Another icon not to miss is the **Port Washington 1860 Light Station**, located on Johnson Street on Saint Mary's Hill. The station is the epitome of a Great Lakes coastal lighthouse. A combination keeper's dwelling and lighthouse, the station was an active navigation aid from 1860 to 1903. If you visit Port Washington in late November to mid-December, stop by for the **Light Station Victorian Christmas Showhouse**, when you can tour the lighthouse with a costumed guide.

AFTERNOON

Following this morning's big breakfast, you'll probably want a lighter lunch. **Kasha's Old World Café** offers homemade sandwiches and soups, such as cream of potato, which should hit the spot. They also have an extensive list of winter warm-up drinks: Christmas Kahlua Cappuccino; Peppermint Patty Latte; Mexican Spiced Cocoa; and a Frothy the Snowman Fudge Latte made of espresso, chocolate, macadamia nut, and vanilla flavoring, and topped with whipped cream.

This afternoon, spend some time at the Lake Michigan shoreline—in a wintry way—at **Harrington Beach State Park** located in nearby Belgium, a seven-mile drive north on I-43. You'll find that this 637-acre park has a myriad of treasures: a wild beach stretching more than a mile along Lake Michigan, a white cedar swamp, old field grasslands, and a limestone quarry lake ringed by cedars. The cooling effect of Lake Michigan makes the area hospitable for cedars and other northern plant species, which usually do not grow this far south. **Winter hike** around Quarry Lake on a trail or amble through a forest filled with ash, maple, birch, and quaking aspen before its footpaths lead you to a spectacular view of Lake Michigan. There are three miles of groomed **cross-country ski trails**, and **snowmobiling** is allowed. Call the Ozaukee County Trails Snowphone at (262) 284-8259 for more details on snowmobiling in the area.

If you missed the **Ozaukee Interurban Trail** in Cedarburg yesterday, today is another chance to **cross-country ski** on a portion of it. You can pick it up as it winds near the Port Washington 1860 Light Station or marina.

The winter sun is just beginning to rise over Port Washington, a picturesque Great Lakes fishing town.

EVENING

Eat in an historical venue tonight at **Smith Brothers Fish Shanty** *[see "A Winter Mystery: Loss of the* Linda E.*" sidebar]*. In a prime position overlooking the Port Washington Harbor, Smith Brothers offers you a choice of dining style: sit in the brewpub for oak-planked

A WINTER MYSTERY: LOSS OF THE *LINDA E.*
by Richard D. Smith

Richard D. Smith is a retired science teacher, scuba diver, Great Lakes historian, and co-director and curator of the Port Washington 1860 Light Station Museum. He was born and raised in Menominee, Michigan, where his father once fished the waters of Green Bay. He had many close friends on the crew of the Linda E. *and often went with them to help lift their nets on Lake Michigan and document the work of Great Lakes fishermen.*

Early on the morning of December 11, 1998, Lief Weborg, Scott Matta, and Warren Olson, Jr., left Port Washington on a routine run to lift their nets southeast of the harbor. It was a beautiful, warm, clear December day. They called in to Smith Brothers wholesale fish processing plant at 9:45 a.m., reported their catch to Bruce Rasmussen, the Smith Brothers foreman, and gave their approximate arrival time back at the dock. That was the last that was heard from them.

That night, Lief's wife, Sherry, called my home and asked me to go down to the dock, see whether the boat was in, and find out why Lief had not called home. I checked the marina, then went up on the North Bluff to see if I could see the boat's lights. Sadly, I could not and called Sherry back. She then contacted Danny Anderson, a Milwaukee fisherman and friend, who was already on his way out onto the lake to look for the crew. He searched all night but found nothing. The next day, a land, air, and sea search failed to turn up any sign of the *Linda E.* We all began to fear that something catastrophic had occurred; Lief always kept his cell phone within easy reach.

A couple of days later, I walked the beach for five miles in 20-degree temperatures and still found nothing. The lack of wreckage seemed to confirm that whatever happened occurred very rapidly, leaving the crew with no chance to escape.

Most of the fishermen I talked with felt that the *Linda E.* had been run down by a barge, because a leak or fire would have allowed enough time for the crew to call for help and don survival suits. This theory proved correct: On June 18, 2000, the U.S. Navy minesweeper *Defender*, built in Warren Olson's hometown of Marinette, Wisconsin, located the *Linda E.'s* partially caved-in hull in 265 feet of water southeast of Port Washington. The *Linda E.* had been plowed under by a 500-foot tug and barge; the crew never had a chance. They died quickly, and commercial fishing out of Port Washington died with them. The *Linda E.* was one of the last two fishing boats out of Port Washington. Lief and Sherry also owned the remaining boat, the *Oliver H. Smith*, which was docked in Milwaukee at the time the *Linda E.* went down. Due to the high cost of upkeep, Sherry soon had to sell the *Oliver.*

Lief, Scott, and Werny, rest in peace.

pizzas, sandwich plates, and salads, or choose the Harbor Room for Great Lakes fish, pasta, and steaks. Listen to the jazzy saxophone player as you enjoy some of the best-prepared meals in town.

After dinner, the evening is just about to begin if you're in town for the **Christmas on** the **Corners** festival. Horse-drawn wagons will take you on a ride through the city streets, where live musicians play holiday tunes. Have your picture taken with real reindeer housed in a corral at the corner of Main and Franklin Streets. The lights from the stores and art galleries shine on Black Peter and St. Nicholas, as they visit with youngsters on the sidewalks.

Day Three
MORNING

One winter moment you'll never forget is watching the red-and-yellow glow of the sunrise over Lake Michigan and the Ozaukee County Courthouse belfry from Dorothy's Room at the Port Washington Inn. Savor the view as you partake in your inn's provided breakfast, or go to the **Port Hotel** on East Main Street for an elegant Sunday brunch. After breakfast, take a walk down to the marina and listen to the Sunday-morning quiet.

JOHN T. ANDREWS

St. Mary's Church, with its tall spire, stands watch over Port Washington on an early winter morning.

AFTERNOON

After checking out of your inn or bed and breakfast, take a countryside drive to the 350-acre **Riveredge Nature Center** in nearby Newburg, just northwest of Port Washington on Highway 33. Situated along the Milwaukee River and Riveredge Creek, the center is one of the largest and most diverse nature preserves in southeastern Wisconsin, consisting of prairies, forests, meadows, ponds, rivers, and marshes. It is the region's first nature center, founded in 1968 with the dual mission of preservation and education. Deer, foxes, and coyotes live in the

SNOWFLAKES ON SLIDES

Wilson Alwyn Bentley had always had a passion for fragile environments. Born on a Vermont farm in 1865, Bentley was home-schooled by his mother and early on became fascinated by studying water, whether it was clouds, dew, frost, rain, or snowflakes.

As a teenager, Bentley began experimenting with the new medium of photography. He developed a way to attach his camera to his microscope and produced the first photomicrograph ever taken of an ice crystal on January 15, 1885. Although a snowflake is usually composed of several ice crystals that stick together as they fall, Bentley isolated individual ice crystals and took more than 5,000 photomicrographs of them over the course of his life.

The research of a farmer with no formal education, however, was not popular with the scientific community. Bentley's tendency to infuse his writings with observations about the beauty of nature further worked to assure that his research would generally be ignored.

Around 1900, believing that his photomicrographs belonged to the world, Bentley prepared boxes of lantern slides and sold the majority of them to colleges and universities in the United States. Some of them found their way to the University of Wisconsin–Madison and eventually to the Department of Atmospheric and Oceanic Sciences. In 2000, the department donated its collection to the Schwerdtfeger Library, a joint effort between the Department of Meteorology and the Space Science and Engineering Center. Shortly after, the library obtained partial funding through UW–Madison Friends of the Libraries to preserve almost 1,200 of Bentley's slides and provide Internet access.

In 2002, the Schwerdtfeger digitized the images and put them online. Now, you can make your own observations about the fragility of nature—through the lens of a single snowflake. Find the collection at http://library.ssec.wisc.edu/bentley.

---

preserve, along with nearly 190 species of birds. Wood ducks, great blue herons, Cooper's hawks, the state-threatened red-shouldered hawks, and many songbirds have been recorded here. There are 10 miles of **winter hiking** trails and 6.5 miles of trails east of the river groomed and tracked for **cross-country skiing**. This includes an extra mile through the **Riveredge Creek and Ephemeral Pond State Natural Area** in the southeast portion of the property. The natural area is open only in the winter, in order to protect its fragile environment *[see "Snowflakes on Slides" sidebar]*.

The education and visitors center with hands-on displays is open from 8:00 a.m. to 5:00 p.m. on Friday and from noon until 4:00 p.m. on Saturday and Sunday. **Hike-alongs** occur once a month from October to March in the afternoons, with **snowshoes** if there is enough snow.

In late February through early April, you can visit Riveredge's 30-acre sugar bush, where you can follow a self-guided trail to learn more about and watch syrup being made. On one of the last days of the **sugar-mapling** process, you can eat pancakes cooked right in the bush, alongside the trees that provided the boiling syrup in the pans next to you.

And that's a sweet rite-of-winter festival, all in itself.

FOR MORE INFORMATION

**CEDARBURG VISITOR
INFORMATION CENTER
CEDARBURG GENERAL STORE MUSEUM**
W61 N480 Washington Ave.
Cedarburg, WI 53012
(262) 377-9620 or (800) 237-2874
www.cedarburg.org

**PORT WASHINGTON VISITOR CENTER AND
CHAMBER OF COMMERCE**
126 E. Grand Ave., Port Washington, WI 53074
(262) 284-0900 or (800) 719-4881
www.portwashingtonchamber.com

WINTER ATTRACTIONS

CEDAR CREEK SETTLEMENT
N70 W6340 Bridge Rd., Cedarburg, WI 53012
(262) 377-4763 or (866) 377-4788
www.cedarcreeksettlement.com

CEDAR CREEK WINERY
Cedar Creek Settlement, N70 W6340 Bridge Rd.
Cedarburg, WI 53012, (262) 377-8020 or
(800) 827-8020, www.cedarcreekwinery.com

CEDARBURG GENERAL STORE MUSEUM
W61N480 Washington Ave. , Cedarburg, WI
53012, (262) 375-3676
www.cedarburgculturalcenter.org

COVERED BRIDGE COUNTY PARK
Highway 143 (Washington Ave.) and Highway
60, Covered Bridge Rd., Cedarburg, WI 53012,
(262) 284-8257 or (800) 237-2874

HARRINGTON BEACH STATE PARK
531 County Road D, Belgium, WI 53004
(262) 285-3015, www.wiparks.net

OZAUKEE ICE CENTER
5505 W. Pioneer Rd., Mequon, WI 53097
(262) 375-1100, www.co.ozaukee.wi.us/Parks/
IceCenter/Index.htm

OZAUKEE INTERURBAN TRAIL
PO Box 143, Port Washington, WI 53074
(262) 284-9288 or (800) 403-9898
www.interurbantrail.us

PEBBLE HOUSE VISITOR CENTER
(Edward Dodge House)
126 E. Grand Ave., Port Washington, WI 53074
(262) 284-0900 or (800) 719-4881

PORT WASHINGTON 1860 LIGHT STATION
311 Johnson St., Port Washington, WI 53074
(262) 284-7240, www.portlightstation.org

RIVEREDGE NATURE CENTER
4458 W. Hawthorne Dr., Newburg, WI 53060
(262) 375-2715, www.riveredgenc.org

WINTER FESTIVALS

**FESTIVE FRIDAY EVES AT CEDAR CREEK
SETTLEMENT—mid-November to mid-December.** During the five weeks before Christmas,
visitors can enjoy music, holiday-themed demonstrations, winter cookouts, and shopping.
(800) 237-2874.

PORT CHRISTMAS PARADE—late November.
The annual Christmas parade in Port Washington. (800) 719-4881.

**LIGHT STATION VICTORIAN CHRISTMAS
SHOWHOUSE—late November to mid-December.** Enjoy the Port Washington 1860 Light
Station decorated in Victorian style for Christmas.
(262) 284-6000 or www.portwashingtonhistorical
society.org.

CHRISTMAS IN THE COUNTRY—early December. Arts-and-crafts show featuring more
than 50 artists, located in Cedar Creek Settlement. (800) 237-2874.

SILVERBELL MARKETPLACE—early December. Annual fine arts-and-crafts show and sale
with more than 40 juried artisans. Cedarburg
Community Center. (800) 237-2874 or www.
cedarburgjuniors.org.

CHRISTMAS ON THE CORNERS—early December. Port Washington. A day filled with
Christmas traditions, sights, and sounds.
Highlights include St. Nicholas and Black Peter,
horse-drawn wagon rides, musicians throughout
the historic district and strolling carolers. (262)
305-4220 or www.portbid.com.

POLAR BEAR DIP—January 1. Port Washington. At the end of Jackson Street, join other brave
swimmers for a dip in Lake Michigan. (800) 719-4881 or www.ozaukeetourism.com.

**CANDLELIGHT SKI-HIKE AT HARRINGTON
BEACH STATE PARK—early January and early
February.** A .5- or 2.5-mile candlelight cross-country ski or hike through the woods. (262)
285-3015.

**CURE FOR CABIN FEVER ANTIQUE SHOW
& SALE—late January.** At this long-running
annual event, more than 20 high-quality dealers
from the tri-state area exhibit furniture, toys,
sporting goods, and more. Cedarburg Community Center. (262) 377-9620, (800) 237-2874,
or www.cedarburg.org.

WINTER FESTIVAL—early February. One of
the oldest winter festivals in the state. Bed and
barrel races (a team of four skaters pushes a bed
or barrel along with a passenger across the ice)
on frozen Cedar Creek, hayrides, ice-carving

contest, Alaskan malamute weight-pulling contest, pancake breakfast, chili-cooking contest, Frosty the Snowman Look-A-Like Contest, and live music. Downtown Cedarburg. (800) 237-2874 or www. cedarburgfestivals.org.

CEDAR CREEK WINERY & SETTLEMENT OPEN HOUSE—late March. Tour the winery and taste award-winning wines from Wisconsin—even barrel tasting with a winemaker. Food demonstrations and more. Cedar Creek Winery & Settlement. www.cedarcreekwinery.com or (800) 827-8020.

RESTAURANTS
CEDARBURG COFFEE ROASTERY
W62 N603 Washington Ave., Cedarburg, WI 53012, (262) 375-4321, www.cedarburgcoffee.com

CREAM & CREPE CAFÉ
(Friday–Saturday, breakfast, lunch, and dinner; Sunday, lunch and early dinner)
Cedar Creek Settlement, N70 W6340 Bridge Rd.
Cedarburg, WI 53012, (262) 377-0900
www.cedarcreeksettlement.com/cream&crepe

DANCING GOAT ESPRESSO BAR & CAFÉ
(breakfast, lunch, and dinner)
W62 N605 Washington Ave.
Cedarburg, WI 53012, (262) 376-1366

THE FARMSTEAD
(Friday–Saturday, lunch and dinner)
W62 N238 Washington Ave.
Cedarburg, WI 53012, (262) 375-2655

THE FISH SHANTY *(lunch and dinner)*
100 Franklin St., Port Washington, WI 53074
(262) 284-5592

KASHA'S OLD WORLD CAFÉ
(breakfast, lunch, and dinner)
309 Franklin St., Port Washington, WI 53074
(262) 268-9133

KLUG'S CREEKSIDE INN *(Friday–Saturday. lunch and dinner; Sunday brunch)*
N58 W6194 Columbia Rd.
Cedarburg, WI 53012, (262) 377-0660
www.foodspot.com/klugs

PORT HOTEL *(Friday, lunch and dinner; Saturday, dinner; Sunday brunch)*
101 E. Main St., Port Washington, WI 53074
(262) 284-9473, www.theporthotel.com

SMITH BROTHERS FISH SHANTY *(dinner)*
100 N. Franklin St., Port Washington, WI 53074
(262) 284-5592
www.co.ozaukee.wi.us/history/fishshanty.htm

TOMASO'S ITALIAN AMERICAN RESTAURANT *(lunch and dinner)*
W63 N688 Washington Ave.
Cedarburg, WI 53012, (414) 377-7630

LODGING
AMERICAN COUNTRY FARM
12112 N. Wauwatosa Rd., Mequon, WI 53097
(262) 242-0194
www.americancountryfarm-bedandbreakfast.com

PORT WASHINGTON INN
308 W. Washington St., Port Washington, WI 53074, (262) 284-5583 or (877) 794-1903
www.port-washington-inn.com

THE STAGECOACH INN BED AND BREAKFAST
W61 N520 Washington Ave.
Cedarburg, WI 53012, (262) 375-0208
or (888) 375-0208, www.stagecoach-inn-wi.com

THE WASHINGTON HOUSE INN
W62 N573 Washington Ave.
Cedarburg, WI 53012, (262) 375-3550
or (800) 554-4717
www.washingtonhouseinn.com

Chapter Five
ART IN WINTER
Dodgeville/Spring Green/Mineral Point/New Glarus

ALL KINDS OF ARTS AND ARTWORKS thrive in a cluster of communities in Wisconsin's southwest corner. The city of Dodgeville is known internationally as the home of builder Alex Jordan's unusual brainchild, The House on the Rock. Nearby, serene Spring Green showcases the imaginative endeavors of another native artist, Frank Lloyd Wright, and has a robust schedule of Shakespearean performances in the warmer months. Mineral Point has become largely a community of artists and their galleries, and New Glarus is pure homage to Swiss culture, music, and traditions.

Dodgeville, at the intersection of Highways 18 and 151, has been praised for its preservation efforts in the historic downtown district. Not only are manmade creations valued and protected here, but also an incredible artwork of nature, Governor Dodge State Park, has been set aside for all to enjoy.

On the edge of Wisconsin's Wyoming Valley sits the village of Spring Green, on the north side of an unimaginably pretty Wisconsin River bight. The area's pastoral beauty even caught the eye of Frank Lloyd Wright, perhaps Wisconsin's best known curmudgeon, who decided that this was the perfect spot to build his own home and to start his groundbreaking design school. Today, Spring Green has a full count of art galleries and upscale boutiques.

Many say that Mineral Point is the birthplace of Wisconsin. Native Americans had long used the area's lead deposits that were once so plentiful that they lay mixed in with the topsoil. As far as historians can tell, the first European to barter for the metal was Nicholas Perrot around 1690. By the 1830s, news of the abundant lead had reached as far as Cornwall, England, and Cornish miners started arriving in Mineral Point. They brought with them their advanced hard-rock and deep-mining skills. Digging long hours on the hillsides, they scraped gouges into the bluffs where they could catch some rest and escape bad weather. Because of the holes they built, the miners were dubbed "Badgers."

On July 4, 1836, a pioneer resident of the area, Henry Dodge, was sworn in as the first governor of the Wisconsin Territory. He kept his office in Mineral Point until October of

Every brick, stone, and dog is fair game for artistic expression in Mineral Point's historic downtown.

that year, thus earning the village the honor of being the place where the state of Wisconsin began. Today, more than 500 buildings in Mineral Point still stand on 1837 plats. Most contain locally quarried limestone and display the distinctive stone designs of those early Cornish immigrants.

Escaping an economic crisis in the canton of Glarus, Switzerland, in 1845, 108 immigrants came to Wisconsin and settled. Since then, a steady stream of new Swiss immigrants has kept New Glarus's Swiss–German language, folk traditions, and music alive for visitors to experience today.

On this winter weekend, you'll travel to some of the best of Wisconsin's artist communities and admire their works made from nature. In artistic terms, you might describe the next three days' attractions as *trompe l'oeil:* houses on rocks, houses of rocks, and a whole village that looks as if it were transplanted from a green valley in Switzerland.

Day One
MORNING AND AFTERNOON

This weekend will start by impressing you with Wisconsin's commitment to preservation as an art form. Upon arriving in downtown Dodgeville, take a few minutes to look at the historic facades. In fact, the Iowa County Courthouse, at 222 N. Iowa Street, was built in 1859 by masons who immigrated to Wisconsin from Cornwall, England, and it is the oldest courthouse in continuous use in the state.

A block down from the courthouse is **Grace Café**. The menu changes daily here, to take advantage of fresh seasonal ingredients. Stop for a hot bowl of home-cooked soup, such as potato pesto or smoky turkey vegetable, or a plate of vegetarian lasagna.

Plan to spend the majority of today at the second-largest state park in Wisconsin, **Governor Dodge State Park** (Devil's Lake State Park is the largest). Just north of Dodgeville on Highway 23, the massive 5,270-acre park lies in the Driftless Area, untouched by a great glacier that left its print on most of the state. Because of the lack of "drift," or glacial debris, we can now revel in Governor Dodge's rugged sandstone bluffs, forested ridges, and secluded, deep valleys, fashioned by wind and water over the last 400 million years. A vast prairie once characterized the ridges with no natural lakes in the well-drained land. But as

JUST TAKE OFF WALKING: GOVERNOR DODGE STATE PARK

"For me, Governor Dodge State Park was a living laboratory," says Gary Walz, park naturalist from 1976 to 1991. "It was all there, just for the looking."

A biology teacher at Dodgeville High School from 1963 to 1995, Walz took on the part-time job of naturalist "with a passion," he says. "Many people don't have a working knowledge of the outdoors. So I tried to get them close-up, take them to the hidden recesses of the park, and show them how all nature works together." Walz did just that. In fact, he did his job so well that Governor Dodge ended up having the largest program attendance of any state park in Wisconsin during his tenure.

"When I first became the park's naturalist," recalls Walz, "I would just take off walking. There's 5,270 acres out there. I knew if I wanted to show the park to other people, I would really have to know it myself. So I would just take off and go. No compass or anything. I liked the adventure of just heading somewhere, not knowing where I was going or where I'd end up," he says.

Some of Walz's most popular programs were his night hikes. He added special elements to his walks that brought Governor Dodge State Park alive for his groups. "We'd walk out to a stand of timber that I thought was good owl habitat, and then I'd turn on a battery tape recorder and play the hoots of a barn or great horned owl. Owls tend to fly toward hoots," he explains. "People would often see a big owl fly in the night sky and alight in the trees just above them. I showed people the things that were always there, but just hidden from them."

Walz introduced programs such as night hiking with an astronomer and hikes where people learned to trust their senses in new ways. "I'd instruct my group to turn off their flashlights to get their 'night eyes.' Then I'd tell them to go single file on the trail and let their feet guide them," he states. "That way, we got to see things like glowing fungi. It added a certain mystique to our hikes that I'm sure people remember to this day."

Glowing fungi, the sounds of owls, the starry sky. Walz is still exploring the natural wonders in Governor Dodge State Park, only the group he's leading today is a little different. "I take my grandchildren there now," he says. "I do the things I used to do with my groups, but now I can pass this information on to them."

---

the park evolved from an original homesteader's 160 acres, two manmade lakes, Cox Hollow and Twin Valley, were formed with earthen dams.

Many spectacular outcroppings and valleys hidden in foliage during the summer months now magically appear on the landscape. **Cross-country ski**, **winter hike**, **snowmobile**, **winter camp**, **ice fish**, **snowshoe**, **ice-skate**, **sled**, or **toboggan** in the beauty of this natural Wisconsin sculpture.

Governor Dodge's **cross-country ski** and **winter hiking** trails wander around the lakes, through stands of hardwoods and across open fields on some of the park's most awesome scenery. Three loops totaling 22 miles of groomed and tracked trails accommodate classic skiing for whatever your degree of expertise.

Both the 1.25-mile **Lakeview Trail** and the 2.5-mile **Gold Mine Trail** cater to less-experienced skiers. The trails run through woods, deep valleys, and meadows without steep grades. The **Mill Creek Trail**, which begins at the Cox Hollow Beach picnic area, is a 3.3-mile loop winding around meadows and wooded valleys with spectacular views of Cox Hollow and Twin Valley Lakes. The more difficult 6.8-mile **Meadow Valley Trail** also begins at the Cox Hollow Beach picnic area, but it has steeper downgrades than Lakeview or Gold Mine Trails. The **Lost Canyon Trail** is an 8.1-mile trail that is rated advanced for its length and number of steep grades. You'll tour through mostly wooded terrain and pass scenic Lost Canyon, Stephens Falls, and Twin Valley Lake—the payoff for your hard work.

Even winter is an artist, as seen by this ice sculpture at Stephen's Falls in Governor Dodge State Park.

© GARI WALZ

When walking or skiing the trails, make sure to take frequent breaks to savor the sacred place that Governor Dodge State Park truly is *[see "Just Take Off Walking: Governor Dodge State Park" sidebar]*. Lean against a sandstone ridge or pause in front of an expanse of frozen lake. Take out your camera and press panoramic mode, watching for ruffed grouse or wild turkeys. If you're lucky, you may even spot a rare bobcat. Breathe in deeply the crisp winter air and solitude of the season in this natural land.

The Mill Creek Trail hooks up with the **Military Ridge State Trail**, a popular **snowmobile, winter hiking**, and **cross-country ski** trail. Eight to 10 feet wide and composed of compacted limestone, the trail has a storied history. Running 40 miles from Dodgeville east to Fitchburg and passing through Barneveld, Blue Mounds, and Mt. Horeb, the trail follows the natural divide between the Wisconsin River and the Pecatonia River watersheds. For hundreds of years it has been a route for bison and French explorers, and for American soldiers during the Blackhawk War. With a gentle grade of only 2 to 5 percent, the trail travels primarily along prairies, woods, wetlands, the Sugar River Valley, and cow ranges. There are 48 bridges, all with planked decks. The 15-mile snowmobile trail inside Governor Dodge State Park hooks up with the Military Ridge State Trail.

Some people come to Governor Dodge in winter just to **winter camp** *[see "Why Would Anyone Winter Camp?" sidebar]* at one of the 33 plowed or 6 walk-in campsites in the Twin Valley campground. **Ice fishers** regularly score walleyes and pan fish. **Snowshoers** travel freely in the park, and a large **ice-skating** rink is maintained at Cox Hollow Lake. **Sledding** and **tobogganing** can be done on any hill.

Finish out the afternoon by checking into your weekend accommodations. **The House on the Rock Inn** offers a choice of two complexes: the 114-room Main Lodge or the 63-room

WHY WOULD ANYONE WINTER CAMP?

I know what you're thinking. "Why would anyone camp out in winter when you could be far more comfortable inside, under your warm covers, with a mug of hot chocolate?"

There are reasons to camp in winter, and yes, one of them is that winter camping will make you appreciate more deeply than ever before the comforts you take for granted every day. But one of my favorite reasons to go winter camping is that it's the fastest way to lose weight. Experts say you can expect to burn twice as many calories traveling and camping in winter as you do in your day-to-day life.

Then, there are the soul-restoring reasons to camp. State park campsites that become populated with luxurious RVs and crowds in summer can seem remote and wild in winter. You can enjoy the solitude of having a forest practically to yourself. There is the awe in waking up to discover an ice sculpture nature created just for those who dare to see it. Wildlife tends to take more of an interest in you, as a fellow winter traveler. All this and no bugs!

High-tech advances in cold-weather gear have made winter camping accessible for everyone. Here's a basic primer on things to consider when winter camping:

❄ **CAMPSITE LOCATION.** Find a flat spot in a wooded area, with tall trees to shield you from the wind. A dry patch of ground (or shovel down to dry ground) on a south slope also makes a good spot. Stay away from tree boughs heavily laden with snow or hillsides that could create snow slides.

❄ **TENT.** The smaller the tent, the warmer you'll be. Choose a tent that withstands winds and is easy to erect. Breathable synthetic fibers keep the heat in and allow air to circulate. Floors and walls should be waterproof, and a water-resistant fly should cover the outside of the tent. A pitched roof will avoid snow buildup. A vestibule over the door will allow you to cook in inclement weather.

❄ **SLEEPING BAGS.** A hooded "mummy bag" is recommended. A mummy bag hugs your body so that you don't have to warm up a lot of empty air space. But buy the mummy bag with enough roominess to wear heavy clothing inside it if necessary. A nylon shell will keep water out. The zipper should be made of materials that won't freeze. Bags filled with goose down or insulated with synthetic, high-quality materials are among the best. You also need a mat, preferably full-length, for insulation against the cold ground.

❄ **STOVE AND FUEL.** A reliable stove is crucial on a winter-camping trip, not only to heat food but to melt snow to provide drinking water if you're not packing it with you or you don't have access to it. A weak stove will make you feel like you're waiting for hours to melt a pot of snow. A stove should not be used inside a tent unless there is absolutely no other choice. Make sure to check with park rangers to see whether campfires are allowed at your campsite.

❄ **FOOD.** Your body needs more calories for energy in cold weather, especially if you're cross-country skiing, hiking, or snowshoeing. A standard dinner for winter campers is either freeze-dried, prepurchased food supplemented by snacks or a one-pot meal of macaroni, rice, or instant potatoes to which you can add dried vegetables, canned meats, or soup bases. Breakfast is typically oatmeal or instant noodles, flavored with butter or cheese. Lunch is often eaten on the trails and is made of cheese, bread, crackers, peanut butter, salami, or Gorp (dried fruits, nuts, raisins, and chocolate bits). Add lots of hot drinks such as tea or cocoa. If you don't bring your own water, you'll have to melt snow; given that fluffy, new snow can be up to 98 percent air, be prepared to melt lots of it to get a cup of water. Protect your water bottle or canteen from freezing by keeping it under your clothing, or insulate it well and stow it in your pack. At night, share your sleeping bag with it.

❄ **EMERGENCIES.** Many emergencies can be avoided by traveling with a companion or telling someone your travel plans. Maps, a compass, extra food and clothing, a flashlight, matches, a fire starter, a candle, a knife, sunglasses, and a first-aid kit should be included in your gear. Learn how to watch for and treat frostbite and hypothermia.

Winter campsites can be found on the Wisconsin Department of Natural Resources Web site at www.wiparks.net. And in case you wondered, warm covers and mugs of hot chocolate just seem better on the trail.

There are soul-restoring reasons to winter camp in Wisconsin's state parks.

JOHN T. ANDREWS

North Lodge. An inviting, 16-foot-wide by 30-foot-high native-stone fireplace greets you in the Main Lodge's lobby. Stuffed armchairs encourage good conversation around the warmth and glow. There's an indoor whirlpool and swimming pool with a play area for kids, featuring a 45-foot-long submarine nestled in a coral reef, complete with waterfalls and slides.

EVENING

Tonight you'll dine in a comfortable, 1950s-style restaurant, **Thym's Supper Club** on Highway 23. Thym's gracious staff serves broiled walleye, cod, steaks, hickory-smoked pork chops, and pastas.

If you've still got some energy to burn this evening, take a few turns on the **ice rink** at **Ley Pavilion** in Harris Park. Public skating is held on Fridays from 6:30 to 9:30 p.m. and on Saturdays from 6:00 to 9:00 p.m. There is a small fee for skate rental.

Day Two
MORNING

Today, you'll have more encounters with Wisconsin artworks—only this time it will be more cultural than geological art.

Breakfast is served all day at the **Courthouse Inn** across from the Iowa County Courthouse on Iowa Street. In what looks like a courtyard inside this historic building, you can get good coffee to accompany your Belgian waffles with whipped cream and strawberries. A large mural by artist Jeb Prazak graces one wall of this eatery that has one of the largest

JOHN T. ANDREWS

Santas in all shapes—even life-sized—decorate the special edition Christmas at The House on the Rock.

menus in town.

If your winter visit falls between mid-November and the end of December, don't miss **Christmas at The House on the Rock**. Nothing says Dodgeville more than the singular house that sits atop the pinnacle of Deer Shelter Rock, 450 feet above the floor of the Wyoming Valley near the Baraboo Range. The famous home that was built in the 1940s by Alex Jordan, a noted Wisconsin art collector, is decked out with 6,000 Santas and lots of holiday cheer. The Santas come in all shapes and sizes—from life-sized and themed Santas to the simplest plastic Santa toy or drinking cup. This special-edition of The House on the Rock is a scaled-down version of the regular season's tour at a discounted price to fit holiday schedules and budgets. However, you'll still want to set aside several hours to roam around the original house, the Gate House, the Mill House, the Streets of Yesterday, the Heritage of the Sea, the Transportation Building, the Music of Yesterday, and the World's Largest Carousel, with 20,000 lights and not a single horse.

Nearby **Spring Green** holds more winter arts options. Early in December, the city transforms itself into an old-time town during a **Spring Green Country Christmas**. For three days, the downtown area hosts a gingerbread house contest, horse-drawn carriage rides, caroling, a Christmas tree lighting, holiday art festival, fireworks display synchronized to holiday music, a homemade quilt show, and more.

AFTERNOON

The **Spring Green Café and General Store** recalls a less complicated time. Order your lunch at the kitchen window, and then select a table in the bright dining area, amid small freezers stocked with cheeses and twirling stationery racks. Located in a converted cheese warehouse, the café and store combine homemade meals with a chance to explore aisles of scented candles, jewelry, toys, housewares, and alternative magazines. Daily lunch specials here are as familiar and comfortable as a hot bowl of chili, or as exotic as potato and kalamata olive stew.

From the days of general stores, keep driving back in time—right into Wisconsin's oldest

JOHN T. ANDREWS

The beauty of Spring Green caught the eye of Frank Lloyd Wright, who built his home, Taliesin, here. The snowy Wisconsin River is seen through the windows of the Frank Lloyd Wright® Visitor Center.

settlement, **Mineral Point.** When Cornish miners began arriving here in the 1830s to work the lead mines, they introduced a style of stone building construction that resembled what was done in western England. Many of their buildings have been painstakingly restored and are part of Mineral Point's historic district. The district contains more than 500 structures, including rock houses and Victorian homes, and was the first in the state to be placed on the National Register of Historic Places. Spend the later part of the afternoon walking this city's steep and narrow streets. If you visit in early December, stay for the annual **Candlelight Shopping and Gallery Night,** when downtown artisans keep their shops open past 5:00 p.m. for visitors on the candlelit streets. At least 18 artist-owned galleries here introduce new pieces on this night. Stop to chat with the artists, and stay for dinner.

EVENING

For a traditional Cornish pasty, with beef, potato, and onion baked in pastry dough, enjoy dinner at the **Brewery Creek Brewpub.** In this 1880s building of wood and stone, relax with a home-brewed beer amid the large oak posts, beams, and original ceiling joists.

Just six miles east of Dodgeville on County Highway BB is the nationally recognized heritage center, **Folklore Village.** A folk arts programming and educational pioneer since 1967, the organization presents a year-round schedule of dances, concerts, folk culture retreats, and craft workshops. Check their schedule for specific weekend events. The **German Tree Lighting** and **Festival of Christmas and Midwinter Traditions** are annual celebrations.

Day Three

MORNING

The House on the Rock Inn serves its guests a complimentary continental breakfast of cereal, bagels, doughnuts, muffins, toast, coffee, and juices. Or enjoy the fare at your bed and breakfast. Better yet, save room for some of the best stollen and Swiss-style baked goods you've ever had.

After checking out of your room, you'll visit another city full of history, culture, and arts: **New Glarus.**

New Glarus has been dubbed "America's Little Switzerland" by its residents and has been recently designated as the home for the Swiss Center of North America. When leaders of Swiss organizations in the U. S. and Canada decided they needed a central location to highlight their contributions to society, the historic community of New Glarus was chosen. Full of white-and-brown architecture, Swiss flags, and music piped throughout the village, New Glarus sits on a small rise off Highway 69. Here you'll find Swiss dairy products—some of the best cheese in Wisconsin, and that's saying a lot!—and holiday and special-occasion gifts. You'll also find the headquarters of the **Sugar River State Trail.**

If you've held off on breakfast, make your first stop at the **New Glarus Bakery & Tea Room** on First Street. The bakery was established in 1912. The current building, built for the bakery in 1916, is a registered historical landmark. The cookies, breads, pastries, doughnuts, and desserts are baked from scratch every day. In November and December, you'll find *lebkuchen* (a Swiss cookie similar to gingerbread), hand cut and iced with images of Hansel, Gretel, and Santa. It's traditional to hang the cookies with a ribbon from your mantle or Christmas tree.

ICE AGE NATIONAL SCENIC TRAIL

Wisconsin's Ice Age National Scenic Trail is one of only eight national scenic trails in the United States. When completed, it will be a 1,000-mile walking/hiking trail that runs from the western border of Wisconsin at the St. Croix River, turns south at Langlade down to Janesville, and works its way up north again to the state's eastern border in Door County. About 600 miles of the trail are now available for use.

The route of the trail roughly follows the terminal edge of the most recent Wisconsin glacier, between 75,000 and 10,000 years ago. It varies at points to include other nearby geological features of interest, portions of the Driftless Area, and local communities, such as Hartland, Janesville, Lodi, Madison, Portage, Saint Croix Falls, and Sturgeon Bay.

Two hundred named lakes and hundreds more unnamed lakes and ponds are along the trail. Features like moraines, eskers, erratics, drumlins, kettles, and kames are prevalent. The trail is meant to be used for low-impact activities such as walking, hiking, cross-country skiing, and snowshoeing. Segments of the trail are owned by different entities, so some segments may coincide with biking trails, horse paths, and snowmobile rail-trails.

For more information on the Ice Age National Scenic Trail, visit www.iceagetrail.org.

Speaking of sugar, you'll need to drop some of those calories you picked up at the bakery on the **Sugar River State Trail**, which connects the villages of New Glarus, Monticello, and Albany and the city of Brodhead with more than 24 miles of trail. Start your **winter hike** or **snowmobile** tour in New Glarus at the century-old Railroad Depot. Built on an old railroad right-of-way, the limestone-surfaced Sugar River Trail crosses the Little Sugar and Sugar rivers more than a dozen times along the way and is part of the **Ice Age National Scenic Trail** *[see "Ice Age National Scenic Trail" sidebar]*. The trail corridor covers 265 acres and is home to deer, foxes, coyotes, bobcats, beavers, otters, woodchucks, minks, and gray squirrels. Adding to the path's enchantment are trestle bridges and even a covered bridge that is over 100 feet in length. The towns along the way provide great places to stop for a hot cappuccino.

If you'd like to get in one more **snowshoeing** or **cross-country skiing** outing, the 411-acre **New Glarus Woods State Park** has seven ungroomed hiking miles through dense woods and deep valleys that are favorites with local residents.

AFTERNOON

For lunch, stop at the immensely popular **Glarner Stube** for some Swiss–American cuisine. The pork schnitzel sandwich is utterly delicious; other delectable Swiss specialties include *schüblig, kalberwurst,* and *wiener schnitzel.* The house specialty is a cheese fondue dinner: bubbling Swiss cheese flavored with wine, garlic, and kirsch that is served with cubes of crusty bread for dipping.

Before stepping outside, get a "Hot Buttered Chocolate": hot chocolate, butterscotch schnapps, and whipped cream; or the "Stube Warmer": hot chocolate, peppermint schnapps, and whipped cream. On a cold winter day, such artistic creations can be greatly appreciated.

FOR MORE INFORMATION

DODGEVILLE AREA CHAMBER OF COMMERCE
338 N. Iowa St., Dodgeville, WI 53533
(608) 935-5993, www.dodgeville.com

MINERAL POINT CHAMBER OF COMMERCE
225 High St., Mineral Point, WI 53565
(608) 987-3201 or (888) 764-6894
www.mineralpoint.com

NEW GLARUS CHAMBER OF COMMERCE & TOURIST INFORMATION
418 Railroad St.
New Glarus, WI 53574
(608) 527-2095 or (800) 527-6838
www.swisstown.com

SPRING GREEN AREA CHAMBER OF COMMERCE
150 E. Jefferson St.
Spring Green, WI 53588
(608) 588-2054 or (800) 588-2042
www.springgreen.com

WINTER ATTRACTIONS

FOLKLORE VILLAGE
3210 Highway BB
Dodgeville, WI 53533
(608) 924-4000, www.folklorevillage.org

GOVERNOR DODGE STATE PARK
4175 Highway 23 North
Dodgeville, WI 53533
(608) 935-2315 or (888) 947-2757
www.wiparks.net

THE HOUSE ON THE ROCK
3637 Highway 23, Dodgeville, WI 53533
(608) 935-3770 or (800) 947-2799
www.thehouseontherock.com

ICE AGE PARK & TRAIL FOUNDATION
207 E. Buffalo St., Suite 515
Milwaukee, WI 53202, (414) 278-8518
or (800) 227-0046, www.iceagetrail.org

LEY PAVILION
1600 Bennett Rd., Dodgeville, WI 53533
(608) 935-9971

MILITARY RIDGE STATE TRAIL
4350 Mounds Park Rd., Blue Mounds, WI 53517
(608) 437-7393, www.wiparks.net

NEW GLARUS WOODS STATE PARK
W5446 Highway NN, New Glarus, WI 53574
(608) 527-2335 or (888) 947-2757
www.wiparks.net

SUGAR RIVER STATE TRAIL
W5446 Highway NN, New Glarus, WI 53574
(608) 527-2334, www.wiparks.net

WINTER FESTIVALS

**CHRISTMAS AT THE HOUSE ON THE ROCK
—mid-November to late December.** Take a special tour of The House on the Rock, decorated for the holidays. (608) 935-3639 or www.thehouseontherock.com.

MINERAL POINT CANDLELIGHT SHOPPING AND GALLERY NIGHT—early December. 5:00 p.m. to 9:00 p.m. The streets of Mineral Point are nostalgically lit with candles as you visit the artists and their unique works, newly introduced for this night. (608) 987-3201 or www.mineralpoint.com.

MINERAL POINT HOLIDAY TOUR OF HOMES —early December. The Mineral Point Historical Society sponsors this annual benefit that features tours of historic homes and Orchard Lawn, a home built shortly after the Civil War. (608) 987-2884 or www.mineralpoint.com.

NEW GLARUS ST. NICHOLAS DAY—early December. Downtown New Glarus is decorated for the holidays, and shop owners welcome customers with holiday specials, lunch with Santa, a cookie sale, and a craft show. (608) 527-2095 or www.swisstown.com.

SPRING GREEN COUNTRY CHRISTMAS— early December. Downtown Spring Green. A three-day event with winter favorites such as a gingerbread house contest, horse-drawn carriage rides, caroling, Christmas tree lighting, holiday art festival, fireworks, free movies, and more. (800) 588-2042 or www.springgreen.com/countrychristmas.

FOLKLORE VILLAGE GERMAN TREE LIGHTING—mid-December. A pot-luck supper, followed by lighting the candles on a 14-foot tree, singing, and dancing. Call in advance to reserve a spot for this popular event. (608) 924-4000 or www.folklorevillage.org.

FOLKLORE VILLAGE FESTIVAL OF CHRISTMAS AND MID-WINTER TRADITIONS—end of December. After five days of dance and art sessions, traditional meals, and afternoon teas, New Year's Eve is marked by an Old World celebration.

As the clock strikes 12, a bonfire of 50 Christmas trees sends flames 30 feet high while guests sing songs in the snowy outdoors. To participate on New Year's Eve, you must be registered for other festival events. (608) 924-4000 or www.folklorevillage.org.

NEW GLARUS WINTERFEST—mid-January. Dressed in Swiss costumes, yodelers and alphorn players send sounds of Switzerland over the hills of southern Wisconsin. This weekend celebrates winter with a dance, parade, bonfire, guided hike on the Ice Age National Scenic Trail, sleigh rides, snowmobiling, and cross-country skiing. (608) 527-2095 or www.swisstown.com.

CANDLELIGHT SKI/WALK AT GOVERNOR DODGE STATE PARK—late January/early February. 6:00 to 9:00 p.m. Ski or walk a trail lit with glowing candlelight. Warm yourself by a bonfire at trail's end. Hot drinks and snacks available. (608) 935-2315 or www.wiparks.net.

RESTAURANTS

BREWERY CREEK BREWPUB
(Friday and Saturday, lunch and dinner; closed Sunday)
23 Commerce St., Mineral Point, WI 53565
(608) 987-3298, www.brewerycreek.com

COURTHOUSE INN
(breakfast, lunch, and dinner)
237 N. Iowa St., Dodgeville, WI 53533
(608) 935-3663

GLARNER STUBE *(lunch and dinner)*
518 First St., New Glarus, WI 53574
(608) 527-2216

GRACE CAFÉ
(Friday and Saturday, lunch; closed Sunday)
138 N. Iowa St., Dodgeville, WI 53533
(608) 930-2233
www.gracecafedodgeville.com

NEW GLARUS BAKERY & TEA ROOM
(breakfast and lunch)
534 First St., New Glarus, WI 53574
(608) 527-2916 or (866) 805-5536
www.newglarusbakery.com

THE ROYAL SUPPER CLUB *(dinner)*
43 High St., Mineral Point, WI 53565
(608) 987-1545

SPOTTED DOG GALLERY *(breakfast and lunch; teas, coffees, pastries)*
148 High St., Mineral Point, WI 53565
(608) 987-2855

SPRING GREEN CAFÉ AND GENERAL STORE *(breakfast, lunch, and early dinner)*

137 S. Albany St., Spring Green, WI 53588
(608) 588-7070
www.springreengeneralstore.com

THYM'S SUPPER CLUB *(dinner)*
3625 State Road 23, Dodgeville, WI 53533
(608) 935-3344

DODGEVILLE ACCOMMODATIONS
DON Q INN
Highway 23 North, Dodgeville, WI 53533
(608) 935-2321 or (800) 666-7848
www.fantasuite.com/Location.asp?LocationId=2

GRANDVIEW BED & BREAKFAST
4717 Miess Rd., Dodgeville, WI 53533
(608) 935-3261, www.grandviewbb.com

THE HOUSE ON THE ROCK INN
3591 Highway 23, Dodgeville, WI 53533
(608) 935-3711 or (888) 935-3960
www.thehouseontherock.com

MINERAL POINT ACCOMMODATIONS
THE BREWERY CREEK INN
23 Commerce St., Mineral Point, WI 53565
(608) 987-3298, www.brewerycreek.com
(Guest cottage on Shake Rag Street)

RED SHUTTERS BED & BREAKFAST
221 Clowney St., Mineral Point, WI 53565
(608) 987-2268, www.redshutters.com

SPRING GREEN ACCOMMODATIONS
HILL STREET BED & BREAKFAST
353 W. Hill St., Spring Green, WI 53588
(608) 588-7751, www.hillstreetbb.com

PRAIRIE HOUSE MOTEL
E4884 Highway 14, Spring Green, WI 53588
(608) 588-2088 or (800) 588-2088
www.execpc.com/~phouse

SPRING VALLEY INN
6279 Highway C, Spring Green, WI 53588
(608) 588-7828, www.springvalleyinn.com

Chapter Six
A TWO-SIDED ROMANCE
Door County

O N ONE 75-MILE-LONG peninsula, you can find five state parks, 18 county parks, more than a dozen community parks, 10 historic lighthouses, and more than 300 miles of shoreline. That peninsula is Wisconsin's Door County.

A Wisconsin point of pride is that there are more miles of shoreline, state parks and lighthouses in Door County than in any other county in the United States. Four of those pristine state parks are accessible in winter: Potawatomi State Park, Peninsula State Park, Newport State Park (the wildest of them all) and Whitefish Dunes State Park. Rock Island State Park, at the very tip of the peninsula, is not as accessible in winter, but with all of the other parks, wildlife sanctuaries, and state trails—even a national trail—your weekend will be full of sights and one-of-a-kind adventures.

Door County is often called Wisconsin's "thumb," and its natural configuration makes traveling up one side of the digit and returning down the other the natural thing to do. Experiencing the county that way makes the two sides' distinct personalities that much more apparent. Start on the busier, more populated Green Bay side of the peninsula. Located in the lee of the Niagara Escarpment, the bay is usually calm. Driving up this side of the county, you'll find awe-inspiring Potowatomi and Peninsula state parks, picturesque villages, charming bed and breakfasts, and incredible restaurants.

The Lake Michigan side of the Door Peninsula is wild in comparison. The unpredictable lake and its churning waters make this the quieter—people-wise—side; it's the county's less developed, more natural expression. Whitefish Dunes and Newport state parks are on this side of the peninsula. Newport is so rugged, in fact, that signs will warn you of the dangers of engaging in activities here without adequate knowledge and expertise. The Ridges Sanctuary, a preserve for wildlife and rare plants, is also on this side, as is the Cana Island Lighthouse, which has been guiding ships on the turbid Lake Michigan waters since 1869. Living in the lighthouse side by side with the Great Lake's stormy temperament was tough in the early years, and the keeper's day logs are filled with stories of struggle.

While there was a strife-filled side to everyday life in historic Door County, today's Door

County shows yet another face: Luxurious and impressive spas are here to treat you to the good life. And how lucky for you that you are visiting Door County in the off-season: You'll find your winter visit is far different from one in the summer. In winter, there are no horrendous traffic jams, no long waits for dinner, and no problems securing lodging.

It's easy to get close to Door County's two distinct sides in winter—and fall in love with them both.

Day One
LATE MORNING AND AFTERNOON

Although this is technically a Door County weekend and some say the "door" doesn't start until you cross into Sturgeon Bay, stop for an early lunch in Green Bay—the city is, after all, the oldest community in Wisconsin and *any* great Wisconsin weekend should include a brief homage to the state's roots.

Located in the heart of downtown Green Bay in an 1899 Chicago & North Western railroad station on the banks of the Fox River is **Titletown Brewing Company**. Stepping in the front door is like stepping into history: from the original fireplaces to the hardwood floors to the "Railroads of Northeastern Wisconsin" murals decorating the walls. Choose one of Titletown's eight to 10 specialty beers and ales brewed onsite to go along with your "Bison Melt." Or order the Sno-Cap root beer, based on the recipe of the owner's grandma.

Pay your respects to Wisconsin's oldest community by getting outdoors to see a little of it. After lunch, visit a 700-acre urban wildlife refuge. The **Bay Beach Wildlife Sanctuary** has live animal exhibits, educational displays, and seven miles of groomed and tracked **cross-county ski** trails. **Winter hiking** and **snowshoeing** are also allowed.

Cana Island Lighthouse, north of Baileys Harbor along the Lake Michigan shore, has been guiding ships since 1869.

DOOR COUNTY CHAMBER OF COMMERCE/VCB

The Bay Beach refuge and rehabilitation center supports a large waterfowl flock, and don't be surprised if hundreds of resident geese follow you as you trek through the outdoor pens. The pens are temporary homes for animals whose injuries prevent them from being released into the wild. Here may be the closest you will ever get to a family of timber wolves, who reside in a one-acre habitat. You'll also walk or stride by cougars, coyotes, otters, and raccoons. From a 30-foot lookout tower, you can get an overview of the deer habitat. The Woodland Building is a side trip of note: you'll see flying squirrels, owls, skunks, and other nighttime creatures in their darkened environment.

THE STATE PARK YOU DIDN'T GET TO THIS WINTER

At the far tip of the Door Peninsula is the isolated, 912-acre Rock Island State Park. The state of Wisconsin purchased the island in 1964 from the estate of Charles H. Thordarson, an electrical inventor. Born in Iceland in 1868, Thordarson moved to Milwaukee at the age of five. He purchased the island in 1910 and hoped to create his own Icelandic-like retreat there. Washington Island, just a mile away, has the oldest Icelandic community in the United States, perhaps the reason for his purchase.

As many as 12 Native American nations had lived on the island before Thordarson bought it, including Ottawa, Ojibwa, Huron, and Potawatomi.

During the 1920s, Thordarson built the massive Viking Hall and boathouse out of Rock Island limestone. He ferried Icelandic artisans and workmen from Washington Island over to Rock Island to build the structures in the Icelandic style, although he never built the summer mansion he had planned. Viking Hall is now a museum with natural history displays. The oldest lighthouse in the state, the 1858 Pottawatomie Lighthouse, also sits in the state park, on the northwest corner of the island. The original Pottawatomie Lighthouse was constructed in 1836 on the same site. It was torn down when inferior mortar and moisture damage began to compromise its structural integrity.

In the winter, the only way to get to the primitive Rock Island State Park is when the channel between Washington and Rock Islands freezes, allowing you to walk there. (Private boats are allowed to dock at the pier, but it is extremely expensive to arrange for one.) It should be stressed that you must check locally for ice conditions before you attempt such a feat. But planning starts well before even getting within walking distance to the island, as January through March, ferry crossings between Washington Island and the mainland are very infrequent, and there are no services to Rock Island itself. Cross-country skiing and snowshoeing are allowed in Rock Island State Park, though no trails are maintained.

That stretch of water between the mainland and Washington Island is called Porte des Morts Passage, which means "Passage of Death" or "Door of Death" in French. The name was assigned by a group of French fur traders who wanted to commemorate Native American friends who died there during a storm.

If you are resourceful and do make it to Rock Island State Park in winter, you can count on having one of Wisconsin's most isolated nature experiences.

For more on Rock Island State Park, go to www.wiparks.net.

In Sturgeon Bay's shipyards, near Potowatomi State Park, you can see monstrous freighters locked in their winter homes.

The cross-country ski trail leads out from the Woodland Building area and runs through forest, marshes, and fields, eventually connecting with the University of Wisconsin–Green Bay's **Cofrin Memorial Arboretum** trail system, creating a total of 12 miles of skiing trail.

After your outing at the sanctuary, get ready: It's time to step over the threshold and enter Door County.

You'll get to visit four of the county's five state parks this winter weekend [see "The State Park You Didn't Get to This Winter" sidebar], and the first one will astound you with its vistas of rocky, steep, limestone cliffs. **Potawatomi State Park** is approximately one mile south of Sturgeon Bay, north off of Highways 42 and 57 on County Road PD. This nationally acclaimed 1,225-acre park that sits on top of the Niagara Escarpment is known for its birch-lined trails. The escarpment is a 650-mile rock formation that began 420 million years ago at the outer rim of a shallow, saltwater sea and that extends all the way from eastern Wisconsin to Niagara Falls. The park stands guard over the waters of Green Bay and the Sturgeon Bay ship canal and marks the beginning of the **Ice Age National Scenic Trail. Cross-country skiers, winter hikers, snowshoers, winter campers, snowmobilers,** and those who love a good, old-fashioned **sledding hill** will be kept intrigued by this Sturgeon Bay retreat all afternoon.

Seventeen miles of **cross-country ski** trails wind and turn through the park. The five-mile **Black Loop** is groomed and tracked with a skate-ski lane. The trail follows flat to gently rolling terrain, with one short, steep hill. Farther along the trail and turning inland, you'll traverse a rocky bluff through maple, oak, pine, and birch trees before angling up the only steep climb. The 6.5-mile **Red Loop** and 3.1-mile **Blue Loop** are both rated easy and are designated for classic and skate-skiing, while the 2.7-mile **Green Loop** is for classic striding only.

Winter hikers and **snowshoers** can follow a pair of two-way trails: the .5-mile **Ancient Shores Nature Trail** or the 1.5-mile section of the **Ice Age National Scenic Trail.** For those who like off-trail hiking and snowshoeing, a trip to the observation tower is a don't-miss event. At the northern end of the park standing on top of a ridge, off the Red Loop cross-country ski trail and close to the snowmobile trail, is a 75-foot-tall tower. Take your camera, climb to the top, and stand 225 feet above Sawyer Harbor in Sturgeon Bay. With the benefit of clear, winter air and less foliage, you'll be able to see Michigan's Upper Peninsula, all across Green Bay and over crystal-blue islets.

There are at least seven plowed sites for **winter camping** at Potawatomi, and **snowmobilers** will find an 8.3-mile, two-way trail that mostly follows the park roads. **Sledders**

WHITE LACE INN WINTER RECIPES

An advantage to staying at the White Lace Inn in winter is having access to its hot cocoa mix, 24 hours a day. Below is the recipe for you to use at home, a memento from your great Wisconsin winter weekend in Door County. As an added bonus and extra treat, here is a nut bread recipe, featuring Door County cherries.

Door County knows how to do bed and breakfasts right. The White Lace Inn in Sturgeon Bay encompasses a main, Victorian house and four historic homes linked by garden paths.

White Lace Inn Hot Cocoa Mix

3 cups Nestlé's Quick powder mix
8 cups instant dry milk
8 oz. powdered coffee creamer
½ cup powdered sugar (or to taste)
⅔ cup Hershey cocoa powder

Blend all in a large bowl. Fill your cup with half hot cocoa mix and half hot water.

Mary's Holiday Cherry Almond Nut Bread

8 oz. cream cheese
1 cup butter
1½ cups sugar
1½ tsp. almond extract
4 eggs
2½ cups flour
1½ tsp. baking powder
1 cup chopped nuts
3 cups rinsed and drained Door County cherries

Preheat the oven to 350 degrees. Grease three small or two large bread pans. Cream together the cream cheese, butter, sugar, and almond extract. Beat in the eggs one at a time. Sift in the flour and the baking powder. Stir in nuts and cherries. Divide batter into pans. Bake 50 to 60 minutes.

have a hill conveniently located next to the warming shelter, where dry wood is ready near the fireplace. Build a fire and make a cup of hot chocolate before you leave the winter beauty and solitude of Potawatomi.

Snowmobilers, cross-country skiers, or **winter hikers** who want to continue their adventures can access the 33-mile **Ahnapee State Trail** that runs from downtown Sturgeon Bay through Casco in Kewaunee County. The Ahnapee is a mostly level trail that passes through wetlands and farmlands. It, in turn, connects with 95 miles of snowmobile trails in Kewaunee County and more than 250 miles of trails in Door County.

DOOR COUNTY CHAMBER OF COMMERCE/VCB

Ephraim, on the north side of Peninsula State Park, is just one of the picturesque communities on Door County's calm bay side.

If you've never experienced the charms of Door County's many bed and breakfasts, you're in for a treat this weekend. The county knows how to do B&Bs right. And Sturgeon Bay's **White Lace Inn** has to be one of the best.

The White Lace Inn encompasses a main Victorian house and 18 guest rooms in four separate historic homes linked by garden paths. The Hadley House, for example, holds four suites. Your room there will be romantic and cozy with a cherry wood, gas fireplace and hearth, whirlpool tub, in-floor radiant heat, and kitchen just outside your room door. Use the special White Lace Inn hot cocoa mix *[see "White Lace Inn Winter Recipes" sidebar]* in the kitchen to make yourself a warm mug, then sit in the Adirondack chairs on your private porch to watch light snow fall on the gazebo and trees. Or walk the short distance to the main house, and sit in the parlor for a while with a cup of hazelnut coffee or tea and a homemade, chocolate-chunk cookie.

EVENING

Make sure you only indulge in one or two of those White Lace Inn cookies, because tonight's dinner will be at one of Sturgeon Bay's most renowned eating establishments, the **Sage Restaurant and Wine Bar**.

The Sage is just three blocks from the White Lace Inn, so if you can, leave your car behind and enjoy the sights of the historic downtown district on your walk. With an Asian-style, intimate dining room, a Sage dinner experience is sophisticated, yet relaxing. You won't hear any kitchen clanging, no matter where you're seated. The menu is creative; try the duck in black tea leaves with blueberry merlot sauce or the whitefish encrusted in thinly sliced potatoes with clam broth. The live jazz is an added touch of class.

Check with your bed and breakfast proprietors to see whether there are any special festivals *[see "Jacksonport Polar Bear Club" sidebar]* in town, or spend the rest of the evening relaxing by the fireplace in your room.

JACKSONPORT POLAR BEAR CLUB

by Joe Jarosh

A 12-year veteran of the Jacksonport Polar Bear Club, Joe Jarosh was born and raised in Manitowoc, Wisconsin. He is a retired teacher and the father of two sons: J.R., founder of the Jacksonport Polar Bear Club, and Jon, marketing director for the Door County Chamber of Commerce. He and his wife, Sue, own the Jacksonport Craft Cottage Gift Shop.

Billed as the "biggest one-minute event in Door County," the Jacksonport Polar Bear Club's New Year's Day Swim is now an area tradition and has become one of the biggest in the entire country. The swim takes place at noon at Lakeside Park in Jacksonport, Wisconsin.

The club began in 1986 when 13-year-old J.R. Jarosh took a dip in icy Lake Michigan as two young friends watched. In 2005, just shy of the event's 20th anniversary, 700 swimmers and 3,000 spectators took part. Over the years, participants have come from 18 other states and even several foreign countries. The Jacksonport Polar Bear Club received national recognition when it was asked to participate in the 2002 movie premiere of the award-winning, animated film *Ice Age* at the Mall of America in Minnesota.

Safety is a prime concern in the cold temperatures, and the Jacksonport Fire Department provides assistance. A number of firemen don special cold-water suits and form a large semicircle in waist deep water to keep the swimmers contained to a limited area. Swimmers are required to wear some kind of foot protection. Extra proceeds from the sale of Jacksonport Polar Bear Club sweatshirts, T-shirts, caps, and lapel pins go to the fire department to help offset expenses and thank them for their help.

Today, J.R. Jarosh is the club's president—and rightly so. Says J.R., "Any idiot can throw himself in freezing water, but it takes a real Polar Bear to do it 16 years in a row."

The invigorating Jacksonport Polar Bear Club has a popular Internet site with a year-by-year history of the club and helpful hints for first-time swimmers at www.doorbell.net/pbc.

Day Two
MORNING

Because a visit to Door County absolutely must include a stay at one or two of its renowned bed and breakfast inns, you'll want to eat breakfast at your lodgings. At the White Lace Inn, you'll stroll the short pathway to the main house anytime between 8:00 and 10:30 a.m. and be served a sumptuous meal at one of four tables-for-two in the sunlit parlor. Cherry-stuffed, baked French toast, a homemade breakfast cookie of banana and apple, old-fashioned rice pudding, cranberry-orange juice, and a steaming cup of cinnamon-hazelnut coffee are standard fare here.

Today, you'll continue up the bay side of Door County, circle the tip, experience two more of its magnificent state parks, and then stay at an incredible English inn, all with an opportunity for some luxurious treatment in between.

One of those chances for a little winter pick-me-up will come this morning as you travel up the county to Egg Harbor. If you have time, stop at **Lucia Luxury Day Spa** for a

60-minute facial or massage. The relaxing, heated steam on your face or muscle warm-up will get you ready for this afternoon's physical activities.

JOHN T. ANDREWS

Sledders and snow tubers have a wide, steep hill to themselves in Door County's Peninsula State Park.

And you'll have an opportunity for plenty of activities at **Peninsula State Park** in Fish Creek. This enormous, 3,776-acre park draws more people per year than Yellowstone National Park. How lucky you are to see this inspiring and picturesque property in the relative solitude of winter. You could spend a week here, and each sunset of every evening you'd swear is lovelier than the day's before.

Stretching from the north edge of Fish Creek, past Eagle Bluff and Nicolet Bay to Eagle Harbor and Ephraim, this peninsular park was deeded to the state in 1909. It is the second-oldest park in the state system. The peninsula itself, for which the park was named, rises 180 feet above the waters at Eagle Bluff, a result of the western edge of the Niagara Escarpment.

The ecosystem in the park is unparalleled, and it's just another reason to spend as much time as you can here. Near **Weborg Point** in the southwest, the **Peninsula Park White Cedar Forest Na-tural Area** is a 53-acre stand of spruce, hemlock, cedar, and balsam, and the boggy remains of an ancient lake. South of Eagle Tower on the north of the peninsula is the 80-acre **Peninsula Park Beech Forest Natural Area.** Not only does this area contain a range of forest types, but it also holds a relatively uncommon stand of American beech. Both natural areas are sanctuaries for threatened species, including several native orchids and the dwarf lake iris. Watch for wild turkeys, winter wrens, red-shouldered hawks, deer, foxes, coyotes, and even a few bears.

Peninsula State Park has something for just about every winter sport enthusiast. Here, you can **cross-country ski, snowmobile, snowshoe, sled, tube, winter hike, winter camp,** or **ice fish.** You can ski the most advanced hill trails in the county here on the **Purple Loop.** At the northern section of the loop, the hills are many, but if you're up to the challenge, you'll come away with fantastic views of Green Bay from high atop Sven's Bluff. You'll even find a white cedar on Sven's Bluff that is more than 500 years old.

Sixteen miles of groomed and tracked **cross-country trails** for classic skiing and 18 miles of **snowmobile trails** are waiting for you to explore in Peninsula State Park. Six-and-a-half miles of trails can accommodate **skate-skiing.** The **Minnehaha Trail** and sections of the **Eagle and Sentinel Trails** are designated as a two-mile **snowshoeing** trail. Another trail loops near the nature center between Bluff and Skyline Roads. The snowshoeing trails travel some of the most peaceful and remote regions of the park. The Minnehaha and a Sentinel Trail section will take you to the 75-foot Eagle Tower, from where you'll be able to see, in the north, Horseshoe Island, a 38-acre island that is part of the state park. The top of the platform is 250 feet above the lake, and it gets windy up there, so dress warmly *[see Chapter 13: The Resort Life, Winter Style (Lake Geneva/Delevan/Williams Bay)]*.

Back down on the ground, magnificent ice sculptures along the shoreline may tempt you to leave the trail, but use extreme caution. Always carry ski poles with you so that if you should fall through, you can use them to pound the tips into the ice and pull yourself out.

The western edge of the **snowmobile trail** will take you past the **Eagle Bluff Lighthouse**. Built shortly after the Civil War, it was the second of the peninsula's lighthouses. A 45-foot-tall square tower attached to the keeper's house, it stands on top of Eagle Bluff and can be seen for 15 miles. History is also apparent at the pioneer cemetery, where etched stones have dates of birth going back to 1795. In fact, one stone dated 1834 denotes the first white settler in Door County.

Sledders and **snow tubers** will find a steep hill on the No. 17 fairway of the **Peninsula State Park Golf Course**, and one of four campground sectors (10 plowed sites) is open to accommodate **winter campers**. **Ice fishing** is another popular activity at the park. Peninsula State Park offers a year-round nature program, and the **White Cedar Nature Center** is open most Saturdays in winter.

While in Fish Creek, keep in mind that the **Orchard Country Winery & Market** on Highway 42 offers **horse-drawn sleigh rides** by **Mayberry's Carriages** at various times throughout weekends (usually 11:00 a.m. to 4:00 p.m., depending on snow conditions). Reservations are recommended, however, so call Orchard Country at (920) 868-3479. You can call Mayberry's Carriages directly at (920) 743-2352.

AFTERNOON

In Fish Creek, you can have your lunch at the oldest inn in Door County. The **White Gull Inn** was built in 1896 and set the style for most of the architecture in the rest of the bayside villages, with its white wood, black shutters and long front porch. In winter, the dining room is especially inviting with a wood-burning fireplace. The grilled sandwiches are great here; try the "Closed Doorwich," a smoked turkey, caramelized apple and mozzarella cheese sandwich or the "Creek's Fish Sandwich," half a fillet of Lake Michigan whitefish, seasoned with lemon pepper and served on rye bread.

After lunch, you'll be winding around the tip of the county to experience the wild but quiet side. The Lake Michigan side of the Door is a real wonderland of pristine environments—healed-over forests, rocky sea caves, postcard-worthy heaths and nature preserves, and two of the state's most untamed state parks.

Five miles northeast of Ellison Bay on County Road NP off State Highway 42 is **Newport State Park**, a real Wisconsin wilderness. In fact, the Department of Natural Resources has designated the 2,373-acre park for minimal development to protect its wild character. For that reason, only **cross-country skiing**, **winter hiking**, **snowshoeing**, and **backpack winter camping** are allowed. A sign at the park entrance cautions you not to go beyond your abilities or limits—wise advice in such a secluded, quiet, and wild spot.

This isolated and rough wilderness park constitutes half of Door County's tip and stretches for almost 12 miles along the Lake Michigan coast. The eco-diversity is astounding: bogs, wetlands, untrammeled forests of hardwoods, conifers, and hidden coves along the lakeshore make **cross-country skiing**, **winter hiking**, and **snowshoeing** the area mystical. The 140-acre **Newport Conifer-Hardwoods State Natural Area** at the southern end of the park includes northern and boreal-like forests and protects many rare plants.

Newport was once a place where schooners came in from Lake Michigan to acquire Christmas trees to sell in large cities such as Milwaukee and Chicago. Today, the remnants of the Newport ghost town have been reclaimed by the wilderness.

Twenty miles of trails are maintained for **cross-country skiing** at Newport—beautiful, isolated, wooded skiing. The seven-mile **Europe Bay/Hotz Loop** leads to the pristine Europe Lake through a sandy forest with dune-like mounds that isolate the lake from Lake Michigan. Europe Lake is one of the county's largest inland lakes. The 2.2-mile **Lynd Point/Fern Loop** passes a rocky beach, and the five-mile **Newport Loop** weaves through large stands of conifer. **Rowleys Bay Loop**, a four-miler mostly along old logging roads, alternately runs through wooded areas, meadows, and limestone headlands on the coast. The two-mile **Upland Loop** circles just north of the park office, and the 1.8-mile, open field **Monarch Loop** is groomed for **skate-skiers**.

Winter hikers and **snowshoers** are allowed to walk parallel to the ski tracks on the **Lynd Point/Fern Loop** and **Upland Loop.** The **Sugarbush Loop** is exclusively for hiking and snowshoeing and runs through an old sugar-mapling area with a mature pine forest at the back end. Coming to Newport in winter means you'll get to feel the stillness of a snowy Wisconsin forest as it might have been years ago. Snowy owls and white-winged crossbills come to Newport in winter, too, to keep company with the coyotes, foxes, porcupines, and occasional bears. You may hear the silence broken by the tapping of a pileated woodpecker or, out of the corner of your eye, see a deer watching you.

Outstanding wilderness **winter camping** can be found at Newport State Park, and hearty campers who love solitude can reach the walk-in-only sites. The shortest hike in is a half mile; the longest is nearly four miles. One of the rewards will be incredible sunsets.

A short swing back to the bay side of the Door will get you into Sister Bay and the **Church Hill Inn**, your accommodations this evening. This English-style inn provides the best of a bed and breakfast with the size of a larger inn. Each of its 34 rooms have their own theme, such as the Songbird, Rose, Afternoon Tea, Willow, Ladies Costume, and Garden Room. All of the rooms have antique and reproduction furnishings, their own porches or balconies, and triple-sheeted, four-poster beds. Four parlor areas (two upstairs and two downstairs) with warm, welcoming fireplaces invite you to sit and relax, read, or get to know other guests. Complimentary hors d'oeuvres are served in the lobby from 4:00 to 6:00 p.m., and tea and coffee are available from 7:00 a.m. to 9:00 p.m.

EVENING

After relaxing and unpacking at the inn, walk the short distance down the hill to the junction of Highways 42 and 57 for dinner at the **Mission Grille**. From 1911 to 1984, the building was the home of St. Rosalia's, Door County's first Catholic church and mission. The menu includes fresh fish flown in from Hawaii, Alaska, and North Carolina, and the beef entrées list certified Black Angus steaks and prime rib, among other specialties. *Wine*

Spectator magazine recognized the Mission Grille seven times from 1999 to 2005 for being one of the best restaurants for wine the world has to offer and, in 2005, as one of only five restaurants in Wisconsin to receive the Best of Award of Excellence. *Gourmet Magazine* has rated it one of the top 12 restaurants in Wisconsin.

Tonight, check to see whether **Newport State Park** is holding its **candlelight ski**, or head over to **Teresa K. Hilander Ice Rink** on Autumn Court for a glide on the silver blades by moonlight.

Day Three
MORNING

Today, you'll visit two more of Door County's spiritual, natural areas—or indulge in a spiritual retreat—so rise for a sumptuous breakfast at the Church Hill Inn. Breakfast is anytime from 8:30 to 9:30 a.m. in the cozy dining room and features hot egg dishes, coffee cakes, homemade granola, fresh fruit, and hot beverages.

If a little more relaxation sounds good to you, head over to **The Spa at Sacred Grounds**, halfway between the village of Ephraim and Sister Bay. Starting at 9:30 on Sunday morning, you can slip away for any of a number of healing and well-being sessions, including Swedish massage, craniosacral therapy, Door County stone massage, raindrop therapy, reflexology, and herbal wraps in one of six treatment rooms or the Holy Hut, a chink-and-log, one-room building.

If you'd rather find your spirituality in the great outdoors, **The Ridges Sanctuary** on Highway 57 in Baileys Harbor will be your morning retreat. Sometimes called the state's "most beloved ecological haven," The Ridges Sanctuary stretches along the Lake Michigan shoreline in 1,200 acres of boreal forest, swales, and dunes. It has one of the largest concentrations of rare plants in the Midwest: More than 500 different plant species have been identified, including all of Wisconsin's more than 25 native orchids and 13 endangered species of flora. The sanctuary was established in the 1930s as the result of one of the state's first environmental controversies: The area had been suggested as a site for a trailer park. Early ecologists championed the sanctuary, and it became the first State Natural Area in Wisconsin in 1967. The U.S. Department of the Interior lists the preserve as one of the most ecologically precious in the region.

Five miles of rustic and ungroomed trails and bridges at The Ridges are open for exploration by **winter hikers, snowshoers,** or **cross-country skiers** from 10:00 a.m. to 5:00 p.m. Just pay the fee at the trailhead kiosk. Boardwalks allow you to explore the area without disturbing the plants, bogs, and dunes.

Within the grounds of The Ridges is perhaps the most beautiful of Door County's many lighthouses, the brilliantly white **Cana Island Lighthouse**. Standing tall and framed by white birch, it stands off the coast on a rocky landform jutting into Lake Michigan. Built in 1870, it was one of the most crucial lighthouses in the country and considered a hardship station during storm season.

Also accessible via the trails and boardwalks are the 1869 **Baileys Harbor Range Lights**, two small but powerful lighthouses. The Lower Range Light is a short, wooden octagon on the beach; and the Upper Range Light, 900 feet inland, was the lightkeeper's one-and-a-half story, seven-room home, with a rectangular tower on the south gable, directly above the front door. From the water, a sailor got "on range" by vertically lining up the white light in the Upper Range Light, which shone 39 feet above the water, with the red Lower Range Light, 22 feet above the water.

AFTERNOON

Before leaving Baileys Harbor, stop for lunch at the **Harbor Fish Market & Grille** on Highway 57. Savor a cup of chowder or enjoy a "Walleye Cake Sandwich" while taking in a beautiful, wintry view of the shoreline.

After lunch, as you travel down the Door's wild side, you'll have one last, exceptional state park stop in this unique county.

The 863-acre **Whitefish Dunes State Park** has miles and miles of wind-sculpted, mocha-colored dunes formed by the advances and retreats of ancient lakes and countless storms. Sand banks first enclosed Clark Lake in what is now the mainland. As plants slowly began to take hold, wind deposits piled up atop the sandbar. The result is a biome that couldn't possibly occur on the bay side of the Door Peninsula: a wide beach rising to forested dunes. The tallest dune, Old Baldy, stands 93 feet high. *Wisconsin Trails* magazine once called this beach the best in Wisconsin.

As you photograph and enjoy this park's many treasures, make sure that you always stay off the dunes. The dune grasses that hold the mounds together, such as beach pea and a rare quack grass, are peculiar to this park and fragile to human touch. Your feet can easily uproot them. Once the grasses are gone, the dunes will be gone.

There are 13.5 miles of groomed and tracked trails for classic **cross-country skiing** amid the vast, rolling dunes and along the shoreline. **Winter hikers** and **snowshoers** are allowed on 4.5 miles of those trails. Even the **beach** is considered a winter trail area here and is open to **cross-country skiing, hiking**, and **snowshoeing**.

The popular 2.8-mile **Red Trail** follows the Whitefish Bay shoreline and then branches away through mixed hardwood, red pine, and wooded dune areas. At its southern end, you can access Old Baldy, which has an observation platform from which you can get a panoramic view of Lake Michigan and Clark Lake. A boardwalk and stairs lead to the top; you must remove your skis before attempting to climb, however. The 1.8-mile **Green Trail** is heavily forested and will take you to the shore of Clark Lake, while the **Yellow Trail,** at 4.2 miles, starts and finishes on the Green Trail and passes through a red pine plantation.

The 2.5-mile **Black Trail** is an ungroomed trail for **cross-country skiing, hiking**, and **snowshoeing**, which will take you to a forest of hardwoods and exposed rocks. The two-mile **Brachiopod Trail** branches off the Black Trail and ends at the boardwalk over a wetland area. **No winter camping** is allowed in the park, and **ice fishers** are asked to be cautious since the park does not monitor ice conditions. **No snowmobiling** is allowed in the park.

Walking the Black and Brachiopod Trails will take you to a truly fantastic land. **Cave Point County Park**, 19 acres within Whitefish Dunes State Park, is a special place for photographers and those who love nature. The breaking waves here make a booming sound that can be heard a quarter mile away. As six-footers pound the shore, the ground at Cave Point trembles. Amazing in the summertime, Cave Point is even more spectacular in winter, when gigantic icicles hang from water-sculpted limestone sea caves and rocks—a side of the park that summer-only visitors never get to see.

FOR MORE INFORMATION

DOOR COUNTY CHAMBER OF COMMERCE
Visitor & Convention Bureau
1015 Green Bay Rd., Sturgeon Bay, WI 54235
(920) 743-4456 or (800) 527-3529
www.doorcounty.com

STURGEON BAY VISITOR &
CONVENTION BUREAU
23 N. Fifth Ave., Sturgeon Bay, WI 54235
(920) 743-6246 or (800) 301-6695
www.sturgeonbay.net

WINTER ATTRACTIONS

AHNAPEE STATE TRAIL
3538 Park Dr., Sturgeon Bay, WI 54235
(920) 746-9959, www.ahnapeetrail.org

BAY BEACH WILDLIFE SANCTUARY
1660 E. Shore Dr., Green Bay, WI 54302
(920) 391-3671
www.baybeachwildlife.com

COFRIN MEMORIAL ARBORETUM
University of Wisconsin–Green Bay
2420 Nicolet Dr., Green Bay, WI 54311
(920) 465-2111
www.uwgb.edu/biodiversity/arboretum

ICE AGE PARK & TRAIL FOUNDATION
207 E. Buffalo St., Suite 515
Milwaukee, WI 53202, (414) 278-8518 or
(800) 227-0046, www.iceagetrail.org

LUCIA LUXURY DAY SPA
7821 Highway 42, Egg Harbor, WI 54209
(920) 868-1597, www.luciaspa.com

MAYBERRY'S CARRIAGES
4044 County Trunk V, Egg Harbor, WI 54209
(920) 743-2352, www.mayberryscarriages.com

NEWPORT STATE PARK
475 Highway NP, Ellison Bay, WI 54210
(920) 854-2500
www.dcty.com/newport or www.wiparks.net

ORCHARD COUNTRY WINERY & MARKET
9179 Highway 42, Fish Creek, WI 54212
(920) 868-3479, www.orchardcountry.com

PENINSULA STATE PARK
9462 Shore Rd., Fish Creek, WI 54212
(920) 868-3258, www.wiparks.net

POTAWATOMI STATE PARK
3740 Park Dr. (Highway PD), Sturgeon Bay, WI
54235, (920) 746-2890, www.wiparks.net

TERESA K. HILANDER ICE RINK
111 Autumn Ct., Sister Bay, WI 54234
(920) 854-7014, www.sisterbay.com/parks.htm

THE RIDGES SANCTUARY
8270 Highway 57, Baileys Harbor, WI 54202
(920) 839-2802, www.ridgesanctuary.org

THE SPA AT SACRED GROUNDS
10450 Townline Rd., Ephraim, WI 54211
(920) 854-4733, www.sacredgroundsspa.com

WHITEFISH DUNES STATE PARK
3275 Clark Lake Rd., Sturgeon Bay, WI 54235
(920) 823-2400, www.wiparks.net

WINTER FESTIVALS

EGG HARBOR HOLLY DAYS—late November.
Horse-drawn wagon rides, breakfast with Santa, children's scavenger hunt, tree-lighting ceremony, and hospitality throughout the village. (800) 527-3529 or www.eggharbor-wi.com.

STURGEON BAY'S CHRISTMAS BY THE BAY —late November. Tree lighting, caroling, and Santa parade on Friday at 7:00 p.m. Hay and trolley rides through historic downtown, special children's activities, photos with Santa, and Christmas Tea. (800) 301-6695 or www.sturgeon bay.net.

JACKSONPORT POLAR BEAR SWIM—January 1. Lakeside Park. Noon. Join hundreds of hearty souls as they storm into the freezing water of Lake Michigan. Refreshments available. All proceeds go to the Jacksonport Fire Department. (920) 823-2231 or www.doorbell.net/pbc.

EGG HARBOR'S NEW YEAR'S PARADE— January 1. The Midwest's goofiest parade takes to the streets at 1:00 p.m. The fun is in never knowing what or who will show up to take part in this impromptu tradition. The parade goes on, no matter what the weather. (920) 868-3717 or www.doorcounty.com.

SNOWSHOEING AT THE RIDGES SANCTUARY—Fridays in January and February. Baileys Harbor. 1:00 p.m. Naturalist-guided snowshoe tour through the Ridges Sanctuary. Different location each time. The tour meets at the Upper Range Light on Ridges Road. Bring your own snowshoes or call ahead to arrange a loaner pair. (920) 839-2802 or www.doorcounty. com.

CANDLELIGHT RIDE AT KURTZ CORRAL RIDING STABLES—Saturdays in January and February. Egg Harbor. Enjoy a candlelight horseback ride through Door County's winter landscape and then warm up by the fireplace with a hot cider. The ride begins around sunset and lasts for an hour and a half. Kurtz Corral Riding stables, 5712 Howard Lane, 10 miles north of Sturgeon Bay. Reservations required by calling (920) 743-6742 or www.kurtzcorral.com.

GREEN BAY'S WINTERFEST ON BROADWAY —late January. Ice sculptors line the streets, creating their masterpieces, while event-goers can race each other in the beer barrel races, learn how to curl from the Green Bay Curling Club, and more. (920) 437-2531 or www.onbroadway.org.

WHITEFISH DUNES STATE PARK CANDLELIGHT SKI—late January. 6:00–8:00 p.m. Evening ski on candlelit trails, snow conditions permitting. (920) 823-2400 or www.doorcounty.com.

FISH CREEK WINTER FESTIVAL—early February. The harbor in Clark Park. Twelve days of winter fun, with games such as ice bowling, ice golf, and minnow races. Food, entertainment, candlelight ski, kites on the bay, ice sculptures, and more. (800) 577-1880 or www.fishcreek.info.

PENINSULA STATE PARK CANDLELIGHT SKI—first weekend in February. 5:30–8:30 p.m. Evening ski on candlelit trails, snow conditions permitting. (920) 868-3258 or www.doorcounty.com.

FISHING DERBY WEEK, WASHINGTON ISLAND—mid-February. Cash prizes for the top three entries in several categories. (920) 847-2179 or www.doorcounty.com.

NEWPORT STATE PARK CANDLELIGHT SKI, HIKE & SNOWSHOE—mid-February. Ellison Bay. 6:00–9:00 p.m. One-mile trail lighted by homemade candles, bonfire, and refreshments. (920) 854-2500 or www.doorcounty.com.

POTAWATOMI STATE PARK CANDLELIGHT SKI—late February. Sturgeon Bay. 5:00–9:00 p.m. Evening ski on a one-mile, candlelit trail. Bonfire and refreshments. Hike will take place if there is lack of snow. (920) 746-2890 or www.doorcounty. com.

STURGEON BAY'S "FIRE & ICE" ICESCAPE— late February. 9:00 a.m.–9:00 p.m. Ice-carving competition throughout the Sturgeon Bay business district. Carvers turn 400-pound blocks of ice into works of art, and the evenings are filled with hot music in local bars and restaurants. Vote in the popular People's Choice Awards. Judging at 2:30 p.m. (800) 301-6695 or www.sturgeonbay.net.

STURGEON BAY'S ST. PATRICK'S DAY PARADE —mid-March. 11:00 a.m. Sturgeon Bay will be green for a day. (800) 301-6695 or www.sturgeonbay.net.

RESTAURANTS
AL JOHNSON'S SWEDISH RESTAURANT & BUTIK *(breakfast, lunch, and dinner)* 704 N. Bay Shore Dr., Sister Bay, WI 54234, (920) 854-2626

HARBOR FISH MARKET & GRILLE *(breakfast, lunch, and dinner)* 8080 Highway 57, Baileys Harbor, WI 54202 (920) 839-9999 www.harborfishmarket-grille.com

MISSION GRILLE *(dinner)* Highways 42 and 57, Sister Bay, WI 54234 (920) 854-9070, www.missiongrille.com

SAGE RESTAURANT AND WINE BAR *(dinner)* 136 N. Third Ave., Sturgeon Bay, WI 54235 (920) 746-1100, www.sagedoorcounty.com

TITLETOWN BREWING COMPANY *(lunch and dinner)* 200 Dousman St., Green Bay, WI 54303 (920) 437-2337, www.titletownbrewing.com

WHITE GULL INN *(breakfast, lunch, and dinner)* 4225 Main St., Fish Creek, WI 54212 (920) 868-3517 www.whitegullinn.com

LODGING
CHURCH HILL INN 425 Gateway Dr., Sister Bay, WI 54234 (920) 854-4885 or (800) 422-4906 www.churchhillinn.com

INN AT CEDAR CROSSING 336 Louisiana St., Sturgeon Bay, WI 54235 (920) 743-4200, www.innatcedarcrossing.com

INN ON MAPLE 414 Maple Dr., Sister Bay, WI 54234 (920) 854-5107, www.innonmaple.com

REYNOLDS HOUSE 111 S. Seventh Ave., Sturgeon Bay, WI 54235 (920) 746-9771 or (877) 269-7401 www.reynoldshousebandb.com

SCOFIELD HOUSE 908 Michigan St., Sturgeon Bay, WI 54235 (920) 743-7727 or (888) 463-0204 www.scofieldhouse.com

WHITE GULL INN 4255 Main St., Fish Creek, WI 54212 (920) 868-3517 or (888) 364-9542 www.whitegullinn.com

WHITE LACE INN 16 N. Fifth Ave., Sturgeon Bay, WI 54235 (920) 743-1105 or (877) 948-5223 www.whitelaceinn.com

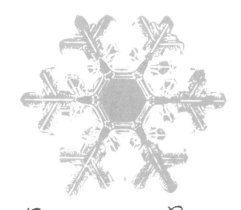

Chapter Seven
SOUNDS OF THE NORTH WOODS
Eagle River

THERE'S ONE WINTER SOUND that is probably heard more often than any other in Eagle River—and you can be sure that you'll hear it, too, on your winter weekend here. It's the schwoose-schwoose of people walking in snowmobile pants. Snowmobiles—and their riders—are everywhere: alongside every road, outside every restaurant and hotel, and at every gas pump.

Eagle River has long been a tourist destination. Vilas County has the greatest number of inland lakes in the world, and the town of Eagle River lies along an interlinked chain of 28 of them. In summer, swimmers, boaters, and fishermen fill the waters.

But it is the winter season that really gives Eagle River its personality and its reputation for recreation. Snowmobiling is ingrained in the culture here. Numerous snowmobile clubs groom and maintain a scenic, wooded 500-mile network of trails known as the "Eagle River 500." Local snowmobile dealers rent machines and helmets by the day or hour, and scores of local groups offer guided tours ranging from three to seven days that even include meals and lodging. Fittingly enough, Eagle River is host to the annual World Championship Snowmobile Derby on the Ice Oval, the first racetrack exclusively dedicated to snowmobile racing.

But there are pioneer-types in Eagle River who fill the air with other winter sounds. The annual Klondike Days is the biggest winter rendezvous in the country and brings to Eagle River's North Woods the buzz of chain saws and the ring of axes as lumberjacks compete in feats of sawing, chopping, and climbing. Over at River Country Red's encampment, there are the sounds of muzzle-loaders shooting, blacksmiths hammering, and muffled horse hooves on the snow.

Quieter sounds often accompany your own weekend activities in Eagle River. Picture a day in the Nicolet National Forest, mantled in white. Stands of virgin pines, with frosted boughs, reach so high into the sky that you can't see their tops. Clumps of white birch glisten in the winter sunlight. You hear only your skis cutting through the soft snow and the birds that flit around and above you.

An old-fashioned sleigh takes Klondike Days visitors through the encampment and surrounding grounds.

The roar of snowmobiles. The whirring of chainsaws. The quiet of the North Woods. It all sounds like a great way to spend a winter weekend.

Day One
MORNING

For an introduction into the North Woods, stop for breakfast at the **Copper Kettle Restaurant** in downtown Eagle River. Here the servers all wear different plaid flannel shirts amid the wood-paneled dining rooms. While you'll find some standard favorites on the thick menu, such as omelets, Belgian waffles, French toast, salads, and club-style sand-wiches, you'll also find more unusual fare such as the Braunwich—braunschweiger (smoked liverwurst), hard-boiled egg, tomato, and bacon—and liver. You even have a chance to get *on* the menu at the Copper Kettle. If you order the "All You Can Eat Pancake Breakfast" and eat 10 pancakes or more, you'll be listed in the "Pancake Hall of Fame." The roster began on August 18, 1977, when a 15-year-old boy from Manawa, Wisconsin, ate 10 of the restaurant's giant-size pancakes. Since then, the menu has listed the names of the hall of famers, one of whom managed to ingest 30 pancakes.

After your brush with fame at the Copper Kettle, walk off a little of the meal by going to see the **Eagle River Ice Castle**, erected between Christmas and New Year's Day near the train depot on Railroad Street. The castle usually stands for about five to seven weeks after construction. Every winter, community volunteers—more than 60 people cutting 16-inch blocks from Silver Lake, with another 63 people building the castle—construct a newly designed, magnificent ice castle. The Eagle River Area Fire Department designs the castle and implements the construction, with the help of the Lions Club and other organizations. The frozen masterpiece is illuminated with dozens of colored floodlights every evening. The castle has become so popular that travelers often plan their trips to Eagle River around the date of its construction.

To further acquaint yourself with Eagle River's history and lore, make a quick stop at the **Snowmobile Hall of Fame and Museum**, located 10 miles west of Eagle River off Highway 70 on the west side of St. Germain. Open since 1993, the museum contains famous championship trail sleds, from a 1964 Polaris snowmobile raced in the first snowmobile derby in Eagle River to the winning Black Magic Arctic Cat snowmobile driven by Blair Morgan in the 2001 X Games. Other cool snowmobile memorabilia rests here, such as uniforms, jerseys, and a history of the 30-plus inductees. The nonprofit organization inducts both racing and recreational snowmobilers each year in January. Watch action-packed videos of famous races in the mini-theater, focusing on the biggest race of them all, the World Championship Snowmobile Derby held in Eagle River every January.

AFTERNOON

Tomorrow you'll have a chance to watch the World Championship Snowmobile Derby in person, but this afternoon you'll be the action hero.

Back in downtown Eagle River, have lunch at the nostalgic **Soda Pops**. The owner collects old-time soda machines, and the restored Victorian tin ceilings and old booths embody the flavor of the late 1800s. Soda Pops is one of the oldest operating soda fountains in Wisconsin. Besides more than 200 varieties of bottled sodas, you can choose from some 70 condiments and toppings for sandwiches, soups, and salads at the "Fresh Produce Filling Station."

Today you'll spend time cross-country skiing, snowshoeing, or snowmobiling, and several outlets in downtown Eagle River will rent you the equipment you may need. Cross-country ski and snowshoe rentals are available at **Chain of Lakes Cyclery & Ski** on Railroad Street. Snowmobiles can be rented at **Boat S'Port Marina**, **Heckel's Marina**, or **Track Side**.

This afternoon, explore close-up what the North Woods is all about. At the 661,000-acre **Nicolet National Forest**, you'll be able to **snowmobile**, **cross-country ski**, or **snowshoe** with white pines, spruce, hemlocks, and aspens as your companions. Encompassing parts of Wisconsin and the Upper Peninsula of Michigan, the Nicolet National Forest has more than 500 miles of trails designated for snowmobilers. Cross-country skiers will find five trails catering to their interests. From Eagle River, the two most easily accessed are the **Nicolet North Trail** and the **Anvil National Recreation Tail**, which intersect. On both, you can cover more than 27 miles of terrain.

The **Anvil National Recreation Trail** is one of the oldest and most popular cross-country ski trails in the Eagle River area. Twelve miles of groomed and tracked trails accommodate classic and skate-skiing. The trailhead for the level, wooded, and sometimes hilly Anvil Trail is found 8.5 miles east of Eagle River on Highway 70.

Connected to the Anvil National Recreation Trail is the 15-mile **Nicolet North Trail**. Its gently rolling terrain has a few steep hills and is groomed and tracked for both classic and skate-skiing. From Eagle River, the trailhead is 11 miles out on Highway 70 east, then right (south) on Fornier Road about three miles. If groomed trails are too civilized, you can **snowshoe** throughout the woods.

Right within town is another popular cross-country skiing venue—some local residents claim it's the best in the area—the 6.8-mile **Nordmarka and Norge Ski Trails** on the north side of Eagle River at the Eagle River Municipal Golf Course on Eagle Waters Road. The **Nordmarka's** groomed and tracked trails on the golf course handle both classic and skate-skiing techniques and contain challenging hills. The nearby four loops of **Norge Trails** cover 3.1 miles of gentle terrain. These wooded trails are groomed only for classic skiing. A .6-mile classic-only section connects the Nordmarka and Norge Trails.

EVENING

Capture the feeling of having your own North Woods lodge home by staying at the **Wild Eagle Lodge** this weekend *[see "The Changing Face of Wisconsin Resorts" sidebar]*. One mile north of Eagle River on Highway 45, this resort has several buildings with two floors of "lodge homes" in each—and every room has a view of either Duck or Lynx Lakes. The one-, two-, and three-bedroom homes have a full kitchen—with a range, dishwasher, refrigerator, coffeemaker, toaster, microwave, and kitchenware—and two full bathrooms. A fieldstone, gas fireplace in the living room makes winter nights comfortable. The balcony overlooking the lake comes with chairs, table, a grill, and a nightly show of brilliant stars. Before unpacking, take a moment to have a Dreamy Winter hot cocoa or Bavarian Blizzard hot coffee drink at the Boondocker's Lounge.

Dinner tonight comes with a view of Lake Voyager, brought to you by the **Chanticleer Inn**. The inn has an elegant but casual atmosphere. Its menu ranges from a Chanti burger to lobster, with nightly specials and a Friday fish fry.

Staying at the Wild Eagle Lodge is like having your own North Woods lodge home.

THE CHANGING FACE OF WISCONSIN RESORTS

by Jo Haverkampf Daniel

Jo Haverkampf Daniel moved to St. Germain in 1969 when her family purchased Sunrise Shores Resort. She now lives in Sayner, Wisconsin, and works as special events coordinator and sales director for the Wild Eagle Lodge, an Eliason family resort.

Having grown up on a small mom-and-pop resort in St. Germain, Wisconsin, I remember well most of the families that stayed with us. Year after year, the same groups returned for their vacations, and to this day a lot of them have remained my friends. Some even became part of our family. Every week brought a new group of old friends, filled with sun-drenched days on the lake, fishing, swimming, bonfires, and cookouts. I couldn't imagine a better childhood.

The resort was sold about 15 years ago when my parents retired. It was eventually split up and turned into condos. We all moved on to other careers. It was sad to see this era come to an end. Now, after all these years I find myself back in the Wisconsin resort business. I came on staff at the Wild Eagle Lodge during the 2004 construction. This is one of the new breed of resorts: large properties with amenities galore to satisfy every taste in every season.

I was pleasantly surprised to discover, however, that the size of the property cannot change the people. By personally greeting and getting to know our guests, I have made many new friends and memories. There have been times when I've laughed until I cried, went home with wet clothes from playing with kids on our beach, and even joined in a sing-along beside a campfire. For me, Wisconsin resort life hasn't changed much at all— just a few of the faces are different.

Day Two
MORNING

Inside the Vilas Village Mall, you'll find one of the best places in Wisconsin to get a bowl of hot oatmeal. The "porridge" at **Terra Nicole's Espresso Cafe**, inside the locally owned bookstore, Jabberwocky, should be part of at least one of your Eagle River winter mornings. The presentation alone is awesome: oatmeal served with whipped milk in a small creamer, with a cup of raisins and a cup of brown sugar on the side. The cheese/herb bagels with cream cheese are another excellent option. A sign on the wall of the cafe claims that Terra Nicole's has the "best coffee on earth," and there's no reason to argue. The café is just a couple of blocks away from two winter festivals, either of which you should consider planning your weekend around: the World Championship Snowmobile Derby and Klondike Days.

The most recognized professional snowmobile race in the world, the **World Championship Snowmobile Derby** *[see "The First Snowmobile" sidebar]* draws almost 500 racers, some from as far away as Japan, to compete in 20 classes for nearly $90,000 in prize money. The event is held at the famed Ice Oval, the first racetrack constructed exclusively for snowmobile racing. The egg-shaped ice oval has banked corners and is a half mile in length on the outside wall. It is a demanding configuration for drivers. Sitting pit-side is a dramatic winter experience: the ground shakes, the sleds roar, and ice kicked up by 400-pound sleds going over 100 miles per hour stings your face. If you prefer to keep out of the ice-spray zone, a two-story viewing stand holds 500 "Hot Seats," with restrooms, beverage service, closed circuit TV, and a panoramic view of the racing action.

The Ice Oval races are complemented by the high-flying Sno-Cross competition on a snow-covered course with big bumps, jumps, and moguls. Different types of sleds and techniques are used in the two types of racing, but both hold thrills and excitement for the more than 50,000 attendees. Friday and Saturday are the exhibition races and elimination heats. The championships are held Sunday afternoon.

On the following weekend in Eagle River is **Klondike Days,** the nation's largest winter rendezvous *[see "Living History at Klondike Days" sidebar].* The two-day festival features dog and horse weight-pulls, the **Great Northern Lumberjack Exhibition**, chainsaw log carvings, dog sled rides, and **River Country Red's Rendezvous encampment**. Re-creators in authentic-looking, 18th-century clothing reflect the period in a living history camp. "Buckskinners" and "fur trappers" can be found trading, muzzle-loader shooting, black-smithing, and testing their tomahawk- and knife-throwing skills against one another.

THE FIRST SNOWMOBILE

Wisconsin has the nation's most extensive network of snowmobile trails: over 25,000 miles are maintained by dozens of clubs through-out the state. One quarter of the snowmobiles in the United States are in Wisconsin; registered snowmobiles here number more than 200,000.

But long before the first World Championship Snowmobile Derby in Eagle River and riders jumping moguls on sleek sleds, the first snowmobile was patched together with skis, a small motor, and parts from a Model T Ford and a bicycle. An avid hunter in Sayner, Wisconsin, Carl Eliason, had grown tired of always lagging behind his hunting buddies because of his crippled foot. He put together the first snowmobile, or engine-powered ski machine, in his workshop in 1924.

Suddenly, Eliason was moving faster than his friends afoot in the woods. He'd often arrive at a destination an hour ahead of them. In 1927, he patented the machine and con-tinued to make improvements. His neighbors began asking for sleds of their own, so Eliason built more of them during the winter months. No two were alike, and he charged about $350 per machine. In the early 1930s, *Popular Mechanics* magazine publicized his creation, and more requests for the sleds poured in. When an order for 200 machines came in from the Finnish government, which recognized the snow sled's potential in winter com-bat, Eliason realized he could not keep up with the demand. He sold the patent to the Four Wheel Drive Company of Clintonville, Wisconsin, which assembled the machines in Appleton and later in Canada.

When Eliason died at age 80 in the winter of 1979, his funeral procession consisted of a mile-long parade of snowmobiles. His original sled can be seen at the Vilas County Historical Museum in Sayner, Wisconsin.

Mapmakers set up their tents next to teepees, and squirrel and bear meat is likely to be cooking on outside spits.

At the Great Northern Lumberjack Exhibition, you'll catch events like the Women's Hot Start Chainsaw competition and the Men's Pole Climbing and Topping Off competitions. In the Topping Off event, the men are given a tall tree stump. They must cut into the stump, insert a board to stand on to reach a higher level, repeat the process two more times, then top off the stump. Often you'll find representatives from Canada, Wisconsin, and Minnesota pitted against each other.

During Klondike Days, you can travel through time at River Country Red's Rendezvous encampment.

Located in the Eagle River Northland Pines Middle School is a craft fair, and the **Native American Cultural Exposition** in the high school offers a living museum of Ojibwe culture through plays, storytelling, drumming, songs, and dancing in authentic dress.

Klondike Days activities are held at the World Championship Snowmobile Derby Track, Northland Pines High School, Northland Pines Middle School, and other venues around Eagle River. More than 15,000 people attend this two-day event each year.

AFTERNOON

You'll probably want to stay at the festivals all day, but if you're not partaking in a buffalo burger or wild rice soup at Klondike Days, head over to the **Braywood Resort** on Catfish Lake for lunch. Choose an Italian beef, steak, or BBQ pork sandwich.

If your winter weekend doesn't coincide with one of the two festivals, consider taking a **snowmobile tour** with a guide company. **Decker Sno-Venture Tours** has been in the business for more than 25 years. For 12 years, the company has been recognized as the top tour operator by the readers of *Snowgoer Magazine*. Although Decker conducts snowmobile

LIVING HISTORY AT KLONDIKE DAYS

Walk the path into the encampment at Klondike Days and you walk into history. The camp is a living museum depicting what life was like during upper Wisconsin's fur-trading era, a period that lasted from 1600 to 1840. Bill Kroll has been involved with Klondike Days for the past 10 years as historical interpreter and is currently the camp's administrator.

Bill's own foray into living history began 25 years ago. Both Bill and his wife, Lillian, were avid campers. While Lillian favored "Coleman camping," a style of camping with niceties such as stoves and battery-powered lanterns, Bill preferred more primitive stays in the outdoors. On one of their outings, they met a man who is a historical interpreter at Heritage Hill State Park in Green Bay. He convinced them to check out "history camping."

The Krolls started slowly by setting up day camps with friends who had done historical re-enactments. At night, they'd go to a hotel. But feeling like they were missing out on a lot of the camaraderie, the Krolls finally splurged and bought a teepee. That purchase brought them into the second phase of evolving into true historical interpreters, "buckskinning."

Buckskinning is a type of hobby camping where the point is to get out outside and

Bill Kroll, history interpreter, wears authentic-looking, 18th-century clothing at Klondike Days living history encounter.

experiment with authenticity. Says Bill, "Buckskinners don't necessarily try to be historically accurate with everything they do. For example, you'll see a lot of ironware around a buckskinner's campfire. Since most people in this area of Wisconsin traveled by foot or canoe, they wouldn't have carried all that heavy ironware with them. And, a lot of folks will get carried away with the mountain-man character. But the mountain man didn't really get started until after the 1800s when the fur trade started pushing west of the Mississippi and people started using horses for transport. There's nothing wrong with buckskinning; it's a lot of fun. But as long as Lillian and I were going to do this, we wanted to do it with accuracy."

Learning that a teepee was not historically correct for northern Wisconsin, Bill and Lillian stopped using it. "We now use an A-frame or wedge-tent, which is typical for Wisconsin from the late 1600s up to the 1800s," says Bill.

Developing a historical persona was the next step to becoming a true historical interpreter. "We had to come up with characters who were our ages and appropriate for this region. And not wanting to wear white lace, we needed to portray people low on the social scale. After some initial research, I came up with a character who would have been employed by the fur-trading North West Company at Lac du Flambeau in 1793. Lillian's job was tougher; there weren't a lot of white women in the region at the time. There were a few at the fur trading post at Grand Portage, so my wife bases her portrayal on a woman who would have worked there."

While at a living history encounter, which typically lasts three days, the two try to stay in their characters. "Because we are in the 21st century, there are some things we're not permitted to do, like hunt for meat. But nothing says you can't bring in a venison haunch from the previous deer season and cook it," notes Bill.

Today, Bill hires history interpreters from Wisconsin, Minnesota, Kentucky, and Virginia to appear at Klondike Days. His favorite part of the experience every year is seeing the families who come—not only the ones visiting the camp, but the families that choose to participate as history interpreters. "Buckskinning is truly a family hobby," says Bill. "Even young kids can play an important role, and they certainly won't get bored."

According to Bill, the only pitfall in historical camping is impatience. "Don't try to get everything at once," he cautions. "You can get caught up in getting a lot of equipment you really don't need, and that can be expensive. Learn to make a lot of things as they would have back then. If you can't make it, find someone who can, and then start trading."

---

tours around the world—the Midwest, Alaska, Canada, and Iceland—they will arrange for guided one-, two-, or three-day rides out of Eagle River. The **Sno-Eagles Snowmobile Club** also offers guided tours in the area.

If you'd like to make tracks of another kind, let the blades of your **ice skates** carve into one of the area's many frozen lakes.

EVENING

Tonight, dine among eight huge aquariums at **Captain Nemo's Supper Club**. The tanks are filled with North Woods native fish: muskie, walleye, northern pike, pan fish, and bass. Seafood, Cajun cooking, and "blackening" are the specialties.

For after-dinner entertainment, attend the **Bluegrass Festival at Klondike Days** in the Snowmobile Derby Track pavilion or catch an **Eagle River Falcons hockey game** at the **Eagle River Sports Arena**.

Day Three
MORNING AND AFTERNOON

Before leaving the Wild Eagle Lodge, take the early morning hours to **snowshoe** the trail winding through the lodge's 18-acre site. Walk along the lakes and watch the sunrise. After checking out, stop for breakfast at the **Brew Moon Coffeehouse** on South Railroad Street, an inviting espresso bar and café.

Spend the rest of your weekend in Eagle River either with a return visit to **Klondike Days,** by checking out the action at the **Sno-Cross World Championship Race** at 2:00 p.m. and the **World Championship Snowmobile Derby Title Race** at 3:00 p.m., or by sampling Eagle River's quieter sports side, with a **skiing** or **snowshoeing** outing at **Razorback Ridges** near Sayner.

For both classic and skate-skiers, Razorback Ridges has become one of the more acclaimed **cross-country ski** trail systems in Wisconsin. Located two miles west of Sayner at the intersection of Highway N and Razorback Road, Razorback Ridges is a community service project of the Sayner/Star Lake Lions Club and is dedicated to silent sports. The trails begin at Mel and Emma Long Memorial Park, which includes a warming building, the lighted Bernie VanAcker Memorial **ice-skating rink** and a four-mile **snowshoe trail**. The 12.4 miles of ski trails range from the gently rolling **Doug's Folly**, a 3.7-mile loop through a wide mixture of oak, pine, and aspen forests, to **Suicide Hill**, a steep, fast tour with a compression bump and blind approach. Spend some of your time here, and it just could be that the last sounds you hear in Eagle River are the happy shouts of skiers flying down the hill.

FOR MORE INFORMATION
**EAGLE RIVER CHAMBER OF COMMERCE
AND VISITOR CENTER**
201 N. Railroad St., Eagle River, WI 54521
(715) 479-8575 or (800) 359-6315
www.eagleriver.org

ST. GERMAIN CHAMBER OF COMMERCE
PO Box 155, St. Germain, WI 54558
(715) 477-2205 or (800) 727-7203
www.st-germain.com

**SAYNER/STAR LAKE CHAMBER OF
COMMERCE**
203 Main St., Sayner, WI 54560, (715) 542-3789
or (888) 722-3789, www.sayner-starlake.org

*For a map showing the county's 550 miles
of snowmobile trails:*
**VILAS COUNTY ADVERTISING &
PUBLICITY**
(715) 479-3649 or (800) 236-3649, www.vilas.org

For a free map of snowmobile trails around the state:
WISCONSIN DIVISION OF TOURISM
(800) 432-8757

WINTER ATTRACTIONS
**ASSOCIATION OF WISCONSIN
SNOWMOBILE CLUBS**
5497 Waterford Ln., Suite B, Appleton, WI
54913, (920) 734-5530, www.awsc.org

BOAT S'PORT MARINA *(rents snowmobiles)*
3624 Highway 70 East, Eagle River, WI 54521
(715) 479-8000 or (800) 315-7737
www.boatsport.com

CHAIN OF LAKES CYCLERY & SKI
(rents skis and snowshoes)
107 N. Railroad St., Eagle River, WI 54521
(715) 479-3920

DECKER SNO-VENTURE TOURS
1311 N. Railroad St., Eagle River, WI 54521
(715) 479-2764, www.sno-venture.com

EAGLE RIVER SPORTS ARENA
4149 Highway 70 East
Eagle River, WI 54521
(715) 479-4858

EAGLE RIVER ICE CASTLE
(constructed near the train depot on Railroad Street)

HECKEL'S MARINA *(rents snowmobiles)*
437 W. Division St., Eagle River, WI 54521
(715) 479-4471 or (800) 432-5357
www.heckels.com

NICOLET NATIONAL FOREST: ANVIL NATIONAL RECREATION TRAIL AND NICOLET NORTH TRAIL
Forest Supervisor's Office, 68 S. Stevens St.
Rhinelander, WI 54501
(715) 362-1300, www.fs.fed.us/r9/cnnf

NORDMARKA AND NORGE SKI TRAILS
3801 Eagle Waters Rd., Eagle River, WI 54521
(800) 838-9472

RAZORBACK RIDGES *(Intersection of Highway N and Razorback Road)*
Sayner/Star Lake Lions Club
3126 Razorback Rd., Sayner, WI 54560
(715) 542-3019, www.vilas.org/sa-xctrls.htm

SNO-EAGLES SNOWMOBILE CLUB
PO Box 866, Eagle River, WI 54521
(715) 479-1712

SNOWMOBILE HALL OF FAME AND MUSEUM
6035 Highway 70 East, St. Germain, WI 54558
(715) 542-4488, www.snowmobilehalloffame.com

TRACK SIDE *(rents snowmobiles)*
1651 Highway 45 North, Eagle River, WI 54521
(715) 479-2200, www.tracksideinc.com

WINTER FESTIVALS

CHRISTMAS KICK-OFF—late November. Parade with Santa Claus and live reindeer, hayrides, cookies, and more. Downtown. (800) 359-6315 or www.eagleriver.org.

WORLD CHAMPIONSHIP SNOWMOBILE DERBY—early January. The world's premier snowmobile racing event. More than 500 entrants compete for oval and sno-cross championships. World Championship Snowmobile Derby Track. (715) 479-4424 or www.derbytrack.com.

WOMEN ON SNOW TOUR—late January. Women ride the snowmobile trails of Vilas County. Leave Eagle River early Monday morning for three full days of riding. Pre-registration is recommended. (715) 479-3301 or www.womenonsnow.org.

KLONDIKE DAYS—mid-February. World Championship Snowmobile Derby Track. 9:00 a.m.–4:00 p.m. Winter festival featuring an 1800s encampment and fur-trade rendezvous, lumber-jack competition, horse and dog weight-pull competition, snow sculpting, art-and-craft show, music, and Native American cultural demonstrations. The World Championship Oval Sled Dog Sprints take place on the same track as the snowmobile races of the previous month. Four-, six-, and ten-dog teams compete over two days in three classes for $20,000 in prize money. (800) 359-6315 or www.klondikedays.org.

SAYNER ANNUAL CHAMBER ICE FISHING TOURNAMENT—mid-February. Held on Plum Lake from 6:00 a.m. to 4:00 p.m. with registration at South Plum Lake public boat landing. Entry fee required. (888) 722-3789.

GLACIAL ICE TRIALS—late February. The Hardwoods Motor Sports Association, Chanticleer Inn, and Wisconsin Autosports Group host automotive, two-day ice trials on Dollar Lake. The object is to complete the course in the least amount of time. (715) 546-3927.

SNOWSHOE BLAZE—early March. St. Germain. 10:00 a.m.–4:00 p.m. Take a scenic, guided snowshoe adventure, with a campfire along the way. There will also be a moonlight trek. (715) 479-4545 or www.st-germain.com.

SILVER BLADES ICE SHOW—mid-March. Eagle River Hockey & Sports Arena. More than 30 years old, the Silver Blades Ice Show features more than 100 participants in figure-skating numbers choreographed to music and lighting. Evening, Saturday, and Sunday afternoon performances. (715) 479-7640.

RESTAURANTS

BRAYWOOD RESORT *(lunch and dinner)*
1084 Catfish Lake Rd., Eagle River, WI 54521
(715) 479-6494, www.braywoodresort.com

BREW MOON COFFEEHOUSE
(breakfast and lunch)
113 S. Railroad St., Eagle River, WI 54521
(715) 479-1555

CAPTAIN NEMO'S SUPPER CLUB *(dinner)*
3310 Highway 70 East, Eagle River, WI 54521
(715) 479-2250

CHANTICLEER INN *(breakfast and dinner)*
1458 E. Dollar Lake Rd.
Eagle River, WI 54521
(715) 479-4486 or (800) 752-9193
www.chanticleerinn.com

COPPER KETTLE RESTAURANT
(breakfast, lunch, and dinner)
207 E. Wall St., Eagle River, WI 54521
(715) 479-4049

SODA POPS *(lunch and dinner)*
125 S. Railroad St., Eagle River, WI 54521
(715) 479-9424, www.soda-pops.com

TERRA NICOLE'S ESPRESSO CAFE
(breakfast and lunch)
Vilas Village Mall, 711D Highway 45 North
Eagle River, WI 54521
(715) 479-8215 or (866) 479-8215
www.terranicoles.com

LODGING
CHANTICLEER INN
1458 E. Dollar Lake Rd., Eagle River, WI 54521
(715) 479-4486 or (800) 752-9193
www.chanticleerinn.com

EAGLE RIVER INN & RESORT
5260 Highway 70 West, Eagle River, WI 54521
(715) 479-2000 or (866) 479-2020
www.eriver-inn.com

GYPSY VILLA RESORT
950 Circle Dr., Eagle River, WI 54521
(715) 479-8644 or (800) 232-9714
www.gypsyvilla.com

INN AT PINEWOOD, INC.
1820 Silver Forest Ln., Eagle River, WI 54521
(715) 477-2377, www.inn-at-pinewood.com

PITLIK'S SAND BEACH RESORT
4833 Sand Beach Dr., Eagle River, WI 54521
(715) 479-4340, www.pitliksresort.com

WILD EAGLE LODGE
4443 Chain O'Lakes Rd., Eagle River, WI 54521
(715) 479-3151 or (877) 945-3965
www.wildeaglelodge.com

Chapter Eight

THE START OF SOMETHING BIG
Eau Claire/Chippewa Falls

GLORIOUS, TALL STANDS of timber brought the first people to the Chippewa River Valley. The trees provided homes for moose, elk, bison, cougars, timber wolves, black bears, and other wildlife, and the Ojibwa (Chippewa) Indians used these animals for food, clothing, and shelter material. They caught fish where the Chippewa and Eau Claire rivers converged in present-day downtown Eau Claire. Explorers and trappers came when they learned of the waterways, too, and then the loggers. They cut the valley's trees, then used the two rivers to transport the logs to mills downstream. The timber industry dominated the area's economy in the latter half of the 1800s. After the virgin timber was gone, farmers cleared the stumps and turned the land to agriculture.

Today, the trees have rebounded into second-growth forests and state parks. Eau Claire, which means "clear water" in French, now proudly considers itself to be west-central Wisconsin's border city to the Great North Woods.

While Eau Claire may be named the city of clear water, Chippewa Falls considers itself the "City of Pure Water" for the natural springs that flow into the Chippewa River, which once floated millions of logs. In fact, in 1969 the city called in a private laboratory based in Minneapolis to settle a friendly dispute between it and Deming, New Mexico, which also claimed to have the country's purest water. The lab gave Chippewa Falls a nearly perfect quality rating, thus ending the debate. That pure water is the main ingredient in Leinenkugel Beer, known affectionately to locals as "Leinie's." The Jacob Leinenkugel Brewing Company is the oldest business in Chippewa Falls, established in 1867. The city was recently named one of the nation's Top 12 most preservation-minded cities by the National Trust for Historic Preservation, and *Time* magazine has rated it one of the country's Top 10 small towns.

Ice skaters and ice fishers in Chippewa Falls routinely enjoy the pure waters in a frozen state, gliding over them and pulling up from them walleyes, northerns, and bluegills. Snowmobilers and cross-country skiers can't get enough of the many state trails that offer breathtaking views within the forests and along the Chippewa and Eau Claire rivers. Adding to the charm is that Chippewa Falls harbors a herd of buffalo right in the city's heart, in the 318-acre Irvine Park.

In Eau Claire and Chippewa Falls, the loggers have long since departed. The trees have come back. Here the North Woods begin—and during this winter weekend, that could be the start of something big.

Fragrant wreaths, boughs and garland delight your senses at Lowes Creek Tree Farm.

MORNING AND AFTERNOON

If only the walls of the **Grand Avenue Café** in downtown Eau Claire could talk. The century-old building with its tin ceiling was at one time a dairy, then a pharmacy, and then a hardware store. It certainly could tell stories about the city of Eau Claire and the changes it's seen. Even the sandwiches here will remind you of olden tales: Choose the Hamlet (ham) sandwich, the Moby Tuna, or Great Expectations (turkey, bacon, and cheese). Then order the warm Bistro Bread Pudding for dessert, filled with nuts, spices, and chocolate, and covered with cream sauces.

This morning and early afternoon, you'll get familiar with outdoor Eau Claire's Great North Woods. The **Chippewa River State Trail**, a 26-miler linking Eau Claire with the Red

88

Cedar State Trail near the city of Menomonie, runs through prairies, mixed forests, and Eau Claire's river corridor. The trail is open for **winter hiking** and **snowmobiling**, and sections of it are groomed for **cross-country skiing.**

You can access the 14.5-mile **Red Cedar State Trail** portion of the Chippewa Valley Trail System at Carson Park on Lake or Menomonie Streets or at the University of Wisconsin–Eau Claire campus. The 15-mile trail, which can be used for **winter hiking**, **snowmobiling**, **cross-country skiing**, and **snowshoeing**, shadows the Red Cedar River from the Chippewa River to Menomonie. The Red Cedar is a fast-flowing river that freezes only in the coldest winter temperatures. Bring your camera because it is usually open water, and you are likely to spot a bald eagle soaring against the steep walls of the valley, looking for fish.

For **snowshoeing** or a city **cross-country skiing** experience, head to **Irvine Park** in Chippewa Falls. The early afternoon is a good time to explore this 318-acre, one-of-a-kind park. The grounds hold a zoo, a museum, a 100-year-old schoolhouse, a 1936 fire truck, and antique machinery. At Christmas, thousands of lights and 100 displays change the look of the park into an old-time Christmas Village. There are three miles of groomed cross-country ski trails through the woods and over the hills. Snowshoe trails run next to the cross-country ski trails. If not enough snow has fallen yet, take a **winter hike** to the top of the park up Flag Hill. Stop by the overlook above Duncan Creek, where you can see Glen Loch, a dam built in 1875.

Mary E. Marshall Park on Bridgewater Avenue, right across the street from Irvine Park,

CHIPPEWA VALLEY CONVENTION & VISITORS BUREAU

Winter paints Wisconsin's many all-season trails with a new, dramatic look.

has an **ice-skating** rink and warming house. In December, you can look at the Christmas Village in Irvine Park as you glide across the frozen pond.

By 4:00 p.m., it's time to check into **The Atrium Bed and Breakfast** in Eau Claire, your home for this winter weekend. Set along Otter Creek on 15 wooded acres, the Atrium is a half mile off of Highway 53 on Prill Road. The bed and breakfast is aptly named since an atrium with a 20-foot glass ceiling and a fountain is built into the middle of the house. The stained glass windows in the dining, Willow, Wicker, and Woodland rooms were crafted in the 1850s and rescued from old Czech churches. Upon your arrival, you'll be treated to wine and cheese in the atrium. The bed and breakfast maintains its own **hiking** trails, and **snowshoeing** is encouraged on its wooded creekside acres.

EVENING

After your day of traveling, enjoy a casual dinner at Eau Claire's only brewery, the **Northwoods Brewpub & Grill**. The menu tells you that "Bumblin' Bubbas Buzzin' Brew," a light golden ale brewed with honey, is an Eau Claire favorite. Try a dinner from the "wild side," such as an elk or bison burger, a plate of elk meatloaf, or an elk brat—or for something less adventurous, salmon on a cedar plank. The brewpub also serves winter warmers such as Tom and Jerrys and a "Mountain Pass"—butterscotch schnapps and hot chocolate topped with whipped cream.

If you're in town in late November, check out the **Sinterklaas Market** held in downtown Eau Claire. This annual holiday arts-and-crafts show draws more than 90 Midwest artists. The market is open on Fridays from 5:00 to 9:00 p.m.

Day Two
MORNING

Wake up this morning at the Atrium to the smells of freshly brewed coffee, delivered to your room on a tray along with fresh-baked breads. It's only the beginning, because you'll also be served a three-course breakfast in the location of your choice: in the dining room, in the atrium, or in your room.

Be prepared for many woodsy outings today. Just 10 miles east of Eau Claire in Fall Creek is **Beaver Creek Reserve**. This county-owned land is 360 acres of forest, wetlands, prairies, and oak savannas along the Eau Claire River, which form the reserve's southern and western boundaries. A natural habitat for deer, raccoons, beavers, weasels, foxes, bears, owls, wild turkeys, grouse, and rabbits *[see "Stories in Snow: Animal Tracking" sidebar]*, the grounds are also home to an observatory, butterfly house, and Citizen Science Center.

The center trains ordinary citizens to help with scientific research. Citizen scientists monitor the flow, turbidity, and temperature of streams, note the invasion of purple loosestrife into wetlands, and record wildlife sightings on an interactive Internet site to help resource agencies with planning and management decisions.

From the reserve's **Ralph H. Wise Nature Center**, which sits atop a ridge overlooking Beaver Creek, you can rent **snowshoes** or **cross-country skis** and take the three-mile hike to Big Falls. The center contains displays and hands-on nature exhibits, and was built using renewable energy resources and energy conservation methods. Check the day's schedule of

STORIES IN SNOW: ANIMAL TRACKING

Animals reveal far more of their lives to you in winter than they do in summer. In the warm months, you usually have to count on seeing them to learn of their proximity; and often, they prefer not to share that information with you. In the winter, however, snow is the medium upon which their daily diaries are written.

Voles, shrews, and mice are as active in winter as they are in summer, scurrying about to maintain a high body temperature and find food. They are sometimes working and living right beneath your cross-country skis and snowshoes. The presence of a deer is recorded by a bowl-like depression under a conifer where he slept; if needles on the lower branches of a tree are missing, he most likely dined there. If tiny paw prints end abruptly in a large, fan-like pattern in the snow, it is safe to surmise that a hawk swept out of the sky and scooped up a scurrying mouse in a life-and-death drama.

The next time you're cross-country skiing or snowshoeing, consider taking a field guide with you to decipher the tracks. Guidebooks have their limitations, however; they illustrate the perfect pattern, while in the field you'll most usually come across partial, obscured, and hastily left tracks.

The best way to train yourself to identify real-world tracks is to begin in your own back yard. Four toes on each of the front and hind feet means you're looking at a track from the dog family: foxes, coyotes, or most likely a neighbor's pet. Now, try to become an expert on which breed of dog the track was left by: a retriever, poodle, or greyhound. You may even get to know which retriever it was, by his gait. Move up to identifying the prints of small rodents: Four toes on the front foot and five toes on the hind foot means a mouse, vole, chipmunk, squirrel, or woodchuck.

Then the next time you're in Wisconsin's Great North Woods, remember these tips:

❋ Most mammals are active nocturnally, so the best time to find tracks is in the early morning. A good place to look is where two habitats meet, such as a forest's edge or a riverbank.

❋ Use the sun to your advantage. Keep the track between you and the sun; that way the track will stand out better.

❋ Imagine you are the animal you are tracking. When the tracks end and you lose them, ask yourself where you would have gone. What would have been the best thing to do in that situation in order to survive?

❋ If a track looks very strange and you can't seem to identify it, look up. A branch of a tree, an icicle, the eave of a house, or a power line can dribble down and create something that looks like a footprint.

❋ Never walk on or destroy a track you find. It could prove to be a reference for you if you get lost and need to find your way back.

As long as we have snow, we'll have animal stories to read.

---

classes; you just might find **a snowshoe-making workshop**, **a timber wolf ecology class**, or **a winter camping symposium**. There's even **a snowshoe furniture class**—what better decor for someone who loves winter than a snowshoe-seat rocker or snowshoe-latticed end table? The Wise Nature Center is open on Saturdays from 9:00 a.m. to 4:00 p.m., on Sundays from noon until 4:00 p.m., and on Fridays from 8:00 a.m. to 4:30 p.m.

AFTERNOON

Back in Eau Claire, have lunch at the **Acoustic Café**. Enjoy a latte or gourmet coffee with a hot hoagie sandwich. The buns are baked fresh every day from scratch using the café's own recipe. Try the turkey, tomato, provolone, and Swiss cheese hoagie, made with an exceptional special sauce.

If you planned your weekend in the Chippewa Valley for early February, you're in for a thrill. The annual **Silvermine Invitational Ski Jumping Tournament** attracts more than 60 top jumpers from the United States and Canada. The jumpers literally "fly" off the 295-foot hill to compete for prize money. The tournament has been going on for more than 100 years, and almost 3,000 spectators attend. You can't miss the jump site; the Silvermine scaffold stands tall against the Eau Claire skyline.

If you're in Eau Claire on any other winter weekend, go to the **Tower Ridge Recreation Area** located just outside of the city near Lake Altoona in the town of Seymour. To get there, take Highway Q to Highway L and follow the signs. Tower Ridge is the **largest cross-country ski trail complex** in west-central Wisconsin. Many skiers like to train for the American Birkebeiner here *[see Chapter 10: Birkie Bound (Hayward/Cable)]*; the 12 miles

www.travelwisconsin.com

Being on the fringe of the Great North Woods creates an abundance of cross-country skiing opportunities.

WINTER DRIVING: DEBUNKING THE MYTHS

Winter driving is a rich source of lore handed down the generations and dispersed freely to newcomers—and, like most lore, it's often mainly fiction. Here are some common winter driving myths and what you should do in some winter conditions:

❄ MYTH: Following a salt truck is safe. You may think that driving on top of freshly dropped salt will give you traction, but road salt only works if it's warmer than 17 degrees. If it's colder, the salt will just sit inertly on the top of the ice.

❄ MYTH: A heavier vehicle has better traction than a lighter vehicle. A heavy SUV with a high center of gravity is more prone to rolling over than an economy car with a wider wheelbase. While piling sandbags or cat litter into your trunk may help you get started on ice and snow, it won't help you once you're going. In fact, thanks to inertia, the heavier the car is, the harder it will be to bring to a stop.

❄ MYTH: It's safe to keep up with traffic flow. Don't be tempted to keep pace with an 18-wheeler whizzing by with all that tread on the road. Speed limits are meant for ideal conditions; it can take a vehicle nine times longer to come to a stop in wintry weather. Rather than judging how fast to go by other traffic, just keep a safe distance between you and the cars in front of you.

❄ MYTH: Steer into a skid. This is one we all learned at our father's knee—but Dad was driving a rear-wheel drive car. Since most cars now have front-wheel drive, most skids occur when the front wheels lose their grip while taking a turn too fast. If you start to skid, look in the direction that you want to go, and steer in that direction.

❄ MYTH: Shift down to slow down. Downshifting causes a momentary increase in the speed of the drive wheels, which makes them lose grip on icy roads. Better to ease on the brakes or pump them. If you have antilock brakes, brake firmly without tapping.

❄ MYTH: Leave the car to seek help if you get stuck. Don't do it. You could get hit by another car or become frostbitten. Unless you're stalled in a traffic lane, the safest thing to do is stay in the car. Turn on your emergency flashers (unless there is blinding snow or fog, since drivers will tend to go toward them thinking they are an exit sign) and hang something on the antenna to make your car more visible. Use your cell phone to call for help, and run the engine for a few minutes when you need more heat.

❄ MYTH: Lower your tire pressure to put more rubber on the road. This might have worked with Dad's old balloon tires, but an underinflated radial tire bows inward, leaving less tread on the road. And tire pressure drops one pound per square inch for every 10 degrees the outside temperature falls. Make sure to check your tire pressure when it starts getting cold. Even better get four radial snow tires, which are made from rubber compounds that are designed to stay flexible in the cold.

In winter, remember: Don't use cruise control, keep your gas tank full, and always drive with your lights on. And one piece of Dad's advice is still good as gold: Slow down. You'll get there.

of groomed and tracked ski trails include woods and rolling terrain for all levels of skiing expertise. The recreation area also includes approximately two miles of **lighted ski trails** and a **snowshoe** trail adjacent to—but separate from—the lighted ski trails.

Another option for afternoon activities is in nearby Menomonie at **Hoffman Hills State Recreation Area**, which lies east via I-94, then north on Highway 40. Set on 707 acres, the area has 10 miles of multiuse trails. A 60-foot observation tower set on a 1,400-foot hill offers sweeping views of wetlands, restored prairies, and rugged country. On **cross-country skis**, tour through nine miles of hills and valleys on trails that wind along hardwood ridges, climb up and down aspen and birch slopes, and pass through pine plantations and under the eyes of lots of wildlife.

JOHN T. ANDREWS

Winter hikers will find Glen Loch, a dam built in 1875, near the top of Irvine Park in Chippewa Falls.

For yet another afternoon choice, take a daytrip *[see "Winter Driving: Debunking the Myths" sidebar]* back into Chippewa Falls. **Winter camping, ice fishing, snowshoeing, cross-country skiing, snowmobiling,** and **winter hiking** can all be done within **Lake Wissota State Park's** borders. This 1,062-acre park sits opposite Chippewa Falls on the 6,300-acre lake created by the 1916 damming of the Chippewa River. Young, rich forests and prairies surround the lake, and 18 miles of hiking trails feature 35 educational stations. Look for deer, foxes, beavers, minks, weasels, porcupines, otters, and badgers.

There are eight easy miles of groomed **cross-country ski trails**, including the **Red Pine, Jack Pine, Plantation,** and **Staghorn Trails,** and the southern part of the **Lake Trail.** On the Lake Trail, you'll pass two long panther effigy mounds and gain great lake views. All but the Staghorn Trail can accommodate **skate-skiing.** You are free to explore anywhere in the park on **snowshoes,** which can be rented in the park office, except on the established cross-country ski loops. **Ice fishers** routinely take walleyes, northerns, and pan fish, and a five-mile stretch of the county **snowmobile** trail system, which connects with another 150 miles of county trails, passes along the east end of the park.

You can even access one of the most recent additions to Wisconsin's extensive recreational trail network from Lake Wissota State Park. The **Old Abe State Trail,** a **snowmobile** trail, and **winter hiking** route that follows the Chippewa River, starts in the park and runs 20 miles to **Brunet Island State Park** in the city of Cornell to the north. **Ice fishing, cross-country skiing, snowshoeing,** and **ice-skating** are popular activities in the Brunet Island park.

EVENING

Now that you've seen Lake Wissota in the great outdoors, enjoy it from a great indoor perspective at **High Shores Supper Club** in Chippewa Falls. The supper club has floor-to-ceiling windows positioned in front of the lake. At a candlelit table, choose from more than 50 entrées, from fried lake perch to broiled or fried Cajun alligator.

After dinner, take the **holiday drive** through the **Irvine Park Christmas Village,** decorated with more than 75,000 lights.

Day Three

Linger at your inn with a relaxing late breakfast. If you're staying at The Atrium, this morning would be a good time to take a **winter hike** around the grounds near Otter Creek.

After check-out, there's one more stop you'll want to make in the Chippewa Valley area that will excite your senses with winter. Take your camera and travel just five miles south of Eau Claire to **Lowes Creek Tree Farm and Log Cabin Christmas Market,** one of the prettiest tree farms in Wisconsin. Featured in the December 2004 issue of *Midwest Living* magazine, Lowes is a 240-acre, family-owned woods, with choose-and-cut holiday trees.

Your ears will be filled with the sound of jingle bells on **horse-drawn sleighs,** your nose will be delighted by the piney scents of a wreath-packed porch, your skin will glow in the warmth of the wood-burning stove inside the cabin, and your taste buds will awaken with a cup of hot cider. Take a fresh, handmade evergreen wreath or swag home in your trunk, or arrange to have wreaths and trees shipped to friends and family—a fragrant gift from

CREATE A FAMILY TRADITION: SELECTING AND CARING FOR A REAL CHRISTMAS TREE

by Therese Olson

A Wisconsin native, Therese Olson co-owns and operates Lowes Creek Tree Farm, a 250-acre, family-owned, choose-and-cut Christmas tree farm near Eau Claire. Lowes Farm, the collective dream of the Olson family, was created in 1981 from a worn-out soybean field and the initial novice planting of 9,000 trees. Today, Lowes Creek Tree Farm includes a log cabin built in the old, Norwegian-notched method that sits among the fields of fir and pine trees. You can read more about Lowes Farm at www.lowescreektreefarm.com.

One of the most common inquiries we receive each Christmas season is "How do you pick the perfect Christmas tree, and what is the best way to keep it fresh through the holidays?" Every year, we strive to help people choose the tree that is best for them and teach them how to care for their special tree.

Keeping a real Christmas tree fresh is fairly simple once you learn to separate proper care from the many tales that continue to circulate. Here are some basic tips:

❋ 1. **Test for freshness.** The freshness of the tree depends on the care the trees have received as they were grown, harvested, and displayed. One simple test for freshness is to gently grasp a branch between your thumb and forefinger and pull it toward you. Very few needles should come off in your hand if the tree is fresh. Remember that the loss of interior brown or off-color needles is normal and will occur over the lifetime of the tree. The cut-your-own option provides optimal freshness because you can see exactly where the tree has been growing for the past 10 to 14 years, and you'll be bringing it home usually within a short time of cutting.

❋ 2. **Make a fresh cut off the bottom of the tree trunk before putting it in the stand.** At our farm, we make an additional fresh cut after we process the trees through our mechanical shaker to clean out the interior needles of the previous year's growth. The fresh cut will reopen the tree's pores, which may have started to seal over with sap, so it can take up water. This is especially important after purchasing a precut tree from either a farm or retail lot.

❋ 3. **Keep adequate water in your tree stand.** Using a tree stand that holds at least one gallon of water is recommended for a typical six-foot tree. The tree "drinks" moisture in the cells directly underneath the bark—not in the center wood of the trunk. We suggest cutting the tree bottom to fit the tree stand versus shaving the bark to taper the trunk, which would remove the woody areas that transport water throughout the entire tree.

❋ 4. **Which tree is the best Christmas tree?** There are many varieties to choose from in the Midwest. Balsam, Canaan, and Fraser fir are the most popular real Christmas trees in Wisconsin, with white and Scotch pine ranking next. Whichever variety you choose, a fragrant, real tree will provide your family with happy memories. The "best" Christmas tree is the one that fits your home and your family's ornaments, is a delight to decorate, and is the one you'll remember as the "most perfect tree ever."

LOWES CREEK TREE FARM

Lowes Creek Tree Farm and Log Cabin Christmas Market is a popular destination during the winter holiday season.

the North Woods *[see "Create a Family Tradition: Selecting and Caring for a Real Christmas Tree" sidebar]*. Belgian horses will take you to the tree fields in a sleigh, over Lowes Creek on a wooden bridge and "through the woods."

As the Lowes Creek Tree Farm history goes, in 1982 Therese and Tim Olson stood among the stubble of a worn-out soybean field and envisioned an area of perfect Christmas trees. They planted—all by hand, with the help of a Ford pickup truck—the 40 acres of thousands of mature trees that now stand on the farm. It was the restart of a forest and the beginning of a north woods.

FOR MORE INFORMATION
**CHIPPEWA FALLS AREA
CHAMBER OF COMMERCE**
10 S. Bridge St., Chippewa Falls, WI 54729
(715) 723-0331 or (866) 723-0340
www.chippewachamber.org

**THE CHIPPEWA VALLEY CONVENTION
& VISITORS BUREAU**
3625 Gateway Dr., Suite F, Eau Claire, WI 54701
(715) 831-2345 or (888) 523-3866
www.chippewavalley.net

WINTER ATTRACTIONS
BEAVER CREEK RESERVE
S1 Highway K, Fall Creek, WI 54742
(715) 877-2212, www.beavercreekreserve.org

BRUNET ISLAND STATE PARK
23125 255th St., Cornell, WI 54732, www.wiparks.net

CHIPPEWA RIVER STATE TRAIL
Wisconsin Department of Natural Resources
1300 W. Clairemont Ave., Eau Claire, WI 54702
(715) 839-1607, www.wiparks.net

**HOFFMAN HILLS STATE
RECREATION AREA**
921 Brickyard Rd., Menomonie, WI 54751
(715) 232-1242, www.wiparks.net

IRVINE PARK
Bridgewater Ave. and Jefferson Ave.
Chippewa Falls, WI 54729, (715) 723-0051
www.chippewachamber.org/parks

LAKE WISSOTA STATE PARK
18127 Highway O, Chippewa Falls, WI 54729
(715) 382-4574, www.wiparks.net

LOWES CREEK TREE FARM AND LOG CABIN CHRISTMAS MARKET
S9475 Lowes Creek Rd., Eleva, WI 54738
(715) 878-4166 or (888) 878-4166
www.lowescreektreefarm.com

MARY E. MARSHALL PARK
Bridgewater Ave., Chippewa Falls, WI 54729
(715) 723-0331
www.chippewachamber.org/parks

OLD ABE STATE TRAIL
Chippewa County Forest and Parks
711 N. Bridge St., Chippewa Falls, WI 54729
(715) 726-7880, www.wiparks.net

RED CEDAR STATE TRAIL
Wisconsin Department of Natural Resources
921 Brickyard Rd., Menomonie, WI 54751
(715) 232-1242, www.wiparks.net

TOWER RIDGE RECREATION AREA
955 S. 82nd Ave. (Highway L), Seymour, WI 54165
(715) 839-4738, www.co.eau-claire.wi.us

WINTER FESTIVALS

SINTERKLAAS MARKET—mid-November. Eau Claire. This annual holiday art-and-craft fair features 90 artists from throughout the Midwest, selling handcrafted gifts, artworks, and home accessories. Live music and strolling carolers. (715) 552-5568 or www.chippewavalley.net.

CHRISTMAS VILLAGE IN IRVINE PARK—late November through December. The day after Thanksgiving, Irvine Park is illuminated with more than 75,000 Christmas lights, life-size Christmas scenes reminiscent of the Victorian era, and local historical replicas. (715) 723-0051 or www.chippewachamber.org.

VICTORIAN OPEN HOUSE—early December. Chippewa Falls. Savor the season at the Cook–Rutledge Mansion filled with Victorian Christmas decorations, caroling, and old-fashioned treats. 505 W. Grand Ave., Chippewa Falls. Saturday, 6:00 –9:00 p.m. and Sunday, 1:00–4:00 p.m. (715) 723-7181 or www.chippewachamber.org.

A WALK THROUGH THE PARK—early December. Enjoy the holiday lights and displays in the Christmas Village in Irvine Park. Caroling, Santa Claus, and cookies. (715) 723-0051 or www.chippewachamber.org.

ICE FISHING CONTEST AND RAFFLE—early February. The Chippewa Falls Lions Club hosts its annual fishing contest on Glen Loch from 11:00 a.m. to 3:00 p.m. Cash prizes for first, second, and third place in each of three categories: northerns, bluegills, and perch. Lions Club members will be available to drill holes on request.

Food and refreshments will be served on the ice. (715) 723-7181 or www.chippewachamber.org.

SILVERMINE INVITATIONAL SKI JUMPING TOURNAMENT—early February. Eau Claire. Top ski jumpers from the United States and Canada soar off the 295-foot hill to compete for prize money at this annual tournament going on for more than 100 years. (715) 831-8996.

RESTAURANTS

ACOUSTIC CAFÉ *(breakfast, lunch, and dinner)*
505 S. Barstow St., Eau Claire, WI 54701
(715) 832-9090, www.theacoustic.com

DRAGANETTI'S RISTORANTE *(dinner)*
3120 Hillcrest Pkwy., Altoona, WI 54720
(715) 834-9234, www.draganettis.com

GRAND AVENUE CAFÉ *(Friday–Saturday, breakfast, lunch, and dinner; Sunday breakfast and lunch)*
119 W. Grand Ave., Eau Claire, WI 54703
(715) 831-1100

HECKEL'S FAMILY RESTAURANT
(breakfast, lunch, and dinner)
805 S. Hastings Way, Eau Claire, WI 54701
(715) 834-2076

HIGH SHORES SUPPER CLUB
(Friday–Saturday, dinner; Sunday breakfast, lunch, and dinner)
17985 Highway X, Chippewa Falls, WI 54729
(715) 723-9854, www.highshores.com

HOULIGANS STEAK & SEAFOOD PUB
(dinner)
415 S. Barstow St., Eau Claire, WI 54701
(715) 835-6621

MIKE'S SMOKEHOUSE *(lunch and dinner)*
2235 N. Clairemont Ave., Eau Claire, WI 54703
(715) 834-8153

NORTHWOODS BREWPUB & GRILL
(lunch and dinner)
3560 Oakwood Mall Dr., Eau Claire, WI 54701
(715) 552-0510, www.northwoodsbrewpub.com

LODGING

THE ATRIUM BED & BREAKFAST
5572 Prill Rd., Eau Claire, WI 54701
(715) 833-9045 or (888) 733-0094
www.atriumbb.com

FANNY HILL VICTORIAN INN
3919 Crescent Ave., Eau Claire, WI 54701
(715) 836-8184 or (800) 292-8026
www.fannyhill.com

**MCGILVRAY'S VICTORIAN BED
AND BREAKFAST**
312 W. Columbia St., Chippewa Falls, WI 54729
(715) 720-1600 or (888) 324-1893
www.mcgilvraysbb.com

OTTER CREEK INN
2536 Highway 12, Eau Claire, WI 54702
(715) 832-2945 or (866) 832-2945
www.ottercreekinn.com

PLEASANT VIEW BED & BREAKFAST
16649 96th Ave., Chippewa Falls, WI 54729
(715) 382-4401 or (866) 947-7682
www.pleasantviewbb.com

Chapter Nine
A CLASSIC, OLD WORLD WINTER
Green Lake/Princeton

DISPITE ITS HISTORY and reputation as a resort community, Green Lake has managed to keep a lot of its quietness, accessibility, and Old World charm. The area was settled in 1840, and by 1867 the Oakwood Hotel, the first resort west of Niagara Falls, had been built. Vacationing Chicagoans began to flock to the area, and within three decades, there were several more extravagant resorts on Green Lake's shores. But for some reason, the city never seemed to take on an affected air, never seemed to paint itself as an exclusive playground primarily for the rich. It has always remained a classic resort town, catering to hard-working Midwesterners who were looking for a summer retreat and a winter hideaway.

The spring-fed lake around which the elegant resorts were built is the deepest inland lake in the state. It is 230 feet deep, measures 7,320 acres and has 27 miles of shoreline. The beautiful, Swiss-looking Green Lake is why the region became a vacation destination in the first place. And understandably, a lot of the area's winter recreational opportunities center on the lake: ice fishing, iceboating, ice-skating, and even cross-country skiing around the perimeter on trails that pass through pine and maple woodlands.

Today's quintessential Green Lake resort is the Heidel House Resort, an elegant but casual hotel with breathtaking lake views and gorgeous shoreline woods. Here, you can feel comfortable dining at its exceptional restaurants after just hanging up your ice skates, leaning your cross-country skis against the wall, or stacking together your snowshoes.

Just eight miles from Green Lake is another Old World–style gem, the village of Princeton. Sitting near the Fox River, it is an enchanting town full of boutiques and general stores. It was once known as "Beantown" because steamboats on the Fox stopped here to pick up and deliver lima and green beans that were grown in the region.

In Green Lake and Princeton, privacy is plentiful, kicking back is contagious, and putting all your problems on ice is encouraged.

HARD-WATER FISHING

By John H. Gaukel

John H. Gaukel was born in Madison, Wisconsin. From an early age, his grandfather taught him how to hunt and fish. Growing up in Madison, he had plenty of access to fishing waters, with four lakes right at his doorstep. He fishes in both summer and winter, but the winter holds a special fascination for him.

Hard-water fishing—that's what I like. What's "hard water?" It's ice, and fishing for pan fish on it is what I have been doing for 50 years. Every trip is a new adventure.

Throughout my years of ice fishing, I have seen a lot of changes in equipment and techniques. I started ice fishing with "hand lines," using a big, six-inch cork, with which you had to actually grab the line and jerk it up, trying to hook the fish. If the fish was hooked, you pulled up the line hand-over-hand until the fish landed on the ice, making your fingers wet and numb. Now we have graphite ice rods with reels and mini-stealth bobbers, which allow you to reel the fish in—just like in summer.

Holes used to be chiseled out with "ice spuds," a long, handheld chisel. I think almost every old-timer at least once in his lifetime has had a chisel slip through his cold hands and end up on the bottom of the lake. Now we have hand-turned and gas-powered augers that cut through the ice like butter. From sitting out in the open weather on a five-gallon pail, we have gone to modern, lightweight portable shelters that offer protection from the wind, the enemy of the ice fisherman.

Before, I had to go out on the lake to well-known, winter fishing spots and start searching for fish by chiseling many holes and fishing them until I found what I was looking for or got tired and went home. Now, ice fishermen have depth finders that don't even need a hole. Just place it on the ice, and it will tell you whether fish are present and at what depth.

As I hunted in the fall, I'd gather goldenrod bulbs for ice fishing bait. I'd cut the bulb open, take the little grubs out and put them in a jar filled with cornmeal. I kept them in the refrigerator until ice fishing season. Now, at local bait stations, you can get wax worms, spikes, black-eyed Susans, and various sizes of minnows to use with a myriad of jigs and small spoons to tempt the fish into biting. Some of the jigs even glow in the dark!

I treasure my knowledge of old techniques and learning new ones as I venture out on Wisconsin lakes I've never tried before in order to catch a few fish for a delicious meal. It can be a very peaceful trip out on ice all alone with your thoughts, or you can go with a friend and enjoy the company. To me, fishing is not about how many fish I can catch; rather, it is about being outdoors and experiencing the winter season.

When ice fishing, my senses seem to come alive with every snow-crunching footstep in this now-frozen wilderness, with the sounds of "lake thunder" rumbling around me. In this new, frozen land that didn't exist just a few months before, I can watch beautiful sunrises and sunsets. As each new winter approaches, I can't wait to start my search for those slab-sized pan fish I love to catch.

Day One
LATE MORNING AND AFTERNOON

A bustling town of unique shops and crowded boutiques in summer, Princeton is sedate, old-fashioned, and softly quiet in winter. Nestled between the bending Fox River and pristine Green Lake, it appears to be a Victorian Christmas card. Browsing the Water Street shop windows alongside the sweeping river reminds you of what towns were like before shopping malls.

Stop for lunch at one of those restored Victorian storefronts. **Mimi's** is a casual Northern Italian restaurant with intimate tables, exposed brick walls, and a large bar. Try one of the pizzas made with fresh mozzarella and herbs or the unparalleled crispy spaghetti with toasted noodles tossed with bacon, tomatoes, onions, and eggs.

You'll return to the Princeton area tomorrow, but after lunch drive a short six miles east on Highway 23 to the city of Green Lake, where you'll start your classic outdoor winter activities. On the southwest end of Green Lake lies **Dodge Memorial Park**. Also known locally as "County Park," Dodge is popular with **ice fishers** [see "Hard-Water Fishing" sidebar] and **ice-skaters**. Engaging in either of these pursuits is a great way to get an introduction to Green Lake. **Dennis Walker's Pontoon Guide Service** in Green Lake and **Mike Norton's All Season Fishing** in Princeton can set you up with heated ice shanties and equipment.

From your room at the Heidel House, you'll have a myriad of winter activity choices just outside your doorstep.

If you're in the area in early December through early January, Norton's can take you **cisco fishing from a heated houseboat**. An open-water fishing experience is quite a novel way to enjoy the early winter season on Green Lake.

Ice-skaters can lace up their skates for a glide on a clear area of ice at Dodge Memorial Park or swing around to the northeast side of the lake to downtown's **Deacon Mills Park** on the 500 block of South Street.

If you're a **snowmobile** enthusiast, you may want to use the morning and early afternoon to explore the more than 150 miles of trails in Green County [see "When It's Safe to Go on the Ice: Guidelines" sidebar]. Check with the Princeton snowmobile club, the **Princeton Sno-Barons**, at (920) 295-3416 or with the **Green Lake Terrace Snostreakers** at www.snostreakers.homestead.com for suggested trails and itineraries.

Check into your weekend's lodgings at the elegant and luxurious **Heidel House Resort** as soon as you can this afternoon. This 20-acre, self-contained winter universe will keep you busy with **winter hiking, snowshoeing, cross-country skiing, sledding, ice fishing,** and **ice-skating**—all right on the grounds.

Ice-skating is one of winter's simple pleasures—always made more fun with a few friends.

Located on the shores of Green Lake, the Heidel House has 200 rooms from which to choose, including main lodge guest rooms with awesome lake views, La Verde Lodge suites with private balconies, estate rooms with whirlpool tubs, cozy cottages, a carriage house, a stable house, and a bungalow. Ask for one of two fireplace suites in the main lodge and enjoy the warmth all weekend. From your private balcony, you'll be able to gaze out at the cross-country skiers skimming the shoreline and colorful **ice-boats** gliding across the frozen waters of Green Lake.

From the front desk at the Heidel House, you can rent **snowshoes** and **cross-country skis** for a nominal fee and use its **ice skates** for free. An ice-skating rink is onsite under the carriage tent's metal framework, and cross-country skiing can be done on the grounds and across the road on the golf course. A winter weekend at the Heidel House comes fully equipped with all of the season's fun.

EVENING

Tonight, stay on the Heidel House grounds and eat at the **Grey Rock Mansion Restaurant**, housed in a palatial 1890s residence. Consistently rated one of the top 25 restaurants in Wisconsin, the Grey Rock in winter is an evening outing to kick back and linger over. Arrive at least 30 minutes before your reservation time and enjoy a drink at the bar on the main level. Listen to the jazz pianist amid a backdrop of rich wood interiors and warm fireplaces. Your dinner will be served in the windowed dining room where every table affords a vista of Green Lake. The rainbow trout with crabmeat stuffing and walleye entrées are superb.

Day Two
MORNING

Soak in the morning sun as you eat breakfast at the **Sunroom Café** at the Heidel House. Eggs Benedict, French toast, and tasty blueberry blintzes are served with beautiful sunrise views of Green Lake. If you're really anxious to get going this morning, the Sunroom has a "to-go" window where you can grab a sandwich and coffee.

And you just may want to get moving, because you'll be spending a large part of the day at **Mecan River Outfitters & Lodge** in Princeton. **Cross-country skiing, sleigh rides,** and

WHEN IT'S SAFE TO GO ON THE ICE: GUIDELINES

Green Lake (and all large lakes) usually freeze around the edges first before freezing to the center. Ice-skaters and ice fishers should be very careful when venturing out onto frozen waters. Use an ice bar or auger to check the thickness of the ice before you move about on the lake. If you aren't sure how frozen the lake is, ask the advice of someone in the area who knows.

ICE THICKNESS	TRAVEL MODE
Less than 3 inches	Unsafe—stay off
3 inches	On foot—though anglers should spread out
4 inches	On foot—group fishing acceptable
5–6 inches	Snowmobiling
12 inches or more	Cars and light trucks

pheasant hunting are all a part of this property near the Mecan River on Highway 23.

Ten miles of groomed and tracked **Red Pine cross-country ski** trails for classic and skate-skiing will take you through the stillness of tall pines, hardwoods, and marshlands on this winter morning. The terrain varies from flat to gently rolling for beginning skiers to some trails with steep hills for those with more experience. Ski rentals are available at the lodge.

For cross-country skiers who want to immerse themselves in a rustic, outdoor weekend, **cabins are located on the ski trails**. Located in the woods without phones or electricity, these cabins will keep you in a relaxed and unhurried state of mind all weekend. Bring your own sleeping bags, towels, and food. The outfitters will furnish cooking and eating equipment, firewood, and gaslights. The cabins have outdoor fire pits, and his and hers outdoor bathrooms. Showers are available at the lodge. There are also five rooms in the lodge itself; the rooms have shared baths, but towels and linens are supplied.

JOHN T. ANDREWS

Traveling by horse-drawn sleigh through snowy terrain is a classic way to experience Wisconsin's winter beauty.

105

HEIDEL HOUSE RESORT

Since 1867, the Green Lake area has been home to some of the country's most extravagant resorts and winter hideaways.

From mid-December to the end of February, you can take a 45-minute **sleigh ride** through the Mecan River Outfitters' snowy woods. If the woods are less than snowy, a wagon ride is offered. Two Belgians, Ben and Judy, will take you on an old-time trip through the country. Afterward, get a hot chocolate at the lodge and sit next to its 35-foot, fieldstone fireplace. Reservations for sleigh rides are required.

October through mid-March, Mecan River Outfitters offers **pheasant hunts** *[see "Pheasant Hunting in Wisconsin" sidebar]* on 500 privately owned acres. Daily hunts may take you to open marshes, cornfields, and set-aside land—prime pheasant habitat. The hunts are especially helpful for first-time bird hunters or young dogs because of the quantity of birds. There are no bag limits, and no license is required. A guide and dogs are available, or you may bring your own dog. Be sure to wear something orange and call ahead for times available.

AFTERNOON

Have lunch at the Mecan River Lodge before leaving Princeton or return to downtown Green Lake and order what locals rate the "no. 1 homemade pizza" at the **Goose Blind Grill and Bar**.

You'll spend this afternoon as a winter cowboy or cowgirl. Between nearby Ripon to the east and Green Lake is **Cedar Ridge Ranch**, a 250-acre farm with wooded riding trails. An afternoon with the horses at Cedar Ridge promises to be unlike any other ride you may have taken. Here, you'll interact with your horse before the two of you take to the trails. You'll start with a lesson on how horses think and learn how best to communicate with them. Then you'll help catch, groom, and saddle your own horse before the both of you ride off into the sunset. Indoor and outdoor riding arenas are available, so your ride can take place in any kind of weather. Reservations are required by calling (920) 748-8405.

If you have time this afternoon, head back to the Heidel House for some **ice-skating**, **cross-country skiing**, **snowshoeing**, or **sledding** fun on the grounds.

PHEASANT HUNTING IN WISCONSIN

The ring-necked pheasant is a large (21–33 inches), long-tailed game bird that was introduced to Wisconsin in the late 1800s. A native of Asia, the bird establishes itself in open country, and the farmlands of Wisconsin proved to be ideal habitat. The population flourished, and pheasant hunting became a Wisconsin tradition.

The male ring-necked pheasant is an iridescent bronze color with a blue-black belly and has a glossy, green-black head with red eye patches. The female is buff-colored overall. A fast runner, a pheasant will rise up noisily when flushed.

In the 1940s, however, the pheasant population began to decline in Wisconsin. Urbanization and modern agricultural practices took a toll on available habitat, and today most pheasants are found in the southeast one-third of the state and in a few Pheasant Management Zones in west-central Wisconsin.

The state's pheasant-hunting season usually runs from mid-October to the end of December, and a small game license is required. A pheasant stamp is also required to hunt these birds in Pheasant Management Zones (Green Lake County is in one of the zones.) The stamp was created in 1991 to provide funds for pheasant restoration. Habitat projects partially funded by pheasant stamp dollars have managed and preserved thousands of acres of the bird's nesting and winter habitat.

The Wisconsin Department of Natural Resources (DNR) has two annual publications for pheasant hunters: the Special Pheasant Hunting Regulations guide and the Small Game Hunting Regulations booklet. A small game license and pheasant stamp can be purchased at any licensing vendor or DNR service center, at the DNR Web site at www.wildlife license.com/wi, or by calling 1-877-WI-LICENSE.

For information on where to hunt in Wisconsin, visit the Public Recreation Lands in Wisconsin Web site at www.dnr.state.wi.us/org/land/wildlife/reclands.

EVENING

Located on the north shore, **Norton's of Green Lake** on South Lawson Drive has been an area restaurant tradition since 1948. Norton's knows steaks and seafood, from tender filet mignons to Alaskan king crab legs with lemon and drawn butter.

After dinner, check the performance schedule at the **Thrasher Opera House**, built by local resident Charlie Thrasher in 1910 to host vaudeville acts and show silent movies. For decades, it was used as a community center and later became a warehouse. Renovated in the 1990s, the building now serves as a beloved arts venue. The 200-seat theatre has welcomed Irish singers, blues musicians, and bluegrass legends to its stage.

Day Three
MORNING AND AFTERNOON

This morning, enjoy a champagne brunch at the **Grey Rock Mansion Restaurant**. Amaretto-flamed pancakes, roast prime rib and pit ham, and made-to-order omelets and pastas are just some of the reasons the Grey Rock has received the *Wine Spectator* award for the "Best Wisconsin Brunch" for four consecutive years.

After leaving your accommodations at the Heidel House, relax—and digest—with a 40-

minute drive north to **Nordic Mountain Ski Area** in Mt. Morris. This **downhill ski** and **snowboard area** has 14 runs ranging from the easy "Gentle Giant" to the challenging "Lightning." The vertical drop is 265 feet, and the longest run is one mile. Nordic Mountain rents downhill skis and snowboards, and one-hour private and two-person ski and snowboard lessons are available. There's no better time than after an Old World winter weekend to take up a new classic winter sport.

FOR MORE INFORMATION

GREEN LAKE AREA CHAMBER OF COMMERCE
PO Box 337, Green Lake, WI 54941
(920) 294-3231 or (800) 253-7354
www.greenlakecc.com

PRINCETON CHAMBER OF COMMERCE
708 W. Water St., Princeton, WI 54968
(920) 295-3877, www.princetonwi.com

WINTER ATTRACTIONS

CEDAR RIDGE RANCH
W14471 Dartford Rd., Ripon, WI 54971
(920) 748-8405, www.cedarridgeranch.net

DEACON MILLS PARK
500 Block of South St., Green Lake, WI 54941
(920) 294-6912, www.visitgreenlake.com/greenlakecc/boatlaunches.asp

DENNIS WALKER'S PONTOON GUIDE SERVICE
370 Palmer Ave., Green Lake, WI 54941
(920) 294-0611, www.greenlakefishing.com

DODGE MEMORIAL PARK
W3306 Highway K, Green Lake, WI 54941
(920) 294-4005, www.visitgreenlake.com/greenlakecc/boatlaunches.asp

GREEN LAKE TERRACE SNOSTREAKERS SNOWMOBILE CLUB
www.snostreakers.homestead.com

MECAN RIVER OUTFITTERS & LODGE
W720 Highway 23, Princeton, WI 54968
(920) 295-3439
www.mecanriveroutfitters.com

MIKE NORTON'S ALL SEASON FISHING
W4410 Huckleberry Rd., Princeton, WI 54968,
(920) 295-3617, www.nortonsfishing.com

NORDIC MOUNTAIN SKI AREA
W5806 Highway W, Wautoma, WI 54982
(immediately east of the town of Mt. Morris)
(920) 787-3324 or (800) 253-7266,
www.nordicmountain.com

PRINCETON SNO-BARONS SNOWMOBILE CLUB
(920) 295-3416

THRASHER OPERA HOUSE
506 Mill St., Green Lake, WI 54941
(920) 294-4279 or (888) 441-0140
www.thrashersoperahouse.com

WINTER FESTIVALS

CHRISTMAS BY THE LAKE—early December. Green Lake. Musical entertainment at the Thrasher Opera House, lunch with Santa, horse and wagon rides, a craft fair, and cookie decorating. (800) 253-7354 or www.greenlakecc.com.

OLD-FASHIONED COUNTRY CHRISTMAS—early December. Green Lake Conference Center, W2511 Highway 23, Green Lake, WI 54941. A gourmet buffet dinner followed by a musical Christmas show and more. (800) 558-8898 or www.glcc.org.

HOLIDAY HOUSE AT HEIDEL HOUSE—first two weekends in December. Heidel House Resort. Breakfast and photos with Santa, horse-drawn carriage rides through the decorated grounds, Christmas cookie workshop, and more. (800) 444-2812 or www.heidelhouse.com.

PRINCETON'S CANDLELIT CHRISTMAS—mid-December. Enjoy Princeton's Water Street by luminaries. Christmas story readings, carolers, gallery receptions, candlelight dinners, and concerts. Shops open 10:00 a.m.–6:00 p.m. (920) 295-3877 or www.princetonwi.com.

GREEN LAKE WINTERFEST—second weekend in February. Deacon Mills Park. Two-day event including a dance at the Goose Blind Grill and Bar, baked-bean contest, ice-carving competition, carriage rides, fishing seminars, ice bowling, ice golf, snowman decorating, and a snowmobile safety demonstration. (800) 253-7354 or www.greenlakecc.com.

RESTAURANTS

BERNIE'S ITALIAN STEAKHOUSE
(dinner)
W3919 Highways 23 and 73, Princeton, WI 54968, (920) 295-3721
www.princetonwi.com/food-spirits.cfm

BOATHOUSE LOUNGE AND EATERY
(lunch and dinner)
At the Heidel House Resort

643 Illinois Ave., Green Lake, WI 54941
(920) 294-3344 or (800) 444-2812
www.heidelhouse.com

GOOSE BLIND GRILL AND BAR
(lunch and dinner)
512 Gold St., Green Lake, WI 54941
(920) 294-6363, www.gooseblind.com

GREY ROCK MANSION RESTAURANT
(Friday–Sunday, dinner; Sunday brunch)
At the Heidel House Resort
643 Illinois Ave., Green Lake, WI 54941
(920) 294-3344 or (800) 444-2812
www.heidelhouse.com/dining/greyrock.asp

J.J.'S SUPPER CLUB *(dinner and Sunday brunch)*
402 S. Fulton St., Princeton, WI 54968
(920) 295-3882
www.princetonwi.com/food-spirits.cfm

MECAN RIVER OUTFITTERS & LODGE
(breakfast, lunch, and dinner)
W720 Highway 23, Princeton, WI 54968
(920) 295-3439, www.mecanriveroutfitters.com

MIMI'S *(Friday–Saturday, lunch and dinner; closed Sunday)*
523 Water St., Princeton, WI 54968
(920) 295-6775
www.princetonwi.com/food-spirits.cfm

NORTON'S OF GREEN LAKE *(lunch and dinner)*
380 S. Lawson Dr., Green Lake, WI 54941
(920) 294-6577, www.nortonsofgreenlake.com

SUNROOM CAFÉ *(breakfast and lunch)*
At the Heidel House Resort
643 Illinois Ave., Green Lake, WI 54941
(920) 294-3344 or (800) 444-2812
www.heidelhouse.com

LODGING

ANGEL INN BED & BREAKFAST
372 S. Lawson Dr., Green Lake, WI 54941
(920) 294-3087, www.angelinns.com

BAY VIEW MOTEL & RESORT
439 Lake St., Green Lake, WI 54941
(920) 294-6504
http://home.centurytel.net/bayview

HEIDEL HOUSE RESORT
643 Illinois Ave., Green Lake, WI 54941
(920) 294-3344 or (800) 444-2812
www.heidelhouse.com

McCONNELL INN BED & BREAKFAST
497 S. Lawson Dr., Green Lake, WI 54941
(920) 294-6430 or (888) 238-8625
www.mcconnellinn.com

MECAN RIVER OUTFITTERS & LODGE
W720 Highway 23, Princeton, WI 54968
(920) 295-3439
www.mecanriveroutfitters.com

MILLER'S DAUGHTER BED & BREAKFAST
453 North St., Green Lake, WI 54941
(920) 294-0717 or (866) 266-0717
www.millersdaughter.com

OAKWOOD LODGE
365 Lake St., Green Lake, WI 54941
(920) 294-6580
www.wisvacations.com/oakwoodlodge

Chapter Ten
BIRKIE BOUND
Hayward/Cable

S ET IN THE ENVIRONS of Wisconsin's great, 1.5-million-acre Chequamegon–
Nicolet National Forest are the towns of Hayward and Cable. Seventeen miles of
Highway 63 stretch between them, but they are soul-mate cities joined in their fer-
vor for cross-country skiing. The two are the beginning and endpoint for the annual
American Birkebeiner, the largest cross-county ski race in the United States.

"Birkie" fever and the opportune locale for outdoor recreation enliven these two cities
in winter. Both the Chequamegon National Forest (858,400 acres) and the Nicolet National
Forest (661,400 acres) were established by presidential proclamations in 1933. Since 1993,
these two national forests have been managed as one, but each has retained its individual
identity and signage. Cable sits right on the edge of one of the three sections of the mighty
Chequamegon, a land filled with woodlands, wetlands, and lakes—800 total in the national forest's boundaries. Also within the forest are 200 miles of designated cross-country ski
trails, 11,500 miles of roads for nature and wildlife viewing, more than 800 miles of snowmobile routes, and 285 miles of ATV trails.

Ten thousand years ago, the Hayward–Cable area was inhabited by Paleo-Indians. They
were followed by Archaic Indians and, finally, Woodland Indians. After a stream of
European missionaries and fur traders, the lumbermen came. Hayward was the site of the
area's first lumber mills, and Cable, a railroad center and headquarters, became pivotal in
moving the product out. Lumbering reached its peak in the forest in the 1920s.

The cutover land was soon sold to immigrants for farms and homesteads, but the soil
turned out to be better for growing trees. Many of the farms were abandoned, and by 1928
the federal government, under the authority of the Weeks Law of 1911, began buying tax-
delinquent land with the intent of establishing a national forest. In 1929, a forest service
office was established in Park Falls to oversee land acquisitions.

Today, Cable and Hayward have been restored to much of what pre-lumbering Wisconsin looked like. The forest is resilient, and second-growth trees are abundant in this picturesque area next to the Namekagon River.

And the best way to see as much as you can of it is on a pair of cross-country skis.

Day One
MØRNING

This weekend is going to be a cross-country ski extravaganza! Be prepared to travel between the two cities of Hayward and Cable—often—to take advantage of all the area has to offer.

Get a good start on the morning by stopping for breakfast at **Mulberry Street** on Highway 63 in Cable. Get a latte to go for the short car ride just down the highway to **New Moon Ski Shop** in Hayward. There, you can rent equipment for all the cross-country skiing and snowshoeing in store for the next three days.

After getting outfitted at New Moon, you'll jump right in with both feet by **cross-country skiing** or **snowshoeing** at **Rock Lake Ski Trail**. From Highway 63 in Cable, drive 7.5 miles east on Highway M. Here, you'll find 26 miles of groomed and tracked trails for classic cross-country skiing. Tucked inside the beautiful **Chequamegon National Forest**, this system of loops can seem like the middle of a remote and secluded "nowhere," which is why they are favorites with local residents and visitors. More than 20 years ago, the National Forest Service chose the rugged Rock Lake area for its first ski trail. Today, the loops retain their original character: narrow and single tracked, making for an intimate ski experience as you glide through trees so close you'll feel like the forest's first intruder.

JOHN T. ANDREWS

The thousands of high-energy skiers participating in the American Birkebeiner take off in 10 separate "waves."

Take the long, isolated 9.9-mile Rock Lake loop. It rates on the low end of "most difficult" because of its distance, rolling terrain, and steep grades. But traveling through a maple and oak forest that has occasional stands of large, white pines where heavy snows bend limbs almost to the ground, you'll appreciate why Rock Lake is such a sought-after trail.

AFTERNOON

If a warm meal sounds good, head for Hayward and eat lunch at **Coops Pizza Parloure**. Try one of the Italian pies on a hand-rolled crust, or order a large plate of spaghetti or lasagna. You'll also find a menu rarity: pressure-fried chicken.

If you happen to be in Hayward during one of Wisconsin's most signature events, the **American Birkebeiner** *[see "History of the American Birkebeiner" sidebar]*, stake out your spot on Main Street at 2:00 p.m. to watch the **Hayward Chamber of Commerce Citizen Sprints**. It's just one of the many competitions included in the biggest cross-country ski race in the United States.

The place to stay if you want to be in the middle of the Birkebeiner excitement is the **Telemark Resort and Convention Center**. On County Road M east of Cable, the Telemark is not only a lodging establishment, but also a winter hub. With **cross-country ski trails,** a **snowboarding area, ice-skating pond, sleigh rides,** and **snow tubing, snowshoeing, ATVing,** and **snowmobiling** access right outside the door, you'd never have to even leave the grounds to keep your three-day schedule full.

The Telemark is surrounded by 900 acres of protected forest, mountains and meadows. The main lodge has 129 guestrooms, along with 62 suites and condos. The resort itself is a **Nordic ski center,** and the first American Birkebeiner was held here in 1973. It has 40 miles of groomed and tracked trails on 16 loops. If you're not up to the challenge of the winding **World Cup Loop,** take an easier tour on the **Martha Rockwell** or 1.2-mile **Birkebeiner Loop.** The Telemark rents cross-country skis; so if you're a beginner, take a one-hour ski lesson and by the end of the weekend, you'll be striding like an old hand.

For some downhill fun, hit the 90-foot-high **snow tubing hill**. There are two chutes and a rope tow. The hill is open for tubing Friday from 3:00 to 8:00 p.m., and Saturday and Sunday from 9:00 a.m. to 8:00 p.m.

Telemark offers **snowboarders** their own slopes with sculpted jumps and a quarter-pipe. A rope tow services the Berard slope. **Snowshoers** can hit 20 miles of marked trails. Some are easy treks, such as the 1.2-mile trip to the

JOHN T. ANDREWS

Various checkpoints along the trail, like this one on Mosquito Road, give spectators a chance to cheer on the American Birkebeiner contestants.

warming cabin. Others are hour-long wilderness adventures, such as to the top of Mount Telemark for a 30-mile overview of the forest. You can rent snowshoes at the resort. On winter weekends, you can take a horse-drawn **sleigh ride** right from the main lodge.

You may want to use the afternoon to do more exploring in the Chequamegon National Forest—by **snowmobile** this time. There are more than 800 miles of groomed snowmobile trails in the forest, and the Telemark is right on a Bayfield County trail.

Just four miles from the Telemark is the **Bayfield County Forest Island Lake Loop ATV trail**. The trail connects to 100 miles of year-round-use trails. Do transport your ATV to the trailhead, however, since access via roads on snowmobile trails is prohibited.

With all the options for winter activities, expect a late dinner.

EVENING

The wait will be worth it. Tonight, you'll eat dinner at the Bavarian and Old World–style **Garmisch USA Restaurant & Lounge** in Cable. Featuring traditional German entrées, the restaurant overlooks Lake Namekagon. On Friday nights, you can take advantage of the all-

HISTORY OF THE AMERICAN BIRKEBEINER

Between the years of 1130 to 1217, Norway was the scene of a civil war between the Bagler faction, a group of aristocracy, clergy, and merchants, and the Birkebeiners (named for their protective birch-bark leggings), essentially made up of peasants. The conflict pertained to royal succession laws, the power struggle between church and king, and social conditions.

When King Haakon Sverrirson died in 1204, leaving his baby son Haakon Haakonsson in a Bagler-controlled territory, a group of Birkebeiners set off in 1206 on a mission through treacherous terrain to rescue the now 18-month-old child and bring him to safety in Trondheim. On the journey back, they ran into a blizzard. Only the two strongest warriors, Torstein Skevla and Skjervald Skrukka, could continue on skis, carrying the child in their arms. They managed to bring the heir to safety, and their courage is still commemorated in Norway's annual Birkebeiner ski race.

More than 750 years later, in the winter of 1973, a group of Midwesterners—34 men and one woman, some on skis for the first time—headed out of Hayward and skied 32 miles to the Telemark Resort in Cable. They were attempting to recreate the famous Norwegian Birkebeiner race, but they had no idea they, too, were making history.

That small group in 1973 has grown today to nearly 8,000 skiers who show up in the small towns of Cable and Hayward in late February to share in the spirit of the American Birkebeiner, now the largest and most prestigious ski event in North America.

---

you-can-eat fish fry, with a choice of fried perch or baked haddock almondine.

Back at the Telemark, check to see whether the **Friday evening candlelight ski/snow-shoe** is being offered. If not, head out to the **ice-skating pond**. Glide on the smooth ice under the lights in Wisconsin's great North Woods. On Friday and Saturday evenings, a pond-side bonfire makes things even more bright and beautiful.

Day Two
MORNING

This morning, you'll want to get up early to watch the high-energy "waves" of Birkebeiner participants take off.

If you're staying at the Telemark, grab a bite at the **Outpost Restaurant**, or go to the **Robin's Nest Café** in Hayward. The Outpost has a Wisconsin history theme, with fur-trader-type wallpaper and old maps on the wall. Also situated on a snowmobile trail, the Robin's Nest can get you fed and off with a hot omelet breakfast, such as the tasty blue cheese western.

If you've never witnessed an **American Birkebeiner** start, make sure this is the winter you do! "High-spirited" doesn't even begin to describe the atmosphere, as thousands of cross-country skiers anxiously wait their time to depart. Songs such as "Wild Thing" blast from outdoor speakers, and people of all ages and skiing abilities stand—and dance—at the ready. That's what's so special about the Birkebeiner: It is a pure celebration of winter.

Starting at 8:20 a.m. in Cable at the Telemark Resort, different classes of skiers take off in the first of 10 waves of starts *[see "Competing in the Birkie: A Personal Account" sidebar]*. The race runs a course of 31 miles, ending in downtown Hayward. The elite skiers may come in after only two hours. Watch a few of the waves take off, then drive to one of the course's checkpoints on Mosquito Road. The whole communities of Hayward and Cable come out to cheer the skiers on, shake cowbells, and shout encouragement.

Make your next stop the finish line in Hayward. Over a loudspeaker, the participants' names, the number of Birkies they've been in, and their home cities—and in some instances, countries—are announced as they cross the finish line. Cheer on our Wisconsin heroes; Italians have dominated the race in the last few years.

COMPETING IN THE BIRKIE: A PERSONAL ACCOUNT
by Mike Ivey

Mike Ivey is a business reporter and columnist at The Capital Times *in Madison, Wisconsin. A past president of the Madison Nordic Ski Club, Ivey lives with his wife, Vicki Elkin, and their son, Alex.*

I grew up playing team sports like baseball and basketball, and actually didn't discover cross-country-ski racing until I hit my 30s.

But now I'm hooked and couldn't imagine going through a winter without entering the American Birkebeiner cross-country ski marathon.

I used to race bicycles quite a bit and still try to hang with the front pack on the Sunday morning Bombay Bicycle Club rides out of Madison, but it's skiing that keeps my competitive juices flowing most of the time. Even on those steamy July mornings on the bike, the Birkie is still in the back of my mind, driving me to stay fit all year round.

When the leaves start to turn in the fall, it's time to pull out the roller skis, which are the closest thing you can get to skiing without the snow. Heck, with our globally warmed Wisconsin climate, sometimes roller-skiing has to pass for the real thing.

It's a challenge to keep the training going through the dreary days of November and December, when the sun sets so early that flashing lights and reflective vests are needed if you want to continue roller-skiing. I also make a point of attending yoga class at least once a week—a key strength, balance, and flexibility workout for aging athletes.

In early December, there's usually enough snow in the Lake Superior snowbelt to make a trip north to Ironwood, Michigan, about a four-hour drive north of Madison. What a thrill to get on snow for the first time each season, although the initial outing on those skinny skis can be a challenge to one's balance and breathing.

During January and February, the goal is to get out skiing every day there's snow on the ground, do as many local races as possible, and hopefully stay healthy and injury-free.

Fortunately, I've managed to complete 18 straight Birkies without ever being sick and have even gotten more competitive over the years. I had the second-fastest Birkie of my career in 2005 at age 47, keeping my Wave One starting position for the 15th straight year.

Therein lies the great thing about Nordic skiing: Good technique and smart training can trump youth. That's why it's called a "Sport for Life."

115

CLASSIC VS. SKATE-SKIING

Cross-country skiing used to come in one style: straight forward in a set of tracks—or not. But about 20 years ago, a different, faster technique called "skate-skiing" began to take hold across the country, after having appeared in the Winter Olympics. To distinguish itself, the first style became known as "classic."

Classic-style skiing is when your skis are parallel to each other and you perform a "walk-gliding motion" by pushing off on the planted ski and gliding on the other, and then repeating the motion on the opposite leg. Classic skiing can be done in a track set, on ungroomed trails, or in the backcountry on touring skis.

Skate-skiing simulates the movement of inline skating. The skis are set in a V shape, and the skier propels forward by pushing off in a skater's side-to-side motion and also pushing with ski poles.

The two types of skiing require separate grooming techniques. A classical trail is packed down, then set with two parallel tracks for the skis to run in. A skate-ski trail is packed and left smooth and usually requires a wider berth. Skate-ski trails can be groomed with less snow.

Skate skiers should avoid classically groomed trails in order not to damage the tracks.

Thirty-one miles from the starting line in Cable, contestants make their way into downtown Hayward.

In addition to the 31-mile Birkebeiner, the ski event has shorter races such as the 14.2-mile Kortelopet, the citizen sprints on Friday night, the Barnebirkie for kids ages 3 to 13 and the Junior Birkie for children ages 10 to 18. Every year, more than 15,000 spectators attend the Birkie, and the whole city welcomes them. Even the folks working the stores and gas stations will wish you a "good day"; the locals seem to enjoy playing host to visitors from all over the world.

If you prefer to try **skiing the Birkie Trail** by yourself before taking on all comers, go to

JOHN T. ANDREWS

The setting sun enhances the geometric patterns of tracks in the snow.

Cable on any other winter weekend. The Birkie Trail is free and open to the public whenever sufficient snow is on the ground. The trail is big, wide, and tough—the hills just keep coming. Trailheads are located at County Road OO in Seeley, on Mosquito Brook Road and in Fish Hatchery Park in Hayward, and at the Telemark Resort in Cable. Lighted sections for nighttime skiing are located on the east and west side of the trail at County Road OO and Fish Hatchery. The Birkie Trail is groomed weekly by the American Birkebeiner Ski Foundation and accommodates both classic and skate-skiing styles. *[See "Classic vs. Skate-Skiing" sidebar.]*

AFTERNOON

Between watching groups of Birkie skiers cross the finish line, stop for lunch at the **Sawmill Saloon & Mooselips Java Joint** in Seeley, between Hayward and Cable on Highway 63. Grab a River Pig Chili Dog amid logging antiques.

If the Birkebeiner Trail sounded a little daunting, you'll have a chance to sample an easy-to-intermediate **cross-country ski** trail this afternoon. Eleven miles east of Cable on Highway M is the **Namekagon Ski Trail** in the Chequamegon National Forest. Turn left (north) on Highway D and go 5.5 miles to Forest Road 209. Turn left (west), and drive .5 mile to the trailhead. The three loops of the trail total 4.3 miles and are groomed for classic cross-country skiing. The Namekagon Trail is filled with forest beauty and side trips to fantastic spots. On Forest Road 203, you can view a bog; and at the south end's Lynch Creek Overlook, you can stop to photograph an expansive landscape of streams and tamarack trees.

EVENING

This evening, you'll dine in a Turkish atmosphere in a restaurant that has been serving the area for more than 75 years. **Turk's Inn** is a quirky, delightful supper club that is still owned and operated by the family of the original "Turk." Start with a Mediterranean appetizer, but be advised that Turk's is most famous for its steaks. Each piece of meat is aged for five weeks and hand cut when you order it. A Turk's steak will always be one of the biggest and best you've ever tasted.

117

Day Three
MORNING

You've burned a lot of calories this weekend; now it's time to replenish them. Sunday brunch at **Lakewoods Resort** on Lake Namekagon in Cable serves a crab leg buffet, along with choices of roast beef, barbecue ribs, chicken, made-to-order omelets, and hand-tossed pastas. There are salads, fresh-baked breads, and even a make-your-own sundae bar.

AFTERNOON

This afternoon, fit in an outing on one of the area trails that have eluded you so far on your weekend's activity-packed agenda. One great option for a change of pace from cross-country skiing is the **North End Snowshoe Trail**.

The three loops of the North End Trail offer a short 1.1-mile hike to a hike of almost six miles. On old, abandonded roads and rustic paths that are mapped and marked for snowshoeing, you'll walk deep into the woods. A variety of terrain is not too difficult. The trailhead can be found on Randysek Road just two miles south of Cable.

If you long to go back to the Chequamegon National Forest, the **Drummond Ski Trail** has more than 30 groomed miles on its **Boulevard, Antler, Antler Chute, Jackrabbit, Racetrack, Playground**, and **North Country loops**. The Drummond Ski Trail system is located in a hardwood forest with white pines on gentle terrain and is groomed for classic cross-country skiing. The trailhead is located .1 mile off Forest Road 213.

Also in the national forest, you'll find 27 miles of **Mukwonago Ski Trail** loops for both classic and skate-skiing. The trails flow easily over rolling to hilly terrain. Beginner and novice skiers may want to try the 1.4- and 2.7-mile loops. The uphills are located on moderate slopes, making the trail easy to ski. The 8.4-mile loop has several long downhills. You'll travel through an oak and white pine forest and see several small lakes and ponds. From Highway 63 in Hayward, drive 18.5 miles east on Highway 77. The parking lot is located on the right (south) side of the road just past the Chequamegon-Nicolet National Forest entrance sign.

The many beautiful lakes in the Chequamegon National Forest make for exhilarating snowmobile tours.

For more trails, such as the lighted **Hatchery Park Trail**, the **Hayward Hospital Ski Trails**, the **Lost Land Lake Ski Trail**, and the **West Torch River Ski Trail** in Hayward, go to www.haywardlakes.com/skiing.html or call (715) 634-8685.

You'll no doubt leave the Cable/Hayward area this weekend impressed with the number of fit and healthy people you've seen in the Wisconsin North Woods. It's probably because of all the time they spend on cross-country skis.

FOR MORE INFORMATION

CABLE AREA CHAMBER OF COMMERCE VISITOR CENTER
Highway 63 and County Road M
Cable, WI 54821, (800) 533-7454
www.cable4fun.com

HAYWARD LAKES VISITOR & CONVENTION BUREAU
Highway 63 and Highway 27 Junction
Hayward, WI 54843, (715) 634-4801
or (800) 724-2992, www.haywardlakes.com

WINTER ATTRACTIONS

CHEQUAMEGON–NICOLET NATIONAL FOREST
Great Divide Ranger Station
10650 Nyman Ave. Hayward, WI 54843
(715) 634-4821, www.fs.fed.us/r9/cnnf

DRUMMOND SKI TRAIL
Washburn Ranger District
113 Bayfield St. East, Washburn, WI 54891
(715) 373-2667, www.norwiski.com

MUKWONAGO SKI TRAIL
Hayward, WI 54843, (715) 634-4821
www.norwiski.com

NAMEKAGON SKI TRAIL (off Forest Road 209)
Mogasheen Resort
23380 Missionary Point Rd.
Cable, WI 54821
(715) 634-4821, www.norwiski.com

NEW MOON SKI SHOP
(cross-country ski and snowshoe rentals)
Highway 63 North, Hayward, WI 54843
(715) 634-8685, www.newmoonski.com

NORTH END SNOWSHOE TRAIL
41640 Randysek Rd. (two miles south of Cable)
Cable, WI 54821, (715) 798-3599

ROCK LAKE SKI TRAIL
Great Divide Ranger Station
10650 Nyman Ave. Hayward, WI 54843
(715) 634-4821, www.norwiski.com

WINTER FESTIVALS

CHRISTMAS IN CABLE—early December. Start the day with breakfast with Santa at Lakewoods Resort. Head to Telemark Resort for the Christmas Arts & Crafts Fair. Then on to Cable for the Trinity Lutheran Church bazaar and luncheon. (800) 533-7454 or www.cable4fun.com.

WORLD POWER SPORTS ASSOCIATION/ NORTHWOODS CHALLENGE SNO-CROSS RACES—early December. Telemark Resort, Cable. Snowmobiles race on manmade jumps on Mt. Telemark. (715) 746-4521 or www.wpsaracing.com.

24 HOURS OF TELEMARK—early January. Cross-country team relay at the Telemark Resort in Cable. Skiers take turns skiing a 6.2-mile loop for a continuous 24-hour period. Categories for all abilities. (715) 798-3571 or www.telemark resort.com.

WINTERFEST—early February. Lake Hayward. Snowmobile drag races (Saturday) and speed runs (Sunday). All racers and race fans welcome. (715) 634-2102 or www.logboy.com/winterfest.

HAYWARD LIONS PRE-BIRKIE—mid-February. Telemark Resort. 11:00 a.m. Annual 15.5-mile, cross-country ski race. Awards in 25 classes, plus the top three men and women. (715) 634-6456 or www.haywardlakes.com/lionsprebirkie.

AMERICAN BIRKEBEINER CROSS-COUNTRY SKI RACE—late February. Cable to Hayward. Spanning 31.6 miles from Cable to Hayward, the Birkie is part of the esteemed World Loppet series of 14 international races, part of the International Ski Federation Marathon Cup series of eight races and part of the American Ski Marathon series of 11 races. More than 8,000 skiers of both genders, and all ages and nationalities participate in the Birkebeiner, the 16.1-mile Kortelopet, the children's Barnebirkie, Junior Birkie, and citizen sprints. (800) 872-2753 or www.birkie.com.

WORLD'S LONGEST WEENIE ROAST—early March. Lakewoods Resort. More than 700 men, women, and children line up shoulder to shoulder along a 1,000-foot (environmentally approved) fire trench on the ice of Lake Namekagon to roast their way into the record books. Anyone can become a link in the weenie roast chain. All you have to do is buy a foot-long hot dog and join the line-up. (715) 794-2561 or www.lakewoodsresort.com.

LAKEWOODS BALLOON RALLY AND SNOW-SHOE RACE—mid-March. Lakewoods Resort. Help set up a hot-air balloon and then climb aboard with an experienced pilot for a truly fantastic flight over Lake Namekagon. Take part in a 3.1-mile and 6.2-mile snowshoe race that is part of the Midwest Championship Snowshoe Series. (715) 794-2561 or www.lakewoodsresort.com.

RESTAURANTS

COOPS PIZZA PARLOURE *(lunch and dinner)*
10588 California Ave. (and Highway 63 North), Hayward, WI 54843
(715) 634-3027
www.haywardlakes.com/coops.htm

GARMISCH USA RESTAURANT & LOUNGE *(dinner)*
23040 Garmisch Rd., Cable, WI 54821
(715) 794-2204
www.garmischresort.com/rest.htm

LAKEWOODS RESORT *(dinner; Sunday brunch)*
21540 County Road M, Cable, WI 54821
(715) 794-2561, www.lakewoodsresort.com

MULBERRY STREET *(Friday–Saturday, breakfast, lunch, and early dinner; Sunday, breakfast and lunch)*
41410 Highway 63, Cable, WI 54821
(715) 798-4237, www.shopmulberry.com

OUTPOST RESTAURANT
Telemark Resort and Convention Center
42225 Telemark Rd., Cable, WI 54821
(715) 798-3999 or (877) 798-4718
www.telemarkresort.com

ROBIN'S NEST CAFÉ *(Saturday–Sunday, breakfast and lunch)*
11014 Highway B, Hayward, WI 54843
(715) 462-3132, www.robinsnest-hayward.com

SAWMILL SALOON & MOOSELIPS JAVA JOINT *(breakfast, lunch, and dinner)*
15560 Highway 63, Seeley, WI 54843
(715) 634-5660 or (715) 634-1006
www.seeleywis.com/saloon.htm

TURK'S INN *(dinner)*
11320 Highway 63 North, Hayward, WI 54843
(715) 634-2597

LODGING

FOREST MOON BED & BREAKFAST
12546 W. County Road OO, Hayward, WI 54843
(715) 634-5188 or (866) 666-6044
www.forestmoonbb.com

GARMISCH USA
23040 Garmisch Rd., Cable, WI 54821
(715) 794-2204 or (800) 794-2204
www.garmischresort.com

LAKE OWEN RESORT
14580 Resort Rd., Cable, WI 54821
(715) 798-3603 or (800) 872-9370
www.lakeowenresort.com

LAKEWOODS RESORT
21540 County Road M, Cable, WI 54821
(715) 794-2561 or (800) 255-5937
www.lakewoodsresort.com

SPIDER LAKE LODGE BED & BREAKFAST
10472 W. Murphy Blvd., Hayward, WI 54843
(715) 462-3793 or (800) 653-9472
www.spiderlakelodge.com

TELEMARK RESORT AND CONVENTION CENTER
42225 Telemark Rd., Cable, WI 54821
(715) 798-3999 or (877) 798-4718
www.telemarkresort.com

TREELAND RESORTS
9630 N. Treeland Rd., Hayward, WI 54843
(715) 462-3874, www.treelandresorts.com

Chapter Eleven
WINTER WATERS
Kohler/Sheboygan

S HEBOYGAN IS A FIXTURE ON THE WATERS of Lake Michigan, and water fixtures built the town of Kohler. The name "Sheboygan," in fact, comes from the Ojibwa name "Shaw-bwah-way-gun," translated as "the sound like the wind of the rushing waters."

As in so many other Wisconsin towns in 1835, the sawmills were buzzing in Sheboygan. But it was the city's location—along the Lake Michigan shipping lane and equidistant from Milwaukee and Manitowoc—that really fueled its development. By constructing one of the first decent piers along the lake, Sheboygan became home to German, Dutch, and English immigrants who poured off lake schooners and ferries.

The final wave of German immigration occurred between 1880 and 1890, when 20,000 northern Germans came into Sheboygan. Today, some townships in the county are 95 percent German, and neighborhood butchers still turn out family-secret-recipe bratwurst, leading to the town's proclamation of "Bratwurst Capital of the World."

Located just minutes away from Sheboygan and one hour north of Milwaukee is the "planned" community of Kohler. In 1883, an Austrian immigrant named John Michael Kohler built the first one-piece bathtub by pouring hot enamel over a horse trough and adding four legs. He sold the first tub to a farmwoman for a cow and 14 chickens. By 1887, the Kohler Company had 65 employees, and today it has 42,000 worldwide.

Built in 1918, the American Club originally served as housing for the hundreds of immigrants who worked at the Kohler Company, now a world-famous maker of porcelain fixtures. In the early 1900s, Walter Kohler, John Michael's son, envisioned a safe and clean place for his immigrant employees to live—a place where they could share a sense of community while they contributed to the growth of the Kohler Company. Today, that housing establishment is known as the American Club, the state's most highly ranked resort, restaurant, and nature preserve for hiking, fishing, and hunting.

Experiencing the American Club is a special luxury any time of the year, but staying there during Christmas Kohler—a four-week-long winter celebration when the resort is backlit by 180,000 tiny, white lights that sparkle on the Wisconsin snowscape—is sublime.

Heated horse-drawn carriage rides offer a relaxing trot through the village of Kohler.

COURTESY OF KOHLER CO.

The Kohler Waters Spa even has the perfect antidote for dry, winter skin: bathe in a tub with its own waterfall, not far from the waters of a Great Lake.

Day One
MORNING

Start your weekend just south of Sheboygan, on one of the last natural preserves along the Lake Michigan shoreline. The 988-acre **Kohler–Andrae State Park** is known for its two-mile, windswept Lake Michigan beach in the summer; but in the winter, it is an attractive **winter hiking**, **snowshoeing**, **sledding**, **tobogganing**, **cross-country skiing**, and **winter camping** venue.

If you're in Sheboygan on a cold winter day, make sure to wander the shoreline to photograph the ice sculptures designed by the lake waves. The place has an almost sacred quality, when you stop to consider that those chilly waters are the last resting spots for some 50 shipwrecks.

As you continue your **winter hike** at the Kohler–Andrae State Park inland, the pine and hardwoods forest will come alive with deer and other wildlife. The park has two self-guided nature trails. The **Creeping Juniper Trail**, an easy half-mile loop just south of the **Sanderling Nature Center**, winds through some of the park's scenic sand dunes, while the **Woodland Dunes Trail** loops through the wooded southern end of the park. You can pick up a brochure at the nature center that describes the various trees found along the way.

The park also includes the fantastic 2.5-mile **Kohler Dunes Cordwalk**, a board-and-rope trail that meanders through the fragile, 135-acre **Kohler Park Dunes State Natural Area.** One mile of the Lake Michigan beach is included in the natural area. An interdunal wetland, it is one of the state's rarest habitats. The planks ride over the gorgeous, chocolate drop–shaped dunes through stark sand blow—when lakefront sand gets blown back and intermingles with grassy areas of lakeshore rush and sedges. Common plants stabilizing the dunes are sand reed, marram grass, Canada wild rye, common and trailing junipers, sand cherry, and willow species. Three plants on the state's threatened list are found here: clustered broomrape, dune goldenrod, and dune thistle. Rumor has it the dunes also may still harbor the only known Wisconsin population of the endangered prairie moonwort, a tiny fern last observed here in 1985.

Cross-country skiers at Kohler–Andrae can glide through a magical white pine forest and the heavily wooded south campground area on a 2.5-mile, groomed trail, which encompasses part of the Woodland Dunes Trail. **Winter campers** may use one of the wooded campsites, with electrical hookups in the north campground that are kept open during the snow season. You can **snowshoe** anywhere in the park, except on the groomed cross-country ski trail.

Although Kohler–Andrae has no facilities for **snowmobilers**, a short section of trail in the park's northwest corner connects with other local trails. A better option would be the **Old Plank Road Trail**, which parallels Highway 23. In 1843, the territorial legislature began building the first all-weather plank road. They wanted to accommodate the many immigrants who they hoped would permanently settle in the Sheboygan County region. It was completed in 1852. Today, the Old Plank Road Trail is a paved, 17-mile, multipurpose recreation trail running from western Sheboygan to Greenbush and the **Kettle Moraine State Forest–Northern Unit** via Kohler and Plymouth. **Snowmobilers**, **winter hikers**, and **cross-country skiers** can pass each other on 10 feet of asphalt and eight feet of turf. It's seldom flat, making for more interest and exertion than many other trails.

AFTERNOON

When in Rome—well, since this *is* the Bratwurst Capital of the World, lunch should include the famous sausage. Go to the **Charcoal Inn** for a brat or, if you must forego the city emblem, try the **Scenic Bar & Restaurant** for a noon Friday fish fry.

Before leaving Sheboygan, consider three last afternoon visits. The largest city park is the 120-acre **Ellwood H. May Environmental Park (Maywood)**. Located on the Pigeon

River corridor on Sheboygan's far northwest side, Maywood features spring-fed ponds, wetlands, restored prairie, and maple and pine forests. In addition to diverse ecosystems, you'll find plenty of environmental programs, miles of free **cross-country skiing** trails, and—should your visit fall in March—a flapjack day.

If you'd like to take a leisurely **winter walk**, consider **Indian Mound Park**, located on Sheboygan's far south side. There are more effigy burial mounds in southern Wisconsin than in any other spot in the world. Here, you can respectfully wander on paths among 18 mounds in animal and geometric forms that were built between A.D. 500 and 1000. Your tour is self-guided and free.

If you're a snowshoe purist, try **Evergreen Park**. With no groomed trails for cross-country skiing, **snowshoers** rule.

This is the weekend to treat yourself to the Midwest's only AAA Five-Diamond hotel, the **American Club** in Kohler. Kohler, less than four miles from Sheboygan, started as a fac-

Light passing through the American Club's stained-glass windows bathes the courtyard snow.

COURTESY OF KOHLER CO.

tory town for the Kohler Company. The Tudor-style inn, a member of Historic Hotels of America, has guest rooms with hand-carved oak trimmings, sky-lit rooms, and Kohler-manufactured whirlpool baths, whose styles range from luxurious, marble-columned retreats to enclosed habitat chambers where weather—wind, rain, and sun—is at your fingertip control.

EVENING

After unpacking, stop in the American Club's library for wine during the evening cocktail hour and listen to the pianist. Then eat dinner at the American Club's signature restaurant, **The Immigrant Dining Room & Winery Bar**. The restaurant is often ranked the state's best on numerous surveys and scales. It has seven dining rooms, each with a different European theme (such as France, Holland, Germany, Scandinavia, and England). Expect impressive dishes such as Maine lobster bisque, pan-roasted black bass, and white truffle-crusted lamb loin. Men are required to wear jackets to dinner; resort evening attire is appropriate for women.

Just before bed, enjoy the waters in your relaxing, massaging, and feature-heavy Kohler tub.

Day Two
MORNING

Rise for a breakfast with history in the **Wisconsin Room** in the American Club. Set in the former dining hall for the Kohler Company's immigrant employees, this restaurant serves regional food in a room decorated with an ethnographic map of Wisconsin hanging on the wall, leaded glass windows etched with labor-related axioms, oak paneling, and antique chandeliers. Linger in the hall just outside the Wisconsin Room, where you can look at the line illustrations and read about famous Wisconsinites and people important to Wisconsin, such as Father Jacques Marquette, Soloman Juneau (the "father of Milwaukee"), John Bascom, John Muir, and Edward A. Birge.

After breakfast, take the resort's free shuttle to the 500-acre **River Wildlife** for the 9:00 a.m. **winter bird hike**. *[See "A Winter Walk at River Wildlife" sidebar.]* River Wildlife is the American Club's private hunting and wilderness preserve located along the Sheboygan River near the Blackwolf Run golf course. After the bird hike, for a day-pass access fee, you can **winter hike** 25 miles of trails or **cross-country ski** on three miles through some of the most pristine and unspoiled lands in Wisconsin. River Wildlife also offers **clay and trap shooting** and **pheasant hunting**.

And every Saturday at 12:30 p.m., you can attend a **snowshoe clinic** at the American Club's **Sports Core**, after which you are encouraged to rent snowshoes and take off exploring out the facility's back door. *[See "A Snowshoe for You" sidebar.]*

AFTERNOON

Back at the American Club, eat lunch at **The Horse & Plow** restaurant. The building was the former taproom for Kohler Company employees. You'll eat on tables made from the floors of the company's old bowling alley and soak in the ambiance of a they-don't-make-'em-like-this-anymore pub with brass fixtures and stained-glass windows. There are more than 80 regional bottled beers and 12 Wisconsin beers on tap to accompany hearty sandwiches and burgers, such as the Wisconsin burger, topped with Wisconsin cheddar cheese on a Sheboygan hard roll.

If you planned your weekend to coincide with **Christmas Kohler**, you can spend the rest of the day partaking in all of the festivities. Attend the Holiday Afternoon Tea in the Wisconsin Room or listen to the carolers in the library. On the American Club grounds at the Waelderhaus, a replica of a house found in Bergenzerald, Austria, you can vote for your favorite display at the Annual Gingerbread Village Festival.

If a quieter weekend is more your style, you may want to make the trip to the **Kettle Moraine State Forest–Northern Unit** a short distance away in Cambellsport. Sheboygan County's portion of the state forest includes 14,865 acres along the western boundary of the county. Across the impressive terrain created by gouging glaciers are 71 miles of picturesque **winter hiking** trails, 58 miles of groomed **snowmobile** trails, 15 miles of **cross-country ski** trails, as well as extensive areas and facilities for **winter camping, tobogganing,** and just plain, old appreciation of the outdoors.

One of the most popular events at the American Club is the **Dessert/Wine Tasting** every Saturday from 3:00 p.m. to 4:00 p.m.—offered *only* in winter [*see "An Afternoon of Wine Tasting" sidebar*]. Held in the American Club Winery, the event treats you to tastings of several wines with samples of delectable desserts, all under the tutelage of an expert sommelier. Imagine experiencing the flavors of late-harvest wines accompanied by tidbits of rich cheeses and chocolates.

The American Club's winery is a showcase for "Le Verre de Vin," the most state-of-the-art wine preservation system available. Early in spring, wineries vie to get their products on the club's prestigious list of over 600 wines. If you must spend this winter afternoon indoors, you couldn't ask for a better way to pass the time.

EVENING

This evening, you'll dine at the site of the 2004 Professional Golfers' Association (PGA) championship, **Whistling Straits**. Nine miles northeast of Kohler at the Pete Dye–designed golf course along Lake Michigan, the Whistling Straits Clubhouse resembles a farmhouse in the Irish countryside. Feast on American cuisine with a British Isles flair in a rustic setting—post-and-beam ceiling, fireplace, wood floors, and soft music. This intimate restaurant features not only excellent food, but also exceptional service. The emphasis is on seafood, and the sea bass is delectable. Add potato leek soup, a spinach salad, and New York–style, deep-fried cheesecake with bananas-foster sauce for dessert. The restaurant is closed in January and February, so indulge here in November, December, or March.

Back at the American Club, take a romantic **carriage ride** around the village of Kohler.

Day Three
MORNING

If you're an early riser, enjoy a breakfast buffet at The Horse & Plow or wait until 10:00 a.m. and have Sunday brunch in the Wisconsin Room.

A visit to Kohler at any time of year wouldn't be considered complete without a stop at the 36,000-square-foot **Kohler Design Center**. Here, the international manufacturer of bathroom

A WINTER WALK AT RIVER WILDLIFE

You can hear voices in the woods at River Wildlife every Saturday morning. At this 500-acre wilderness preserve, naturalist Debbie Denzer leads a group of American Club visitors on weekend walks, teaching them how to identify the trees, animals, and topographical features they see as they travel along the woodland trails. Winter walks are a special favorite for Debbie: first of all, the ground is harder, making the trails easier to traverse; and the snow and quiet in the winter woods makes animal tracks and sounds stand out in relief.

Debbie's tours start out from the Blackwolf Run Clubhouse with a walk over the Sheboygan River on a footbridge. She happily advises her charges to be on the lookout for foxes, coyotes, pheasants, and geese. It is soon clear that her trained eyes notice things in the woods that most of us never see. She points out a trail the deer have carved to the river and a great horned owl perched in a bur oak. She mentions that downy hawthorns are forest-edge trees and that they are "allelopathic"—meaning they reduce competing plant species in an area. Ash trees are growing here, too, which could, in turn, shade out the hawthorns. Debbie even draws attention to the shapes beside the trail that look like Indian mounds. The area has a strong tradition of mound builders, and she wonders whether the same people who built the mounds in nearby Sheboygan also came here. A gull cries overhead.

Debbie names the trees all around and points out their distinguishing features:

❄ Aspen trees are the first to bloom; they have a yellow-green leaf. They seem to like wet feet, preferring sand and clay.

❄ American beech has a smooth bark.

❄ The bark of an ash has a diamond-shape pattern. Its branches are big and heavy.

❄ Red oak has smooth, flat bark. If you look up the tree, the bark takes on a shiny-looking appearance on its plates.

❄ White pine has needle bundles in fives.

❄ Black cherry has bark that peels up in square plates. If you have a very straight black cherry tree, it is valuable in lumber terms.

There is a math formula to determine the age of a tree, which involves the diameter of the tree at breast height. Debbie hugs a tree she thinks is 85 years old. Three white-tailed deer watch quietly as the hikers turn to make their way back. The deer, at least, are easy to identify. Passing under the bur oak, the great horned owl takes flight, stretching its wings out the full eight feet. Debbie says it is the largest nighttime raptor in this area.

Fall leaves crunch underfoot as the hikers walk the winter-hardened trails. A cold wind kicks up, and the trees bend and moan. There are voices in the winter woods at River Wildlife. But this time, it's the trees who are talking.

A SNOWSHOE FOR YOU

We can thank North American Indians for inventing snowshoes. Native Americans living in the sub-Arctic, Northeast, and Northern Woodlands wore snowshoes so they could travel on top of the snow— much easier than trying to break a trail through the deep stuff.

Snowshoes act essentially like a flotation device; the wider distribution of your weight keeps you on top of the snow.

Native Americans made snowshoes by bending steamed wood to form a frame and then filling it with netting made of sinew. They fastened the snowshoes to their feet with leather straps. Modern wooden snowshoes still retain this design and come in three styles:

❉ **BEAR PAW:** the type trappers used. Oblong and short, they can get into small areas.

❉ **ALASKAN:** for open-country areas. They are narrower than a bear-paw shoe, with a long tail for going distances in deep powder.

❉ **OJIBWA:** a shoe designed for distance, with a flat nose. These shoes were designed for brushier areas (such as you find in Wisconsin); the flat nose of the shoe displaces grasses as you walk.

Bindings for wooden snowshoes today come in two styles: "A" and "H" bindings, each of which looks like the letter it's named for.

If you can walk, you can snowshoe. It's probably the most accessible winter sport there is, to get to the most inaccessible places—those beyond the trails.

Debbie Denzer describes the difference between the various types of snowshoes at the American Club's Sports Core.

JOHN T. ANDREWS

AN AFTERNOON OF WINE TASTING

I once thought tasting wine was a matter of removing the cork and drinking. That is, until I attended the Dessert/Wine Tasting held in the American Club Winery one winter afternoon.

Wine, I learned, is not only a matter of taste but of sight, smell, and feel of the glass in your hand and on your lips. Sight: is it star-bright or dull? Smell: do you detect fruits, or spices? What is its "nose"? The glass: everything that comes in contact when you drink wine affects its flavor. A thin piece of glass should touch your lips when you taste wine; it just enhances the experience.

In fact, said our sommelier that afternoon, one glassware company makes a different glass for every grape. A wider glass will put the wine at the center of your palette; a narrower one puts it in the front. Wine should be poured so it sits far below the center of the glass. The Immigrant uses real glassware and stemware, and the glasses are all hand polished.

The American Club has 600 wines on its list, and during my afternoon we were offered several "late harvest wines." These are wines produced from grapes that were allowed to overripen and dry on the vine, making their flavor more concentrated and complex.

Wine taste is determined by a lot of things. Like the soil the grapes were grown in. Or how hard they had to work to get water. The more stress, the better the wine. I thought they

The American Club's sommelier instructs guests on the subtleties of combining wine with food at the Dessert/Wine Tasting presentation.

all tasted wonderful.

But then the cheese and chocolates—"the allies of wine"—were brought out, and I didn't know which tasted better. We were served three-, five-, and seven-year cheddars along with chocolate-covered strawberries made only in the fall. Chocolates, we were told, pair well with the sweet nature of dessert wines. I know they always paired well with me.

We then heard about what went into pricing wines. The high cost of the late harvest wines we were enjoying is due to the process of making it: how many grapes were left on the branch, how long they took to dry (raisinating), and the quantity of a particular wine produced. Some wines are "allocated"; for instance, the United States may get only 500 cases of a certain wine, and Wisconsin may get three of those cases. Luckily for me that afternoon, the American Club is a dominant player in the wine market in Wisconsin. Some bottles in the club's collection sell for as much as $1,400.

We talked about oak barrels, which impart their oaken flavor to the wine. A new oak barrel can cost $700. A good vintner will use a barrel until the oakiness is waning—then sell it on the secondary market. Some will cheat and use sawdust or oak chips to extend the oak flavor.

As we were getting ready to leave our comfy chairs, delicious wines, and delectable chocolates and cheeses, we heard some good news. Our sommelier assured us that we would be able to purchase some very good wines at our local retailers. Good wines, he said, can come in every price range, from $30 to $200.

And didn't he say that drinking wine is all about "your perception" anyway? The sight, smell, and feel of the wine in your glass and on your tongue? Sitting at home now in my living room on a winter night, with the smell of wood burning in my fireplace and a real glass in my hand, my $20 wine tastes better than I thought it would. Or maybe I have just learned how to appreciate it more.

---

fixtures showcases the company's early factory and factory-town history in an incredible "Great Wall of China," a floor-to-ceiling display of plumbing fixtures in all shapes, sizes, and colors. Also featured are a theater and ceramic art gallery. In the basement is the famous "toilet museum." Admission to the museum is free, and the hours are 8:00 a.m. to 5:00 p.m. on weekdays, and 10:00 a.m. to 4:00 p.m. on weekends and holidays (closed Thanksgiving and Christmas).

EVENING

Conclude your weekend in Kohler "dashing through the snow" with a **sleigh ride** at **Bulitz Carriage & Sleigh Rides,** just minutes away from the American Club, or by having the most relaxing time you've ever had in a tub at the **Kohler Waters Spa.**

From among a list of 50 luxurious treatment options at the Kohler Waters Spa, the most wonderful is the "River Bath." Once dressed in your plush robe and slippers, you'll be led past a cascading waterfall and pool to your soothing "bath room," outfitted with a gas fireplace, pots of bamboo shoots, soft lights, and New Age music. First, you'll be asked to walk across a smooth-stone path in your bare feet to connect you with the earth's elements. Then watch as seaweed extracts and special salts are added to the water flowing into your huge, Jacuzzi-type tub. Surrounded by the smell of hollyhock, you'll lower yourself in privacy into a tub equipped with its own waterfall and light therapy: beautiful blues, tangerines, and soft beiges envelope the room at your command. You'll swear the water is the softest you've ever had next to your skin.

After the River Bath, you'll receive a warm oil massage that will relax you down to every toe and finger. The only motivation to get up will be the thought of walking by the very calming sound of the cascading waters you passed on the way in and walking out into your next glorious winter weekend.

FOR MORE INFORMATION

KOHLER VISITOR INFORMATION
444 Highland Dr., Kohler, WI 53044
(920) 457-8000 or (800) 344-2838
www.destinationkohler.com

SHEBOYGAN COUNTY CHAMBER OF COMMERCE & CONVENTION AND VISITOR BUREAU
712 Riverfront Dr. Suite 101
Sheboygan, WI 53081, (920) 457-9495
or (800) 457-9497, www.sheboygan.org

WINTER ATTRACTIONS

BULITZ CARRIAGE & SLEIGH RIDES
(Carriage rides at the American Club. Sleigh and hayrides on the farm, with a warming house and bonfire.) N5924 Range Line Rd. Kohler, WI 53044
(920) 467-6502

ELLWOOD H. MAY ENVIRONMENTAL PARK (MAYWOOD)
3615 Mueller Rd., Sheboygan, WI 53081
(920) 459-3906, www.gomaywood.org

EVERGREEN PARK
3330 Calumet Dr., Sheboygan, WI 53083
(920) 459-3366

INDIAN MOUND PARK
5000 S. Ninth St., Sheboygan, WI 53081
(920) 459-3444

KETTLE MORAINE STATE FOREST–NORTHERN UNIT
Forest Headquarters, N1765 Highway G
Campbellsport, WI 53010
(262) 626-2116, www.wiparks.net

KOHLER–ANDRAE STATE PARK
1020 Beach Park Lane, Sheboygan, WI 53081
(920) 451-4080
www.wiparks.net

KOHLER DESIGN CENTER
444 Highland Dr., Kohler, WI 53044
(920) 457-3699, www.destinationkohler.com

KOHLER PARK DUNES STATE NATURAL AREA
Kohler–Andrae State Park, 1020 Beach Park Ln.
Sheboygan, WI 53081, (920) 451-4080 or (888) 947-2757, www.wiparks.net

KOHLER WATERS SPA
501 Highland Dr., Kohler, WI 53044
(920) 457-7777, www.destinationkohler.com

OLD PLANK ROAD TRAIL
712 Riverfront Dr., Suite 101
Sheboygan, WI 53081
(920) 459-3060 or (800) 457-9497

RIVER WILDLIFE
444 Highland Dr., Kohler, WI 53044
(920) 457-0134, www.destinationkohler.com

SPORTS CORE
100 Willow Creek Dr., Kohler, WI 53044
(920) 457-4444, www.destinationkohler.com

WINTER FESTIVALS

FOOD & WINE EXPERIENCE—late October. The American Club. Enjoy three days of demonstrations, seminars, and tastings by renowned chefs and vintners. (800) 344-2838 or www.destinationkohler.com.

IN CELEBRATION OF CHOCOLATE—Friday prior to Thanksgiving. The American Club. Indulge yourself in an evening of chocolate with an array of desserts, gourmet chocolates, and tortes. (800) 344-2838 or www.destinationkohler.com.

HMONG NEW YEAR CELEBRATION—late November. Sheboygan Armory. Sheboygan's Hmong community invites the public to share in its culture. Children's games, speakers, Hmong clothing, music, and dance. (920) 458-0808 or www.hmaaweb.org.

CHRISTMAS KOHLER—Friday after Thanksgiving to December 23. The American Club kicks off Christmas with a menu of activities. Breakfast with Santa, wine tasting, dancing, and more. (800) 344-2838 or www.destinationkohler.com.

MAYWOOD'S WISHING FOR WINTER—early to mid-December. Ellwood H. May Environmental Park (Maywood). 6:00–9:00 p.m. An indoor and outdoor program that features a self-guided evening hike along trails of twinkling lights with holiday character encounters. Enjoy roasting marshmallows and hot cocoa around the campfire, storytelling, nature crafts, and holiday music. (920) 459-3906 or www.gomaywood.org.

FESTIVAL OF TREES—early December. Sheboygan Armory. View decorated full-size and table-top trees, wreaths, gingerbread houses, and stockings. Music and refreshments. (920) 457-3371 or www. sheboyganfestivaloftrees.org.

POLAR BEAR SWIM—New Year's Day. Northside Beach, Sheboygan. 1:00 p.m. For more than 25 years, hundreds of daring swimmers have charged into Lake Michigan's ice floes dressed as sea monsters, cave people, and diaper-clad New Year's babies. Music, entertainment, brat fry, and refreshments in the Armory. (920) 467-8436.

CANDLELIGHT SKI/HIKE—mid-January and mid-February. Kohler–Andrae State Park. 6:00–9:00 p.m. Cross-country ski or hike by the light of almost 200 tiki torches. Warm up afterwards by the fireplace; refreshments available in the heated shelter. (920) 451-4080 or www.dnr.state.wi.us/ org.

MAYWOOD FLAPJACK DAY—mid-March. Ellwood H. May Environmental Park (Maywood). Celebrate the Wisconsin tradition of sugar-mapling with a guided tour of the forest and observation of the entire process from tapping trees to boiling sap. Taste pure maple syrup on flapjacks. Lumberjack Olympics, live music, and horse-drawn wagon rides. (920) 459-3906 or www.go maywood.org.

RESTAURANTS
CHARCOAL INN *(lunch and dinner)*
1313 S. Eighth St., Sheboygan, WI 53081
(920) 458-6988

CUCINA *(lunch and dinner)*
The Shops at Woodlake Kohler
725 Woodlake Rd., Kohler, WI 53044
(920) 452-3888, www.destinationkohler.com

THE HORSE & PLOW *(lunch and dinner)*
The American Club
444 Highland Dr., Kohler, WI 53044
(920) 457-8888, www.destinationkohler.com

THE IMMIGRANT DINING ROOM & WINERY BAR
(Friday and Saturday, dinner)
The American Club
444 Highland Dr., Kohler, WI 53044
(920) 457-8888, www.destinationkohler.com

NEW YORK ON 8TH *(lunch and dinner)*
632 N. Eighth St., Sheboygan, WI 53081
(920) 457-6565

SCENIC BAR & RESTAURANT
(lunch and dinner)
1635 Indiana Ave., Sheboygan, WI 53081
(920) 452-2881

TRATTORIA STEFANO *(breakfast, lunch, and dinner)*
522 S. Eighth St., Sheboygan, WI 53081
(920) 452-8455

WHISTLING STRAITS CLUBHOUSE
(lunch and dinner)
N8501 Lakeshore Rd., Sheboygan, WI 53083,
(920) 565-4199, www.destinationkohler.com

WISCONSIN ROOM *(breakfast, dinner, and Sunday brunch)*
The American Club
444 Highland Dr., Kohler, WI 53044
(920) 457-8888, www.destinationkohler.com

LODGING
THE AMERICAN CLUB
444 Highland Dr., Kohler, WI 53044
(920) 457-8000 or (800) 344-2838
www.destinationkohler.com

BLUE HARBOR RESORT & CONFERENCE CENTER
725 Blue Harbor Dr., Sheboygan, WI 53081
(920) 452-2900, www.blueharborresort.com

BROWNSTONE INN
1227 N. Seventh St., Sheboygan, WI 53081
(920) 451-0644 or (877) 279-6786
www.brownstoneinn.com

ENGLISH MANOR BED & BREAKFAST
632 Michigan Ave., Sheboygan, WI 53081
(920) 208-1952 or (800) 557-5277
www.english-manor.com

INN ON WOODLAKE
705 Woodlake Rd., Kohler, WI 53044
(920) 452-7800 or (800) 919-3600
www.innonwoodlake.com

LAKE VIEW MANSION BED & BREAKFAST
303 St. Clair Ave., Sheboygan, WI 53081
(920) 457-5253, www.lakeviewmansion.com

Chapter Twelve
RIVER WINTER
La Crosse/Westby/Coon Valley

I T'S IMPOSSIBLE TO GO TO LA CROSSE and not come away with a respect for the greatness of rivers, a feel for the grandeur of nature, and a strong sense of history.

Not only is La Crosse a Mississippi River town, it's also the place where two more rivers meet: the Black and the La Crosse. The three rivers have shaped life in this city, and their influence is seen everywhere, from Riverside Park on the shores of the mighty Mississippi, to the Great River Road and the La Crosse River State Trail. Virtually untouched by the great Ice Age glaciers that scraped across much of Wisconsin, La Crosse has bluffs, coulees, and woods that stand unchanged since the beginning of time. Grandad Bluff dominates the landscape, and from near its top, 500 feet above its surroundings, you can see across three states—Wisconsin, Minnesota, and Iowa.

Just as impressive as its physical beauty is La Crosse's cultural history. French explorers, under the leadership of Father Louis Hennepin, first saw the convergence of the three rivers here in 1680. When the French saw the Winnebago playing a fast-paced game that used long-handled racquets with lattice heads, it reminded them of the aristocratic game of tennis called "la crosse," and thus the city got its name.

During the Civil War, La Crosse's position on the waterways solidified its importance and standing in history. When traffic became obstructed on the lower Mississippi, the U. S. government became convinced it had to reinvest in Mississippi-channel transportation over the next 50 years. Eventually, La Crosse became the major link in the river's travel network between St. Paul and Iowa.

More than 1,600 steamboats stopped in La Crosse in 1879, the most that had docked in any city north of St. Louis at the time. In 1883, former river pilot Samuel Clemens, a.k.a. Mark Twain, wrote about his admiration for the area in his book, *Life on the Mississippi.* He called La Crosse a "choice town." Today, many of the structures he saw are still standing in the downtown district, which has won several awards for its more than 90 historic buildings.

La Crosse, with a population of 51,000, is the state's largest city on the Mississippi, and

Grandad Bluff is the number one scenic spot in western Wisconsin. In winter, it takes on an even more powerful profile, standing in relief from the pared down foliage. Rivers become more complicated and take on a dual personality in winter: Some sections freeze for ice fishing and skating, while open portions act as a homing beacon for eagles, which swoop down to hook a fish. The majestic birds add to the greatness, the grandeur, even the history that is La Crosse.

Day One
MORNING

You can't miss **Grandad Bluff**—the 500-foot cliff looms ahead of you on Main Street as you come into town. Just head straight for it by following Main Street east until it becomes Bliss Road. This aptly named spot will easily become one of your favorites in all of western Wisconsin.

Your reason for heading straight to Grandad Bluff is to acclimate yourself to La Crosse. From where you stand at the top, you'll be able to see the Mississippi Valley and take in three states: Wisconsin, Minnesota, and Iowa. And, after looking out and across at all that lies below you, look down at your feet. You're standing on 15-million-year-old geology that created the great Mississippi Valley.

AFTERNOON

After savoring that sweeping view, head to La Crosse's historic downtown district. Stop for lunch at **Doc Powell's Brewery and Pub.** Order a warm bowl of soup or choose a hearty helping of pasta. Leave room for the bread pudding dessert—Doc Powell's is known for its homemade breads.

Just a short drive from downtown La Crosse is the 800-acre **Hixon Forest,** and you may want to spend the rest of your afternoon exploring its heavy woods, high ridges, and old prairies from an earlier Wisconsin. There, in the shadow of Grandad Bluff, you can **winter hike** or **cross-country ski** on 13 miles of trails. In fact, the **Hixon Forest Nature Center** is the hub of a wide network of trails that extend throughout the city.

We have the Hixon Forest to enjoy today because of one woman's caring for the land. The bluffs just west of La Crosse that the forest comprises had been logged in 1909, and quarrying was set to begin the next year. Logging had left the area virtually bare. *[See "Sustaining Wisconsin's Forests" sidebar.]* To stop the destruction around Grandad Bluff, in the southwest corner of the forest, Mrs. Ellen Hixon bought the land and donated it to the city of La Crosse for a park. Today, many of the forest's steep bluffs harbor remnant prairies, residuals of oak savannas, known as "goat prairies"—left only because they were too steep for agricultural plows. Formerly, there were vast stretches of prairie in the La Crosse area and throughout southern Wisconsin, but only these small patches remain.

During your afternoon outing in the forest, you could meet up with foxes, coyotes, deer, turkey vultures, and hawks. Peregrine falcons, an endangered species, are sometimes sighted here, and bald eagles are common winter visitors.

If you'd prefer to spend the early part of the afternoon indoors on ice, go to the **Green Island Ice Arena** on Seventh Street. Public **ice-skating** is held Monday through Friday, from noon until 2:00 p.m.

LA CROSSE AREA CONVENTION & VISITORS BUREAU

Grandad Bluff is the number-one scenic spot in western Wisconsin. Its ancient features are even more impressive with a dusting of snow.

SUSTAINING WISCONSIN'S FORESTS

The many Wisconsin forests that make our cross-country skiing, snowshoeing, winter hiking, and snowmobiling activities today so scenic and moving weren't here as little as 125 years ago.

But the good news is that today Wisconsin is still actually gaining forest—not losing it. Wisconsin's total land area is 34.7 million acres; and 16 million acres, or 46 percent of our state's lands, are covered with trees. Most of our forested places are in the northern part of the state.

Many southern Wisconsin forests were cleared for agriculture by the late 1800s, and forests in the north were heavily cut for timber by the early 1900s. Almost all of the mature trees standing today are less than 125 years old. Thousands of acres of pines were planted across the state in the 1930s by the Civilian Conservation Corps, and Wisconsinites can be thankful for their forward-looking work. The state now has more forest land than at any time since inventories began in 1936.

Today, logging is still done in the state, and occasionally you may see large trucks carrying timbers on our state highways. According to Vern Everson, forest resource analyst with the Wisconsin Department of Natural Resources Forestry Division, of every 1,000 live trees more than 10 feet tall in Wisconsin, 80 will die this year from severe weather, insect damage, crowding, disease, or old age. Only four of the thousand will be harvested by loggers. However, 98 new trees will grow past the 10-foot mark during the year. Therefore, in Wisconsin, annual wood growth exceeds harvest for most species.

Harvesting trees is not necessarily bad for the forest, either. The forest most hospitable to the greatest diversity of plants and animals is one with young, medium-age, and old trees and a variety of tree species. Since fires, insects, and tree diseases are better controlled today, one way to make room for younger trees is to harvest those nearing the end of their life cycle. Cutting trees properly not only mimics natural events like fire but provides jobs and hundreds of useful wood products. The alternative would be to use wood imported from places that may not manage forests in a sustainable fashion as we do in Wisconsin.

Your base this weekend will have a decidedly historical theme when you stay at one of La Crosse's most historic homes, **The Celtic Inn**. The inn was once the residence of Dr. Wendell A. Anderson, a two-time mayor of La Crosse (1899–1901 and 1907–1909). The 1890 home is on the City of La Crosse Registry of Historic Places and is listed within the 10th and Cass Street National Historic District. The Celtic Inn calls itself an "Irish bed and breakfast," and it lives up to its name. The rooms all have an Irish theme, and every bed is covered with a handmade quilt. Contact the inn for special winter packages, which can include a **carriage ride** around downtown La Crosse, a night's lodging, and dinner in town. The inn is also deaf-friendly.

EVENING

Tonight's dining venue is full of La Crosse history and entertaining tales. The **Freight House Restaurant**, located near downtown's Riverside Park, was once owned by the

JOHN T. ANDREWS

For a change of pace, the Green Island Ice Arena brings some winter fun indoors.

Chicago, Milwaukee, and St. Paul Railroad. The building was constructed in 1880 and is on the National Register of Historic Places. Railroad mementos surround you from the moment you walk in—parked outside, in fact, is an antique railroad car in which Buffalo Bill Cody supposedly once rode. The bar and dining rooms feature large fireplaces, and on Friday and Saturday nights, some of the region's finest musicians appear. The Freight House is famed for its naturally aged, hand-cut steaks, but it also offers a wide selection of seafood entrées. The Freight House's wine selection was recognized by *Wine Spectator* magazine with the Award of Excellence.

After dinner, take a walking tour through **Riverside Park,** located where the La Crosse and Black rivers join the Mississippi. A 25-foot, 25-ton sculpture of Hiawatha stands guard here. Native American legends say that where three rivers meet, no natural disaster will befall. So far, the legend has proved true. If you happen to be in town from late November through the end of December, drive or walk through the **Rotary Lights Display** on the grounds of the park, decorated with more than 750,000 lights and dozens of luminaries. Or go back to the Celtic Inn and curl up with a good book in the great room, called "The Rectory," sitting close to the candlelit fireplace before going off to your comforting and luxurious bed.

The Rotary Lights Display on the grounds of Riverside Park lights up the shores of the Mississippi River on December nights.

Day Two
MORNING

One of the joys of staying at the Celtic Inn is the breakfast basket that you'll find outside your door in the morning. Jumbo homemade muffins or scones, three or four different kinds of fresh seasonal fruit, vanilla yogurt or applesauce, orange juice, and coffee, tea, or hot chocolate appear in a wicker basket as if by magic.

If you'd like to go out for breakfast, go to **Fayze's Restaurant and Bakery**, located on Fourth Street. Often voted the "Best Place for Breakfast and Lunch" by La Crosse *Tribune* newspaper readers, Fayze's is a treat. The vegetarian omelet is a delicious concoction of green olives, tomatoes, mushrooms, and onions and is far bigger than you can imagine. Bakery items include European breads, muffins, cookies, and their world-famous "talame" bread. For a breakfast winter warmer, try the "Indian Summer"—hot apple cider, Berentzen apple schnapps, whipped cream, and a cinnamon stick. Or go for the "Chocolate Heaven," Godiva liqueur and hot chocolate topped with whipped cream. Of course, there's always the Wisconsin favorite, a Tom and Jerry—egg batter with rum and topped with nutmeg.

The heights of Grandad Bluff have probably suggested **downhill skiing** to you a time or two this weekend, and this morning you'll have a chance to hit some slopes. **Mt. La Crosse** is just two miles south of the city on Highway 35 and has been a winter tradition for resi-

EXTREME WINTER: SKI JUMPING

Ski jumping is one of the world's most beautiful and thrilling winter sports, and the Midwest, including Wisconsin, has historically been one of the nation's ski-jumping centers.

Ski jumping began in 1809 when a Norwegian lieutenant named Olaf Rye wanted to show his troops just how brave he was. In front of his soldiers, he made a jump of 31 feet, becoming the first known ski jumper. In 1860, a Norwegian carpenter and ski-maker, Sondre Nordheim, jumped a distance of 98 feet. Local jumping competitions were soon being held across Norway, and referees and rules were added.

In 1880, Scandinavian immigrants introduced ski jumping to Canada. The sport made its first appearance in the Olympics in 1924 in Chamonix, France. In 1985, a Swedish ski jumper named Jan Boklov positioned his airborne skis in a V-shaped position, only to be penalized by the judges, who preferred to see the skis locked together in a parallel alignment under the skier's body. Boklov's innovative technique, however, allowed for 28 percent more lift than the parallel ski style, and it was soon copied by most of his peers.

Skiers start each jump by climbing a hill or tower and skiing down a slick, curved track called the "inrun." Taking a deep breath at the top of the run, skiers push off with one long stride. Crouching low to gather speed, they shoot down the slide toward the lip of the take-off. Once there, the skiers jump hard, spring into the air, and thrust all body weight forward. Now launched into space, the jumpers whistle through the air at nearly 60 miles per hour.

Jumpers stay in the air for three or four seconds, with a little bend at the hips and holding their arms in a "fish" or "torpedo" position for minimum wind resistance. They try to land smoothly, with bent knees, on the landing hill. As they ski toward the finish, the hill flattens to help them slow down. The flatter part is called the "outrun." The jumper snowplows into the outrun and glides to a stop.

Judges lining the incline mark where the ski jumper landed. Form counts just as much as jump distance in determining a jumper's score. The sum of distance and style points for two separate jumps usually gives the skier his total tournament points.

The ski jump barely takes 15 seconds, yet it is one of the most intense performances in all of winter sports.

---

dents and visitors alike since 1959. Mt. La Crosse bundles up the fun in a 516-foot vertical drop, 19 runs and trails, three double-chair lifts, a rope tow, snowmaking, and ski lessons. Skiers can choose from the easy **Mileaway Run** to the expert-only rated **Damnation**. Mt. La Crosse is open until 9:00 p.m. for **nighttime skiing** and also includes a terrain park for **snowboarding.**

AFTERNOON

For lunch, grab a bowl of homemade soup or chili at **Mt. La Crosse's chalet** or head back into town for a "bread cone" sandwich at **Mr. D's Restaurant & Bakery.** The cones are made out of bread and filled with chicken, taco, tuna, or egg salad; or try the hot "Mozambique" sandwich, grilled chicken and smoked ham with walnuts, baby Swiss, and Creole mustard.

You have your choice this afternoon of spending it either as a sports spectator or participant. If you're lucky enough to be in the La Crosse area in mid-February, don't miss the **Snowflake Ski Club Super Tour Jumping Tournament** in Westby *[see "Extreme Winter: Ski Jumping" sidebar]*. The scenic drive there is just the first thrill of the afternoon. You'll pass through horse country, with its rolling, open pastures and sun-drenched fields nestled between snow-covered hills. Westby is located on a ridge between the Mississippi River's Coulee Region and the Kickapoo River Valley at the junction of Highways 14/61 and 27.

Get ready to watch perhaps winter's most extreme sport! More than 70 world-class jumpers from 11 countries, including Norway, Finland, Canada, Japan, Austria, and Germany, soar 300 feet through the air as they jump Timber Coulee, a 374-foot hill—the same size hill used for jumping events in the Winter Olympics. The Westby jump is one of only four of its size in North America. The jumpers often reach speeds of 60 miles per hour traveling down the hill. For your own extreme enjoyment, climb the hundreds of steps to the top of the hill. If you prefer the warmth of your car, park along the outrun and watch the ski jumpers as you listen to results broadcast on a local radio station. Loudspeakers announce the results of each jump, as well.

While in the quaint town of Westby, stop by **Dregne's Scandinavian Gifts**. The store features everything Norwegian, including warm Norwegian sweaters, lefse grills, krumkake irons, Danish wrought-iron candleholders, books on Norway and Iceland, and the area's only year-round Christmas shop.

If you'd rather be part of the action this afternoon, access the **La Crosse River State Trail**, a 24-miler in the La Crosse River Valley between Sparta and La Crosse. **Snowmobile** or **winter hike** on packed limestone screenings along the abandoned grade of the Chicago & North Western Railroad. A link between the Elroy-Sparta Trail and the Great River Trail, the La Crosse River State Trail generally runs parallel to the La Crosse River through coulee country, ridges with steep wooded valleys eroded by water that helped give the La Crosse area its nickname, "God's Country." Stop along the way to photograph the panoramic valley vista spread out before you.

EVENING

Tonight, dine with a view of the mighty Mississippi River from **Piggy's Restaurant.** Pork cuts, aged steaks, and prime rib are smoked on the premises using hickory and apple wood from the surrounding hills. Amid a decor of dark woods, antiques, stained glass, and chandeliers, you can relax and appreciate the gifts—even the fuel that cooked your food—La Crosse has given you this weekend.

Day Three
MORNING AND AFTERNOON

Today will be a mix-and-match menu of winter activities that you can customize for your schedule.

After breakfast and checking out of your accommodations, head to Coon Valley, which takes its name from Coon Creek, a clear, cold stream that runs through the village. The region has miles of pristine Class A trout streams and is rich with Norwegian history and

Open rivers act as a homing beacon for bald eagles, the majestic birds that grace a La Crosse winter.

traditions. The **Norskedalen Nature & Heritage Center** celebrates and preserves them.

Approximately 16 miles southeast of La Crosse, Norskedalen began as an outdoor laboratory in an arboretum and grew to include many surrounding Norwegian and Bohemian homesteader lands. This 400-acre "Norwegian Valley" is a living-history preserve of pioneer settlements, including log cabins, farm buildings, and craft shops. Plenty of ongoing events take place throughout the year; in the winter months, a different program is held every Sunday at 2:00 p.m. Past afternoons have included programs such as "Myths and Legends of Old Norway" and "What Are You Reading this Winter?" Norskedalen has four miles of **cross-country ski trails** that snake through the arboretum.

Within the La Crosse city environs, there are three other venues for cross-country skiing. **Goose Island Park** on County Road GI, just three miles south of downtown La Crosse, offers easy skiing on two 1.9-mile marked trails. **Bluebird Springs Recreation Area** on Smith Valley Road has a moderately difficult five-mile trail through wooded and open spaces. Six miles of trails are groomed at **Raymond C. Bice Forest Preserve** on Fourth Street.

If you'd like to wrap up your weekend with a **snowmobile** outing, there are 130 miles of snowmobile trails in La Crosse County, eventually hooking up with another 650 miles of trails in the surrounding region. Seven local snowmobile clubs ensure that the trails are groomed to what seem to be interstate highway specifications. The La Crosse Area Convention & Visitors Bureau can provide maps.

It's easy to get hooked on the excitement of **ice fishing** in La Crosse—even for those who have never tried it. Here on the Mississippi River and its bountiful backwaters, the Black and La Crosse rivers, you'll find 118 species of fish, including popular game fish such

THE GREAT RIVER ROAD

A great river deserves a great way to see it. And Wisconsin's Great River Road along the Mississippi was developed so that the river's history and beauty could be appreciated and preserved.

The road is a 250-mile stretch of highway that flanks the Mississippi River on Wisconsin's western border. The road starts from Prescott in the north and runs to Kieler just above the Illinois state line in the south. The river towns in between, north to south, are: Diamond Bluff, Hager City, Bay City, Maiden Rock, Stockholm, Pepin, Nelson, Alma, Buffalo City, Cochrane, Fountain City, Centerville, Trempealeau, Holmen, Midway, Onalaska, La Crosse, Stoddard, Genoa, Victory, DeSoto, Ferryville, Lynxville, Prairie du Chien, Wyalusing, Bagley, Glen Haven, Cassville, Potosi, Tennyson, and Dickeyville. The road is nestled between the river on one side and bluffs on the other. Once in a while, it meanders a short way from the river to include scenic valleys and coulees.

The Hopewell Indians who once lived in the area left thousands of mounds here. As their culture evolved, they became known as the Oneota people, who farmed the rich soil of the river valley. By the time Europeans arrived in the area around 1673, the Oneota had been replaced by a group of Sioux Indians.

French missionary Jacques Marquette and explorer Louis Joliet were the first white people to come through the Mississippi River Valley area. Soon after, French forts were established and trading between the Europeans and Native Americans ensued. In a long string of clashes, the area changed hands from the Indians to the French to the British and finally to the Americans. Settlement began in Wisconsin soon after the Black Hawk War of 1832 between the Sauk Indians and American troops. In 1848, Wisconsin became a state.

Wisconsin was soon known for its logging industry and its place on the mighty river. The era of great steamboats, too, is part of the fabric of Wisconsin history. Indian mounds, abandoned quarries, old building ruins, 30-plus historical markers, and the boats that still ply the Mississippi tell the tales of this Wisconsin corridor along the Great River Road.

Whenever you're in one of Wisconsin's Mississippi River towns, look for the Great River Road. Travel a portion of it if you can. In winter's less frenetic traffic flow, you just may begin to know how the early peoples who lived here felt and appreciated its beauty in all seasons.

---

as walleye, northerns, yellow perch, and bluegills.

Be sure to map your route home via the **Great River Road** *[see "The Great River Road" sidebar]*. At the base of the bluffs and adjacent to the Mississippi River, the road goes from Prescott in the north to the Illinois border and is one of seven suggested American Drives per *Reader's Digest* magazine *[see also Chapter 18: Wintering Eagles and Frozen Fish (Prairie du Chien)]*.

What may be most appropriate for the close of your historical weekend is a last call at the 229-acre **Sunset Riding Stables** in La Crosse. You can make reservations to take a **hayride** or **sleigh ride** with Clydesdale horses, truly riding out into the sunset through La Crosse's wooded bluffs and past its great rivers.

Seven local snowmobile clubs in La Crosse keep more than a hundred miles of trails expertly groomed.

FOR MORE INFORMATION

LA CROSSE AREA CONVENTION & VISITORS BUREAU
410 Veterans Memorial Dr., La Crosse, WI 54601
(608) 782-2366 or (800) 658-9424
www.explorelacrosse.com

WINTER ATTRACTIONS

BLUEBIRD SPRINGS RECREATION AREA
N2833 Smith Valley Rd.
La Crosse, WI 54601 (608) 781-2267

DREGNE'S SCANDINAVIAN GIFTS
100 S. Main St., Westby, WI 54667
(688) 634-4414
www.explorewisconsin.com/Dregnes
ScandinavianGifts/index.html

GOOSE ISLAND PARK
W6488 County Road GI *(three miles south of La Crosse)*, Stoddard, WI 54658
(608) 788-7018, www.co.la-crosse.wi.us/
Departments/Facilities/index.htm

GRANDAD BLUFF
3200 Main St., La Crosse, WI 54601
(608) 789-7533

GREAT RIVER ROAD
(800) 658-9480 or www.greatriverroad.org

GREEN ISLAND ICE ARENA
2312 S. Seventh St., La Crosse, WI 54601
(608) 789-7199

HIXON FOREST AND NATURE CENTER
2702 Quarry Rd., La Crosse, WI 54601
(608) 784-0303, www.explorelacrosse.com

LA CROSSE RIVER STATE TRAIL
111 Milwaukee St., Sparta, WI 54656
(608) 269-4123 or (888) 540-8434
www.lacrosseriverstatetrail.org

MT. LA CROSSE
5460 S. Second St., La Crosse, WI 54601
(608) 788-0044 or (800) 426-3665
www.mtlacrosse.com

NORSKEDALEN NATURE & HERITAGE CENTER *(Friday, 8:00 a.m.-4:00 p.m.; Sunday, noon to 4:00 p.m)*
N455 O Ophus Rd.
Coon Valley, WI 54623
(608) 452-3424, www.norskedalen.org

RAYMOND C. BICE FOREST PRESERVE
400 N. Fourth St., La Crosse, WI 54601
(608) 785-9770
www.co.la-crosse.wi.us/Departments/Facilities/index.htm

RIVERSIDE PARK
410 E. Veterans Memorial Dr., La Crosse, WI
54601, (608) 782-2467

SUNSET RIDING STABLES
W4803 Meyer Rd., La Crosse, WI 54601
(608) 788-6629

WINTER FESTIVALS

HOLIDAY FOLK FAIR—mid-November. La
Crosse Center, 300 Harborview Plaza, La Crosse,
WI 54601. Wares showcased by more than 130
arts-and-crafts exhibitors. Items are geared
specifically to the holidays. (608) 255-4646 or
www.lacrossecenter.com.

**ROTARY LIGHTS DISPLAY—late November
through December.** Riverside Park. The park is
decorated with more than 750,000 lights and
dozens of luminaries during the holiday season.
Santa and his live reindeer greet visitors each
evening. Stroll or drive through the display from
5:00 to 10:00 p.m. (800) 658-9424 or www.
rotarylights.org.

**NORSKEDALEN OLD-FASHIONED CHRIST-
MAS—early December.** Norskedalen Nature &
Heritage Center. 10:00 a.m.–4:00 p.m. Experience
Norwegian holiday traditions with favorite foods,
entertainment, a bake sale, decorated pioneer
homesteads, wagon rides, Santa, and more. (608)
452-3424 or www.norskedalen.org.

**SKYROCKERS NEW YEAR'S EVE FIREWORKS
—late December.** Grandad Bluff. Midnight fireworks on Grandad Bluff light up the Mississippi
Valley. Folks watch from the bluff, downtown,
while ice fishing on the river, cross-country skiing, or sledding. Early show for kids at 6:00 p.m.
(608) 792-0763 or www.explorelacrosse.com.

WINTER REC FEST—late January. Skating
party, figure-skating show, torchlight ski/hike,
snow sculpture contest, ice fishing derby, and
more. (608) 789-7533 or www.cityoflacrosse.org.

MARDI GRAS—February just before Lent. La
Crosse Center. Entertainment, raffle, food, a mas-
querade ball, and more. (608) 782-3169 or www.
lacrossemardigras.com.

**SNOWFLAKE SKI CLUB SUPER TOUR JUMP-
ING TOURNAMENT—mid-February.** Snowflake
Ski Club grounds, Westby. International ski
jumping competition on an Olympic-sized hill.
Top skiers from the U.S. and more than 11 foreign
countries will soar 300 feet on Timber Coulee.
(608) 634-3211 or www.snowflakeskiclub.com.

RESTAURANTS

DOC POWELL'S BREWERY AND PUB *(lunch
and dinner 11 am.-midnight, Friday–Saturday;
closed Sunday),* 200 Main St.
La Crosse, WI 54601, (608) 785-7026

FAYZE'S RESTAURANT AND BAKERY
(breakfast, lunch, and dinner)
135 S. Fourth St., La Crosse, WI 54601
(608) 784-9546, www.explorelacrosse.com

FREIGHT HOUSE RESTAURANT *(dinner)*
107 Vine St., La Crosse, WI 54601
(608) 784-6211
www.freighthouserestaurant.com

MR. D'S RESTAURANT & BAKERY
(breakfast and lunch)
1146 State St., La Crosse, WI 54601
(608) 784-6737, www.mrdsrestaurant.com

PIGGY'S RESTAURANT *(dinner)*
501 Front St. South, La Crosse, WI 54601
(608) 784-4877, www.piggys.com

LODGING

BENTLY WHEELER BED & BREAKFAST
938 and 950 Cass St., La Crosse, WI 54601
(608) 784-9360 or (877) 889-8585
www.bentley-wheeler.com

THE CELTIC INN
924 Cass St., La Crosse, WI 54601,
(608) 782-7040, www.celticbb.com

CHATEAU LA CROSSE
410 Cass St., La Crosse, WI 54601
(608) 796-1090 or (800) 442-7969
http://chateaulacrosse.castlesofamerica.com

FOUR GABLES BED & BREAKFAST
W5648 Highway 14/61, La Crosse, WI 54601
(608) 788-7958, www.bedandbreakfast.com/
wisconsin/four-gables-bed-breakfast.html

GUEST HOUSE MOTEL
810 S. Fourth St., La Crosse, WI 54601
(608) 784-8840 or (800) 274-6873
www.guesthousemotel.com

WESTBY HOUSE VICTORIAN INN
200 W. State St., Westby, WI 54667
(608) 634-4112 or (800) 434-7439
www.westbyhouse.com/pages/
westbyhouse.html

WILSON SCHOOLHOUSE INN
W5720 Highway 14/61, La Crosse, WI 54601
(608) 787-1982
www.wilsonschoolhouseinn.com

Chapter Thirteen
THE RESORT LIFE, WINTER STYLE
Lake Geneva/Delavan/Williams Bay

"LAKE GENEVA IS THE CITY; Geneva Lake is the lake." It's a statement you'll hear often from local residents during your winter weekend in one of Wisconsin's most upscale resort destinations. The distinction is made, most probably, out of a sense of pride in this lovely community, which could very well remind you of a pristine hamlet in Switzerland.

The Potawatomi were the original settlers of the area, but by the early 1830s, it had become a stagecoach stop on the route between Kenosha and Beloit. The first industries were water power plants and mills. By the 1860s, when the Chicago & North Western Railroad extended its line 75 miles north from Chicago, that city's elite began to discover what a gorgeous summertime respite the area provided. But it was the Great Chicago Fire of 1871 that really propelled Lake Geneva into a bona fide getaway when it became a haven for the city's moneyed refugees. They soon built magnificent estates along Geneva Lake's shores, and the city earned the moniker "Newport of the West." By 1879, 10 trains a day were pulling into Geneva Station. By 1910, the whole lakeshore, with the exception of a few public beaches, had been recast as private estates and grand resorts.

Four lakes actually grace the area: Delavan Lake, Lake Como, Lake Comus, and Geneva Lake. And around Geneva Lake itself are three picturesque communities: Lake Geneva on the northeast, Williams Bay to the north, and Fontana to the southwest. The city of Delavan sits 10 miles to the west of Lake Geneva, between Lake Comus and Delavan Lake.

The Potawatomi Indians called Lake Geneva "Kishwauketoe," meaning "clear water." With a surface area of 5,262 acres (7.6 miles long and 2.1 miles wide) and a depth of 135 feet, Geneva Lake is one of the larger lakes in southern Wisconsin, the second-deepest natural lake in the state, and one of the cleanest. Fed by natural aquifers from Lake Superior and from small streams that originate from springs, Geneva Lake was carved out by two glaciers approximately 30,000 and 14,000 years ago. A 20.6-mile footpath circles the lake and makes an excellent winter hike—access it along the lakefront, and you'll walk past stately mansions, a state park, and a state of natural beauty.

145

The city of Lake Geneva has alternately been called the iceboat and ice fishing "Capital of the World." Ice fishermen surely dot the lake in the winter, trying for northerns, walleyes, ciscoes, and pan fish. And although Madison and Lake Geneva engage in a friendly rivalry regarding rights to the iceboat title *[see Chapter 14: Winter Sports Capital (Madison)]*, boaters here take to the lake as soon as conditions permit. You'll most likely see their craft going 130 miles per hour jumping the fault: the narrowest point of Lake Geneva.

This is the weekend to experience the high-style resort life, complete with mansions, fast boats, and scenery reminiscent of a European vacation. The best part is, your particular brand of holiday comes cloaked in a rich, powdery white.

Lake Geneva has been called the "Ice Fishing Capital of the World" and shantytowns dot the area's rich lakes in winter.

Day One
LATE MORNING

One of the bonuses that comes with traveling to Lake Geneva for a winter weekend is bumping into the wonderful communities nearby. Plan to begin your weekend with a stop in **Delavan**. Founded in 1836, it is one of Wisconsin's early cities, still retaining much of its 19th-century charm. Brick streets and restored buildings decorate the downtown area. And like Baraboo, Delavan has a circus history *[see Chapter 2: A Natural Winter (Baraboo/Prairie du Sac)]*. Between 1847 and 1894, the city was the winter quarters for 28 traveling circus troupes, including P.T. Barnum's first. That explains the statue of a giant, rearing elephant and giraffe in the town square.

After photographing those rather large animals downtown (after all, how often do you get the chance?), enjoy a walk on the old streets. Pick up a coffee at **Elizabeth's Cafe** or **Remember When Antiques & Collectibles** on East Walworth Avenue, or check out the rare, out-of-print, and used books at **Bibliomaniacs** next door, which holds two levels of literary treasures.

Delavan has one of the best city **sledding** hills in Wisconsin, located one block off

DRESSING FOR WINTER

The single most important factor for enjoying the outdoors in winter is dressing correctly to keep warm. In fact, there are almost no winter weather conditions in which you cannot be perfectly comfortable, as long as you abide by one important rule: dress in layers.

Several layers of clothing will trap body heat and air inside your garments while allowing moisture to evaporate so your inside clothing stays dry. Using three layers works the best:

Starting closest to your skin is the **vapor layer**. Polypropylene or Capilene underwear that fits close to the skin will wick body moisture away to keep you dry.

The second, **insulation layer** holds body-produced heat within your garments. The insulation layer should be more loose-fitting and made from fleece, felt pile, or Synchilla, a fleece made from recycled plastic products. Avoid cotton, which retains moisture and wicks poorly.

The third layer and first defense against the elements is the **protective layer**. Its main purpose is to be your shell and keep you dry; a goose-down-filled, wind-and-water-resistant jacket and wind-and-water resistant pants work the best. A jacket with a hood and waist and wrist cords to keep out drafts is preferable. Garments made with Gore-Tex act like a one-way valve. Gore-Tex is a laminate bonded to polyester or nylon that contains pores too small to let water in, yet large enough to allow water vapor to escape.

Deerskin mittens lined with wool or silk store heat better than gloves. Boots should be waterproofed with wool or synthetic liners. Separate the liners from the boots and let them air dry every evening. Your body loses most of its heat from your head, so always wear a hat, even under a jacket hood. A knit cap that can be pulled over your ears or a hat with earflaps is essential. Facemasks, balaclavas, and scarves add layered protection against getting a frostbitten face. And don't forget sun block when you're on the snow in bright sunshine.

Walworth Avenue on Terrace Street. **Rudy Lange Sledding Hill** (see cover photo) is open from 8:00 a.m. until 10:00 p.m. daily, so get your sled, tube, or a piece of cardboard from the trunk of your car and winter like a kid. The fun is free, and the park is lit at night for extended sliding.

Still on Terrace Street, you can **winter hike** or warm up your **cross-country ski** muscles at the **Paul Lange Memorial Arboretum** on the north side of the city. Many of the arboretum's more than 200 trees are labeled to create a self-guided tour.

If riding rather than striding sounds good this morning, **Fantasy Hills Ranch** about three and a half miles out on Highway 50 to Town Hall Road can put you on **horseback** or in a **sleigh**. Ride through 65 acres of rolling hills and woodlands, freshly covered in a blanket of snow.

If a faster pace is what you had in mind, head to the **Interlaken Resort and Country Spa** for a **snowmobile outing**. Interlaken is just five minutes away from downtown Lake Geneva on Lake Como. The resort rents snowmobiles by the half hour or hour.

JOHN T. ANDREWS

How often do you get the chance to photograph large circus animals downtown?

AFTERNOON

Whether on a snowmobile or not, before leaving Delavan, catch lunch at the **Lake Bluff Dining Room at the Interlaken Resort**. Enjoy a "Como Catch Super Sandwich"—a beer-battered cod fillet—or a half-pound Black Angus burger along with your ceiling-to-table-top view of Lake Como.

Five minutes southeast on Highway 50 will take you into the heart of **Lake Geneva**. This southernmost, Wisconsin-lakes playground draws 60 percent of its annual visitors from Chicago, and another 25 percent come from Milwaukee—mostly in the summertime. As a winter visitor, you'll be able to enjoy this resort-land with plenty of breathing room.

Although you'll want to spend most of your winter weekend enjoying the outdoor beauty of the Lake Geneva area, make a practical stop downtown. Family-owned and operated since 1973, the **Overland Sheepskin Co.** is one retailer you won't want to miss in winter. Here, you'll find warm sheepskin outer ware: shearling coats, mittens, and hats *[see*

148

"Dressing for Winter" sidebar]. The warm clothing will make your outing this afternoon an entirely comfortable one.

Located two miles south of Lake Geneva on Geneva Lake is the small, 271-acre **Big Foot Beach State Park**. Named for a Potawatomi chief, the park is a popular and crowded place in summertime because of its large, beach frontage. In winter, however, you'll more likely be sharing it with squirrels, rabbits, hawks, ducks, deer, raccoons, foxes, and muskrats. **Winter hikers** and **snowshoers** will travel to oak-hickory woods, open fields, prairie remnants, marshes, and shorelines. **Cross-country skiers** will find six miles of groomed trails that pass by Geneva Lake and hundreds of **ice fishers** hoping for walleyes and northerns. *[See "How a Lake Freezes" sidebar.]* This is the part where you'll be thankful you stopped at Overland Sheepskin Co.—from Big Foot Beach State Park, you can access the **20-mile trail that circles Geneva Lake**. It can get very chilly and breezy along the lake, so don your new duds.

You are going to live the resort life this weekend, so check into your accommodations at the **Grand Geneva Resort**. And a grand resort it is: here, 1,300 acres are full of winter activities. One of only three AAA Four-Diamond resorts in Wisconsin, the Grand Geneva Resort opened in 1968 as The Playboy Hotel and Country Club. Over the years, it has hosted celebrities such as Sonny and Cher, Tony Bennett, Sammy Davis, Jr., and Bob Hope. The Marcus Corporation purchased the resort in May 1993, and today the resort's rooms are elegantly done in warm colors within a Frank Lloyd Wright–inspired architectural framework.

The biggest event at Grand Geneva Resort is **Christmas in the Country**. If your winter weekend is between mid-November and New Year's Eve, the resort will be decked out in more than 500,000 lights and will offer nightly musical performances, special menus, and fireside teas.

Any time in winter on the resort grounds is fun-filled, however. The Grand Geneva has its own **downhill ski** area called **Mountain Top**, where snowmaking crews can convert 1,200 gallons of water per minute into a perfect blanket of snow. Eighteen challenging slopes with runs up to a quarter mile long, elevations up to 1,086 feet, and a vertical drop of 211 feet can be found at Mountain Top. **Snowboarders** have their own terrain park with a specially designed half-pipe, and you can **cross-country ski** or **snowshoe** on 6.2 miles of trails. Mountain Top is open until 10:00 p.m. every night, and the chalet offers ski lessons and equipment rentals.

EVENING

If you choose to stay at Mountain Top for an evening of fun, get a bite to eat between runs—hot pizza, a sandwich, or snack—at the chalet's upper-level **Timbers Bar & Grill**. If you'd like to go off grounds, **Gilbert's** on Wrigley Drive is a treat for the eyes and palate. This 1885 mansion with 30 rooms is covered in the rich woods of cherry, walnut, oak, maple, mahogany, and fir. There are 13 hand-carved fireplaces, which are inlaid with the original Mediterranean tiles. In winter, they are all lit for guests. The solid cherry staircase, which extends the full three stories of the great hall, is breathtaking. The food, with European and Pacific Rim influences, changes daily, but butter-poached lobster with maitake mushroom and sweet pea fricassee; grilled Hawaiian red snapper with lemon-scented orzo; and cannelloni made with Maui onions, local baby bell peppers, and organic ricotta cheese have been known to appear.

Finish the evening with a romantic, lighted outdoor **ice skate** at **Library Park**, located on Main Street behind the library.

Day Two
LATE MORNING

Today, you'll get an unforgettable opportunity to see a national competition that is often televised on ESPN, spend more time at the resort cross-country skiing, downhill skiing, or snowboarding, or take advantage of Lake Geneva's natural beauty.

Start off the day with a breakfast buffet at **Grand Geneva Resort's Grand Café** or catch the Weekend Champagne Brunch at the **Grandview Restaurant & Lounge in the Geneva Inn**, served from 10:30 a.m. until 2:00 p.m. on Saturday and Sunday. The Grandview's large, panoramic windows offer a view of the lake from every table. The three-course brunch menu includes items such as jumbo crab cakes, and steak and eggs Benedict. Or order à la carte entrées such as shellfish Mornay or special omelets.

This morning, you'll venture out to explore another city on Geneva Lake's shores. The village of **Williams Bay** is located at the north edge of the lake. It's the location for the most intact, undisturbed, and highest quality wetland in the area. The 230-acre **Kishwauketoe Conservancy** is a natural preserve that was established in 1989. The conservancy has more than four miles of **winter hiking trails** that wander through diverse habitats and plant communities. Its main entrance is located just north of Geneva Street.

www.LakeGenevaPhoto.com

Every year, 15 teams of winter artists come to Lake Geneva to vie for top honors in the National Snow Sculpting Competition.

HOW A LAKE FREEZES

A lake begins to freeze long before the first day of winter. Even as early as September, as the days start to get shorter and the weather turns cooler, a lake begins to lose heat into the surrounding colder air. Eventually, the surface water reaches 39.2 degrees Fahrenheit, the point at which water is most dense. The denser, colder water on top sinks to the bottom, displacing the warmer water underneath. That warmer water, in turn, now rises to become cool.

Once this "overturn" of water has brought the whole lake to a relatively consistent 39.2-degree temperature, surface cooling continues until the temperature drops to 32 degrees. Water freezes at 32 degrees as long as there is a nucleus—another ice crystal or mineral speck—to form around (a pure water droplet requires a temperature of -40 degrees before it will freeze).

The ice crystals begin as disks measuring a few millimeters. On a calm, windless night, the disks are able to bond, forming a smooth sheet, which is sometimes called "black ice." The ice then slowly thickens on its underside by forming "candles"—long, hexagonal crystals an inch or two thick—that join together side by side.

Water differs from other liquids in that when it freezes, it expands in size. Most liquids contract when they freeze. Water molecules in an ice-crystal form an airy lattice pattern that spaces them farther apart than in their liquid form. Since ice is lighter than water, it forms on top of a lake first instead of forming from the bottom of the lake up.

The surface ice of a lake will expand and contract as temperatures rise and fall. When two expanding ice sheets bump together, "ice heaves" are created that resemble broken sheets of Styrofoam on the middle of a frozen lake. If there is a stretch of really cold weather, the ice may suddenly contract with cracks and booms that can be heard for miles around the lake.

AFTERNOON

Before leaving Williams Bay, go to the place with homemade donuts and an appropriate time-of-year theme, **Daddy Maxwell's Arctic Circle Diner**. This 65-seat 1940s diner serves nothing but homemade breakfasts and hot lunch specials. If iceboats are out on the lake, take the short drive to nearby Fontana and eat at **Chuck's Lakeshore Inn**, one of the best places to watch Skeeter Ice Boat Club members and their races *[see "Iceboating the Geneva Lake Area" sidebar]*. Chuck's serves burgers and sandwiches and has a seven-mile view of the lake.

This afternoon, you'll have the chance to see a nationwide competition among winter artists: the **National Snow Sculpting Competition**. For the past 10 years, Lake Geneva's **Riviera Park** has been the site for this event that is the centerpiece of early February's **Winterfest**. Almost 50,000 people come to watch 15 teams from throughout the country vie for the national title. Teams must win a major competition in order to even compete in the nationals here. The Wisconsin team each year is the winner of the Flake Out Festival in Wisconsin Dells *[see Chapter 21: Indoor Water Parks and Flake Out Festivals (Wisconsin Dells)]*. Each three-person team, composed of members who are at least 18 years of age and from the same state, spends three days (Wednesday through Friday) carving a three-ton, six-foot-by-six-foot, 10-foot-high block of snow. Only hand tools are permitted, and no

ICEBOATING THE GENEVA LAKE AREA

by Jane Pegel

Jane Pegel is a life member of the Skeeter Ice Boat Club and two-time Detroit News (DN) iceboat class North American champion. She is a 10-time DN iceboat Northwest Ice Yacht Association champion and three-time U.S. Yachtswoman of the Year. In other words, Jane is an accomplished iceboat racer.

The Geneva Lake area and Williams Bay, on the north shore of Geneva Lake in southeast Wisconsin, is known worldwide as the "Iceboat Capital of the World."

Sailing on frozen lakes, rivers, and bays, iceboats are the fastest things under sail on the planet. Typically, an iceboat is a vehicle with mast and sail mounted on a hull, sometimes referred to as "backbone," with a cross-member, referred to as the "runner plank." There is a steel blade runner on each end of the runner plank and a steering runner on either the bow or stern of the hull.

The fastest of all iceboats is the A Division Skeeter that, by class rule, must be bow-steering and have a single sail no larger than 75 square feet. The exact design of the components of the boat and the sail are unrestricted. With its innovative design and high-tech materials, the Skeeter can reach speeds of over 140 mph with ideal wind and ice conditions.

Williams Bay is recognized as the birthplace of the first Skeeter iceboat built by Walter Beauvais in 1932. One of his boats, with Harry Melges, Sr., at the helm, won the Class E (75 square feet of sail) championship in the annual Northwest Ice Yacht Association regatta in 1936. This success caught the attention of iceboating enthusiasts throughout the northern United States and southern Canada. The devotion of these enthusiasts to the sport has led to the evolution of the phenomenal Skeeter Class iceboat, but all recognize that it began in Williams Bay.

When wind and ice conditions permit, members of the Skeeter Ice Boat Club sail and race their iceboats on Geneva Lake. From mid-December to mid-March, the club holds races on Saturdays, Sundays, and Wednesdays, and also hosts championship regattas.

medium other than snow, ice, or water is allowed. Saturday at 11:00 a.m. is "shovels down," and all sculptors must stop for judging. You can be part of the competition by voting in the "Peoples' Choice" award. The awards ceremony takes place on Saturday afternoon, and the champion graduates to the World Winterfest.

If you missed the competition, get a real winter workout in a great Wisconsin forest at the **Kettle Moraine State Forest–Southern Unit**, a short, 30-minute drive away from Lake Geneva. This 22,300-acre forest has 30 miles of groomed **cross-country ski** trails and 56 miles for **snowmobiling**. The level and gently rolling, 12-mile **Nordic Trail**, designated for classic and skate-skiers, is the longest trail in the forest. Its five loops range from 2.5 miles to 9.2 miles, and pass through open and wooded terrain and several small kettle ponds. The mostly wooded, 7.5-mile **Scuppernong** and 6.2-mile **McMiller Trails** will challenge even the most advanced skier. The **McMiller Blue Trail**, for classic or skate-skiing, starts with an easy tour through pine forests and then, after the first mile, moves into the steep climbs of an upland hardwood forest. Good downhill control is a must here. Skiers can experience some rugged backcountry touring on the four-mile **John Muir Orange Trail**. This ungroomed trail is for **skiers, winter hikers**, and **snowshoers**. It travels over prairies before plunging into deep oak, maple forests, and kettle pits left by a glacier.

There are 54 miles of **hiking-only** trails to explore in Kettle Moraine's Southern Unit. **Winter hikers** and **snowshoers** will find that a large section—31 miles—of Wisconsin's statewide **Ice Age National Scenic Trail** enters the forest near the Pine Wood campground. The **Emma Carlin Trail**, with looped routes winding through meadows in rolling oak and pine forest openings, is also designated for those in boots or on snowshoes.

Ice fishing is very popular here, too, as is **tobogganing**. Three backpacking-shelter sites along the Ice Age National Scenic Trail and the Ottawa Lake Campground are open for

JOHN T. ANDREWS

All you really need is a hill, snow, and something smooth to sit on.

adventuresome **winter campers.** And unique to this state forest is the **McMiller Sports Center**, a **target practice facility** for archery and different types of rifles and handguns.

EVENING

This evening, dine inside the Grand Geneva Resort's romantic and sophisticated **Ristorante Brissago**. Entrées such as ravioli filled with chicken and rosemary with Gorgonzola and mushroom pesto sauce are made with fresh ingredients flown in weekly from Italy. After your meal of basil spaghetti and wild mushrooms with a sautéed lobster tail, top it all off with baked chocolate and cocoa mousse.

After dinner, enjoy the musical production of **Christmas in the Country** in the Evergreen Ballroom of the Grand Geneva Resort, or get in some more skiing at **Mountain Top**.

Day Three

MORNING

This morning, have breakfast at **Scuttlebutts Restaurant** on Wrigley Drive. Enjoy a last look at Geneva Lake as you indulge in some of the best Swedish pancakes in Wisconsin.

After breakfast, pick à la carte from a menu of winter activities around the lake. At the Grand Geneva Resort, make arrangements at the **Dan Patch Stables** for a **hay** or **sleigh ride** by one-ton draft horses, who'll pull you along trails of rolling hills and hardwood forests. Or rent a **snowmobile** from **Jerry's Boat and Snowmobile Rentals.** Rent an ice shanty from **Geneva Lake Bait & Tackle** (open from 4:00 a.m. to 6:00 p.m.) and go **ice fishing,** or **ice skate** behind the Field House in Williams Bay. In Delavan, **cross-country ski** at **Lake Lawn Resort** on five miles of groomed trails or **ice-skate** on the rink on Delavan Lake. You can rent cross-country skis or ice skates at Lake Lawn Resort.

If your route home takes you north, you may want to stop by **Alpine Valley Ski & Snowboard Resort** in East Troy. Twenty **downhill ski** runs of varying levels and a **snowboarding** terrain park await you, in grand resort style.

JOHN T. ANDREWS

Ice forms on top of a lake first, here creating a mosaic with surface snow in Riviera Park.

FOR MORE INFORMATION
LAKE GENEVA AREA CONVENTION AND VISITORS BUREAU
201 Wrigley Dr., Lake Geneva, WI 53147
(262) 248-4416 or (800) 345-1020
www.lakegenevawi.com

WINTER ATTRACTIONS
ALPINE VALLEY SKI & SNOWBOARD RESORT
Highway D and Townline Rd.
East Troy, WI 53120, (262) 642-7374 or
(800) 227-9395, www.alpinevalleyresort.com

BIBLIOMANIACS
324 E. Walworth Ave., Delavan, WI 53115
(262) 728-9933
www.abebooks.com/home/BIBLIOMANIACSWI

BIG FOOT BEACH STATE PARK
1452 County Road H *(winter entrance is on Wells Street)*, Lake Geneva, WI 53147
(262) 248-2528, www.wiparks.net

DAN PATCH STABLES
Grand Geneva Resort, 7036 Grand Geneva Way
Lake Geneva, WI 53147, (262) 215-5303
www.grandgeneva.com

FANTASY HILLS RANCH
4978 Town Hall Rd., Delavan, WI 53115
(262) 728-1773, www.fantasyhillsranch.com

GENEVA LAKE BAIT & TACKLE
(by appointment only), 2885 Highway 67
Delavan, WI 53115, (262) 245-6150

JERRY'S BOAT AND SNOWMOBILE RENTALS
Highway 50 West, Lake Geneva, WI 53147
(262) 275-5222

KETTLE MORAINE STATE FOREST–SOUTHERN UNIT
S91W39091 State Road 59, Eagle, WI 53119
(262) 594-6200, www.wiparks.net

KISHWAUKETOE CONSERVANCY
The boardwalk entrance is on Geneva St.
There is also access across from the fieldhouse on Highway 67 *(Elkhorn Road)*.
Williams Bay, WI 53191, (262) 245-2700
www.williamsbay.org/knc.html

LIBRARY PARK
918 W. Main St. *(behind the library)*, Lake Geneva
WI 53147, (262) 248-4416 or (800) 345-1020

MOUNTAIN TOP *(open 10 a.m.–10 p.m., from mid-December through mid-February)*
Grand Geneva Resort, 7036 Grand Geneva Way,
Lake Geneva, WI 53147, (262) 248-8811 or (800) 558-3417, www.grandgeneva.com

OVERLAND SHEEPSKIN CO.
741 W. Main St. , Lake Geneva, WI 53147
(262) 248-1916, www.overlandsheepskinco.com

PAUL LANGE MEMORIAL ARBORETUM
N. Terrace St., Delavan, WI 53115
(262) 728-5585

REMEMBER WHEN ANTIQUES & COLLECTIBLES
313 E. Walworth Ave., Delavan, WI 53115
(262) 728-8670
www.explorewisconsin.com/RememberWhen

RIVIERA PARK
812 Wrigley Drive *(at the lakefront)*
Lake Geneva, WI 53147, (262) 248-3673

RUDY LANGE SLEDDING HILL
100 Block of S. Terrace St., Delavan, WI 53115
(262) 728-5585

WINTER FESTIVALS
DELAVAN TREE LIGHTING CEREMONY— late November. 6:00 p.m. in Tower Park in Delavan. (262) 728-5095.

CHRISTMAS IN THE COUNTRY—Thanksgiving through December. The Grand Geneva Resort presents a six-week-long gala featuring more than half a million lights illuminating the sky and forming dramatic displays across the resort's 1,300 acres. Christmas in the Country is highlighted by "Holiday Magic," a musical/theatrical extravaganza. (262) 249-4741.

WINTERFEST & NATIONAL SNOW SCULPTING COMPETITION—early February. Downtown Lake Geneva and Riviera Park. Fifteen three-member teams from across the United States sculpt 10-foot-blocks of snow throughout the week. Judging is Saturday from noon to 2:00 p.m., with the award presentation at 3:00 p.m. The winning team will represent the U. S. in international competition. A food marketplace in the Riviera Ballroom, demonstrations, outdoor activities, musical entertainment, helicopter, and balloon rides. (262) 248-4416 or (800) 345-1020 or www.lakegenevawi.com.

GRAND GENEVA RESORT'S WINTER CARNIVAL—early February, in conjunction with Winterfest. Ski and snowboard racing, a treasure hunt, chili cook-off, and live entertainment. The fireworks display and torchlight ski parade down Mountain Top's slopes on Sunday night mark the highlight of the weekend. (262) 248-8811 or (800) 558-3417.

BAY WINTERFEST—mid-February. Edgewater Park in Williams Bay. Softball and volleyball atop the frozen waters of Geneva Lake, carriage rides, ice-sculpting demonstrations, food, and a Saturday night dance. (262) 245-2720.

NATIONAL SNO-CROSS COMPETITION— mid-March. Grand finale of the World Snowmobile Association (WSA) season at Grand Geneva Resort's Mountain Top. Nationally televised by ESPN. Sno-cross events are included. (262) 248-8811.

RESTAURANTS
CHUCK'S LAKESHORE INN
(lunch and dinner)
52 Lake St., Fontana, WI 53125, (262) 275-3222
www.chuckslakeshoreinn.com

DADDY MAXWELL'S ARCTIC CIRCLE DINER
(breakfast and lunch)
150 Elkhorn Rd., Williams Bay, WI 53191
(262) 245-5757

ELIZABETH'S CAFE *(lunch and dinner)*
322 E. Walworth Ave., Delavan, WI 53115
(262) 728-3383

GILBERT'S *(dinner)*
327 Wrigley Dr., Lake Geneva, WI 53147
(262) 248-6680, www.gilbertsrestaurant.com

GRAND CAFÉ *(breakfast, lunch, and dinner)*
Grand Geneva Resort, 7036 Grand Geneva Way
Lake Geneva, WI 53147
(262) 248-8811 or (800) 558-3417
www.grandgeneva.com/dining

GRANDVIEW RESTAURANT AND LOUNGE
(Friday and Saturday lunch; dinner daily; brunch on Saturday and Sunday)
Geneva Inn, N2009 S. Lakeshore Dr.
Lake Geneva, WI 53147
(262) 248-5690 or (800) 441-5881,
www.genevainn.com/GrandviewInfo.htm

LAKE BLUFF DINING ROOM *(breakfast, lunch, and dinner)*, Interlaken Resort and Country Spa
W4240 Highway 50, Lake Geneva, WI 53147
www.interlakenresort.com

RISTORANTE BRISSAGO *(dinner)*
Grand Geneva Resort, 7036 Grand Geneva Way,
Lake Geneva, WI 53147
(262) 248-8811 or (800) 558-3417
www.grandgeneva.com/dining

SCUTTLEBUTTS RESTAURANT
(breakfast and lunch)
831 Wrigley Dr., Lake Geneva, WI 53147
(262) 248-1111

TIMBERS BAR & GRILL
Mountain Top at Grand Geneva Resort, 7036
Grand Geneva Way, Lake Geneva, WI 53147
(262) 248-8811 or (800) 558-3417
www.grandgeneva.com/dining

LODGING
FRENCH COUNTRY INN ON THE LAKE
W4190 West End Rd., Lake Geneva, WI 53147
(262) 245-5220, www.frenchcountryinn.com

GENEVA INN
N2009 S. Lakeshore Dr.
Lake Geneva, WI 53147, (262) 248-5680 or
(800) 441-5881, www.genevainn.com

GOLDEN OAKS MANSION BED AND BREAKFAST
421 Baker St., Lake Geneva, WI 53147
(262) 248-9711, www.goldenoaksmansion.com

GRAND GENEVA RESORT
7036 Grand Geneva Way, Lake Geneva, WI
53147, (262) 248-8811 or (800) 558-3417
www.grandgeneva.com

INTERLAKEN RESORT AND COUNTRY SPA
W4240 Highway 50, Delavan, WI 53115
(262) 248-9121, www.interlakenresort.com

LAKE LAWN RESORT
2400 E. Geneva St., Delavan, WI 53115
(262) 728-7950 or (800) 338-5253
www.lakelawnresort.com

LAZY CLOUD LODGE BED AND BREAKFAST
N2025 N. Lakeshore Dr., Fontana, WI 53125
(262) 275-3322, www.lazycloud.com

PEDERSON VICTORIAN BED AND BREAKFAST
1782 Highway 120 North
Lake Geneva, WI 53147, (262) 248-9110 or
(888) 764-9653, www.pedersonvictorian.com

Chapter Fourteen

WINTER SPORTS CAPITAL
Madison

ICE-SKATERS GLIDE ON FROZEN, winding lagoons on a clear winter night. Their silver blades catch the moonlight under the gentle curve of an old arched bridge. Horses pull carriages through the center of town in the dusk of an early evening, their breath made visible in the cool night air. People stroll on the sidewalks, amid winter trees covered with white, twinkling lights. It could almost be a set of Currier and Ives prints. But it's really Madison in winter.

Sitting among four lakes—Lake Mendota, Lake Monona, Lake Waubesa, and Lake Wingra—Madison is a natural center for such winter sports as ice-skating, ice fishing, and even iceboat racing. And with more than 249 parklands, cross-country skiing, sledding, and snowshoeing are just a short walk or drive away. Even downhill skiing is within easy distance. Every day is full of ways to celebrate winter.

Money magazine has often declared Madison the "Best Place to Live in America," and *Men's Health* magazine named the city its "Healthiest City for Men." *Midwest Living* readers have ranked Madison "The Friendliest City in the Midwest," ensuring that visitors here will receive a warm welcome.

Warm food is also welcome in winter, and the city accommodates there as well. Hundreds of restaurants, taverns, and coffee shops—serving exotic hot chocolates—await you. Almost every type of cuisine is cooked in Madison, and, according to Madison Originals, an organization of more than 45 independently owned restaurants dedicated to preserving the area's flavor, the number of restaurants using locally grown produce is at an all-time high.

Madison has a strong environmentalist tradition, counting John Muir, Aldo Leopold, and Gaylord Nelson, founder of Earth Day, in its roster of those who honed their love of the outdoors at the University of Wisconsin–Madison. The university's arboretum is a greenspace paradise for those who like silent winter sports: Ski, hike, or snowshoe through natural communities brought back to resemble the state prior to settlement. For a paradise of another sort, the Olbrich Botanical Gardens will transport you to the tropics. The nearby

Governor Nelson State Park, with views of the stunning, white Capitol building across the lake, was Wisconsin's first urban state park.

The progressive spirit that pervades Madison is also nurturing to the arts. The $205 million Overture Center for the Arts is quickly making downtown a cultural mecca. That's especially true in winter when the performance season is in full swing—convenient for those rare times when you just may want to come in out of the cold!

Madison's State Capitol building is the only one ever built on an isthmus. In winter, its white granite is even more stunning.

JOHN T. ANDREWS

Day One
LATE/MORNING

Wisconsin's capital is a winter sports capital as well, and there are at least 10 cross-country skiing venues within the city limits. One of the most beautiful for **cross-country skiing, winter hiking**, and **snowshoeing** is the **University of Wisconsin–Madison Arboretum**. Its 1,260 acres of prairies, forests, savannas, and wetlands surround Lake Wingra south of the UW–Madison campus. Touring through the arboretum's more than 20 miles of trails puts you in the midst of the oldest and most varied collection of restored ecological communities in the world, including the world's oldest restored tallgrass prairies and sites of the first experiments on the use of fire in forest management, dating back to the 1940s. Not only are there restored communities, but the deciduous forests include one virgin stand dating to the time of European settlement in the lower part of the state, and some Native American burial mounds here date back a thousand years. Admission for cross-country skiing, snowshoeing, or winter hiking is free, but please stay on the trails. Watch carefully in the woods for hares, deer, muskrats, and coyotes.

AFTERNOON

Bordering the arboretum on the north end is Monroe Street, where you'll find **Bluephies**, a restaurant with a flair for vegetables and an ultra-modern decor. For lunch, try one of Bluephies' "Smashed Sammies," such as the "Flattened Athenos Sammie," crispy flat bread filled with tomatoes, red onions, olives, spinach, feta, and ranch dressing. Salads are really big here, both in size and number of choices.

After lunch, head to Wisconsin's first urban state park, the 422-acre **Governor Nelson State Park**. This mix of wetlands, woods, and rolling farmland on Lake Mendota's northwestern edge is another venue for **cross-country skiing, snowshoeing, winter hiking**, and even **ice fishing.** The park has several effigy mounds, the most notable of which is a 358-foot-long panther. As you **ski** or **winter hike** along the 1.8-mile **Woodland Trail**, you'll loop through the forested southern end of the park and pass the panther mound. The 3.5-mile, level **Morningside Trail** circles the northern end of the park and crosses prairie, and oak savanna and marsh. The one-mile **Redtail Hawk Trail** and the 2.1-mile **Oak Savanna Trail** loop over moderate hills and through prairie lands. The Oak Savanna Trail and the Woodland Trail can accommodate skate-skiers. A **snowshoeing** path runs next to the Morningside Trail's groomed ski track. **Ice fishers** here often do well with northerns, walleye, and pan fish.

While skiing or snowshoeing at Governor Nelson, you'll catch photogenic views of the **Wisconsin State Capitol** across the lake. As the sun gets lower in the winter sky, drive toward the Capitol building downtown and check into the **Mansion Hill Inn** three blocks off the Capitol Square. Built in 1858 of Mississippi white sandstone and Carrara marble from Italy, the Mansion Hill Inn was once an elegant home in Madison's **Mansion Hill District**, now listed on the National Register of Historic Places. Four of the inn's 11 guest rooms have fireplaces of brick or marble, and breakfasts are served on silver trays.

Unpack and enjoy the complimentary wine service, held from 4:00 to 7:00 p.m. at the inn.

EVENING

One of Madison's most renowned restaurants is **L'Etoile** on the Capitol Square, located on the second floor of a classy, brick building with Capitol views. Make your reservations here for this evening, and get ready for a three-course meal that couples fresh, organic Midwest ingredients—even in the winter—with French cuisine influences.

After dinner, walk down **State Street,** just off the square, where thousands of white lights strung through the trees create an effect that might make you feel like Jimmy Stewart strolling through Bedford Falls. Attend a performance at the showcase **Overture Center for the Arts,** or if you'd like to squeeze in some more sports—as a spectator this time—take in a **Badger men's hockey game at the Kohl Center,** one of the country's most highly regarded collegiate arenas.

Day Two
MORNING

Enjoy a special breakfast at your bed and breakfast this morning, or eat out at the **Marigold Kitchen** on the Capitol Square. On Saturday mornings, you'll be treated to an out-of-the-ordinary brunch, featuring creative dishes and twists on old favorites, such as challah bread French toast drizzled with pastry cream, seasonal berries and maple syrup, and omelets with artichokes, oven-roasted tomatoes, green onions, and asiago cheese.

A block away, hugging the shores of Lake Monona, is the **Monona Terrace Community and Convention Center,** a building that is both structure and artwork. First designed in 1938 by Wisconsin native and internationally renowned architect Frank Lloyd Wright, the building combines graceful arches, cylinders, and domes. It is, in Wright's words, "the long-

GEOFF SOBERING, http://geoff-s.net

Iceboats race across the lake at speeds up to 140 miles per hour on winter weekends in the "Ice Boat Capital of the Known Universe."

WATCHING AN ICEBOAT RACE
by Debra Whitehorse

Debra Whitehorse grew up above her father's iceboat factory in Monona, Wisconsin. In addition to serving as secretary and Webmaster for Madison's Four Lakes Ice Yacht Club (www.iceboat.org), she has researched and written articles about iceboating history. She still lives in Monona with her daughter and husband, who are also avid iceboaters. On winter weekends, you can find her in the middle of the lake, scoring iceboat races.

Contrary to what my friends who choose to embrace winter at its highest level say, iceboating is a spectator sport. It's best enjoyed from a comfortable red chair in the Community Terrace in Madison's spectacular Monona Terrace Community and Convention Center. Frank Lloyd Wright, famous for his love of all things fast, would approve of making an effort on a cold and windy weekend to watch the unusual boats speed across frozen Lake Monona. Mr. Wright knew Madison's top iceboaters, and an iceboat-building carpenter helped construct his famous Madison Unitarian Church.

When a grandfather brought his grandson to his first iceboat race, I overheard the puzzled boy asking where the racetrack was. The racing lanes he looked for are not painted on the ice, leaving sailors free to choose the quickest route around the course. What looks like aimless fun is quite serious to the skippers, who spend countless hours building and tuning their unique craft.

Forget what you know about automobile racing or even sailboat racing. Iceboat courses are roughly diamond in shape with a fluorescent buoy, or mark, both at the top and bottom of the imaginary diamond. The two marks are lined up directly into the wind about one mile apart. A race usually consists of three laps around the diamond, and the first boat crossing the finish line near the bottom mark wins the race. If the skipper is lucky, an elegant trophy awaits, but there are no cash rewards for iceboat racing.

In 1926, a *Wisconsin State Journal* writer considered the sport of iceboat racing a "sportsman's utopia," stating, "Iceboating is a sport from which absolutely no revenue is derived. It is a matter of everything going out and nothing coming in. In other words, it is a sport for sport's sake in the largest meaning of the term."

---

awaited wedding between the city and beautiful Lake Monona." Wright reworked the plans several times and signed off on the last version seven weeks before his death in 1959. The building finally became reality in July 1997.

From towering windows in the Grand Terrace room on the fourth floor or from the outdoor walkways, Monona Terrace provides a convenient spot for viewing Madison's **iceboat races** *[see "Watching an Iceboat Race" sidebar]*. Races are held on Saturdays and Sundays at 10:00 a.m. and go until 3:00 p.m. on one of Madison's four lakes every weekend, subject to weather conditions.

Since the 1860s, Madison has been home to the sport of iceboat racing. In fact, the **Four Lakes Ice Yacht Club** calls Madison the "Iceboat Capital of the Known Universe"—a title probably only contested by friendly rivals living in Lake Geneva, Wisconsin, who claim their city is "Iceboat Capital of the World" [see Chapter 13: The Resort Life, Winter Style (Lake Geneva/Delavan/Williams Bay)].

The colorful boats with white sails "fly" across the ice at 70 to 140 miles per hour. With a hull attached to three runners, the iceboats have huge triangular mainsails that unfurl in the winter winds.

While iceboat racing is a proud Madison tradition, there's another ice custom with an even longer history: **ice fishing**.

For centuries, Wisconsin's Native Americans have fished in winter. Walleyes, bluegills, crappies, and northern pike are active throughout the cold months. Fishing in winter has its advantages: the lakes are clear of boaters and jet skis, and you don't need a boat! In fact, once you have the proper warm clothing, all you need is an auger or ice drill, a pole and lure, an ice scoop, and a bucket [see "Hard-Water Fishing" sidebar in Chapter 9: A Classic, Old World Winter (Green Lake/Princeton)].

If you'd like to catch the firmest fish you've ever tasted, contact **D & S Bait, Tackle & Archery** on Northport Drive. A guide will pick you up from a designated location, rent you the equipment you'll need, take you safely out on the lake to an ice shanty, and pick you up when you're done. If you're leery of walking on frozen lakes [see "Walking on Ice" sidebar in Chapter 19: It's Elemental: Earth, Water, Wood, Air, and Metal (Superior)], you can ride the "Perch Chariot," a sled with benches pulled by a four-wheeler to a "hot" fishing spot on Lake Mendota.

Two blocks up from the lake and the Monona Terrace Community and Convention Center is the **Wisconsin State Capitol**. Walk inside the state's most venerable edifice, which boasts the only granite dome in the U.S. and is the only state capitol ever built on an isthmus. Of all the U.S. state capitols, the Wisconsin Capitol building most closely resembles the nation's Capitol in Washington, D.C. A free, 50-minute tour will take you inside the Senate chambers, the Assembly chambers, the Supreme Court, governor's conference room, and the impressive rotunda. If you visit in the month of December, be sure to check out the State of Wisconsin holiday tree [see "Choosing the Holiday Tree for the State Capitol Rotunda" sidebar].

AFTERNOON

In the 1850s, George and Anna Fess opened the Fess Hotel, a hotel, livery, and restaurant on the Lake Monona side of the Capitol Square. It stayed in family hands for more than 100 years. In 1973, the building was listed on the National Registry of Historic Places. In 1994, the **Great Dane Pub & Brewing Co.**, Madison's first operating brewery since 1966, moved in. Today, you can get a pub lunch accompanied by a fresh beer or root beer in the main bar overlooking the brewing process or in the dining room with its restored brickwork.

There will be plenty of options for winter sports activities this afternoon, so use a short car ride to digest your meal. **Tyrol Basin Ski and Snowboard Area** in Mount Horeb is just 18 miles west of Madison. **Snowboarders** consider Tyrol's half-pipe the best in the Midwest, and the area has 16 tree-lined, **downhill ski** runs that extend over 40 acres on a 300-foot hill. Three triple chairlifts, two rope tows, and a handle tow provide easy access to the slopes. Skiers can choose from a variety of lift ticket options, and ski/board clinics are held throughout the winter. Ski instructors give free introductory lessons to all first-time

CHOOSING THE HOLIDAY TREE
FOR THE STATE CAPITOL ROTUNDA

If you happen to visit Madison in the month of December, make sure you visit the Capitol rotunda to see the State of Wisconsin holiday tree. Wisconsin's "first tree" is never anything short of majestic: rising 50 feet up from the rotunda floor, it soars beyond the first balcony. The woodsy smell of the giant evergreen and the sight of the richly textured, homemade ornaments carefully crafted by schoolchildren and community organizations make seeing it a one-of-kind winter delight.

According to Bill Beckman, a building superintendent for Wisconsin's Department of Administration in the Division of State Facilities for the State Capitol, the official tree must meet certain requirements. Beckman should know: He's been choosing the tree for more than 26 years. The official holiday tree must be:

❈ **A balsam fir.** Balsam firs are mandatory because they are: (1) lightweight, (2) flexible—important when you have a 52-inch doorway to pull the tree through, and (3) known for holding their needles longer than most other trees.

❈ **Between 45 and 60 feet tall** (25 to 35 years old). The tree will lose about 10 feet in the process of cutting it down.

❈ **Open-grown.** Most balsam firs grow on the edge of a forest. That means while the side of the tree on the outside of the forest may look full, the side of the tree on the inside of the forest may have been shaded to the point of having very few branches. The State Capitol tree needs to be full on all sides because it will be displayed in the rotunda.

❈ **Accessible.** The equipment used to harvest the tree must be able to get to it. And since watching the cutting of the tree is a popular activity for the state's children, school buses must be able to drive close to the tree. The tree is harvested by a processor, which looks like a backhoe with a specialized head. The processor grabs the tree, saws, or pinches off the base, holds the tree upright, walks it to the truck, and lays it on the flatbed. A tarp is laid over the tree so salt damage is minimized on the trip down to Madison.

Beckman says trees come from areas north of Wausau, the cutoff line where balsams occur naturally. But since balsam firs are considered "trash trees" in the north—good only for pulp—it's getting harder and harder to find them.

JAY SALVO, ASSEMBLY PHOTOGRAPHER

Every December, one Wisconsin evergreen is chosen to be the state's holiday tree and to grace the Capitol rotunda.

boarders or skiers, 11 years and older, with the purchase of a ticket and rental.

If **winter hiking** or more **cross-country skiing** are on your mind, also located in Mount Horeb is a section of the 40-mile **Military Ridge State Trail**. Mostly following the former Chicago & North Western Railroad corridor, the trail is an easy ski with a gentle grade of only 2 to 5 percent. Between Mount Horeb and Fitchburg, to the south of Madison, the trail goes through the Sugar River Valley. The Military Ridge State Trail is also open to **snowmobilers**.

Within Madison's city limits, **cross-country skiers** can stride at **Odana Hills Municipal Golf Course** (ski rentals available) or the 227-acre **Elver Park** on the west side of town. Elver Park has a 6.2-mile trail that is groomed for both classic and skate-skiing. Elver has many personalities in winter: It's also a large **sledding** hill, and a **hockey** and **ice-skating rink**.

Ice-skaters can enjoy another outdoor rink at one of the nation's few free zoos, **Henry Vilas Zoo**. After skating, take time to walk the zoo's grounds, a special treat in winter without the crowds. The cold weather makes the animals more active—all 650 of them. Watching polar bears slide in the snow and jump in their icy pool is the very picture of winter joy. Harbor seals, Bactrian camels, alpaca, elk, bison, Siberian tigers, and lions—who guard their heated rocks—await winter explorers. And while the zoo has penguins, these black-footed individuals may need a little encouragement, since their natural habitat is the Southern coast of Africa!

JOHN T. ANDREWS

Cold weather makes the animals at Henry Vilas Zoo more active—all 650 of them. Bison await winter explorers.

EVENING

Make the winter evening romantic with an intimate dinner at **Fyfe's Corner Bistro**, about a mile (12 blocks) off the square. In a 100-year-old building with cobblestone floors, candle-lit tables, and a vintage bar from the Chicago World's Fair, Fyfe's prepares its signature certified Angus steaks with a variety of tasty sauces and rounds out the menu with chicken, pork, salmon, and lamb entrées.

Continue the romantic aura created by candlelight by engaging in your favorite winter sport under lamplight. A quarter of a mile from Fyfe's (one mile north of the Capitol Square) is the 23-acre **Tenney Park**. Here, under soft lights, you can skate on frozen lagoons in a picturesque, friendly neighborhood. Skate rentals are available at the park's warming house, along with cups of hot cocoa. On Madison's west side, you can **ice-skate under lights** on Lake Wingra at **Vilas Park** or **cross-country ski on lighted trails at Elver Park**.

Monthly nighttime winter walks are scheduled on the Saturday closest to the full moon in the **UW–Madison Arboretum**. Excursions teach you how to spot signs of animals in winter, identify trees, and keep a phenology journal that records the timing of natural events.

JOHN T. ANDREWS

Ice-skaters can glide under the gentle curve of an arched bridge that was built in an older time at Madison's Tenney Park.

Day Three
LATE MORNING

Eat at an old-fashioned diner this morning on Madison's east side. At **Monty's Blue Plate Diner**, you can get simple breakfasts such as oatmeal with raisins and milk to the

LIBERTY ON THE LAKE

The Statue of Liberty once paid a visit to Madison's Lake Mendota —or so it seemed for three weeks in 1979.

In February of that year, Madisonians could see the famous statue's head poking up from the lake ice. The story circulating was that the statue had been flown in by helicopter, but when the flight crew attempted to set her on the ice, the cable lowering her broke. She crashed through the ice, until only the top of her head and arm remained above water.

University of Wisconsin–Madison students Jim Mallon and Leon Varjian were responsible for the astonishing event. Mallon and Varjian were leaders of the university's notorious Pail and Shovel (P&S) Party, which had won control of the student government. The P&S Party made bizarre campaign promises, such as a pledge to dump the entire penny value of the student budget on the ground and allow students to scoop up whatever they could with a pail and shovel. They also promised to cover Bascom Hill with pink flamingos—a promise they kept.

After three weeks, Lady Liberty succumbed to arsonists. The next year, she returned, though again her appearance was brief. The Wisconsin Department of Natural Resources, which determined that she resembled a fishing shanty, demanded she be removed to satisfy regulations. She was taken to a shed, where closer examination could detect that she was actually constructed out of chicken wire, papier-mâché, and plywood.

Lady Liberty on Lake Mendota is now a beloved part of the city's lore. You can still find postcards of her on State Street, and today she ranks a respectable fourth place in the Museum of Hoaxes list of "Top 10 College Pranks of All Time."

more adventurous potato-zucchini pancakes.

Don't leave Madison before taking part in one of winter's most simple, uncomplicated pleasures. UW–Madison students *[see "Liberty on the Lake" sidebar]* learn how to slide down the campus's Bascom Hill on University Housing trays their first winter here, but a better option for those of us who travel without cafeteria equipment would be **sledding** or **tobogganing** on the hill at 61-acre **Olbrich Park** , located on Lake Monona about three miles northeast of the Capitol Square. Olbrich offers a skyline view of the Madison isthmus.

After sledding, walk across the street to the 14-acre **Olbrich Botanical Gardens**. During the month of December, the gardens hold a **Holiday Express Flower and Model Train Show**, featuring large-scale model trains and a **Wreath Walk**. For a post-sledding warm-up, walk through the **Bolz Conservatory** on the grounds, an indoor tropical world filled with fragrant orchids, free-flying birds, orange butterflies, and a waterfall. Sit on a bench and listen to the restful cooing of Australian diamond doves and try to spot quail from Africa, canaries from the Canary Islands, and redheaded parrot finches from New Caledonia in the South Pacific.

AFTERNOON

Before heading out of town, pick up a warm drink at **Michelangelo's Coffee House** just

JOHN T. ANDREWS

On Madison's west side, Elver Park has a 6.2-mile trail that is groomed for both clalssic and skate-skiing.

off the Capitol Square on State Street. An urban legend says that a former governor's aide once described Madison as "60 square miles surrounded by reality." After spending a week-end immersed in winter sports and adrift, at least for a time, in a tropical paradise, what could be more fitting than putting your hands around something called a Chocolate Monkey Mocha?

FOR MORE INFORMATION
GREATER MADISON CHAMBER OF COMMERCE
615 E. Washington Ave.
Madison, WI 53701
(608) 256-8348
www.greatermadisonchamber.com

GREATER MADISON CONVENTION & VISITORS BUREAU
615 E. Washington Ave.
Madison, WI 53703
(608) 255-2537 or (800) 373-6376
www.visitmadison.com

WINTER ATTRACTIONS
D & S BAIT, TACKLE & ARCHERY
1411 Northport Dr., Madison, WI 53704
(608) 241-4225, www.dsbait.com

ELVER PARK
1240 McKenna Blvd., Madison, WI 53719
(608) 266-4711, www.ci.madison.wi.us/parks/major/elverPark.html

FOUR LAKES ICE YACHT CLUB
Call the hotline at (608) 233-9744 on Friday afternoon for the location of that weekend's iceboat races, or check www.iceboat.org.

GOVERNOR NELSON STATE PARK
5140 County Road M, Waunakee, WI 53597
(609) 831-3005, www.wiparks.net

KOHL CENTER
601 W. Dayton St., Madison, WI 53715
(608) 263-5645, www.uwbadgers.com

MILITARY RIDGE STATE TRAIL
4350 Mounds Park Rd., Blue Mounds, WI 53517, (608) 437-7393, www.wiparks.net

MONONA TERRACE COMMUNITY AND CONVENTION CENTER
1 John Nolan Dr., Madison, WI 53703
(608) 261-4000, www.mononaterrace.com

ODANA HILLS MUNICIPAL GOLF COURSE
4635 Odana Rd., Madison, WI 53711
(608) 266-4724

OLBRICH BOTANICAL GARDENS AND BOLZ CONSERVATORY
3330 Atwood Ave., Madison, WI 53704
(608) 246-4550, www.olbrich.org

OLBRICH PARK
3527 Atwood Ave., Madison, WI 53704
(608) 266-4711
www.ci.madison.wi.us/parks/major/olbrich.html

OVERTURE CENTER FOR THE ARTS
201 State St., Madison, WI 53703, (608) 258-4141
www.overturecenter.com

TENNEY PARK
1414 E. Johnson St., Madison, WI 53703
(608) 266-4711
www.ci.madison.wi.us/parks/major/tenney.html

TYROL BASIN SKI AND SNOWBOARD AREA
3487 Bohn Rd., Mount Horeb, WI 53572
(608) 437-4135, *Ski report: (608) 437-4FUN*
www.tyrolbasin.com

UNIVERSITY OF WISCONSIN–MADISON ARBORETUM
1207 Seminole Highway, Madison, WI 53711
(608) 263-7888, www.uwarboretum.org

VILAS PARK
702 S. Randall Ave., Madison, WI 53715
(608) 266-4711, www.ci.madison.wi.us/parks/major/vilaspark.html

HENRY VILAS ZOO
702 S. Randall Ave., Madison, WI 53715
(608) 266-4733, www.vilaszoo.org

WISCONSIN STATE CAPITOL
2 E. Main St., Madison, WI 53703
(608) 266-0382
www.doa.state.wi.us/dbps/capitol/index.asp

WINTER FESTIVALS

ANNUAL WINTER ART FESTIVAL—mid-November. Monona Terrace Community and Convention Center. More than 140 Wisconsin artists exhibit their pottery, watercolors, photography, jewelry, graphics, and sculptures. (608) 261-4000 or www.mononaterrace.com.

WINTER SPORTS SHOW—mid-November. Alliant Energy Center. Ice fishing exhibitors, ski swap, snowmobiles, and more. 1919 Alliant Energy Center Way, Madison, WI 53713. (608) 267-3976 or www.alliantenergycenter.com.

GOVERNOR'S MANSION CHRISTMAS TOURS —December. Governor's Mansion, 99 Cambridge Road, Madison, WI 53704. A Madison tradition, the house is decorated for the holidays. (608) 255-2537 or www.visitmadison.com.

OLBRICH'S HOLIDAY EXPRESS FLOWER AND MODEL TRAIN SHOW—December. The Wisconsin Garden Railway Society's large-scale model trains wind through a landscape of castles and circus tents. Outside, enjoy the Wreath Walk. (608) 246-4550 or www.olbrich.org.

MADISON BALLET'S *THE NUTCRACKER*— mid-December. Overture Center for the Arts. (608) 258-4141 or www.madisonballet.org.

U.S. BANK EVE—December 31. Live bands, face painting, museum activities, and fireworks in venues around the city. (608) 255-2537 or www. visitmadison.com.

CAPITOL SQUARE SPRINTS—mid-January. Athletes from throughout the U.S. and Canada circle the Wisconsin State Capitol in a North American Continental Cup cross-country ski race. The public can try out the course during citizens' races and open-ski periods. (608) 385-8864 or www.capitolsquaresprints.org.

GROUNDHOG DAY CELEBRATION—early February. The city of Sun Prairie welcomes visitors to celebrate in the unofficial "Groundhog Capital of the World." Enjoy a breakfast at 6:30 a.m., followed by Jimmy the Groundhog's prognostication around 7:00 a.m. (608) 837-4547 or www.sunprairiechamber.com.

WISCONSIN FILM FESTIVAL—late March/ early April. Filmgoers fill various Madison venues to see more than 100 films, including independent features, experimental films, documentaries, and shorts. (608) 262-9009 or www.wifilmfest.org.

RESTAURANTS

BLUEPHIES *(lunch and dinner; Saturday and Sunday brunch, 8:00 a.m.–2:00 p.m.)*
2701 Monroe St., No. 700, Madison, WI 53711
(608) 231-3663
www.foodfightinc.com/bluephies.htm

FYFE'S CORNER BISTRO *(lunch and dinner)*
1344 E. Washington Ave., Madison, WI 53703
(608) 251-8700, www.foodspot.com/fyfes

GREAT DANE PUB & BREWING CO.
(lunch and dinner)
123 E. Doty St., Madison, WI 53703
(608) 284-0000, www.greatdanepub.com

L'ETOILE *(dinner)*
25 N. Pinckney St., Madison, WI 53703
(608) 251-0500, www.letoile-restaurant.com

MARIGOLD KITCHEN *(breakfast and lunch; Saturday and Sunday brunch)*
118 S. Pinckney St., Madison, WI 53703
(608) 661-5559, www.marigoldkitchen.com

MICHELANGELO'S COFFEE HOUSE
(7 a.m.-11 p.m. daily)
114 State St.., Madison, WI 53704
(608) 251-5299

MONTY'S BLUE PLATE DINER
(breakfast, lunch, and dinner)
2089 Atwood Ave., Madison, WI 53704
(608) 244-8505
www.foodfightinc.com/montys.htm

RESTAURANT MAGNUS *(dinner)*
120 E. Wilson St., Madison, WI 53703
(608) 258-8787, www.restaurantmagnus.com

THE WHITE HORSE INN *(dinner)*
202 N. Henry St., Madison, WI 53703
(608) 255-9933, www.thewhitehorseinn.com

LODGING
ARBOR HOUSE, AN ENVIRONMENTAL INN
3402 Monroe St., Madison, WI 53711
(608) 238-2981, www.arbor-house.com

CANTERBURY INN
315 W. Gorham St., Madison, WI 53703
(608) 258-8899 or (800) 838-3850
www.madisoncanterbury.com

COLLINS HOUSE BED & BREAKFAST
704 E. Gorham St., Madison, WI 53703
(608) 255-4230, www.collinshouse.com

THE EDGEWATER
666 Wisconsin Ave., Madison, WI 53703
(608) 256-9071 or (800) 922-5512
www.theedgewater.com

MANSION HILL INN
424 N. Pinckney St., Madison, WI 53703
(608) 255-3999 or (800) 798-9070
www.mansionhillinn.com

Chapter Fifteen
A GREAT LAKE WEEKEND
Manitowoc/Two Rivers

LAKE MICHIGAN IS THE LARGEST body of fresh water in the United States. Its overwhelming power and sheer force of personality can't help but color life in two of its Wisconsin shore towns: Manitowoc and Two Rivers.

Originally home to Ojibwa, Ottawa, and Potawatomi Native Americans, the lake area around present-day Manitowoc soon drew European settlers and fur traders. By 1795, the Northwest Fur Company had established a post, and shipbuilding and fishing industries began to prosper. Although the waters were soon overfished, the building of ships endured—from clippers first produced in the 1800s to submarines constructed during World War II. In fact, during the war years, Manitowoc's shipyards became one of the most important naval production facilities in the country, outdoing even the builders on the East Coast. Only with the coming of ore supercarriers, which were too large to be built in Manitowoc's channel, did the golden age of ship production end.

Today, a memorial to Manitowoc's shipbuilding heyday can be found at the city's Wisconsin Maritime Museum. Outside the $2 million riverfront edifice sits the USS *Cobia* submarine. Similar to the ones built in Manitowoc in World War II, the *Cobia* is a National Historic Landmark: it sank 13 Japanese vessels in 1944 and 1945. After being decommissioned, the 311-foot-long *Cobia* was used as a training ship for Milwaukee's reserve units. She is now permanently docked in Manitowoc as a tribute to the city's factory workers who built 28 subs during the war. The Wisconsin Maritime Museum also presides over the nation's best collection of Great Lakes maritime memorabilia and historical re-creations, such as old port towns and harbor fronts.

Just six miles north of Manitowoc is a second lakeshore town, Two Rivers. The two rivers that inspired the name are the East Twin (Mishicot) and the West Twin (Neshota) rivers, which effectively trisect the city as they flow into Lake Michigan.

Although Two Rivers calls itself the "Fishing Capital of Lake Michigan," it is duly proud of another title: "Birthplace of the Ice Cream Sundae." The story goes that on a hot, humid Sunday in 1881, Ed Berner, owner of a soda fountain at 1404 15th Street, was asked by a

The Rawley Point Lighthouse is a bright beacon that warns Lake Michigan ships but beckons visitors.

JOHN T. ANDREWS

man named George Hallauer to top off a dish of ice cream with chocolate sauce. At the time, the sauce had only been used to make sodas. Once the town's youngsters heard about the new dish and tried it, the popularity of the concoction grew. Berner purportedly just served ice cream covered with chocolate sauce on Sundays, until one day a 10-year-old girl insisted upon having it. After that, chocolate-topped ice cream was served daily and became known as the "ice cream sundae." Another local tale says that an enterprising glass vendor saw sales potential in the new recipe and ordered special sets of canoe-shaped dishes for Berner, calling them "sundae dishes." Although Berner's soda fountain no longer stands in Two Rivers, a plaque commemorating the historic invention can be found downtown.

But fish and dessert titles are only asides to Two Rivers. Lake Michigan has placed its profound mark here, as well. And nowhere can it be better felt than at Point Beach State Forest. The waves of the Great Lake crash up on the snowy, sandy shores here, on some of the largest lakeshore dunes in the world. And just as the sun sets and the last natural lights of the sky pale, a two-million-candlepower lighthouse lamp takes over the night watch, respectfully illuminating the Great Lake's dark and churning distance.

Day One
MORNING

The third largest of the five Great Lakes, Lake Michigan is the only one entirely within the United States. On this winter weekend, you'll discover the historic, beautiful, and recreational gifts this very American lake gives us.

You'll first get to know Lake Michigan this weekend by visiting one of its most beautiful creations. Near the town of **Two Rivers** on Highway 310 is the **Woodland Dunes Nature Center.** Here, on the center's 1,150 acres, you'll be able to **winter hike**, **cross-country ski**, or **snowshoe.** Woodland Dunes is a private, nonprofit organization that owns and protects this natural area between Manitowoc and Two Rivers. The spot was first used as a bird-banding center by researchers studying migration. Bird-watchers and local citizens got together and initially purchased 40 acres in 1974 to ensure that this migratory stopover would be preserved. Today, bird-banding programs continue on its larger protectorate.

Although the Woodland Dunes area is home to deer, coyotes, badgers, minks, and weasels, its most famous resident may be the tiny, saw-whet owl. Named for its twittering call, the owl is the featured guest at the annual Owl-Fest in October. The area is also of note because it lies in an ecological "tension zone" between northern and southern habitats. Thus, birds from both habitats commonly nest here; more than 130 species have been recorded in summer surveys.

Woodland Dunes has six trails, which total about six miles, and all are very easy. Two of the six trails begin at the nature center. The .5-mile **Cattail Trail** is a boardwalk though the swamp and marsh, and the two-mile **Willow Trail** passes through open meadow, and then loops around a small pond, an alder thicket, an old tree farm, and through an unusual plot that resembles a tamarack bog, but with cedars. It also goes to the shore of the West Twin River and passes Manitowoc's largest tree, with an 18-foot girth.

Three other wooded trails start at the end of Goodwin Road. The **Yellow Birch Trail** is a boardwalk less than a half mile long. The .75-mile **Black Cherry Trail** and the 1.5-mile **Trillium Trail** are narrow but easy to follow; the Trillium crosses numerous ridges and swales, and boardwalks lead over wet sections of both. The **Conifer Trail** is a .50-mile loop that follows two beach ridges and goes past 11 species of conifer.

The sandy ridges that you see in Woodland Dunes were formed thousands of years ago by a much-higher Lake Michigan. And unlike the beach ridges you'll see later in the weekend at Point Beach State Forest, where the dunes formed parallel to Lake Michigan, Woodland Dunes' ridges lie in a spread-out, fan-shaped pattern.

The Woodland Dunes Nature Center, located in an 1800s stone farmhouse, is open on Friday from 9:00 a.m. to 4:00 p.m., Saturday from 9:00 a.m. to 11:00 a.m., and closed on Sunday, but the trails are accessible 24 hours a day.

AFTERNOON

At the corner of Jackson and 22nd Streets in Two Rivers is **Café Alkamye**, where you'll stop for lunch. In this light and airy café, local artists display their work, and the windows exhibit a view of the East Twin River and the historic North Pier Lighthouse. Have a bowl of Neshota chowder—chunks of boneless whitefish, corn, and white and wild rice flavored with bacon—or a plate of pasta "carnivora" with roasted roma tomatoes and sweet Italian sausage.

After lunch, drive six miles south to Manitowoc, your second Lake Michigan port this weekend. The city of Manitowoc contains several parks, and two are **cross-country ski** enthusiasts' favorites. The 67-acre **Henry Schuette Park** on Broadway Street has three miles of groomed trails for classic and skate-skiing. The 78-acre **Silver Creek Park** on Tenth Street also has three miles of groomed trails for both types of skiing but comes with **sledding and tubing hills**, and an **ice-skating rink**.

From the city parks, it's a short hop to the **Westport Bed and Breakfast** located six blocks from Lake Michigan and downtown. In this 1879 historic home, most of the guest rooms are appointed with double whirlpool tubs and gas fireplaces. All have rose-scented, crisply ironed sheets, and you'll find the refrigerator in your room stocked with wine and sparkling cider. Make sure you partake of the warm cookies in the dining room before you unpack.

EVENING

A bonus for staying at the Westport is a free dessert at the **Courthouse Pub** in Manitowoc. Even if you're not staying at the bed and breakfast, make the Courthouse Pub your choice for dinner tonight. Start with the sizzling artichoke hearts for an appetizer, and move on to the Chicken Tuscany entrée. Hopefully, you'll still have room for the cranberry upside-down cake or the decadent Oblivion Flourless Chocolate Cake. The pub handcrafts its own brews, such as the Chief Wawatam Steam Lager, and has received the *Wine Spectator* Award of Excellence for its wine list and menu three years in a row.

Relax with a whirlpool soak back at the bed and breakfast tonight, or check the schedule for the **Capital Civic Centre**. In November and December, several holiday productions and performances are planned.

Day Two
MORNING

Enjoy a candlelight breakfast at the Westport Bed and Breakfast, or have a basket delivered to your room. Expect a feast: stuffed French toast, grapefruit, orange juice, coffee, muffins, bacon, and sausage are typical morning fare. If you'd like to go out for breakfast, the **Culture Cafe** on Calumet Avenue has bagels with cream cheese, cucumbers, and tomatoes or a hot ham, eggs, and cheese sandwich—and 12 varieties of fresh-roasted fair-trade and organic coffees.

Manitowoc is steeped in Lake Michigan maritime history, and most of it is remembered at the **Wisconsin Maritime Museum**. In early December, the museum re-enacts one of the most unique Wisconsin holiday traditions, the **Lake Michigan Christmas Tree Ship Celebration**. A ship loaded with Christmas trees sails into Manitowoc, arriving at the harbor by the museum. Santa is on board, along with shipmates who help him unload the trees and hand out candy to the children waiting on shore. The trees are donated by a local tree farm and are given to area families designated by the Salvation Army. Those with tickets pick up their free trees on the shore. If you're in town for this event, don't miss it. It is a true treasure of Wisconsin's heritage.

Another holiday event worth planning to catch is **Pinecrest Historical Village's "A Holiday in History."** The 60-acre village, three miles west of Manitowoc off Highway JJ, is an ensemble of

JOHN T. ANDREWS

Loaded with holiday trees—and Santa—the annual Lake Michigan Christmas Tree Ship prepares to dock near the Wisconsin Maritime Museum.

THE TREE IN YOUR FRONT YARD

by Larry J. Schweiger
President and Chief Executive Officer
National Wildlife Federation

Book Author's Note: I was captivated by this article when it first appeared in the June/July 2005 issue of National Wildlife, *the magazine of the National Wildlife Federation (NWF). Larry Schweiger, the organization's president, has graciously allowed us to reprint this article in its entirety.—C.G.A.*

Our children are disconnecting with nature. The average suburban young person has little relationship to increasingly distant wild places. By the time they are seven years old, most youngsters have been exposed to more than 20,000 advertisements. They can identify 200 corporate logos but cannot identify the trees growing in their front yards. They can navigate the Web with ease, but few of them have climbed a tree and even fewer have the love of nature needed to be good stewards. How can a person be a good steward if they don't care about trees, wildlife, or wild places?

Trees always inspired me as a child, so when my seventh-grade science teacher asked each student to do a project, my choice was an easy one. I set out to make a leaf collection of every native tree in the Pittsburgh area. I spent countless hours hiking forests, identifying trees, pressing leaves. In the process, I developed a deeper appreciation of the richness of our forests. In many ways, that leaf collection helped launch my career in conservation.

Trees are amazing. They give meaning to the notion of "multitasking." Their shade cools us during summer. In winter, their tossing branches buffer harsh winds. They bear tasty fruits and nuts, often in extravagant abundance. They provide us with wood and paper products. All the while, trees produce oxygen, sequester carbon dioxide, and help reduce global warming. They build soil and reduce water runoff and pollution.

Trees even make us well when we are sick. Aspirin is derived from willows. The breast-cancer fighting compound Taxol is extracted from western yews. Chemicals from gingko trees are widely used as memory enhancers.

Though often overlooked, trees are an essential element of local beauty. They quietly define place. Imagine giant redwoods reaching skyward in a northern California coastal forest, mature ponderosa pines in the Rockies, stately live oaks draped with Spanish moss on a Southern plantation, massive white oaks with widely outspread branches on Midwestern farms, multicolored autumn landscapes of mixed forests in New England.

What would these places be like without their unique trees?

In recent times, we have been taking down trees by the millions and replacing them with highways and shopping malls. Along with the loss of trees, we lose the understory of native wild plants and wildlife that they shelter.

I wish every conservation-minded adult would take a moment to introduce just one child to just one tree. It's a small step but who knows what little actions like this can do to stimulate childhood curiosity? How can we expect our children to care if you and I don't help them make the critical connections to nature while they are young enough to have their values shaped? If you need help with tree identification, visit our resource library at enature.com.

Trees give us so much and they desperately need our attention—and the attention of our children. If you want to do something for nature this season, plant a tree and while you are at it, plant a seed in the heart of a future steward.

more than 20 buildings dating from as far back as the 1840s, brought here and painstakingly restored. During this special winter weekend, the village puts on an old-fashioned, living-history Christmas, with holiday trees decorating the homes, "villagers" singing carols in the church, and Santa walking the footpaths in a long robe. Make sure you pay a visit to the old-time bank and listen to the banker tell his favorite stories about the "big" robberies of 1937 (the robber got away with $4,000) and 1957. If it's a particularly cold day, just go over to the blacksmith shop and stand near as he works in the heat of his large fire.

JOHN T. ANDREWS

**At Pinecrest Historical Village's "A Holiday in History,"
volunteer "villagers" demonstrate century-old skills,
such as stringing cranberries for holiday decorations.**

THE ANNUAL CHRISTMAS TREE SHIP CELEBRATION IN MANITOWOC, WISCONSIN
by Sarah Spude-Olson

Sarah Spude-Olson was born and raised in Sturgeon Bay, Wisconsin. After graduating from UW–Stevens Point in 1998, she worked for a publishing company before becoming marketing associate for the Wisconsin Maritime Museum in Manitowoc. Spude-Olson now lives in Collins, Wisconsin, with her husband, daughter, and three Labrador retrievers.

In the waning years of the 19th century and early years of the 20th century, many vessels on Lake Michigan served as Christmas Tree Ships. Each year, schooners would sail to Manistique, Michigan, to cut fresh trees and then make the weeklong journey south to Chicago, arriving just after Thanksgiving. Many families in Wisconsin and Illinois bought their Christmas trees from the decks of sailing schooners moored along the waterfront in communities up and down the Lake Michigan coast. The sight of these ships became a Christmas tradition.

More than 50 Christmas tree schooners have been documented on the Great Lakes alone. And the practice of hauling trees via boat was not exclusive to the lakes. Schooners often carried trees to markets throughout the Northeast, and there's at least one account of a ship taking refrigerated trees to Hawaii.

The most famous was the three-masted schooner, *Rouse Simmons*. Bound for Chicago, it vanished in a gale off the coast of Two Rivers, Wisconsin, on November 23, 1912. All 17 crew members were lost.

Today, the Christmas Tree Ships are remembered and celebrated. The Wisconsin Maritime Museum relives those days as a ship loaded with trees—and Santa—sails into the Manitowoc harbor during the annual Christmas Tree Ship Celebration. The ship docks just west of the museum, where the trees are distributed to needy area families. The event celebrates the people who took pride in braving early winter storms to ensure that their cargos of trees arrived in time for the holidays.

AFTERNOON

In accordance with this morning's dip into history and the weekend's Lake Michigan theme, have lunch at **Kurtz's Pub & Deli** in Two Rivers. Since 1904, Kurtz's has been serving beer and drinks by the yard and half-yard to sailing merchants docked nearby. Today, you'll still find a wide variety of brews, as well as a long menu of hot and cold sandwiches, melts, wraps and salads. They also offer great hot-fudge sundaes: the "Kurtz's Delight" is a combination of Door county cherries, homemade hot fudge, and real whipped cream.

For superlative **snowshoeing**, **winter hiking**, **cross-country skiing**, **snowmobiling**, or **winter camping**, plan to spend the afternoon at **Point Beach State Forest**, four miles north of Two Rivers on Highway O (Rustic Road 16). This long, thin, six-mile forest and dunes area tucked up against Lake Michigan was once considered for a national park. When the plans fell through, local citizens convinced the Wisconsin State Legislature to establish a state forest instead. The first parcel of land was acquired in 1937, and today Point Beach State Forest covers 2,903 acres.

In this hard-fought and locally treasured forest *[see "The Tree in Your Front Yard" sidebar]*, the dune ridges along the shoreline, residual effects of a glacial lake that retreated 5,500 years ago, have been designated a National Natural Landmark and are one reason the entire forest is a State Scientific Area.

Not only are Point Beach State Forest's natural features renowned, but a manmade feature is also of historic and aesthetic note. The **Rawley Point Lighthouse**, located near the park office, is one of the largest and brightest on the Great Lakes and has been listed on the National Register of Historic Places. Nineteen miles off shore, sailors can see the lighthouse's two-million-candle-power beacon.

Snowshoeing or **winter hiking** at the forest on the five-mile, limestone **Rawley Point Bicycle Trail** will take you right by the picturesque lighthouse. Dress warm for this flat-to-rolling trek next to the winter waves and wind of Lake Michigan. At the spot where the cur-

A highlight of any cross-country skier's season is a candlelight ski. With only candles and moonlight to show the way on a crisp, winter night, all your senses come alive.

MANITOWOC AREA VISITOR & CONVENTION BUREAU

rent 113-foot-tall Rawley Point Lighthouse stands, there has been a light since 1853. Before the new lighthouse was built, 26 ships foundered or stranded on the point. One of them was the *Rouse Simmons,* a three-masted schooner carrying Christmas trees to Chicago. She went down in a storm in November 1912. No trace of her was found until the spring, when fishermen began pulling up nets tangled with Christmas trees *[see "The Annual Christmas Tree Ship Celebration in Manitowoc, Wisconsin" sidebar].* With your camera, capture a shot of the dunes, the majestic, white lighthouse towering over the sandy pines, and the crashing lake waves. For more dramatic light effects, come back to this spot tomorrow morning at sunrise.

There are 11 miles of groomed **cross-country ski** trails here for both classic and skate-skiing techniques. The easy, flat-to-rolling, 3.4-mile **Red Pine Trail** can be used for traditional striding. Starting at the nature center, you'll ski over old, wooded dunes and through a beautiful stand of birch and hemlock. The **Ridges Trail** offers three loops: start with the three-mile **Red Loop**. Add the **Blue Loop** for a total of 5.5 miles and then the **Yellow Loop** for a total trail length of 7.25 miles. While on your skis, watch for wild turkeys, deer, foxes, coyotes, weasels, and minks.

Snowmobilers will find a through-trail at Point Beach that connects the forest with the county snowmobile trail system and the city of Two Rivers. Vehicles and trailers may be

---

 ## AN ODE TO MY ALUMINUM CHRISTMAS TREE

As a child growing up in the early 1960s, I remember the first time an aluminum Christmas tree made its appearance in our home. We had always had real trees before, and the aluminum tree was so different—so metallic, so "unreal"—that it seemed futuristic. I felt like my family was the "coolest" on the block.

My father placed the tree in front of the "picture window" of our 1950s-built home. Every evening, my mother would dutifully plug in the plastic color-wheel projector that sat on the floor next to the tree and changed its look from red to green to yellow to blue.

What I didn't know then was that the trees were manufactured in my own state of Wisconsin, at Manitowoc's Aluminum Specialty Company. For 100 years, the Manitowoc plant had been making pots, pans, and kitchen utensils, earning the city the title "Aluminum Cookware Capital of the World." In 1959, however, they hit a nerve in America with their "Evergleam," an all-aluminum Christmas tree. The trees even became popular throughout the world, and millions were shipped out from the Manitowoc plant.

In 1965, *A Charlie Brown Christmas* was first aired on TV. Charlie despairs about the commercialism of Christmas and bucks the fashion of the time by buying a real—albeit small and fragile—Christmas tree, despite Lucy's instructions to get the "biggest aluminum tree you can find." Shortly after that year, my family, and millions of others, turned away from the aluminum trees and went back to the more natural variety.

Forty years later, I do, though, still think nostalgically about that very unusual tree and wonder where it is now. Is it sitting in a museum somewhere or coloring the home of a collector? Perhaps it's the one that now stands at Manitowoc's Visitor Information Center—perhaps it has returned to its roots.

parked at Port Sandy Bay. At least five plowed **winter camping** sites are kept open. What better time to camp here than in the winter, when you can have the forest practically to yourself?

If you arrive back in Manitowoc early, you'll be able to do a few laps and several spins at the **Manitowoc County Ice Center**. Call for public **ice-skating** times, which usually run from 2:15 to 4:15 p.m. on Saturdays.

EVENING

Tonight, get ready for some tasty Lake Michigan whitefish at **Machut's Supper Club** in Two Rivers. Machut's was voted the 2002 No. 1 Supper Club in Wisconsin by *Wisconsin Trails* magazine. Along with seafood, the restaurant features steaks and broasted chicken or pork chops, a specialty they started in 1964.

This evening, check to see whether **Pinecrest Historical Village** or **Point Beach State Forest** is offering their **candlelight ski/hikes**, typically held in late February at Pinecrest. You can ski or hike a three-quarter-mile loop around the village from 7:00 to 9:00 p.m. Point Beach State Forest's Candlelight Ski/Hike is often held in early January.

Day Three
MORNING AND AFTERNOON

After another hearty and romantic breakfast at your bed and breakfast, ease into the day by taking a tour of the **Rahr–West Art Museum** in Manitowoc. Located on Eighth Street, the museum is housed in a Victorian home of one of Manitowoc's pioneer families. This

MANITOWOC AREA VISITOR & CONVENTION BUREAU

"Hard-water fishing" can be a peaceful time alone or a shared trip with a good buddy.

mansion, with its intricate woodworking, beamed ceilings, and stained-glass windows, is listed on the National Register of Historic Places and boasts one of the finer collections of art in the Midwest. Exhibitions are mounted in three galleries featuring thematic presentations of works from the museum's 2,000-plus collection of American art. From mid-November to early January, you can experience **"Christmas in the Mansion,"** where each room is decorated in holiday accoutrements. Special exhibits take place during this event, such as the tribute to the aluminum Christmas tree. The trees were once made by the Aluminum Specialty Company, a cookware manufacturer that was an icon in Manitowoc for more than 100 years. The company turned out more aluminum Christmas trees than anywhere else during the rage in the early 1960s—an estimated four million between 1959 and 1969 *[see "An Ode to My Aluminum Christmas Tree" sidebar]*.

For more **snowmobiling**, take to the 222 miles of trails maintained by nine clubs of the Manitowoc County Snowmobile Alliance. Call the snowmobile hotline at (800) 627-4896 for a trail map. To learn about snow conditions, call the Manitowoc County Park and Recreation Department at (920) 758-7669.

For a last look at the stunning Lake Michigan shoreline, **winter hike** on the six-mile **Mariners Trail**, which runs between Manitowoc and Two Rivers. You can pick up the trail in downtown Manitowoc at the Eighth Street Bridge near the Wisconsin Maritime Museum and the USS *Cobia* submarine.

Touted as one of the finest paved promenades in the Midwest, the Mariners Trail connects your weekend's two port towns—and you with the longest continuous view of Lake Michigan in the state of Wisconsin.

FOR MORE INFORMATION

MANITOWOC/TWO RIVERS AREA CHAMBER OF COMMERCE
1515 Memorial Dr., Manitowoc, WI 54221
(920) 684-5575 or (800) 262-7892
www.manitowocchamber.com

MANITOWOC AREA VISITOR & CONVENTION BUREAU
4221 Calumet Ave.
Manitowoc, WI 54221
(920) 683-4388 or (800) 627-4896
www.manitowoc.org

WASHINGTON HOUSE MUSEUM AND VISITOR CENTER
1622 Jefferson St., Two Rivers, WI 54241
(920) 793-2490, www.lhinn.com/history.html

WINTER ATTRACTIONS

CAPITOL CIVIC CENTRE
917 S. Eighth St., Manitowoc, WI 54220
(920) 683-2184, www.cccshows.org

HENRY SCHUETTE PARK
3700 Broadway St.
Manitowoc, WI 54220
(920) 683-4530, www.manitowoc.org

MANITOWOC COUNTY ICE CENTER
(call for public skating schedule; typically Friday 11:00 a.m.–2:00 p.m.; Saturday 2:15 p.m.–4:15 p.m.; Sunday 2:45 p.m.–4:45 p.m.)
Expo Grounds, 100 Vista Rd.
Manitowoc, WI 54220, (920) 682-2098

PINECREST HISTORICAL VILLAGE
924 Pine Crest Ln., Manitowoc, WI 54220
(920) 684-5110,
www.mchistsoc.org/pinecrest.htm

POINT BEACH STATE FOREST
9400 Highway O, Two Rivers, WI 54241
(920) 794-7480 or (888) 947-2757
www.wiparks.net

RAHR–WEST ART MUSEUM *(open Friday 10:00 a.m.–4:00 p.m.; Saturday and Sunday 11:00 a.m.–4:00 p.m.)*
610 N. Eighth St., Manitowoc, WI 54220
(920) 683-4501, www.rahrwestartmuseum.org

HENRY SCHUETTE PARK
3700 Broadway St., Manitowoc, WI 54220
(920) 683-4530, www.manitowoc.org

SILVER CREEK PARK
3001 S. Tenth St., Manitowoc, WI 54220
(920) 683-4530, www.manitowoc.org

WISCONSIN MARITIME MUSEUM
75 Maritime Dr., Manitowoc, WI 54220
(920) 684-0218 or (866) 724-2356
www.wimaritimemuseum.org

WOODLAND DUNES NATURE CENTER
*(Friday 8:00 a.m.–4:00 p.m.; open weekends for
special events; trails open 24 hours a day)*
3000 Hawthorne Ave. *(Highway 310)*
Two Rivers, WI 54241, (920) 793-4007
www.woodlanddunes.com

WINTER FESTIVALS

CHRISTMAS IN THE MANSION—mid-November to early January. Each room of the
Rahr–West Art Museum Victorian mansion is
decorated by area volunteers, offering a visual
feast. (920) 683-4501 or www.rahrwestartmuseum.org.

A HOLIDAY IN HISTORY—early December.
Pinecrest Historical Village. 12:00 p.m.–4:00 p.m.
The winter season of 100 years ago comes to life
with decorated trees, music, food, historical games,
activities, and storytelling. (920) 684-4445 or
www.mchistsoc.org.

**LAKE MICHIGAN CHRISTMAS TREE SHIP
CELEBRATION—early December.** Celebrate the
days when many Wisconsin families bought their
Christmas trees from the deck of sailing schooners
moored along the waterfront. Ship arrives at 11:30
a.m. Wisconsin Maritime Mu-seum (866) 724-
2356 or www.wimaritimemuseum.org.

WINTERFEST—late February. Vintage snowmobile races, entertainment, and food at the
Manitowoc County Expo, 4921 Expo Drive, Manitowoc, WI 54220, (920) 683-4378.

RESTAURANTS

CAFÉ ALKAMYE *(lunch and dinner)*
1033 22nd St., Two Rivers, WI 54241
(920) 553-2233
www.foodspot.com/cafealkamye

COURTHOUSE PUB *(Friday, lunch and dinner;
Saturday dinner; Sunday closed)*
1001 S. Eighth St., Manitowoc, WI 54220
(920) 686-1166, www.courthousepub.com

CULTURE CAFE *(breakfast, lunch, and dinner)*
3949 Calumet Ave., Manitowoc, WI 54220
(920) 682-6844, www.culture-cafe.com

KURTZ'S PUB & DELI *(lunch and dinner;
closed Sunday)*
1410 Washington St., Two Rivers, WI 54241
(920) 793-1222

MACHUT'S SUPPER CLUB *(Friday and
Saturday dinner; Sunday lunch and dinner)*
3911 Lincoln Ave., Two Rivers, WI 54241
(920) 793-9432, www.machuts.com

NEWEY'S RESTAURANT *(Friday–Saturday,
breakfast, lunch, and dinner; Sunday brunch)*,
914 S. Eighth St., Manitowoc, WI 54220
(920) 769-0259

LODGING

BIRCH CREEK INN
4626 Calumet Ave., Manitowoc, WI 54220
(920) 684-3374 or (800) 424-6126
www.birchcreekinn.com

INN ON MARITIME BAY
101 Maritime Dr., Manitowoc, WI 54220
(920) 682-7000 or (800) 654-5353
www.innonmaritimebay.com

LIGHTHOUSE INN
1515 Memorial Dr., Two Rivers, WI 54241
(920) 793-4524 or (800) 228-6416
www.lhinn.com

WESTPORT BED AND BREAKFAST
635 N. Eighth St., Manitowoc, WI 54220
(920) 686-0465 or (888) 686-0465
www.thewestport.com

RED FOREST BED AND BREAKFAST
1421 25th St., Two Rivers, WI 54241
(920) 793-1794 or (888) 250-2272
www.redforestbb.com

Chapter Sixteen
A BIG CITY WINTER
Milwaukee

W ISCONSINITES TEND TO THINK of Milwaukee as the "Big City." Home to nearly 600,000 people, it is the largest city in Wisconsin and the 19th largest in the country. Milwaukee has the best of what big cities can offer: world-class museums and cultural outlets, restaurants, and sports venues and events.

But because this big city is made up of several smaller, cohesive communities and groups, Milwaukee also has the best of what small towns offer: roots festivals, lots of ethnic traditions and eateries, and tons of neighborhood parks.

In fact, in the 96 square miles that are known as Milwaukee, there are more acres of parkland per person than anywhere else in the country. Milwaukee County Parks offer nearly 15,000 acres for your recreation and relaxation. On foot, an ice-skating, ice-fishing, sledding, tobogganing, winter hiking, or cross-country skiing excursion is always only minutes and steps away.

By car—only minutes and a few miles away—are two state forests, several state trailheads, and a nature sanctuary. The Schlitz Audubon Nature Center, on the shores of Lake Michigan just 15 minutes from downtown Milwaukee, is 185 acres devoted to communing with the wild and gaining an appreciation for our natural heritage. Twenty minutes from downtown, in Havenwoods State Forest, you can winter hike or cross-country ski through grasslands, forests, and wetlands that will make you think you're far removed from any urban area. Forty minutes from downtown is the Lapham Peak Unit of the Kettle Moraine State Forest, a favorite of cross-country skiers for its enchanting woods, prairies, and oak savannas. The Ice Age National Scenic Trail, with its kettles, moraines, and eskers, can be accessed in the forest and will remove you again not only in place but in time.

The Algonquin Indians called the area that is now Milwaukee "Millioki," which means the "Gathering Place by the Waters." Milwaukee is still that gathering place. Today, diverse groups of people have carved out enclaves for their nationalities and ethnicities, yet they work together to build a single city that is rich in tradition. In Milwaukee, you can get the best in culture, lodgings, and dining establishments, yet still take a walk on a rural trail.

Milwaukee is a big city with a lot of little touches, which serve to make it warm and inviting in winter.

JOHN T. ANDREWS

A beautiful city any time of the year, Milwaukee takes on an almost pristine quality when covered with a layer of snow.

Day One
MORNING

Big Milwaukee is composed of small neighborhoods, so start your weekend by getting to know one of them: the **Historic Third Ward**. Right downtown, the Third Ward boasts the greatest concentration of art galleries in the city and many restaurants with distinctive personalities. Have breakfast at the **Bella Caffé** on N. Milwaukee Street, where you'll find gourmet coffee drinks, baked oatmeal served with apples and maple syrup, and daily quiches such as spinach, mushroom, and parmesan, and asparagus and roasted pepper.

There is a quiet side to the population-dense Milwaukee that you're probably not as familiar with, and winter is a great time to look at the city from a new perspective. Near downtown Milwaukee on North Hopkins Street, about a 20-minute drive from the central city, is a pocket of calm called **Havenwoods State Forest**. This "haven" for outdoor enthusiasts is a 217-acre tract of woods and fields with more than three miles of limestone-surfaced trails. A four-acre pond attracts a variety of wildlife, which makes its hiking trails also popular for **cross-country skiers**—although the trails are ungroomed and untracked. Stop inside the impressive **Havenwoods Environmental Awareness Center**, a 10,000-square-foot, passive solar building, featuring a 70-seat auditorium, display area, classroom, and resource center.

The Milwaukee County Parks System has more than 150 parks and parkways on nearly 15,000 acres of land. If you prefer to **sled**, **ice-skate**, or **ice fish**, use the morning to explore some of this county's parks. **Daytime sledding hills** are found at Columbus (7301 W. Courtland Ave.), Greene (4235 S. Lipton Ave.), Hales Corners (5765 S. New Berlin Rd.), LaFollette (9418 W. Washington St.), Maitland (6001 S. 13th St.), McCarty (8214 W. Cleveland Ave.), McGovern (5400 N. 51st St.), Sheridan (4800 S. Lake Dr.), Whitnall (5879 S. 92nd St.), and Wilson Recreation (4001 S. 20th St.) parks. **Lighted sledding hills** for daytime or nighttime use are located at Brown Deer (7835 N. Green Bay Rd.), Currie (3535 N. Mayfair Rd.), Dretzka (12020 W. Bradley Rd.), Humboldt (3000 S. Howell Ave.), Mitchell (524 S. Layton Blvd.), and Pulaski (2677 S. 16th St.) parks.

PEGGY FLEMING HAD IT ALL:
ICE-SKATING TIPS

I grew up emulating Peggy Fleming. Watching her on TV in the 1968 Winter Olympics, she seemed to bring a grace and elegance to ice-skating that I'd never seen down at my elementary school's flooded parking lot. I remember her knee-length, flowing costumes—so different from the short tutu-like outfits on the other skaters up to then, and which had left me flat.

After watching Peggy, I did manage to teach myself to skate backwards and do a mean cross-over on my school's little rink, but I never made it to the Olympics. I sure did feel like I was Peggy, though. And that's the beauty of ice-skating: by learning just a few basic techniques, anyone can glide across a Wisconsin parking lot, pond, stream, river, or lake and feel like a winner.

Some basics to keep in mind when ice-skating:

❄ **Maintain proper posture for balance.** Keep your chin up, your body upright, and knees slightly bent.

❄ **Think "stroking," not "propelling."** Don't start skating by propelling yourself on the blade or off the pick (the sharp teeth on the front of the skate blade). The picks are there for special feats, like spins or jumps. Get your forward thrust by pushing side to side. A skater moves forward by "stroking": pushing forward on one foot, then gliding, then pushing and gliding with the other foot.

❄ **Learn to stop.** There are three stopping techniques. In the "snowplow," you push your heels outward and your toes inward while moving forward. In the "T-stop," you glide forward on one skate while placing the other skate at a right angle to it, coming to a stop with your feet in a T formation. In a "hockey stop," turn both of your feet sideways and bend your knees, helping your blades to dig into the ice.

❄ **Turn by using a "cross-over."** To turn, alternately cross and uncross your feet while stroking. To turn to the right, for example, cross the left foot over the right while moving forward.

❄ **Don't worry about falling.** You will. Just accept it. The secret to avoiding injury is to relax and keep in mind that vision of how you looked just like Peggy Fleming, the moment before you fell.

Outdoor ice-skating is allowed on the park lagoons when the ice is six inches or more thick. For a great glide on a rink, go to Brown Deer (7835 N. Green Bay Rd.), Dineen (6901 W. Vienna St.), Grant (Oak Creek Parkway at Sixth Ave. in south Milwaukee), Greenfield (2028 S. 124th St.), Humboldt (3000 S. Howell Ave.), Jacobus (6501 W. Hillside Lane), Lake (2975 N. Lake Park Rd.), Scout Lake (5902 W. Loomis Rd.), or Whitnall (5879 S. 92nd St.) parks.

For a very big-city, outdoor ice-skating experience, go to **Slice of Ice in Red Arrow Park** in downtown Milwaukee at 920 N. Water St. The park, redesigned in 1999 with private and public funding, was named to honor the 32nd Red Arrow Division of the U.S. Army. Slice of Ice is an **outdoor refrigerated rink** that can comfortably accommodate 100 skaters at a time *[see "Peggy Fleming Had It All: Ice-Skating Tips" sidebar].* The 128- by 95-foot oval is open from December through February. A cooling system under the concrete allows park officials to keep things icy even if temperatures reach the mid-40s. Skate rental is available.

Either from the warming house's floor-to-ceiling windows or from the rooftop overlook, you can get a great view of all that's happening on the ice.

The Brown Deer, Greenfield, Humboldt, McCarty, McGovern, Scout Lake, Washington (1859 N. 40th St.), and Wilson (1601 W. Howard Ave.) lagoons are popular **ice-fishing** spots.

One of the most scenic county parks is 140-acre **Lake Park,** sitting on a bluff overlooking Lake Michigan. The park was planned by Frederick Law Olmsted's celebrated firm, which also designed New York's Central Park. Here, with a spectacular view of the lake, you'll want to **winter hike** to the south end of the park to the **North Point Lighthouse**, a Romanesque light station built in 1855 and rebuilt in 1912. The 74-foot lighthouse, like many buildings in Milwaukee, was constructed with cream city brick, a light-yellow-colored brick made from clay found in the region. Bring your camera—Lake Park is considered an east side Milwaukee beauty mark, and it is the only park whose grounds are graced by a gourmet French restaurant, **Bartolotta's Lake Park Bistro.**

AFTERNOON

Located on the second floor of the Lake Park pavilion, Bartolotta's Bistro serves dishes made in traditional French-cooking styles. It claims to have Wisconsin's only true French *rotisol* (rotisserie). Tables are positioned in front of the windows, allowing you to look out at the lake as you dine on crepes, sandwiches, and salads. Try the *tranche de saumon au beurre de sancerre* (sautéed Atlantic salmon with whipped potatoes in a white, wine-butter sauce) or *croques monsieur,* a classic Parisian sandwich made of French ham and Gruyère cheese.

After lunch, head back to Milwaukee's lower east side and the **County Clare, an Irish Inn & Pub**. Since Milwaukee is a city of neighborhoods and a mixture of ethnicities, staying at the County Clare—especially if you're in town during the famous St. Patrick's Day Parade—will immerse you in the traditions of one of Milwaukee's proud ethnic groups. The County Clare is the Midwest's only Irish lodging, pub, and restaurant combination. All of its 30 guest rooms have double whirlpool baths and four-poster beds. Celtic music envelops you in the emerald-green lobby.

Another benefit to staying on Milwaukee's east side is that you can literally almost ski

The Schlitz Audubon Nature Center on Lake Michigan offers quiet outdoor escapes from the surrounding urban hustle and bustle.

out the front door. If you're staying at the County Clare, Park East, Knickerbocker, Pfister, or Astor, it's an easy jaunt over to the parks rimming the Lake Michigan shoreline. Just strap on your **cross-country skis**, take a tour along the top of the bluffs that overlook the lake, glide down the slopes, and cruise along the icy lake. Listen to the ice groan on a clear winter evening. All of Milwaukee County Parks allow free cross-country skiing whenever Mother Nature cooperates. Trails are open from dawn until 10:00 p.m.

This afternoon, you'll want to experience another of Milwaukee's less well-known outdoor marvels that lie deep in an urban setting. The **Schlitz Audubon Nature Center** on East Brown Deer Road, just 15 minutes from downtown, is a great place to **winter hike**, **cross-country ski,** or **snowshoe.** This 185-acre nature sanctuary includes prairies, ponds, bluffs, ravines, and an environmentally sensitive nature center with exhibits. The sanctuary represents the largest undeveloped green space along Lake Michigan's shoreline in Milwaukee County. Although the six miles of trails are not groomed or tracked, they are favorites of those who enjoy silent sports. Since the Lake Michigan shoreline is a major migration route, more than 200 bird species have been noted here—see if you can spot a snow bunting. You might also see deer, foxes, and minks. You can even climb a 60-foot observation tower with a parapet for a sweeping lake view.

The Schlitz Audubon's mostly level trails include three loops: the 2.2-mile **Grassland Trail,** the .8-mile **Ravine Trail,** and the 0.7-mile **Beach Trail.** The two-mile **Woodland Trail** leads through a deep ravine and the .35-mile **Green Tree Trail** will take you to the observation tower. Winter hike or snowshoe on any of the five trails. Only the Grassland Trail accommodates cross-country skiing.

Before leaving the sanctuary, be sure to stop inside the Dorothy K. Vallier Environmental Learning Center. This 39,000-square-foot, green facility is one of the most environmentally sensitive buildings in the nation. It employs a well-insulated, massive, and self-shading shell. The building design helps create an energy flywheel, which helps the structure stay cool in summer and warm in winter. Supplemental heating and cooling is provided by a geothermal heat pump, and storm water is collected in an outdoor rain garden. Sustainable wood resourced from Aldo Leopold's homestead, solar power panels, low-flow toilets, and plenty of natural lighting are just a few of the other environmentally friendly features.

If you're in town in early December, try to catch some of the **Christmas in the Ward** festivities. Head to the Third Ward for the tree-lighting ceremony at 5:30 p.m. and fireworks at 6:00 p.m.

EVENING

Tonight, you'll get a taste from another one of Milwaukee's proud ethnic groups when you dine at **Karl Ratzsch's Old World Restaurant**. Amid an extensive stein collection and hand-painted murals, try the tender German *sauerbraten, wiener schnitzel,* or Usinger's bratwurst plate. Bavarian music is often featured entertainment, and a pianist is on hand nightly.

Milwaukee is a beacon for winter sports spectators as well as sports recreationists. Almost 2,000 parking spaces are available downtown within a two- to three-block radius of the Bradley Center. Tickets for a **Milwaukee Bucks** basketball game are hit and miss, but you can usually land them by calling (414) 276-4545 or logging online at www.bucks.com. Also playing in the Bradley Center are the **Milwaukee Admirals** of the International

Hockey League. The IHL is a minor-league, quasi-farm system of the National Hockey League. The top-notch Division 1A **Marquette University Golden Eagles** basketball team also plays at the Bradley Center. Whichever winter sport you like to watch, you'll most likely find it being played somewhere in Milwaukee.

Day Two
MORNING

If you're in town mid-March, you'll want to rise early for the historic **St. Patrick's Day Parade** in downtown Milwaukee. Ask for an early breakfast at your bed and breakfast. Or, if you're staying at the County Clare, you'll be treated to fruit, corned beef hash, French toast, and scrambled eggs. Ask for a table by a window and look out on the Victorian-mansion-filled neighborhood.

Dating back to March 17, 1843, Milwaukee's St. Patrick's Day Parade is one of the oldest in the United States. Before Milwaukee's incorporation as a city and the statehood of Wisconsin, the Milwaukee parade was the first of its kind to be held outside the original 13 colonies. The Shamrock Club of Wisconsin, the state's largest Irish–American organization, and several business partners have been putting on the modern parade since 1967. Featuring over 120 units of Irish dance groups, pipe-and-drum corps, Irish bands, the mayor, and more, the parade begins at noon from Wisconsin Avenue at Old World Third Street. There are excellent viewing spots by the Grand Avenue Mall's front door.

If you're in town on any other weekend, slot out this morning for a trip to **Whitnall Park** in Hales Corners for a **toboggan** outing like you've never had before, with a little **win-**

ter hiking, **cross-country skiing**, and ice-skating thrown in. One of the larger municipal parks in the United States, the 660-acre Whitnall Park includes trails, an ice-skating pond, an education center, and an absolutely awesome **toboggan slide**. You can rent a toboggan there for an exhilarating run on an iced track, open on Friday from 4:00 to 8:00 p.m., Saturday from 1:00 to 8:00 p.m., and Sunday from 1:00 to 5:00 p.m. The trails are even **lighted for nighttime skiing**.

Make a stop inside the park's **Wehr Nature Center**, an environmental education facility with programs for children and adults. The center houses wildlife exhibits and an array of winter programs, such as Maple Sugar Weekends and Moon Walks.

© JOHN T. ANDREWS

Starting in 1843, Milwaukee's St. Patrick's Day parade was among the earliest on record in the United States.

There's no denying that Milwaukee

is a cultural hotspot, and if you'd like to slip in a sampling of some of its famous and well-loved museums, start this morning with a visit to the **Milwaukee Art Museum**. Located on the lakefront, the museum's expansion was designed by world-renowned architect Santiago Calatrava. Its signature Burke Brise Soleil, the moveable, winglike sunscreen that sits on top of the glass-enclosed, vaulted reception hall, is unprecedented in American architecture. The Brise Soleil has a 217-foot wingspan—wider than a Boeing 747 airplane. The wings open at 10:00 a.m. and close at 5:00 p.m. They also close and open each day at noon for visitors' enjoyment. This singular architecture is accompanied by stellar art exhibits. In fact, *Condé Nast Traveller* magazine has called the Milwaukee Art Museum a "Wonder of the World."

©JOHN T. ANDREWS

The Pettit National Ice Center has hosted many world-class competitions, but it also opens its doors for public skating.

AFTERNOON

In keeping with this morning's Irish theme, eat lunch at **Mo's Irish Pub** downtown. Reserve a table by the window, and get a spectacular view of the St. Patrick's Day Parade as you fill up on Irish stew, corned beef and cabbage, or "boxties," a stuffed potato pancake cooked on a griddle.

With Olympic champions like Eric Heiden, Bonnie Blair, Dan Jansen, and Casey FitzRandolph to its credit, Wisconsin has claim to being the home of American speed skating. You can **ice-skate** where the champions did—just 10 minutes west of downtown Milwaukee—at the **Pettit National Ice Center**.

The 200,000-square-foot building houses 97,000 square feet of ice and a 400-meter speed-skating oval. A local philanthropist donated this enormous facility for training U.S.

10 FUN FACTS ABOUT WISCONSIN'S ONLY U.S. OLYMPIC TRAINING FACILITY

by Rob Multerer

Rob Multerer was born in Milwaukee and raised in New Berlin, Wisconsin. A lifelong sports participant, he was a team attendant for the Milwaukee Bucks while attending Catholic Memorial High School in Waukesha. Multerer graduated from UW–La Crosse in 2000 and began his professional sports career with the Milwaukee Wave soccer team. Today, he is the director of marketing for the Pettit National Ice Center.

❄ The Pettit National Ice Center is one of 11 covered (indoor) ovals in the world and is one of three in all of North America.

❄ The center holds 97,000 square feet of ice.

❄ George Steinbrenner was once a member of the Pettit National Ice Center board of directors.

❄ Six-time Olympic speed-skating medalist Bonnie Blair is one of nine current board members.

❄ The Pettit National Ice Center houses a 450-meter indoor track, one of the longest in Wisconsin.

❄ Jane and Lloyd Pettit were well-known philanthropists from Milwaukee who put forth a large share of the financial backing to build Wisconsin's only U.S. Olympic Training Facility.

❄ Before the Pettit National Ice Center opened on December 31, 1992, the site was the home of the Wisconsin Olympic Ice Rink, a training ground for some of the United States' best speed skaters. The Wisconsin Olympic Ice Rink is believed to be the place where U.S. speed skating began. Although U.S. speed-skating supporters sent a team to the Moscow World Championships as far back as 1955, no formal international speed skating association was in existence. When speed skater Terry McDermott won the only gold medal in Innsbruck in the 1964 Winter Olympics, Milwaukeans Phil Krumm and George Howie took the win as their cue to solicit the Wisconsin legislature to support their plan to build an Olympic-caliber speed-skating training facility. As a result of Krumm and Howie's advocacy, the U.S. International Speedskating Association was incorporated in 1966, and the Wisconsin Olympic Ice Rink became a reality.

❄ As of October 20, 2005, the Pettit National Ice Center has used more than 20 million gallons of water exclusively for making ice.

❄ In its 13-year history, the Pettit National Ice Center has hosted three Speed Skating World Championships, two U.S. Olympic Trials, and countless other competitions, special events, tournaments, and meets.

❄ The Pettit National Ice Center is not just for Olympic athletes. Every year, there are more than 700 public skating sessions at the center.

Olympic teams, and national and international competitions are regularly held here. The Pettit National Ice Center is the only one of its kind in the country and only one of five similar ones in the world *[see "10 Fun Facts about Wisconsin's Only U.S. Olympic Training Facility" sidebar]*. Ice-skating lessons are available on Saturday mornings, and a public skate is held from 1:00 to 10:00 p.m.

If your plans include more museum touring, visit **The Eisner American Museum of Advertising & Design**, the only museum in the country to explore advertising and design, and its impact on our culture. The **Milwaukee Public Museum** of human and natural history is always an intriguing spot.

EVENING

What would be the point of going to Milwaukee without going to a brewery? *[See "The Beers of Winter" sidebar.]* Tonight, eat dinner at the **Water Street Brewery** on Water Street. Since 1987, this pub has been brewing a variety of traditional and specialty beers on the premises. A long list of sandwiches, pizzas, pastas, salads, and nightly specials complement the fresh beers.

This evening, check to see whether the **Pettit National Ice Center** is hosting any competitions, such as the U.S. National Long Track Championships in December or the U.S. National Short Track Individual Championships in February. Or take advantage of the winter performance season now in full swing at the **Marcus Center for the Performing Arts**.

Day Three
MORNING

Sunday brunch is a tradition, and in Milwaukee you can enjoy it by Lake Michigan. **Pieces of Eight Restaurant** on Harbor Drive offers a huge brunch buffet, with omelets, pancakes, waffles, roasted meats, salads, fish, seafood, and desserts. Fireplaces invite you to relax for a while with the view.

After checking out of your accommodations, take an easy, 40-minute drive from downtown Milwaukee to the **Kettle Moraine State Forest–Lapham Peak Unit**. At 1,233 feet,

JOHN T. ANDREWS

The Kettle Moraine State Forest's four sections provide winter visitors the opportunity to ski, snowshoe, or take a leisurely walk.

THE BEERS OF WINTER

The many Germans who settled in Wisconsin in the mid-1800s brought with them a fondness and skill for making beer. Soon, small breweries were springing up around the state—especially in Milwaukee, where a large German population stayed. Today, the state produces some of the best handcrafted brews around.

Winter calls for big, bold beers. Brewers especially love this time of year; it's an opportunity for them to exercise their artistry, let their imaginations run wild, and experiment. Winter beers are mostly dark, malty, strong, and more complex than their summer counterparts. They tend to be brewed with lots of grain (which makes beer sweet), balanced by extra hops (which add spicy aroma and bitter flavors), so they're higher in alcohol, flavor, and body than summer varieties.

The December holidays are usually just the start of the winter beer season. While some breweries introduce and release beers that are specifically geared to the holidays, a growing number are introducing winter brews and additional styles in January, February, and March.

Drinking a winter beer should be a special experience for you, as well. These strong, full-bodied beers deserve a robust glass or mug. Heavy goblets work nicely, as does toasting Milwaukee's beer culture by raising a hefty stein.

Below are some common winter beer styles:

❄ **AMBER ALE**—a color, not a style, used to describe a number of American medium-bodied, amber-colored ales.

❄ **BARLEYWINE**—the strongest ale with an alcohol content as high as wines.

❄ **BOCK**—a dark, malty, strong German lager (lager is known for its effervescence or bubbly quality).

❄ **BROWN ALE**—a strong, malty, dark amber ale originally from England; the American version is somewhat sweeter.

❄ **DOPPELBOCK**—a dark, strong, double bock beer.

❄ **DUNKELWEIZEN**—a dark, German wheat beer.

❄ **OLD ALE**—a dark brown, full-bodied, malty sweet ale, but only medium to strong in alcohol content.

❄ **PORTER**—an almost black, roasty beer a shade lighter in body and character than stout.

❄ **SPICED ALE**—a dark, strong ale flavored with spices, such as ginger, cinnamon, nutmeg, and cloves.

❄ **STOUT**—almost black in color from roasted malt. Dry stout has a roasty flavor from the malt and a dryness from hops.

❄ **STRONG ALE**—any number of dark, full-bodied ales with higher alcohol content than typical ales, but less than barleywines.

❄ **WEIZENBOCK**—a bock beer made with wheat.

Lapham Peak is the highest point in Waukesha County. The 1,006-acre unit is the second smallest of the four in the Kettle Moraine State Forest: the Northern Unit covers 29,268 acres, the Southern Unit counts 22,300 acres, and the much smaller Pike Lake Unit comes in at 678 acres. All four sections of the Kettle Moraine State Forest contain portions of the 1,000-mile **Ice Age National Scenic Trail** *[see Chapter 5: Art in Winter (Dodgeville/Spring Green/Mineral Point/New Glarus)]*. **Winter hikers** and **snowshoers** can travel the four miles of the Ice Age National Scenic Trail that cut through the Lapham Peak part of the state forest, passing the 45-foot observation tower along the way. From the top of the tower, you'll be able to see Holy Hill to the north, the site of a Catholic monastery, and about 16 sparkling lakes.

The Lapham Peak Unit is one of southern Wisconsin's most popular **cross-country ski** areas. Approximately 180 hilly miles of extra-wide trails weave a web across the forest for classic and skate-skiing. The main trail is the very scenic, seven-mile **Moraine Ridge Trail** (Black), with the longest and steepest hills. The 5.8-mile **Kettle View Trail** (Blue) follows the same route but bypasses the steepest parts; both traverse open and wooded terrain. The two-mile **Meadow Trail** (Green) has small hills and runs mostly through an open landscape. The Meadow Trail and two short loops branching from it (2.6 miles total) are lit for **night skiing** Monday through Saturday until 10:00 p.m. The two-mile **Kame Terrace Trail** (Purple) is level and travels through the forest. Ski rentals are available on weekends.

The **Prairie Path** (Red) can be used for **snowshoeing, winter hiking**, and **dog sledding**, and winds for 4.8 miles over prairies, meadows, savannas, and medium-sized hills in the western portion of the park. **Homestead Hollow Pond** is kept clear for **ice-skating**, and winter visitors can warm themselves at two shelters. **Winter camping** is allowed at one backpack site along the Ice Age National Scenic Trail. More than 135 species of birds have been recorded at Lapham Peak over the years, with about 80 of those nesting here. Be on the lookout for belted kingfishers and Cooper's hawks. Deer, foxes, and coyotes are some of the many mammalian residents.

If you have time, wander portions of the **Kettle Moraine Scenic Drive** to experience the variety of geology and beauty in this incredible area. The 115-mile route connects the four units of the state forest as well as numerous natural landmarks and historic sites. The roadway is easy to follow. Just look for the green, acorn-shaped signs—a little touch that makes a big city weekend a great part of winter.

FOR MORE INFORMATION
GREATER MILWAUKEE CONVENTION & VISITORS BUREAU
648 N. Plankinton Ave., Suite 425
Milwaukee, WI 53203, (414) 273-3950 or
(800) 231-0903, www.milwaukee.org

VISITOR INFORMATION CALL CENTER
(414) 273-7222 or (800) 554-1448
(Monday–Friday, 8:00 a.m.–5:00 p.m.)

VISITOR INFORMATION CENTER WALK-IN LOCATIONS
Midwest Airlines Center, 400 W. Wisconsin Ave.
Milwaukee, WI 53203, (414) 908-6205
(Monday–Friday, 8:00 a.m.–5:00 p.m.)

WINTER ATTRACTIONS
BRADLEY CENTER
1001 N. Fourth St., Milwaukee, WI 53203
(414) 227-0400, www.bradleycenter.com

THE EISNER AMERICAN MUSEUM OF ADVERTISING & DESIGN *(Friday, 11:00 a.m.–5:00 p.m.; Saturday, 12:00–5:00 p.m.; Sunday, 1:00–5:00 p.m.)*
208 N. Water St., Milwaukee, WI 53202
(414) 847-3290, www.eisnermuseum.org

HAVENWOODS STATE FOREST
6141 N. Hopkins St., Milwaukee, WI 53209
(414) 527-0232, www.wiparks.net

ICE AGE PARK & TRAIL FOUNDATION
207 E. Buffalo St., Suite 515
Milwaukee, WI 53202 (414) 278-8518 or
(800) 227-0046, www.iceagetrail.org

**KETTLE MORAINE STATE
FOREST–LAPHAM PEAK UNIT**
W329 N846 Highway C, Delafield, WI 53018
(262) 646-3025, www.wiparks.net

LAKE PARK
3233 E. Kenwood Blvd., Milwaukee, WI 53211
(414) 962-8809, www.county.milwaukee.gov

**MARCUS CENTER FOR THE
PERFORMING ARTS**
929 N. Water St., Milwaukee, WI 53202
(414) 273-7206, www.marcuscenter.org

**MARQUETTE UNIVERSITY DEPARTMENT
OF ATHLETICS**
1532 W. Clybourn St., Milwaukee, WI 53233
(414) 288-7127 *(tickets)*
www.gomarquette.com

MILWAUKEE ADMIRALS
1001 N. Fourth St. *(games at the Bradley Center)*,
Milwaukee, WI 53203, (414) 276-4545 *(tickets)*
www.milwaukeeadmirals.com

MILWAUKEE ART MUSEUM
(10:00 a.m.–5:00 p.m.)
700 N. Art Museum Dr., Milwaukee, WI 53202
(414) 224-3200, www.mam.org

MILWAUKEE BUCKS
1001 N. Fourth St. *(games at the Bradley Center)*,
Milwaukee, WI 53203
(414) 276-4545 *(tickets)*, www.nba.com/bucks

MILWAUKEE PUBLIC MUSEUM
800 W. Wells St., Milwaukee, WI 53233
(414) 278-2702, www.mpm.edu

PETTIT NATIONAL ICE CENTER
500 S. 84th St., Milwaukee, WI 53214
(414) 266-0100, www.thepettit.com

SCHLITZ AUDUBON NATURE CENTER
(9:00 a.m.–5:00 p.m.)
1111 E. Brown Deer Rd., Milwaukee, WI 53217
(414) 352-2880
www.schlitzaudoboncenter.com

SLICE OF ICE
Red Arrow Park, 920 N. Water St.
Milwaukee, WI 53202, (414) 289-8791
www.county.milwaukee.gov

WEHR NATURE CENTER
9701 W. College Ave., Franklin, WI 53132
(414) 425-8550, www.friendsofwehr.org

WHITNALL PARK
5879 S. 92nd St., Hales Corners, WI 53130
(414) 425-7303
www.county.milwaukee.gov/display

WINTER FESTIVALS

**HOLIDAY FOLK FAIR INTERNATIONAL—
mid-November.** West Allis. The oldest, largest,
indoor, multi-ethnic festival in the country.
Celebrate the traditions of more than 60 ethnic
groups with food, exhibits, demonstrations, attire,
dance, and entertainment. Wisconsin Exposition
Center at State Fair Park, 8200 W. Greenfield Ave.,
West Allis. (414) 273-7222 or (800) 231-0903.

**HOLIDAY LIGHTS FESTIVAL—mid-November
through December.** Downtown Milwaukee. A holiday tree lighting at Red Arrow Park, followed by a
Holiday Lights Kick-Off Extravaganza in Pere Marquette Park, features live music, performances, and
a finale of fireworks. Decorated parks, streets, and
rooflines continue through December. (414) 220-
4700 or www.milwaukeeholidaylights.com.

**A VICTORIAN CHRISTMAS AT THE PABST
MANSION—mid-November through early January.** Captain Frederick Pabst Mansion, 2000 W.
Wisconsin Ave. The historic, nationally recognized
mansion is exquisitely decorated for the holiday
season with traditional Victorian floral arrangements, glass ornaments, and Victorian garlands.
The mansion was built originally for the founder of
the Pabst Brewery in a Flemish Renais-sance style.
(414) 931-0808 or www.pabstmansion.com.

**HOLIDAY NIGHT LIGHTS AT THE ZOO—
weekends in December.** Milwaukee County Zoo,
6:00 to 9:00 p.m. Tour the zoo decked out for the
holidays with thousands of twinkling lights
and decorative displays. Visit the Zoological
Society's "Winter Wonderland," complete with
Santa and Mrs. Claus, holiday gifts, and treats.
10001 W. Blue Mound Road. (414) 771-5500 or
www.milwaukeezoo.org.

**CHRISTMAS IN THE WARD—early Decem-
ber.** 100 and 200 blocks of N. Broadway. Friday,
5:00–8:00 p.m.; Saturday, 11:00 a.m.–4:00 p.m.
Enjoy the holiday spirit of the Historic Third
Ward with Santa, carriage rides, carolers, street
entertainers, and a variety of shops and galleries.
Tree lighting Friday evening at 5:30 p.m., followed by fireworks at 6:00 p.m. (414) 273-1173
or www.historicthirdward.org.

BLESSING OF THE BOCK—mid-March. Serb
Hall. The opening ceremony of the Milwaukee
Beer Festival, this blessing is not a novelty but a
sincere invocation, usually conducted by a
Catholic priest. Attendees can sample a variety of
bocks and other specialty beers from 17 different

brewers, enjoy a lunch buffet, and meet brewery reps. 5101 W. Oklahoma Ave. (414) 372-0749 or www.milwaukeebeerfest.com.

ST. PATRICK'S DAY PARADE—mid-March.
Downtown. Parade starts at noon and lasts about 90 minutes. St. Patrick's Day 5K Run (3.1 miles) beginning at 11:00 a.m. outside Mo's Irish Pub and ending at Pere Marquette Park. Many post-parade parties will take place at various locations featuring Irish entertainment. (414) 276-6696 or www.saintpatricksparade.org.

RESTAURANTS
BARTOLOTTA'S LAKE PARK BISTRO
(Friday, lunch and dinner; Saturday, dinner; Sunday, brunch and dinner)
3133 E. Newberry Blvd., Milwaukee, WI 53211
(414) 962-6300, www.lakeparkbistro.com

BELLA CAFFÉ *(Friday–Saturday, breakfast, lunch, and dinner; Sunday, breakfast and lunch)*
189 N. Milwaukee St., Milwaukee, WI 53202
(414) 273-5620, www.bellacaffe.com

KARL RATZSCH'S OLD WORLD
RESTAURANT *(Friday–Saturday, lunch and dinner; closed Sunday)*
320 E. Mason St., Milwaukee, WI 53202
(414) 276-2720, www.karlratzsch.com

MADER'S RESTAURANT *(Friday–Saturday, lunch; Friday–Sunday, dinner; Sunday, brunch)*
1041 N. Old World Third St.
Milwaukee, WI 53203, (414) 271-3377
www.madersrestaurant.com

MO'S IRISH PUB *(Friday–Saturday, lunch and dinner; closed Sunday)*
142 W. Wisconsin Ave., Milwaukee, WI 53203
(414) 272-0721, www.mosirishpub.com

PIECES OF EIGHT RESTAURANT
(Friday–Saturday, lunch and dinner; Sunday, brunch)
550 N. Harbor Dr., Milwaukee, WI 53202
(414) 271-0597

WATER STREET BREWERY *(Friday–Sunday, lunch and dinner; Sunday, brunch)*
1101 N. Water St., Milwaukee, WI 53202
(414) 272-1195, www.waterstreetbrewery.com

LODGING
ACANTHUS INN BED & BREAKFAST
3009 W. Highland Blvd., Milwaukee, WI 53208
(414) 342-9788 or (877) 468-8740
www.milwaukee-bed-and-breakfast.com

BRUMDER MANSION BED & BREAKFAST
3046 W. Wisconsin Ave., Milwaukee, WI 53208
(414) 342-9767 or (866) 793-3676
www.brumdermansion.com/index-bm.html

COUNTY CLARE, AN IRISH INN & PUB
1234 N. Astor St., Milwaukee, WI 53202
(414) 272-5273 or (800) 942-5273
www.countyclare-inn.com

KNICKERBOCKER BED & BREAKFAST SUITES
1028 E. Juneau Ave., Milwaukee, WI 53202
(414) 276-8500
www.knickerbockeronthelake.com

PARK EAST HOTEL
916 E. State St., Milwaukee, WI 53202
(414) 276-8800 or (800) 328-7275
www.parkeasthotel.com

THE PFISTER HOTEL
424 E. Wisconsin Ave., Milwaukee, WI 53202
(414) 273-8222 or (800) 558-8222
www.thepfisterhotel.com

Chapter Seventeen
ISLAND WINTER
Minocqua/Woodruff/Arbor Vitae

A STRANGELY SHAPED, BUTTERFLY-LIKE PENINSULA jutting into Lake Minocqua, the city of Minocqua is known as the "Island City." Surrounded by water and with another 3,200 lakes, streams, and ponds in Vilas and Oneida Counties, it's no wonder that the Minocqua, Woodruff, and Arbor Vitae area has become a huge recreational destination in all seasons. And with 95 percent of Woodruff and 82 percent of Arbor Vitae on federal, state, or local lands and thus protected from development, it's a sure thing that this tri-city locale will be here for generations to come for people who want to enjoy the great outdoors.

Wisconsin's largest state forest, the Northern Highland/American Legion State Forest is the second big player shaping the character of these three cities. It's one of the reasons that in Minocqua, you'll run into at least a dozen cross-country skiers and snowmobilers on any given winter day. Add to that an average annual snowfall of nearly 65 inches, and it's easy to see why the Island City is a winter paradise.

The early inhabitants of the Minocqua area were Chippewa Indians who may have used the peninsula as a camp during their travels. Early European settlers saw quite a different application for the region: They saw the mammoth forests and believed they were looking at an inexhaustible supply of lumber. By 1887, after the railroads had laid tracks up to the North Woods, the logging town of Maniwaki (which would later become Minocqua) was established.

By 1891, lumberjacks were everywhere in Maniwaki. The town grew to number 29 saloons, 15 homes, two hotels, two general stores, and a small market. The lumberjacks would work at a constant pace through the winter months, harvesting as much timber as possible. At spring thaw, the logs were sent south to the mills. By 1900, the loggers had cut down nearly all of the forests of northern Wisconsin. The "inexhaustible" supply had indeed been exhausted.

But even as the loggers were leaving, the resort industry started to take a foothold. The Minocqua, Woodruff, and Arbor Vitae "lakeland" area began to attract hundreds of visitors wanting to fish the scores of lakes. And in a location with one of the largest concentrations

Silhouetted by early morning light, these skiers prepare for a day of fun on one of Minocqua Winter Park & Nordic Center's cross-country trails.

of bodies of fresh water in the world, the area naturally became an outdoor playground throughout the year.

Today, the Northern Highland/ American Legion State Forest has recovered and stands full of towering trees. It is the headwaters of two of the largest river basins in Wisconsin: the Wisconsin River and the Chippewa– Flambeau River systems. On the same logging roads that once were used for extracting the state's great trees from their homes, cross-country skiers and snowmobilers now marvel at the beauty and solitude the forest provides.

Eagles again soar overhead. The wolves, icons of the wild, are recovering. In their screeches and howls on the wind, the island calls.

Day One
MORNING

Start your morning right in the heart of downtown Minocqua with breakfast at **Tula's Cafe**. Slip into one of the side booths and fill up on an old-fashioned breakfast of eggs and toast, prepared just right in Tula's cheery atmosphere. Cross-country skiing burns a lot of calories, so consider this stop a necessity for your morning's agenda.

Cross-country skiers and **snowshoers** will be impressed with the **Minocqua Winter Park & Nordic Center**. Winter Park, six miles off Highway 70 just west of Minocqua, is one of the Midwest's top 10 all-time favorite cross-country ski facilities. With 46 miles of more than two dozen trails perfectly tracked and groomed for classic and ski-skating, a cozy chalet, and a ski shop with rentals and ski instruction, it is an ideal place for anyone who enjoys the sport.

The intertwining trails represent all levels of difficulty, from the legendary **Nutcracker** to three short loops for children. The Nutcracker climbs steep glacial ridges, with some runs that are considered extreme. Winter Park is definitely an exciting place, where the passion for Nordic skiing is always palpable. There is also a designated trail solely for **snowshoeing**.

If your interests lie in motorized winter sports, another quintessential Minocqua weekend beginning would be to crank up your **snowmobile**. The **Cross Country Cruisers Snowmobile Club** maintains 160 miles of scenic and well-groomed trails throughout Vilas and Oneida Counties.

In fact, Minocqua is the starting point for one of the most scenic snowmobile trails in the state. The picturesque **Bearskin State Trail** *[see "Trail Etiquette" sidebar]* is a railroad grade that travels south of Minocqua for just over 18 miles. It crosses Lake Minocqua on an old train trestle and Bearskin Creek—a tributary of the Tomahawk River—and goes past Baker and Bolger Lakes. You'll travel past hardwood stands of oak and maple and second-growth woods that have stepped in to replace the majestic white pine forests that were cut down in the late 19th century.

AFTERNOON

Snowmobiling, cross-country skiing, or **snowshoeing** in Minocqua could easily occupy you for the whole day, but if you can, break away for a late lunch. At **T. Murtaugh's Pub** on Oneida Street in downtown Minocqua, you can get deli sandwiches, such as a Reuben or prime rib, to go along with your ale or lager.

The great thing about this afternoon's **cross-country ski** trails is that they are in deep

---

TRAIL ETIQUETTE

Whether you're on Wisconsin's trails winter hiking, cross-country skiing, snowshoeing, ATVing, or snowmobiling, there is a code of ethics that comes with traveling on them. Trail etiquette can be described as the polite way to use trails, and subscribing to an ethical code helps protect the natural and aesthetic value of the wilderness, which is why we're all using the trails in the first place.

To ensure that you follow appropriate trail etiquette, keep in mind the following points:

❄ Never discard trash in a natural area, no matter how minimal or seemingly biodegradable. If you pack it in, pack it out.

❄ Never blast loud music in a natural area. Travel as quietly as possible so as not to disturb wildlife and to allow others to enjoy the quiet surroundings.

❄ Let faster travelers on the trail pass, but a basic rule is "Wheels yield to heels." Keep this in mind when approaching other trail users. ATVers and snowmobilers should yield to all other users, while winter hikers and cross-country skiers should yield to horse riders.

❄ When winter hiking, hike on trails whenever possible. In a group, travel in single file to avoid widening the trail. If a puddle is in the middle of a trail, walk right through it. Going around it can create an ever-widening path.

❄ Cross-country skiers should ski on the right side and yield to those coming downhill or who are faster. To step out of a track, lift your skis so you don't disturb the track.

❄ Snowmobilers should operate at appropriate speeds, avoid tracks made for skiers, respect trail closures, and avoid late-night riding near populated areas or lodges.

❄ Stop for photos or breaks off the trail on durable surfaces. Taking a break on the trail blocks it for others.

❄ Leave what you find.

❄ Respect wildlife. Never pursue an animal. Your surroundings are home to many plants and animals, and you are the visitor.

❄ Aspire to be invisible on the trail—leave no impact and no trace.

NORTHERN LIGHTS IN THE GREAT NORTH WOODS

Although it's easier to see the aurora borealis in Alaska or northern Canada, you can see the glowing colors in Wisconsin skies. In fact, in 1991, 2000, and 2005, our state had some spectacular displays. An aurora is a faint, yet often neonlike glow in the Earth's ionosphere. It occurs when there is an interaction between the Earth's magnetic field and the solar wind (charged particles from the sun).

In the northern hemisphere, this phenomenon is called the aurora borealis (also known as the northern lights), and in the southern hemisphere it is called aurora australis (southern lights). The auroral "lights" typically become more pronounced as you get closer to the poles.

The multi-colored arcs, curtains, and rays of light in the night sky have inspired many native peoples for thousands of years. The east Greenland Eskimos thought the lights were produced by the spirits of children who died at birth. The dancing of the children round and round caused the continually moving streamers of light. The state of Wisconsin has the largest number of Native American tribes and bands east of the Mississippi River, and their myths surrounding the phenomenon go back thousands of years.

The Fox Indians regarded the light as an omen of war and pestilence. To them, the lights were the ghosts of their slain enemies who, restless for revenge, tried to rise up again. The Menominee Indians saw the lights as torches used by great, friendly giants in the North to spear fish at night. An Algonquin myth says that when the creator of the Earth, Nanahbozho, had finished his task of creation, he traveled to the North, where he remained. He built large fires, of which the northern lights are the reflections, to remind his people that he still thinks of them.

The next time you are in the Great North Woods, in the middle of a forest or field away from any city lights, watch the night sky for flickers. It is the stuff of legends.

---

forests, and more shade means more snow. Located just off Leary Road, a mile and a half south of downtown Minocqua off Highway 51, the 6.2 miles of **Schlect Lake Ski Trails** are preferred by many locals for their quietness; they usually have less traffic than those in Winter Park. An individual daily pass only costs a few dollars on a purely honor system. Run by the Howard Young Foundation, all of the fees collected are used to maintain the trails. The Schlect Lake Trails are rated on a scale of "easiest," "more difficult," and "most difficult." The trails wind around Schlect and Skida Lakes and skirt the edge of Tomahawk Lake. Portions of the trails are lighted at night until 9:30 p.m.

Toward late afternoon, you'll need to check into your Minocqua accommodations for the weekend. And what could be more magnificent than staying in the midst of the Northern Highland/American Legion State Forest? The **Northwoods Nod-A-Way** on Townline Road in Woodruff is located within Wisconsin's largest state property. At 223,283 acres, this huge state forest overflows with wildlife, more than 900 lakes, and countless streams and rivers. The rustic road to the Northwoods Nod-A-Way will take you between rows and rows of tall pines. If there was ever any doubt, by the time you pull into the driveway, you'll know tonight you'll be sleeping in the arms of a great forest.

EVENING

After unpacking and taking some long, deep breaths of the fresh forest air, drive back into downtown Minocqua for dinner at the **Polecat & Lace Restaurant & Saloon**. Savor the chicken Kiev, baked in a garlic and white sauce, or go with the roast duck.

After dinner, you may want to lace up your skates for some turns on the **ice-skating rink** on Lake Minocqua off Oneida Street; or if you happen to be in town during **Cruiserfest** weekend, attend some of the Friday night activities, such as the lighted snowmobile parade on the lake and a bonfire.

Once you get back to the Nod-A-Way, take a moment to step outside of your car and just listen and look around you. You won't hear a single automobile or any other traffic noises. In winter, the sky in the forest is a rich, deep black, making for the most brilliant stars you've ever seen *[see "Northern Lights in the Great North Woods" sidebar]*.

JOHN T. ANDREWS

The bridge overpass of the Bearskin State Trail looms before this snowmobiler. The various trestles and boardwalks found on this 18-mile trail provide some fascinating viewing opportunities.

Day Two
MORNING

Imagine this scene as you look out the window from your breakfast table: Beyond the big yard lightly covered in snow stand three strong, muscular horses, their warm breath made manifest in a cloud of steam. The snow on the roof of the barn beyond them glistens in the winter sun.

If you can't catch this view from the Northwoods Nod-A-Way, opt for breakfast at the **Northern Cafe**. Part of the Northern Motel in Arbor Vitae on Highway 51, this little, unassuming-looking restaurant claims to have the "best breakfast in the North Woods." Popular with locals, the Northern Cafe serves hearty meals, such as its "Northern legend" French toast.

If you happen to be in Minocqua in mid-February during **Cruiserfest** *[see "Lake Minocqua Comes Alive with Cruiserfest" sidebar]*, you can partake in the event's pancake breakfast. Then head out to the **snowmobile radar runs**. Walk out on the frozen lake and watch as the revved-up machines blast off in a spray of snow and excitement, and their speeds are clocked by radar guns.

Even if you missed Cruiserfest weekend, you still have an opportunity for a wild experience. Just west of Minocqua on Highway 70 across from the 70 West Mall, you can visit a

LAKE MINOCQUA COMES ALIVE WITH CRUISERFEST

by Judy Andreotti

Judy Andreotti is originally from Illinois. She moved to Wisconsin with her husband, Al, in 1992, and they now reside in Lake Tomahawk overlooking the Wisconsin River. Because of their love of snowmobiling, they became active in the Cross Country Cruisers. Al is currently the president of the club, and together they chair the Cruiserfest event every year.

Cruiserfest, held each year on the second weekend of February, is the creation of the Cross Country Cruisers Snowmobile Club of Arbor Vitae, Woodruff, and Minocqua. Tourists, snowmobile enthusiasts, and families from surrounding states come to enjoy the club's biggest event of the year.

The opening ceremony starts on Friday evening with locals and tourists lighting up the night with a snowmobile parade around Lake Minocqua. The public is encouraged to take part in the parade, which ends with a bonfire, food, and beverages. Saturday activities include a breakfast, craft show, snowmobile radar runs, food, and dealer demo rides. Saturday ends with a dance, door prizes, raffles, and our silent auction at the American Legion Hall, where you can bid on everything from a getaway weekend package to motorcycles and snowmobiles.

The Cross Country Cruisers Snowmobile Club originated in 1976 when some local residents became interested in opening snowmobile trails. Today, the club membership numbers more than 300, with members from five states. Our members voluntarily put in over 1,900 man-hours to prepare, maintain, and groom over 100 miles of connecting statewide trails for everyone's riding pleasure. Snowmobilers pay their own way: Funding for the public snowmobile trail systems is paid for by the snowmobile user through snowmobile registration fees, gas tax rebates, trail permits, snowmobile user permits, and volunteer labor. When riding the trails, remember your local snowmobile club and join to show your support.

For more information on Cruiserfest or the trail systems in the North Woods, check out the club's Web site at www.snowmobilewi.com or the Minocqua Chamber of Commerce Web site at www.minocqua.org. Let the North Woods winter playground be your next destination for fun. Until then, safe riding and happy trails.

Snowmobilers take to the ice in downtown Minocqua to test their machines in a series of radar runs.

JOHN T. ANDREWS

real wildlife hospital. Take a free, guided outdoor tour of the **Northwoods Wildlife Center**, offered from 10:00 a.m. to 2:00 p.m. on Saturdays.

Started in 1979, the Northwoods Wildlife Center is a nonprofit, fully operational hospital dedicated to caring for wounded and orphaned wild animals—everything from "hummingbirds to eagles," as the staff proudly tells you. Volunteer veterinarians work in this licensed rehabilitation clinic, treating hundreds of birds, reptiles, and mammals each year in an effort to rehabilitate and release them back into the wild. Currently, the center treats about 1,000 animals a year and releases about 750 back into the wild. In 2004, for example, bears, vultures, loons, deer, and five eagles who were either hit by cars or poisoned by consuming antifreeze were treated. The center also functions as an education and research facility. When you walk in, you'll be able to look at animal x-rays and meet some of the current residents, such as Hortense, a turkey vulture who lost a wing when she was hit by a car.

AFTERNOON

Have your lunch at the **Thirsty Whale**, located on Lake Minocqua off Park Avenue. For 90 years, the Thirsty Whale has been serving signature sandwiches, such as "The Hunger Killer," a Hoagie roll piled high with roast beef, Swiss cheese, sautéed onions, and mushrooms, and the beef and cheddar sandwich with cheddar cheese sauce.

Today, you'll get to take in all that the **Northern Highland/American Legion State Forest** truly is: 223,283 acres of **cross-country skiing, snowshoeing, winter hiking, winter camping, ice fishing, ice-skating**, and **snowmobiling** heaven. Living around its 900 lakes are species such as the spotted salamander and bobcat, along with ospreys, otters, beavers, minks, porcupines, foxes, coyotes, bears, deer, moose, and timber wolves, although you would have to be extremely lucky to see the big cats or wolves.

Cross-country skiers can stride on 72.9 miles of trails, of which 44.9 miles are groomed. Two trails that are easily accessed in Minocqua are the **Madeline Trail** and the **Raven Trail**.

The 13.5 miles of loops on the Raven Trail are hilly, passing scenic Hemlock Lake at the north end. Interpretive panels teach about the plants, animals, and history of the forest. The giant pines on the mostly level, 16.5-mile Madeline Trail loops will almost force you to stop to take photos.

The Raven Trail, Madeline Trail, **Escanaba Trail** (accessed near Boulder Junction), **McNaughton Trail** (located 13 miles from Woodruff), and **Shannon Trail** (near St. Germain) together offer more than 50 miles of expertly groomed cross-country ski trails. Skate-skiing is available on the five-mile loop around the lake on the McNaughton Trail.

It's easier to observe and track wildlife when the forest is buried in snow *[see Chapter 8: The Start of Something Big (Eau Claire/Chippewa Falls)]*. Parking lots at the trailheads of the **Lumberjack, Powell, Fallison, North Trout,** and **Star Lake Trails** are kept clear for **snowshoers**. Snowshoe to one of the wilderness lakes where bald eagles take off from tall, white pines to fish in the headwaters of the Wisconsin River. With a camera under your parka, you'll be able to document your trek in this wildlife haven. Or attempt to capture a lone skier or snowshoer in this vast forest, with the sun peeking though the trees.

There are nearly 400 miles of marked **snowmobile trails** across the forest that link with an extensive network of county trails. Contact one of the many area snowmobile clubs for suggested itineraries or go to www.minocqua.org for snowmobile conditions.

Clear Lake Campground stays open during the winter for those who like their **camping snowy.** And with so many lakes to choose from, you just may find that your **ice fishing** skills exceed your angling abilities in the summer *[see Chapter 9: A Classic, Old World Winter (Green Lake/Princeton)]*. Or pull out your **ice skates** for some graceful turns, with tall trees standing in for your appreciative audience.

EVENING

Bosacki's Boat House opened in 1917, in an 1896 building. Today, Bosacki's has evolved into a tackle-and-bait shop, marina, water–ski operation, guide service, and restaurant. Run by the fourth generation of the Bosacki family, the restaurant is popular and crowded in all seasons. Plan to have your dinner here, but at the very least stop by and go to the hand-carved, 1903 Brunswick oak bar in the back for a hot fudge sundae or homemade candies.

After dinner, continue with the outdoor fun. Outside Bosacki's, join the ice fishers jigging for the big ones. Or just watch them under the moon and stars, waiting for their tip-up flags to fly. You may want to go back to the **Schlect Lake Ski Trails** for classic or skate cross-country skiing on the five miles of lighted trails.

If your Minocqua visit falls around the weekend of Valentine's Day, have a romantic evening by taking part in the **Valentine's Candlelight Ski on the Raven Trail** in the Northern Highland/American Legion State Forest. Glide between hundreds of candles on either the 1.5- or 3-mile loops. **Ski-skating, snowshoeing,** and **winter hiking** are also allowed in the candles' glow. Warming fires will greet you at the start/finish and halfway points on the three-mile loop. Refreshments are available, and for a uniquely romantic evening a grill is provided for those who wish to dine out in the great forest.

Minocqua Winter Park & Nordic Center's 46 miles of professionally groomed ski trails appeal to skiers of all ages and abilities.

Day Three
MORNING

At 7:00 a.m., as the sun is rising, light the candle on your breakfast table at the Northwoods Nod-A-Way. At just about the time that you no longer need the candle, your Belgian waffles, fresh-fruit plate, orange juice, and coffee will be finished. If you prefer to go out to breakfast, try the **Island Cafe** downtown on Oneida Street. The Greek omelet is excellent, and the salmon eggs Benedict is delicious: fresh spinach leaves, poached eggs, hollandaise sauce, and smoked salmon.

The Northwoods Nod-A-Way sits right on the **Madeline Trail** in the Northern Highland/American Legion State Forest. Pack up your car, then strap on your cross-country skis one more time. Take one last tour on the trails of your wild, island paradise that, thankfully, should be here for some time to come.

FOR MORE INFORMATION
MINOCQUA-ARBOR VITAE-WOODRUFF AREA CHAMBER OF COMMERCE
8216 Highway 51, Minocqua, WI 54548
(715) 356-5266 or (800) 446-6784
www.minocqua.org

WINTER ATTRACTIONS
BEARSKIN STATE TRAIL
Wisconsin Department of Natural Resources
518 W. Somo Ave., Tomahawk, WI 54487
(715) 453-1263, www.wiparks.net

CROSS COUNTRY CRUISERS SNOWMOBILE CLUB
PO Box 733, Woodruff, WI 54568
www.snowmobilewi.com

FOREST RIDERS SNOWMOBILE CLUB
PO Box 1161, Minocqua, WI 54548
(715) 588-9041, (715) 356-5054
or (715) 358-3113
www.springprairie.org/forestriders.htm

MINOCQUA WINTER PARK & NORDIC CENTER
12375 Scotchman Lake Rd.
Minocqua, WI 54548, (715) 356-3309
www.skimwp.org

NORTHERN HIGHLAND/AMERICAN LEGION STATE FOREST
Wisconsin Department of Natural Resources, Woodruff Service Center
8770 Highway J , Woodruff, WI 54568
(715) 385-2727, www.wiparks.net

NORTHWOODS WILDLIFE CENTER
8683 Blumenstein Rd., Minocqua, WI 54548
(715) 356-7400
www.northwoodswildlifecenter.com

SCHLECT LAKE SKI TRAIL
Leary Road (*1.5 miles south of downtown*

Minocqua off Highway 51)
Minocqua, WI 54548
(715) 356-5855, www.minocqua.org

TORPY PARK
Highway 51 South (*downtown*)
Minocqua, WI 54548, (715) 356-5266
or (800) 446-6784, www.minocqua.org

WINTER FESTIVALS
CHRISTMAS IN MINOCQUA—late November. Downtown Minocqua and Torpy Park. Noon–5:00 p.m. Decorated Christmas trees along the public ice rink in Torpy Park, official lighting of the Christmas village featuring mini business replicas and Santa's arrival. (715) 356-5266 or www.minocqua.org.

CHILL OUT: A NORTHWOODS CELEBRATION—late January. Arbor Vitae. Friday night fish fry, bonfire with s'mores on Big Arbor Vitae Lake, and candlelight ski by Minocqua Winter Park. Ice fishing tournament on Saturday on Big Arbor Vitae Lake, children's activities, food, sleigh rides, snow-sculpting contest, turkey bowling, ice golf, dogsled rides, and more. (800) 446-6784 or www.minocqua.org.

CRUISERFEST—mid-February. Lake Minocqua and downtown Minocqua. Friday night lighted snowmobile parade on Lake Minocqua with a bonfire to follow. On Saturday, events include a pancake breakfast, craft show, silent auction, brat and chili feed, radar runs on Lake Minocqua, and demo rides with area dealers. (800) 446-6784 or www.snowmobilewi.com.

LAKELAND LOPPET—early March. Minocqua Winter Park & Nordic Center. The park's biggest yearly event kicks off Friday night with a "Pasta Blast" for pre-registrants from 5:00 to 9:00 p.m. Saturday features skate-ski and classic races for all ages. (715) 356-3309 or www.skimwp.org.

CABIN FEVER DAY—early March. The Waters of Minocqua, 8116 Highway 51 South, Minocqua, WI 54548. Enjoy the indoor water park at The Waters of Minocqua hotel.(877) 992-8377 or www.thewatersofminocqua.com.

RESTAURANTS
BOSACKI'S BOAT HOUSE *(lunch and dinner; Sunday brunch)*
305 W. Park Ave., Minocqua, WI 54548
(715) 356-5292, www.bosackis.com

ISLAND CAFE *(breakfast and lunch)*
314 Oneida St., Minocqua, WI 54548
(715) 356-6977

MAMA'S RESTAURANT *(dinner)*
10486 Highway 70 W, Minocqua, WI 54548,
(715) 356-5070
www.mamasrestaurant.biz

NORTHERN CAFE
2685 Highway 51 North, Arbor Vitae, WI 54568
(715) 356-4170

NORWOOD PINES SUPPER CLUB *(dinner)*
10171 Highway 70 W
Minocqua, WI 54548
(715) 356-3666
www.norwoodpines.com

POLECAT & LACE RESTAURANT & SALOON
(lunch and dinner; closed Sunday)
427 Oneida St., Minocqua, WI 54548
(715) 356-3335, www.minocqua.org

SOLEM'S SUPPER CLUB & BANQUETS
(dinner; closed Sunday)
7373 Highway 51 South, Minocqua, WI 54548
(715) 358-6110
www.verizonsupersite.com/solemslake
sidecom/solemsmenu

T. MURTAUGH'S PUB *(lunch and dinner)*
500 Oneida St., Minocqua, WI 54548
(715) 356-7712, www.minocqua.org

THIRSTY WHALE *(lunch and dinner)*
453 Park Ave., Minocqua, WI 54548
(715) 356-7108
www.thirstywhaleminocqua.com

TULA'S CAFE *(breakfast and lunch; Friday dinner fish fry)*
70 West Shopping Center, Minocqua, WI 54548
(715) 356-2847, www.minocqua.org

LODGING
BAY VIEW LODGE
8555 Highway 51, Minocqua, WI 54548
(715) 356-9610 or (877) 215-8051
www.bayviewminocqua.com

NORTHWOODS NOD-A-WAY
10530 Townline Rd., Woodruff, WI 54568
(715) 356-7700, www.minocqua.org

THE POINTE WATERFRONT RESORT HOTEL
8269 Highway 51 South, Minocqua, WI 54548
(715) 356-4431 or (866) 666-6060
www.thepointeresort.com

SILL'S LAKESHORE BED & BREAKFAST RESORT
130 Lake Shore Dr., Minocqua, WI 54548
(715) 356-3384
www.sillslakeshorebandb.com

THE WATERS OF MINOCQUA
8116 Highway 51 South, Minocqua, WI 54548
(877) 992-8377
www.thewatersofminocqua.com

WHITEHAVEN BED & BREAKFAST
1077 Highway F, Minocqua, WI 54548
(715) 356-9097, www.whitehavenbandb.com

Chapter Eighteen
WINTERING EAGLES AND FROZEN FISH
Prairie du Chien

IMAGINE THAT YOU'RE STANDING ALONE on a high, wooded bluff, looking down into the chasm where the Mississippi River meets the Wisconsin River. As you breathe in the clear winter air and contemplate the powerful scene below, suddenly, from somewhere out of the ledges and treetops beneath you, a bald eagle rises up on the wind and ascends over your head on silent wings. Standing there, over the nation's mightiest river and under the nation's icon of freedom, you feel as if you've just witnessed the epitome of America itself.

Prairie du Chien is the oldest community on the Upper Mississippi and Wisconsin's second oldest city (Green Bay takes honors as the oldest). It was once a vibrant community of the Fox people. After French explorers Jacques Marquette and Louis Joliet reached the site by canoe on June 17, 1673, almost all subsequent travel involving French Canada and the Mississippi River passed through Prairie du Chien, making it one of the nation's most important fur-trading centers and river ports.

The only Wisconsin battle in the War of 1812 happened here in July 1814. In the Battle of Prairie du Chien, 150 British troops (with 400 Native American allies) and 60 Americans fought for control of the American-built Fort Shelby. The Yanks eventually surrendered, and the British held the fort until the war ended six months later.

There are at least two theories about how Prairie du Chien got its name. It could be that French trappers saw acres of prairie dog mounds and thus called the area "Field of Dogs." Another theory states that the town was named for "Big Dog," a local tribal leader.

But there's a lot more to this Wisconsin River town than canines or the storied history of the bipeds who dwell on land. What you find in its waters and in the skies overhead is well worth a winter visit. Smoked or fresh fish from the Mississippi is on almost every menu in town, and Wyalusing State Park, often called one of the Midwest's most beautiful spots, has some of the best ice fishing environs in Wisconsin. According to migratory waterfowl experts, this stretch of the Mississippi River also holds one of North America's largest populations of wintering eagles. From the end of November to mid-March, nearly 200 eagles make Prairie du Chien their home. Whether through binocular lenses or the zoom of a camera, an unhurried and reflective traveler is sure to be rewarded with a close-up look at America's symbol of freedom, an experience that will linger in the heart long after this winter weekend has ended.

During winter months in Wyalusing State Park, it's possible to take some fantastic wildlife shots, such as this one of a bald eagle. See "10 Tips for Photographing Wildlife" sidebar.

©PATRICK J. ENDRES/alaskaphotographics.com

Day One
MORNING

Prairie du Chien has one of the nine **Cabela's Outfitters** retail stores in the nation, and your first stop after getting into town should be at this impressive 53,000-square-foot store. Located near the Mississippi River on Highway 35, this outdoors supplier features everything from tuques to toboggans. From the moment you pull into the parking lot, you'll feel like an adventurer. Cabela's is set among beautiful bluffs and landscaped with bronze statues of deer. The front door is your entrance into an inside world that celebrates the outdoors. You'll find a 30-foot mountain and a diorama full of North American animals: bighorn sheep, white-tailed deer, foxes, black bears, a wolf, polar bear, and musk ox. An 8,000-gallon aquarium is stocked with fish native to Wisconsin. If there's anything you anticipate needing for your winter activities, this is the place for hunters, anglers, and outdoor enthusiasts to stock up. Stay for an hour or two; there's a lot to see, try on, and learn about.

10 TIPS FOR PHOTOGRAPHING WILDLIFE
by Patrick Endres

Born and raised in Wisconsin, Patrick Endres traveled to Alaska in 1981, lured north by an innate love for the natural world mixed with a youthful zeal for adventure and travel. He now lives in Fairbanks, Alaska, where he works as a freelance photographer. View his widely published work at www. alaskaphotographics.com.

❄ **Prepare for the physical conditions.** Dress appropriately and have your camera gear well packed and prepared for the type of travel, hiking, or climbing necessary for the task.

❄ **Research your subject and know its natural history.** Understand and respect a comfortable working distance from the wildlife you seek to photograph.

❄ **Go for the light.** If possible, scout the area ahead of time and know the lighting conditions: when, where, and how the morning and evening light and shadows fall.

❄ **Use a tripod with a ball-head camera/lens mount.** This will help you track and follow moving wildlife.

❄ **Try to get images that are on eye-level with your subject.** It will help portray a more natural scene of the animal in its environment.

❄ **Examine your compositional frames and evaluate the full area of your image.** Tunnel vision is a bad habit, easily acquired when shooting moving subjects, especially with the long, telephoto lenses common in wildlife photography.

❄ **Be a quick-change artist.** Have extra film, digital media, or batteries readily accessible should a change be necessary.

❄ **Experiment.** Use telephoto frames, but back off to capture the animal in its environment, too.

❄ **Be patient.** Do your best to blend enjoyment of being out in the natural world with the sheer persistence and patience often necessary to capture the image.

❄ **Be weather wise.** Inclement weather can provide situations for spectacular photos.

AFTERNOON

Before your afternoon with the eagles of the Mississippi River, stop for lunch at **Huckleberry's Restaurant** on Highway 18/35. Huckleberry's is locally owned and operated and offers daily lunch specials—and an attached gift shop—in a bright atmosphere.

Your eagle watching this weekend will begin with an initial foray into **Wyalusing State Park**, just south of Prairie du Chien. Although you won't be able to drive through the entire 2,628-acre park during the winter months, the lack of crowds and relative solitude more than make up for the limited roadways. Often called the most scenic and historically significant of Wisconsin's state parks, Wyalusing is where Father Jacques Marquette and Louis Joliet discovered the Upper Mississippi. Sitting 300 feet above the mingling of the Wisconsin and Mississippi Rivers is **Point Lookout**, perhaps Wyalusing's most popular spot and a great place for **watching the bald eagles** in the winds and waters below you. Eagles soar by catching thermals: rising currents of warm air and updrafts generated by terrain, such as valley edges or Wisconsin bluffs. The year-round open water and craggy variations in the bluffs that provide nesting privacy attract the large birds in winter. Keep quiet, though, because noises will scare them away.

An eagle's vision is at least four times more acute than the average human's. A mature bald eagle has a wingspan of six to eight feet, weighs up to 15 pounds, can reach 30 to 40 miles per hour in flight but, in dives, can achieve 100 miles per hour. Whether you admire eagles for their power, their beauty or their wildness, you'll want to capture these magnificent birds in their winter home with your camera [see "10 Tips for Photographing Wildlife" sidebar].

Wyalusing will be worth another outing tomorrow, but by late afternoon, you'll want to check into your weekend base of operations. A unique place to stay is **The Loghouse**. The kind of old-fashioned, log cabin that you've only read about, it sits on the edge of 65 acres of woods off Highway 27 on Log House Lane. The cabin has a full kitchen (including microwave), living room with a pullout sofa, loft bedroom with two full-size beds, and bath with shower.

From the moment you drive up the lane, The Loghouse sends out a warm welcome. A soft glow emanates from the lights inside, out onto the long, wooden porch. If you're lucky enough to book in December, antique Santas will peer down at you from every crossbeam, and well-loved treasures wait in every cranny. Antique eyeglasses sit atop a stack of books, as if the reader has just stepped outside momentarily. Comfy chairs occupy every corner, for reading, writing, or thinking. The kitchen features a floor salvaged from an 1870s St. Louis warehouse. Upstairs, a dressmaker's form inhabits the loft, and bear-paw slippers rest by the bed, just waiting to warm your feet. A painting of Tom Sawyer and Huck Finn decorates one wall, and, somehow, a childhood spent on the Mississippi River seems very familiar [see "Filming a River" sidebar].

FILMING A RIVER

A silhouetted canoe, enveloped in mist, gliding silently along on the Mississippi River in the golden haze of sunrise. In many ways, this one image captures the essence of Prairie du Chien.

If you'd like to get a pre-trip feel for the ambiance of this river town, view the British Broadcasting Company (BBC) film *Mississippi Tales of the Last River Rat*. Prairie du Chien native Neil Rettig, a nationally renowned cinematographer whose works include nature films for the National Geographic Society, photographed the production.

Rettig shot several of the film's scenes in the Prairie du Chien area. The story is based on the life of Alma, Wisconsin, native Kenny Salwey, who has lived the majority of his life in a shack on the Mississippi's banks. Based on an autobiographical book by Salwey and narrated by him, the film depicts the river's wildlife and scenery and the insights Salwey garnered through the years.

Rettig acknowledged invaluable contributions to the film by another Prairie du Chien native, commercial fisherman and wildlife photographer Don Valley. Valley, whose name also appears in the movie's credits, showed Rettig the best locations to film wildlife and helped get permissions to set up blinds. Rettig was able to shoot bald eagles from just 30 feet away.

The 50-minute film received rave reviews for the BBC in late November 2004 and aired on the Discovery Channel in the United States.

EVENING

It will be hard to leave the warm and inviting Loghouse, even for dinner. But one eatery not to miss in Prairie du Chien is the **Barn Restaurant/Banquet Facility**. True to the city's river theme, the Pond Room, just off the main dining room of this converted barn, features the soothing waters of a fountain, adorned with a statue of a boy fishing. On weekends, you can dance to a live band.

After dinner, pause on the Loghouse porch for some **stargazing**. Out in the country, against the black winter sky, the stars will seem brighter than you're used to seeing them in the city. It's mind-boggling to contemplate that the light you see coming from an average star has been traveling 670 million miles per hour (186,000 miles per second) since the time of the dinosaurs.

Tonight, bask in the glow of the ancient white lights above, and the soft light reaching out to you from your winter cabin of yesteryear within.

Day Two
MORNING

Start an active day with a hearty breakfast at the **Hungry House Cafe**. A variety of breakfasts and lunches are served in this friendly, neighborhood gathering place, to the background sounds of '60s groups such as the Four Seasons, Rolling Stones, and Simon and Garfunkel.

Today, you'll have the chance to experience all the winter fun that **Wyalusing State Park** has to offer. You'll find it not only an optimal locale to watch bald eagles, but a prime place to **cross-country ski, snowshoe, winter hike, winter camp, ice fish**, and even **ice climb**— or at least watch others doing it *[see "Ice Climbing 101" sidebar]*.

"Wyalusing" is a Munsee–Delaware word meaning "home of the warrior," and the park contains a large number of Native American burial mounds, from the earliest type of conical mounds to later animal-shaped effigies. Most of the effigy mounds are along the **Sentinel Ridge Nature Trail**. The rest of the topography is rich with forests and meadows, hills and valleys, bluffs and bottomlands, and caves and waterfalls.

The **Mississippi Ridge Trail**, located in the southwest area of the park, and the **Whitetail Meadows Trail** on the east end are groomed and tracked for **cross-country skiing**. The 3.5-mile Mississippi Ridge Trail has often been described as the easiest cross-country ski trail with the greatest views you'll ever find. This two-way, double-tracked trail starts at the Hugh Harper Group Camp Lodge and Dorms, courses through a hardwood forest to the Mississippi View Picnic Area, and returns up Cathedral Tree Drive, passing the Spook Hill Mound Group. The open-field **Whitetail Meadows Trail** is an easy ski over gently rolling terrain. Located on the west side of the park, the trail is a 3.2-mile loop with a 1.7-mile inner loop. Watch for white-tailed deer and wild turkeys.

The heavily wooded **Sugar Maple Nature Trail**, also located in the southwest area of the park, is the perfect route for those who prefer to **snowshoe** or **winter hike**. Ski poles might be helpful on this 1.5-mile trail, which may challenge you with hills and steps. But your work will be repaid: In a narrow niche between 500-foot-high cliffs is scenic **Pictured Rock Cave**. When winter temperatures drop, a frozen waterfall spills over the limestone entrance from rim to floor. White-tailed deer and red fox are often spotted here, and signage along the path identifies plants and informs you of ecological principles. The 1.7-mile **Sand Cave Trail** is named for a rock overhang that supports a small waterfall. Frozen in winter, it makes for spectacular photos.

Winter camping is permitted at 55 sites in the park, six of them plowed. Electrical hookups and water are available, and reservations are not required. The excellent **ice fishing** on the Mississippi's backwaters draws winter visitors to the park. Bluegills, northerns, and crappies keep anglers occupied.

AFTERNOON

At the end of your vigorous morning, head back to downtown Prairie du Chien for a warm-up coffee and lunch at **Coaches Family Restaurant** on South Marquette Road. A local favorite since 1970, Coaches boasts about its "Flavor Crisp Fried Chicken" and pizzas made to order.

After lunch is a good time to take a leisurely **winter walk** on the **Lawler Park Walk of History** on St. Feriole Island at the end of Blackhawk Avenue. This is the site of the Battle of Prairie du Chien during the War of 1812. Wisconsin's first millionaire, fur dealer Hercules Dousman, built his mansion, **Villa Louis**, here in 1843. The original house was razed 27 years later, and the current Italianate building was constructed. Now owned by the State Historical Society of Wisconsin, you can tour the richly furnished Villa Louis mansion in early December during **A Christmas Holiday on a Victorian Country Estate**. But even if Villa Louis is closed during your winter weekend, the riverfront Lawler Park Walk of History is a relaxing way to see the heart of Prairie du Chien. In winter, it's an excellent location for watching ducks, **spotting eagles**, and taking photos.

Although across the Mississippi River in Iowa, the 2,526-acre **Effigy Mounds National Monument** is a short nine minutes away. **Cross-country skiing**, **winter hiking**, and **snowshoeing** are allowed in the park, and an annual **winter film festival** is held in the visitor center auditorium on Saturdays and Sundays from January through March. The monument provides a quiet respite in winter and contains 195 mounds, 31 of which are effigies. With no roads within its borders, the park has 11 miles of **hiking** trails.

EVENING

After a full day of outdoor exercise and wildlife viewing, enjoy dinner in town at the **Angus Supper Club** on Highway 18. Along with steaks, you'll have a wide variety of pasta, chicken, pork, and seafood dishes to choose from—including frog legs, walleye, and lobster. While waiting for your entrée, bring out the digital camera and look over your Prairie du Chien and eagle photos from the weekend's tours.

If you planned far enough in advance to be in town during New Year's Eve, don't miss the **Droppin' of the Carp** festival that takes place on West Blackhawk Avenue. One Mississippi fish, known as "Lucky the Carp" (although his actual luck is questionable), is lowered in a countdown to the New Year by a 110-foot crane. People from all over the Midwest come just to get bragging rights for having seen a frozen, almost-30-pound carp being lowered in what may be the country's most unusual New Year's Eve event. In fact, national and international news media have checked in on the proceedings. Huge bonfires are lit, starting at 9:00 p.m., and hot chocolate and s'mores help keep the evening warm.

ICE CLIMBING 101

Mountain climbing has always drawn intrepid outdoor enthusiasts, but add the element of ice and you have something bordering on an extreme sport. However, according to Doug Van Horn, an ice climbing devotee of six years, ice climbing has "more of a perceived danger than a real danger." That is, says Van Horn, providing you follow two paramount rules: Always climb with someone else, and always use the correct gear.

Ice climbing is a relatively new sport, but in the past few decades, advances in equipment have allowed even beginners to scale tall walls of solid ice. You swing a short, very sharp axe held in each hand into the ice for handholds and kick sharp, metal points on your boots into the ice for toeholds.

There are two types of ice climbing: top rope and lead. In top rope climbing, an anchor, threaded with a rope, is set where the top of the ice wall is located. Both climbers then walk down to the bottom of the climb. One person ties onto the rope and climbs in what is essentially a one-pulley system. The belayer, the person at the bottom not climbing, pulls against the rope as the climber climbs. If the climber falls, the belayer stops the rope from running through the anchor, and the climber swings from side to side, until getting another toehold or axe into the ice. When finished, the climber hangs back on the rope, and the belayer lowers the climber to the ground.

In lead climbing, both people start at the base, with no gear to begin with on the wall. Both climbers tie onto either end of a rope. The leader, who is usually the more experienced climber, starts out first. The other climber is called the "second." The leader starts climbing, placing screws in the ice wall along the way so that the rope can be clipped to the wall.

Ice climbing is a relatively new sport, and Wisconsin's Wyalusing State Park has some of the region's best ice-climbing opportunities.

213

The second finds a way to get anchored to the ground, ensuring that the rope doesn't snag or tangle as the leader climbs. Once at the top, the leader gets securely anchored and pulls in the slack rope. The leader then belays the second, who removes all the ice screws while climbing. "I don't recommend people start out lead climbing," says Van Horn, "because you really have to understand the ice, know its history, conditions, and its weather, and be able to read it very well."

"Reading" ice is one of the main reasons those new to the sport need to be accompanied by an experienced ice climber. "I once had a chunk of ice about a foot thick and six feet in diameter land near me and my group at Wyalusing State Park," says Van Horn. "Some novice climbers dislodged it after I told them I thought that part of the wall was unsafe. With global warming, the ice has been less safe for more of the season over the last few years."

Ice climbers say that the payoffs for their efforts are spectacular views and a personal interaction with winter not possible in any other way. If you'd like to try ice climbing, go to your local outdoor outfitter and ask for an experienced ice climber recommendation. Outing clubs and university outdoor programs often offer instruction at a nominal charge. You can learn more about ice climbing at www.climbingcentral.com.

"Ice climbing is a blast," says Van Horn. "I have taken people out who have never climbed before, and they've done just fine. Carpenters have a good time with it because they're used to swinging hammers. It's the same motion you use with an ice pick."

In Wyalusing State Park, overlooking the place where the Mississippi River meets the Wisconsin River, you can spend a winter afternoon cross-country skiing, hiking, eagle watching, or just enjoying the view.

JOHN T. ANDREWS

JOHN T. ANDREWS

Kissing "Lucky the Carp" in the first minutes of the New Year is said to bring the kisser good luck for the next 365 days.

Children break a candy-filled carp piñata at 11:00 p.m., while adults munch on smoked carp and crackers, and watch the onstage entertainment. Two minutes and 30 seconds before midnight, Lucky begins his slow descent. At 12:15 a.m., you can take part in the **Carp Plunge** into a livestock water tank near Old Will's Bait Shop, at 400 W. Blackhawk Avenue. You'll receive a souvenir towel to commemorate your bravery!

Day Three
MORNING

Sleep in this morning and plan to eat a leisurely breakfast in The Loghouse. Enjoy a cup of coffee on the porch, followed by a **hike through the woods behind the cabin**. A nature trail leads up the slopes—a path you most likely will share with deer. If it's cold enough, you may be able to fit in an **ice-skating** outing at **Lochner Park**, a 6.3-acre community park on Wacouta and Wells Streets.

Crawford County has miles of **snowmobile** trails, and Corridor 34 leads north out of Prairie du Chien. For more information on snowmobiling in the area, call (608) 326-8682.

On your way out of town, try to travel a section of the **Great River Road** *[see Chapter 12: River Winter (La Crosse/Westby/Coon Valley)]*. One of the nation's oldest and longest national byways, the Great River Road is a 3,000-mile network of highways extending from Canada to the Gulf of Mexico. In Wisconsin, the road flanks the Mississippi River, winding along 250 miles of the state's western border. The Great River Road has been touted as one of the most scenic drives in mid-America, but when the landscape is blanketed in a white mantle of winter, the views become even more serene and idyllic. The road heads into Prairie du Chien from the south along U.S. Highway 18 and State Highway 35, and continues north to La Crosse.

Keep the car windows open and an eye to the sky—you just might glimpse an eagle soaring overhead.

FOR MORE INFORMATION

PRAIRIE DU CHIEN AREA CHAMBER OF COMMERCE
211 S. Main St., Prairie du Chien, WI 53821
(800) 732-1673, www.prairieduchien.org

WINTER ATTRACTIONS

CABELA'S OUTFITTERS
33901 Highway 35, Prairie du Chien, WI 53821
(608) 326-5600, www.cabelas.com

CRAWFORD COUNTY SNOWMOBILE TRAILS
1511 S. Marquette St.
Prairie du Chien, WI 53821, (608) 326-8682

EFFIGY MOUNDS NATIONAL MONUMENT
151 Highway 76, Harpers Ferry, IA 52146
(563) 873-3491
www.nps.gov/efmo/home.htm

GREAT RIVER ROAD
(800) 658-9480, www.wigreatriverroad.org

LAWLER PARK
Water St., off of W. Blackhawk Ave.
Prairie du Chien, WI 53821, (608) 326-7207

LOCHNER PARK
900 S. Wacouta Ave., Prairie du Chien, WI 53821
(608) 326-7207

WYALUSING STATE PARK
13081 State Park Lane, Bagley, WI 53801
(608) 996-2261, www.wiparks.net

WINTER FESTIVALS

BIRDING CRUISES ON THE MISSISSIPPI RIVER—mid-November. Board the *Mississippi Explorer* at the St. Feriole Island riverfront. See migratory birds close-up from the deck, and enjoy peak season for thousands of tundra swans, ducks, geese, bald eagles, and hawks. (563) 586-4444.

A CHRISTMAS HOLIDAY ON A VICTORIAN COUNTRY ESTATE—first two weekends in December. Travel back in time to winter holidays in the late 1890s by touring the Villa Louis historic site on St. Feriole Island, 521 N. Villa Louis Road, from 11:00 a.m. to 4:00 p.m. Evening lamplight tours on two Saturdays. (608) 326-2721 or www.wisconsinhistory.org/villalouis.

HOLIDAY PARADE—early December. Downtown on Blackhawk Avenue. 5:30 p.m. (608) 326-8555.

DROPPIN' OF THE CARP—December 31. Starting at 9:00 p.m., enjoy bonfires, hot chocolate, stage performances, and a countdown to the New Year at the entrance of St. Feriole Island, 400 W. Blackhawk Ave. (608) 326-8602 or (800) 732-1673. The **Carp Plunge** follows immediately after.

WINTER FILM FESTIVAL AT EFFIGY MOUNDS NATIONAL MONUMENT—January through March. Three miles north of Marquette, Iowa. A new movie will be shown each week in the auditorium, along with a special display in the visitor center. Movies will be shown Saturdays and Sundays on the hour, from 10:00 a.m. to 3:00 p.m. Free admission. (563) 873-3491 or www.nps.gov/efmo/activ.htm.

ANNUAL TASTE OF PRAIRIE DU CHIEN— mid-January. Held at the Barn Restaurant on County Road K. (608) 326-8555.

ANNUAL ICE FISHEREE—first weekend in February. Ice fishing competition held on Gremore Lake and headquartered near the Lakeview Marina Bar & Restaurant on County Road K. Ice-sculpting demonstrations, fishing prizes, and evening entertainment. Fishing begins at 7:00 a.m. (800) 732-1673.

BALD EAGLE APPRECIATION DAY—early February. Held on the grounds of the Wisconsin Travel Information Center, 211 S. Main Street. See eagle and raptor exhibits and displays, and bald eagles through spotting scopes. Birding experts are on hand, and short field trips to other bald eagle locations are offered. (800) 732-1673.

CANDLELIGHT SKI AT WYALUSING STATE PARK—second Friday in February.

ST. PATRICK'S DAY PARADE—mid-March. Downtown on Blackhawk Avenue. (608) 326-8555.

RESTAURANTS

ANGUS SUPPER CLUB *(dinner)*
37640 Highway 18 South
Prairie du Chien, WI 5382, (608) 326-2222
www.mwnews.net/html/area_dining.html

BARN RESTAURANT/BANQUET FACILITY
(dinner)
Route 1, County Road K
Prairie du Chien, WI 53821, (608) 326-4941

BUCKHORN GRILL & PUB *(lunch and dinner)*
1801 Cabela's Lane, Prairie du Chien, WI 53821
(608) 326-5716

COACHES FAMILY RESTAURANT
(breakfast, lunch, and dinner)
634 S. Marquette Rd.
Prairie du Chien, WI 53821, (608) 326-8115
www.coachespdc.com

HUCKLEBERRY'S RESTAURANT
(breakfast, lunch, and dinner)
1916 S. Marquette Rd., Highway 18 South Prairie
du Chien, WI 53821
(608) 326-5488, www.huckleberryspdc.com

HUNGRY HOUSE CAFE *(breakfast and lunch)*
531 N. Marquette Rd.
Prairie du Chien, WI 53821, (608) 326-4346

KABER'S RESTAURANT *(dinner)*
225 W. Blackhawk Ave.
Prairie du Chien, WI 53821, (608) 326-6216

LODGING

THE LOGHOUSE
35509 Log House Lane (Highway 27)
Prairie du Chien, WI 53821, (608) 326-4756
www.mhtc.net/~loghouse

SIMPLY LODGING SUITES
204 W. Blackhawk Ave.
Prairie du Chien, WI 53821, (608) 326-7467
www.simplyprairieduchien.com

WINDSOR PLACE INN
1936 S. Marquette Rd., Highway 18 South
Prairie du Chien, WI 53821, (608) 326-7799
www.windsorplaceinnpdc.com

Chapter Nineteen

IT'S ELEMENTAL:
EARTH, WATER, WOOD, AIR, AND METAL
Superior

I T'S ELEMENTARY: Superior is a down-to-earth town filled with basic elements, and the force of nature here rings through the air in the sounds of its waterfalls and the words of its songs.

The largest community in northern Wisconsin, Superior was originally founded as a mining town. But given its natural breakwaters, the place was destined to become the largest and—along with nearby Duluth, Minnesota—the busiest harbor on the Great Lakes. Today, Superior ships 75 million tons of iron ore and grain annually and is one of the farthest inland and deepest freshwater ports in the world.

In fact, Superior's shipyards developed the first "whaleback," a massive ore carrier that gets its name from its whale-like shape that provides it with extra stability in rough waters. You can see the *S.S. Meteor,* a ship launched in 1896 and the world's last remaining whale-back freighter, anchored at the Superior docks off Barkers Island.

Superior is not only linked with Duluth through a shared shipping business but through the element of metal. The Richard I. Bong Memorial Bridge, named for the World War II flying ace born in Popular, 15 minutes east of Superior, stretches between the two port cities. It makes a graceful span over Lake Superior, the largest freshwater lake in the world.

The huge lake seems to have given instruction and inspiration to life's other basic elements here. The coniferous woods in the Superior Municipal Forest make it the second-largest municipal forest in the United States. At the wild and rugged Brule River State Forest, cascades tumble over rocks, and steep river bluffs are forested with aspen and balsam fir. The powerful, tea-colored waterfalls at Amnicon Falls State Park run over ancient lava beds that date back more than a billion years. There is a primal thrill that comes from witnessing the highest waterfall in Wisconsin, Big Manitou Falls at Pattison State Park: hearing the sound of its strength, feeling its mist on your skin, tasting its stray water droplets on your tongue. Just stand in front of Big Manitou, and you're in an actual rain. The smell of pines is stronger here than anywhere else, somehow more pungent in the winter air.

This winter weekend, throw off the extraneous accoutrements of your stressful weekday world. Get down to the basic elements of life. Venture into rugged, natural beauty and release your adventurer within. And just like the words in Gordon Lightfoot's popular song, let the Superior "legend live on."

Day One
MØRNING

If you arrive in Superior early enough for breakfast, make a stop at the **Breakwater West Restaurant** on East Second Street. Reflecting the essence of the city itself, the Breakwater serves good, basic, home-style food that is popular with residents, and the waitstaff is friendly and helpful.

This morning, get ready to have your socks knocked off! Your first stop will be at the **Superior Municipal Forest**, the second-largest municipal forest in the United States, easily accessed on Wyoming Avenue off 28th Street. In this 4,500-acre plot of beauty, you'll find 16 miles of trails for **classic and skate cross-country skiing**, **snowshoeing**, and **winter hiking**, plus trails designated for **snowmobiling**, **skijoring** [see "Dog-Powered Skiing" sidebar], and **ATVing**. In all of these activities, you'll gain an appreciation for this incredible forest. The natural features include a mature coniferous forest, marshes, and wet clay flats where rare plants thrive. The forest borders the fresh water St. Louis River Estuary, which divides the terrain into narrow, steep-sided ridges. Rare Forster's tern and merlin (a small, stocky

falcon) forage here. Your travels through the forest will take you to picturesque views of Pokegama Bay and Kimball Bay, all framed by evergreens, birch, and oak.

A unique feature of the Superior Municipal Forest is its **Archery Course**. Accessed on Billings Drive and 42nd Street, the course is approximately one third of a mile long and set up according to the National Field Archery Association guidelines. Back amid tall pines, scrub brush, and ravines, the course has a total of 39 shots at 14 different targets. **Archery hunting** is allowed within the forest during Wisconsin's archery hunting season (state license and city permit required).

If **ice fishing** is your passion, take along an auger on your outings. With 431 inland lakes in Douglas County and Lake Superior, your weekend will provide plenty of opportunities to snag a walleye.

The late-winter thaw swells the Amnicon River rapids, leaving huge remnants of ice along the rocky shoreline.

JOHN T. ANDREWS

AFTERNOON

Eat your lunch on the waterfront by going to the **Galley Restaurant** in the

DOG-POWERED SKIING

Winter Frisbee aside, there's one winter sport that your dog will probably enjoy just as much as you do. Skijoring is the sport of being pulled on skis by one or more dogs in harness. A line that is about four-to-seven-feet long and equipped with a handlebar for balance and control connects the dog's harness to a waist belt worn by the skier. A typical skijoring kit you can purchase will include a harness, belt, and tow-bar system. Skijoring is usually done with one to three dogs.

Most dogs have a natural instinct to pull, which means that your pet is as likely to take to the sport as a sled dog. A physically fit dog that weighs at least 35 pounds can pull an average-sized adult over moderate terrain. The breed is not important; the primary requirement is a close relationship between you and your dog.

Skijoring is a great way for the two of you to enjoy the winter together. Just make sure that you pay attention to your dog's attitude: it isn't hard to tell if he or she likes to pull or is lethargic, thirsty, or worn out. Remember that your dog may benefit from booties, a coat, and, after heavy exertion, an extra ration of food. A hot chocolate for yourself may be in order, as well.

www.travelwisconsin.com

Willing dogs and a pair of cross-country skis are all you need to start skijoring, a dog-powered sport that is gaining popularity in Wisconsin.

221

Barkers Island Inn & Conference Center at 300 Marina Drive. Order fresh fish or a salad to go along with your splendid view of the bay, sandbar, and Lake Superior before checking into your accommodations at the Barkers Island Inn complex.

The sandbar on which the inn is built is wrapped in an interesting folktale. A Superior legend has it that a man named Charles Barker created the island as the result of a disagreement with lumber baron Martin Pattison, whose home, Fairlawn, sits on the shore of

---

THE SINKING OF THE *EDMUND FITZGERALD*
by Elmer Engman

Elmer Engman was born in Duluth, Minnesota, and grew up just one block from Lake Superior. Watching the ore carriers on the lake, he developed an interest in maritime history and shipwrecks. He learned how to scuba dive in 1968 and has dived on many Lake Superior shipwrecks. He got involved with the S.S. Meteor as a board member in the late 1970s and is still involved with the Meteor as a board member with the Superior Public Museums.

When you look out over Lake Superior on a calm day, it is hard to imagine that more than 500 shipwrecks rest on the lake bottom. The names of most of the ships are known only to a few historians and shipwreck enthusiasts. But one name is known to almost everyone worldwide: the steamer *Edmund Fitzgerald.* Just as the *Titanic* is the most famous ocean shipwreck, the *Edmund Fitzgerald* is the most famous Great Lakes shipwreck. Gordon Lightfoot's song, "The Wreck of the *Edmund Fitzgerald*," told the story well and ensured that the ship and crew would be remembered forever.

The *Edmund Fitzgerald* loaded her last cargo of taconite, 26,000 tons, on November 9, 1975, at the ore docks in Superior, Wisconsin. The *Fitzgerald* was a regular visitor to Superior and sometimes laid up for the winter at the Fraser Shipyards. The day was sunny and calm when the *Fitzgerald* sailed out of the harbor. Nothing in the weather forecast indicated anything bad.

Sailing down the lake to the locks on the eastern end takes around 24 hours, but 24 hours later the *Fitz* found herself in a full gale, with winds blowing at 40 to 70 knots. There was another ship 10 miles behind her, the *Arthur M. Anderson,* and both captains were in radio contact.

Somewhere near Six-Fathom Shoal, Captain Earnest McSorley of the *Fitz* reported two deck vents damaged, the ship listing to port, and both pumps going. Whatever had caused the damage—and there are many theories—it ended up being very serious.

The *Anderson* had the *Fitz* on radar when the doomed ship disappeared in a snow squall and never reappeared. The ship, with 29 crewmen, vanished; there was no mayday call.

I had a chance to hear a couple of other captains talk about the storm. They were about 30 miles behind the *Fitz*, and they described waters that were hitting the stern of their ships as high as the smokestack and sometimes over. Their observations about the severity of the storm made my hair stand on end.

November 10, 2005, marked the 30th anniversary of the sinking of the *Edmund Fitzgerald.* Memorial events around the Great Lakes ensured that, even 30 years later, the legend lives on.

Superior Bay. The story goes that when Barker was in the market for lumber, Pattison raised the price. To show his displeasure, Barker dumped dredge sands in the bay in front of Pattison's home to spoil his view. When lumber prices went up again, more sand was dumped. With more price increases, soon everyone was dumping sand there, and an island was formed. The locals were quick to call it "Barker's Island."

The alternative—and far less colorful—explanation for Barkers Island, however, is that mariners demanded Superior Bay be dredged to enable larger lake freighters to navigate the waters without danger of running aground on a sandbar. Barkers Island, it is said, was named after Captain Barker, who was in charge of the dredging work. Whatever the case, the feud between Barker and Pattison is a great tale, and Barkers Island Inn is a great place to stay and live a Superior legend.

To steep yourself even more in Superior history and in its rugged beauty, spend at least part of the afternoon on the **Osaugie Waterfront Trail**. Starting at the trailhead at the Richard I. Bong World War II Heritage Center, a **winter hike** along this 5.2-mile paved trail will take you on a journey past ocean-going ships and the world's largest ore dock, the Burlington Northern Ore Dock where the ill-fated *S.S. Edmund Fitzgerald* took on cargo before sailing into the treacherous November gale in 1975 *[see "The Sinking of the Edmund Fitzgerald" sidebar]*. If you'd like to continue on the trail, take the 4.4-mile Moccasin Mike Road to **Wisconsin Point**.

Wisconsin Point is a three-mile section of the world's longest freshwater sandbar, which stretches for 10 miles along the Lake Superior shoreline between Superior and Duluth. The point offers a wild, off-the-beaten-path peek into the harbor. In the winter especially, it's a quiet, isolated place with strange pull-offs, numerous forks, and I-think-I'm-lost dead ends. But those moments of "where the heck am I?" will pay off. Keep going until you can spot

www.travelwisconsin.com

A drive or hike along Wisconsin Point will lead to one of the most beautiful lighthouses in Wisconsin. Built in 1913, the Wisconsin Point Lighthouse guards the entrance to Superior harbor.

the **Wisconsin Point Lighthouse** amid the storm-tossed driftwood and crashing waves.

The lighthouse was built in 1913 and still guides all sizes of watercraft to the Superior harbor entrance. Maintained by the U.S. Coast Guard, the lighthouse is not open for tours, but its beauty is really in its exterior setting. If you're lucky and plan well, you'll hit the lighthouse just at sunset. Catch the moment in a photo of the lighthouse on the point, backlit with a dramatic sky and crashing waves. Winter on the sandbar is truly beautiful.

The Osaugie Waterfront Trail links to the 60-mile, crushed limestone **Tri-County Corridor**. The corridor is designated for **hiking, ATVing**, and **snowmobiling**, and parallels Highway 2 east to Ashland. It is a major link to a handful of other trails in Douglas, Bayfield, and Ashland counties. The Tri-County Corridor etches a straight path from Superior through Brule and Iron River to the eastern trailhead in Ashland. A scenic side trip along the way is the spur trail that leads to Amnicon Falls State Park (which you'll visit tomorrow afternoon).

EVENING

The Shack Smokehouse & Grille on Belknap Street has been known for its hickory pit barbecue for more than 20 years. Tonight, order the hickory-smoked half chicken or ribs to learn why the grill has been successful for so long. They also boast the longest happy hour in town: on Friday and Saturday, from 2:00 to 6:00 p.m. and from 10:00 p.m. until midnight. On Sunday, happy hour runs from noon until 6:00 p.m.

On Friday evenings when the sky is at least 75 percent clear and the temperature is above 5 degrees Fahrenheit, the **Schrieber Observatory** in Barstow Hall on the University of Wisconsin–Superior campus holds public viewing sessions at 8:00 p.m. Gaze at galaxies, planets, star clusters, nebulae, and the moon in the Superior sky. The observatory is unheated, so dress warmly.

Day Two
MORNING

This morning will be spent in the wild and rugged **Brule River State Forest**. Before your winter excursion into one of the most untamed areas of the state, get a substantial breakfast at **The Twin Gables Café**. On the corner of Highways 2 and 27, the café has old-time favorites, such as fluffy blueberry pancakes and buttermilk biscuits with sausage gravy.

The Brule is a wild-looking forest. While the river is usually referred to as just the "Brule," the full name is actually the "Bois Brule," French for "burnt wood." The Ojibwa called the river the "Misacoda" or "burnt pine" because the pine barrens in the area frequently caught fire. Forest has now replaced most of the barrens, although some still remain.

The Brule River begins and ends in this narrow 40,882-acre state forest. The river has one of the best trout flowages in the country and travels from Solon Springs into Lake Superior. Presidents Grant, Cleveland, Coolidge, Hoover, and Eisenhower all enjoyed fly-casting in this river, and Calvin Coolidge had his summer White House in a resort here for several years. In winter, **ravens perform an incredible aerial ritual** before roosting for the night. The site for this display changes each year, so ask at the office if you want to see it.

The Brule River State Forest is a territory for **cross-country skiing, snowshoeing, snowmobiling**, or **ATVing**. For classic or skate-skiing, the **After Hours Trail** has a countless variety of loops totaling 8.5 miles. The mostly level trail takes you past aspen, birch, oak, Norway spruce, and red and white pine, although some sections can be a bit challenging. Since this state forest has more diverse species of birds and mammals than any other northern Wisconsin acreage of similar size, keep your eye open and camera ready for deer, ruffed grouse, geese, and bald eagles.

The **Historic Bayfield Road Trail** is dedicated to **snowshoers** and **winter hikers**. The southern half of the two-mile trail follows the 1870 to 1885 route of the first road between Superior and Bayfield, later replaced by a railroad. The thickly wooded trail passes a fire

---

WALKING ON ICE

Winter hiking in Wisconsin's forests and on its trails is an easy, relaxing and healthy way to enjoy four months of the year in our northern climes. It's often simpler than the summer variety—after all, you won't have to haul along insect repellent or netting, and the trails tend to be far less crowded. Your vistas tend to be grander as well. Without the heavy foliage of summer, you often have clear views across miles of lakes, from the tops of bluffs, and over fields. Animal tracks are easy to spot; you're more likely to come across them in the relative solitude, and the songs of birds seem sharper on the crisp air.

What winter hiking has that its summer counterpart doesn't is ice on the trails. But don't let that keep you inside. With just a few minor adjustments to your normal walking stride—and occasionally a simple device strapped to your hiking boots—you may become convinced that winter hiking is "superior" to your summer treks.

Here are a few tips to keep in mind when walking on ice-covered trails:

❋ **WALK SLOWLY.** Ice is easy to traverse if it's flat and you avoid sudden moves. Begin walking with a slow shuffle and build up momentum. A thin layer of snow over ice will lend traction.

❋ **WALK SMALL.** Avoid an erect, marching posture. Instead, emulate the skier's crouch, with knees slightly bent. Keep your shoulders forward of your hips.

❋ **WALK FORWARD.** Especially on sloping ice, use the same shuffle step, but keep your weight forward—about mid-sole or toward the ball of your foot—but never on your heels. When walking downhill on ice, the natural tendency is to lean back; but if you do, your feet will slip out from under you, and you'll land on your backside.

❋ **WALK WITH THE ANIMALS.** If your trail suddenly ends in a snow bank, remember that large animals, such as deer, will often blaze their own convenient trails. If one of their trails is going in your direction, take it. Remember to avoid the combination of deep snow and heavy brush. The vegetation can cause air pockets to form under the snow cover, so that when you break through, you may find yourself in surprisingly deeper snow than expected.

❋ **WALK WITH THE YAKS AND TREES.** Devices such as Yaktrax strapped onto the bottoms of your boots can dramatically help reduce falls and injuries. Yaktrax and similar products are simple strands of rubber and steel coils that are banded together. Clip them onto your regular hiking boots, and they'll crisscross over your soles for instant traction.

For natural traction in Wisconsin's great forests, you'll find that fallen pine needles work wonders.

---

tower and an old mine.

The Brule River State Forest has 32 miles of **snowmobile** trails. The ambitious 26-mile, **Brule–St. Croix Trail** connects to the Douglas and Bayfield County trail system and crosses a continental divide. The trail also connects to the **Tri-County Corridor**.

Snowmobilers, ATVers, and **winter hikers** can also use the **Saunders State Trail**, an 8.4-mile county-operated trail that links with the 98-mile **Gandy Dancer State Trail** near Superior and continues into Minnesota. The county-operated Gandy Dancer crosses the Wisconsin–Minnesota border twice on its way from St. Croix Falls to Superior.

If you'd like to spend the morning going down the slopes, you have two options for **downhill skiing.** Fifteen minutes from downtown Superior—but technically in Duluth— is **Spirit Mountain**, an energetic winter activity area with 22 downhill runs and a 700-foot vertical drop. In fact, Spirit Mountain is home to some of the longest runs in the Midwest—one over a mile long. Those long runs also have fantastic views of Duluth and Lake Superior.

Spirit Mountain's **snowboarding** terrain park is the largest in the Midwest, hosting two half-pipes and a variety of creatively designed terrain features. **Cross-country skiers** aren't left out, either: Spirit Mountain has 13.6 wooded miles of trails that are double-tracked with skating lanes.

A bit farther from downtown Superior is **Mont du Lac**, a **snowboarding** and **downhill ski** area with seven runs and a 310-foot vertical drop. **Snow tubers** can take off from four chutes and ride up the hill with a handle tow.

AFTERNOON

Back in the city, stop for a big burger at **Old Town Bar & Restaurant** on East Second Street before an afternoon at some waterfalls you'll never forget.

Twelve miles southeast along Highways 2 and 53, the 825-acre **Amnicon Falls State Park** has no official **cross-country ski** trails, although skiing is allowed in the park. **Winter hiking** to see the waterfalls and geologic features is popular. Thirty-six sites are open for **winter camping**.

This amazing area was created half a billion years ago by the Douglas Fault, which stretches between Ashland, Wisconsin, and St. Paul, Minnesota. The fault forms the chan-nel of the tea-colored Amnicon River. The color is caused by tannic acid leached from decaying vegetation in the area's bogs. The river splits around an island in the center of the park, just before hitting the fault line, and flows over three impressive falls—Upper, Lower, and Snake Pit—each nearly 30 feet high. Another small waterfall, Now and Then Falls, runs in a river channel that fills only when water levels are high. A 55-foot covered bowstring bridge from the 1930s—often called a "Horton" after its designer—links the banks. The bridge is one of five of its kind remaining in the United States.

The Amnicon River descends 640 feet on its 30-mile trek north to Lake Superior, and almost a third of that drop occurs on the less than two miles of Amnicon River within this park. The watershed and four of its lakes contain the only native muskie population in northwestern Wisconsin, and the Amnicon is a primary spawning run for rainbow trout, Chinook salmon, and smelt from Lake Superior.

There are two beautiful, short **winter hiking trails** in the park. A half-mile trail begins at the bowstring bridge, wraps around the island, and continues south along the river. It has a short spur that drops down to Snake Pit Falls. The .75-mile, wooded, and hilly **Thimbleberry Nature Trail** follows the river west and heads toward a decaying sandstone quarry that dates from the late 1880s. A 1.5-mile **snowshoe trail** parallels the Thimbleberry Nature Trail west and loops beyond the quarry before dropping south and winding back around through the campground.

Your camera will get quite a workout at Amnicon. The park is home to otters, beavers, minks, porcupines, foxes, coyotes, and bears. Although extremely rare, you may even see a moose or timber wolf. More than 140 bird species have been noted here, such as ruffed grouse, turkey vultures, ducks, bald eagles, and ospreys. Of all the waterfalls, Snake Pit Falls seems to be the wildest, and the sounds of its waters will filter through even the thickest of earmuffs. A softer sound is the crunch of pine needles under your boots. *[See "Walking on Ice" sidebar.]* Stand on the bridge or either shore overlooking the falls, and try to get a photo of the tea-colored water during the sepia light of sunset.

EVENING

If you haven't had enough of Superior's famous ribs, catch a full or half rack at **Eddie's World Famous Ribs** on East Fourth Street. If steak is what you're looking for, try **Hammond Steak House** on North Fifth Street. Along with a special every night, Angus beef and prime rib are always on the menu.

Tonight, relax and watch as others play the winter sports. Watch 42-pound granite rocks slide down a 146-foot sheet of ice at the **Superior Curling Club** on the World Champion Bud Somerville Rink. Or catch a face-off at the **Wessman Arena**, home of the **UW–Superior Yellowjackets Hockey Team**, the 2002 NCAA National Champions.

Day Three
MORNING

This morning, rise for breakfast at **Corbin's Harbor Inn,** six miles east of Superior on Highway A. Breakfast is served all day here, so sleep in.

If the Brule River State Forest and Amnicon Falls State Park wowed you, wait until you see **Pattison State Park**, a short, 12-mile drive south of Superior. This absolute jewel-of-Wisconsin park covers 1,476 acres and features the thundering power and graceful lines of 165-foot **Big Manitou Falls**. Dropping over lava deposited a billion years ago, it's the highest waterfall in Wisconsin and the fourth highest east of the Rocky Mountains. The Black River, which bisects the park and runs the color of dark-red amber due to oxides in the soil, tumbles 31 feet over **Little Manitou Falls**, the state's eighth-tallest falls, in the southern end of the park. The Black River forms manmade **Interfalls Lake** before cascading over Big Manitou Falls.

Interfalls Lake is the result of a dam, first built by lumbermen in the 1890s. The Black River flows 22 miles toward Lake Superior from Black Lake along the Wisconsin–Minnesota border and was used to transport lumber. To avoid having their logs splinter and be ripped apart by tumbling over Big Manitou Falls, lumbermen built the dam just 50 yards in front of the cascading waters to act as a holding pen. The result is the 27-acre Interfalls Lake.

It's good to remember as you take in the natural beauty of Big Manitou Falls and its powerful roar that this gem was almost destroyed by a hydroelectric dam that was being planned for the Black River. To prevent that, Martin Pattison, a wealthy Superior business-man, secretly purchased 660 acres along the river in 1917 and donated it to the state for use as a park. The park opened in 1920. While Pattison made his fortune as a lumber baron, he later became successful in the mining and banking industries of Superior, and served as both mayor and sheriff. His 42-room Fairlawn Mansion is now a museum.

Classic **cross-country skiing** can be done in the park on the groomed and tracked 4.5-mile **Logging Camp Trail**. The trail leads to the quieter south end of the park, running alongside the river for much of the way. There are some minor hills, and you may find the remains of Pattison's logging camp on this trail.

For **winter hiking** or **snowshoeing**, the half-mile **Big Falls Hiking Trail** leaves the parking area not far from the shelter and nature center and brings you face-to-face with Big Manitou Falls. Trailing the west side of Interfalls Lake is three-mile **Little Falls Hiking Trail**, which will lead you to Little Manitou Falls. The two-mile **Beaver Slide Nature Trail** is considered an easy snowshoeing outing. Fifty-nine campsites are open year-round for **winter camping**.

While in the park, look for some of the 50 or so species of mammals, such as the rare timber wolf, bobcat or moose, and the more common bear, coyote, fox, deer, mink, beaver, or otter. Over the course of a year, 180 species of birds pass through Pattison State Park, including loons, ducks, bald eagles, and ospreys.

The Ojibwa and their ancestors believed they heard the Great Spirit's voice in the waterfalls. You may find your own spiritual meaning here.

AFTERNOON

If your schedule allows a little extra time in Superior this afternoon, there are two cultural icons you may want to check out.

After a sandwich or plate of pasta at **Grizzly's Grill N' Saloon** on Tower Avenue, head back to Highway 2 and 21st Street. Directly opposite Barkers Island stands **Fairlawn Mansion** museum, one of the most opulent mansions constructed during northwestern Wisconsin's boom days. Built in 1890, it was the home of lumber and iron-ore magnate Martin Pattison, later Superior's second mayor. The mansion is outfitted in a reconstruction of the period's lavish details, and the

At a height of 31 feet, Little Manitou Falls in Pattison State Park seems even more majestic with the addition of melting snow.

JOHN T. ANDREWS

upper floors are a time line of Superior's ethnography, lumber and shipping booms and busts, and mining tales. Pattison's wife, Grace, donated their extravagant home to the Superior Children's Home and Refuge upon his death. Two thousand children lived in Fairlawn between 1920 and 1962. If you're in Superior during December, don't miss **A Fairlawn Christmas** for a succinct way to take in the rich history of Superior.

The **Richard I. Bong World War II Heritage Center** on Harbor View Parkway is a fascinating World War II museum depicting Superior's role in the war effort and the adventures of Wisconsin's flying ace, Richard I. Bong.

By ending your weekend with these two down-to-earth heroes, your own rugged and elemental adventurous spirit may emerge.

JOHN T. ANDREWS

One of Superior's remaining ore docks is viewed at sunset from Wisconsin Point.

FOR MORE INFORMATION

SUPERIOR-DOUGLAS COUNTY CHAMBER OF COMMERCE
205 Belknap St., Superior, WI 54880
(715) 394-7716 or (800) 942-5313
www.superiorwi.net

WINTER ATTRACTIONS

AMNICON FALLS STATE PARK
Highway U near Highway 2, Superior, WI 54880
(715) 398-3000, www.wiparks.net

BRULE RIVER STATE FOREST
6250 S. Ranger Rd., Brule, WI 54820
(715) 372-5678, www.wiparks.net

FAIRLAWN MANSION
906 E. Second St., Superior, WI 54880
(715) 394-5712
www.superiorpublicmuseums.org

GANDY DANCER STATE TRAIL
Douglas County Forestry Department
PO Box 211, Solon Springs, WI 54873
(715) 378-2219
www.burnettcounty.com/tourism/dancer3.html

MONT DU LAC *(Friday 5:30–9:30 p.m;*
Saturday 10:00 a.m.–9:30 p.m.;
Sunday 10:00 a.m.–5:30 p.m.)
3125 Mont du Lac Dr., Superior, WI 54880
(218) 626-3797 or (888) 626-3797
www.skimontdulac.com

OSAUGIE WATERFRONT TRAIL
Superior-Douglas County Travel/Visitor Center
Richard I. Bong World War II Heritage Center
305 Harbor View Pkwy., Superior, WI 54880
www.superiortrails.com/superior.html

PATTISON STATE PARK
6294 Highway 35 South, Superior, WI 54880
(715) 399-3111, www.wiparks.net

RICHARD I. BONG WORLD WAR II HERITAGE CENTER
305 Harbor View Pkwy., Superior, WI 54880
(715) 392-7151 or (888) 816-9944
www.bongheritagecenter.org

SAUNDERS STATE TRAIL
Douglas County Forestry Department
PO Box 211, Solon Springs, WI 54873
(715) 378-2219
www.dnr.state.wi.us/org/land/parks/
specific/Saunders

SCHRIEBER OBSERVATORY
University of Wisconsin–Superior, Barstow Hall
1800 Grand Ave., Superior, WI 54880
(715) 394-8321
http://www2.uwsuper.edu/physics/observatory

SPIRIT MOUNTAIN
9500 Spirit Mountain Place, Duluth, MN 55810
(218) 628-2891 or (800) 642-6377
www.spiritmt.com

SUPERIOR CURLING CLUB
4700 Tower Ave., Superior, WI 54880
(715) 392-2022, www.superiorcurlingclub.com

SUPERIOR MUNICIPAL FOREST
28th St. and Wyoming Ave., Superior, WI 54880
(715) 395-7299, www.dnr.state.wi.us

UW–SUPERIOR YELLOWJACKETS HOCKEY TEAM
University of Wisconsin–Superior, Belknap St.
and Catlin Ave., PO Box 2000
Superior, WI 54880, (715) 395-4693
http://www.uwsuper.edu/athletics/mens/
hockey/index.asp

WESSMAN ARENA
University of Wisconsin–Superior
2701 Catlin Ave., Superior, WI 54880
(715) 394-8361

WISCONSIN POINT LIGHTHOUSE
Superior, WI 54880, (715) 394-7716 or
(800) 942-5313, www.superiorwi.net

WINTER FESTIVALS

A FAIRLAWN CHRISTMAS—month of December. Fairlawn Mansion and Museum. Tour the mansion when the main floor rooms are decorated in holiday finery. The first floor of this 1890 Queen Anne Victorian home has been authentically restored to its original elegance as the home of Martin and Grace Pattison. The sec-

ond floor includes the master suite, nursery, and family bedrooms much as they would have been furnished during the Pattisons' time. On the third floor, a permanent exhibit tells the story of the mansion's 42 years as the Superior Children's Home and Refuge. Guided tours leave from the gift shop on the hour, beginning at 9:00 a.m., with the last tour departing at 4:00 p.m. (715) 394-5712 or www.superiorpublicmuseums.org.

KORBEL INTERNATIONAL SHORT-ICE BROOMBALL TOURNAMENT—mid-January. Men's and women's broomball teams from Ontario, Wisconsin, and Minnesota compete on an outdoor rink. Goodsports Bar & Grill, 2827 Oakes Ave., Superior, WI 54880. (715) 392-2546 or www.biz-profiles.com/goodsports.htm.

SUPERIOR SKI CLASSIC—third weekend of January. Five hundred cross-country skiers gather for a 26-mile trek, a 9.3-mile freestyle, and a 9.3-mile classic in Superior, Wisconsin. Participants and spectators welcome. (800) 385-8842 or www.mzr.com/edu/att/annual.htm.

GREAT LAKES POND HOCKEY CHAMPIONSHIP—late January. Annual outdoor hockey tournament played by up to 60, four-person adult teams on 15 rinks. Barkers Island. (715) 394-4899 or www.sahaice.org.

JOHN BEARGREASE SLED DOG MARATHON—late January. One of the toughest trails in sled dog racing. The 375-mile course winds its way up the north shore of Lake Superior and into the primal wilderness along the Canadian border. John Beargrease, a Chippewa dog-driver from Beaver Bay, Minnesota, carried the U.S. mail to winter-isolated outposts along the north shore of Lake Superior as far as Grand Marais from 1887 to 1900. Admired for his persistence, John challenged weekly the rugged trails and shifting ice of Lake Superior, using his four dogs and sled, a rowboat, and backpack to maintain his schedule. The John Beargrease Sled Dog marathon commemorates his courage and endurance. More than 60 teams with 16 dogs each take part in this race. (218) 722-7631 or www.beargrease.com.

BRULE RIVER TIMBER CRUISE SKI RACE—mid-February. After Hours Ski at the Brule River State Forest. 10:00 a.m. A 9.9-mile and 19.8-mile freestyle cross-country ski race and a 9.9-mile classic cross-country ski race through the Brule River State Forest. (715) 372-5995 or www.brulexcski.com.

RIVER VIEW LOPPET SKI RACE—early March. Brule River State Forest. 10:00 a.m. A 7.4-

mile and 15.4-mile freestyle, and a 7.4-mile classic, and 3.1-mile youth cross-country ski race on the After Hours Ski Trail. (715) 372-5995 or www.brulexc ski.com.

RESTAURANTS

BREAKWATER WEST RESTAURANT
(breakfast, lunch, and dinner)
4927 E. Second St., Superior, WI 54880
(715) 398-7111

CORBIN'S HARBOR INN *(breakfast, lunch, and dinner)*
7804 S. County Road A, Superior, WI 54880
(715) 399-2581

EDDIE'S WORLD FAMOUS RIBS *(dinner)*
5221 E. Fourth St., Superior, WI 54880
(715) 398-0191

GALLEY RESTAURANT *(breakfast, lunch, and dinner)*
Barkers Island Inn & Conference Center
300 Marina Dr., Superior, WI, 54880
(715) 392-7152, www.barkersislandinn.com

GRIZZLY'S GRILL N' SALOON
(lunch and dinner)
3405 Tower Ave., Superior, WI 54880
(715) 392-5210, www.grizzlysgrill.com

HAMMOND STEAK HOUSE *(dinner)*
1402 N. Fifth St., Superior, WI 54880
(715) 392-5210
www.hammondliquor.com/steak.htm
OLD TOWN BAR & RESTAURANT

(lunch and dinner)
2215 E. Second St., Superior, WI 54880
(715) 398-7792

THE SHACK SMOKEHOUSE & GRILLE
(lunch and dinner)
3301 Belknap St., Superior, WI 54880
(715) 392-9836, www.shackonline.com

THE TWIN GABLES CAFÉ *(breakfast, lunch, and dinner)*
13992 E. Highway 2, Brule, WI 54820
(715) 372-4831

LODGING

BARKERS ISLAND INN & CONFERENCE CENTER
300 Marina Dr., Superior, WI 54880
(715) 392-7152 or (800) 344-7515
www.barkersislandinn.com

BEST WESTERN BAY WALK INN
1405 Susquehanna Ave., Superior, WI 54880
(715) 392-7600 or (800) 528-1234

DRIFTWOOD INN
2200 E. Second St. Superior, WI 54880
(715) 398-6661

Chapter Twenty
GETTING HIGH ON WISCONSIN
Wausau/Merrill

W AUSAU IS WATCHED OVER by a singular and stunning piece of geography: Rib Mountain. Once thought to be Wisconsin's highest peak, Rib Mountain actually ranks fourth. Timm's Hill in Price County (1,951.5 feet above sea level) is 27.5 feet higher, and Price County's Pearson Hill (1,950.8 feet) comes in second. The 1,938-foot-high Sugarbush Hill in Forest County is third. Still, perhaps because Wausau is the gateway to Wisconsin's North Woods and the last large city all the way up to Superior, Rib Mountain (1,924 feet) is impressive, rising 670 feet above the surrounding landscape. And Rib Mountain does stand higher above its terrain than any other hill in the state, making it number one in local relief.

Geologically known as a "monadnock," the quartzite Rib Mountain is more than a billion years old. It is thought that at one time, the rock formations that make up the backbone of the mountain were submerged below a sea. Pressures within the earth caused an upheaval, and Rib Mountain was formed. Local Native Americans called the protruding topographical features "ribs," which inspired the name of the 1,528-acre Rib Mountain State Park.

At Granite Peak Ski Area at Rib Mountain, you can swoosh down the longest vertical ski drop in Wisconsin (and the second longest in the Midwest), snowshoe on a groomed, woodland trail, or climb a 60-foot observation tower and look out over what could be the most spectacular view of Wisconsin from one of the oldest geological formations on earth.

About 20 miles northeast of Wausau in rural Marathon County is the secluded Dells of the Eau Claire County Park. This park includes a branch of the Ice Age National Scenic Trail, which awes snowshoers with paths through white and red pines, and maple and birch trees. Here, you'll pass by bluffs and frozen waterfalls that are breathtaking.

Wausau is the home of the Badger State Winter Games, and nearby Merrill hosts the Ice Drags for several weekends each winter. It's a safe bet that on this winter weekend, you'll be spending a lot of time outdoors. You can even ice-skate under the stars in Wausau's historic downtown area.

To many of the area's Native Americans, "Wausau" means "place from which you can see far." Stand atop Rib Mountain, and you'll know the reason for the name. This weekend, your energetic activities—and your elevation—will get you high on Wisconsin.

Day One
MORNING

Just south of Rib Mountain near the village of Rothschild and Schofield on Red Bud Road off Highway N is **Nine-Mile County Forest Recreation Area**, the site of the cross-country ski races of the Badger State Winter Games each February. Start your Wausau winter weekend at this 4,900-acre preserve and get energized. There are a lot of options for winter activities here, including **snowmobiling, snowshoeing, skate-skiing**, and **cross-country skiing** on 20.5 miles of well-groomed trails. The challenging terrain passes through some of the most scenic woods in all of Wisconsin: stretches of Black Creek and Four-Mile Creek, with spruce, oak, and pine trees. You can rent skis at the large, comfortable shelter and watch fellow skiers stride past the windows while enjoying a cup of hot chocolate or coffee. Almost four miles of the trails are lighted for nighttime-skiing challenges.

If your winter weekend falls on the first Saturday in January, attend the **Snekkevik Classic**, a classic cross-country ski race that is one of the oldest races in the Midwest. It was inspired by Asbjorn Snekkevik, a Norwegian who showed the people in Wausau in the early 1970s just how much fun cross-country skiing could be.

AFTERNOON

For a fun and unusual lunch experience, eat at the **Wausau Mine Co.** on Stewart Avenue. You'll be served in a kitschy mineshaft, complete with low lights and rocky walls. Look for Virgil, who keeps a permanent seat at the establishment's bar. Order the Italian fries— lightly fried flat breads that you dip in marinara sauce.

After lunch, check into your weekend accommodations. Wausau has a few cozy bed and breakfasts, several inns, and northern Wisconsin's largest indoor water park hotel, **The Lodge at Cedar Creek**. The lodge sports a sawmill theme, the perfect ambience for your sojourn on the edge of Wisconsin's great North

With 20 miles of groomed cross-country ski trails, Nine-Mile County Forest Recreation Area is a popular destination and boasts eight-foot-wide skating lanes with double tracks on all trails.

JOHN T. ANDREWS

THE BADGER STATE WINTER GAMES

Modeled after the Olympics, Wisconsin's Badger State Winter Games have become the largest winter sports festival in the United States. Over two decades old, the games operate under the philosophy that competitive opportunities should be open to all amateur athletes, regardless of age or skill level. The Winter Games take place predominantly in Wausau and north-central Wisconsin, but several communities throughout the state host events.

To participate in the games, you must have been a legal resident of Wisconsin for at least 30 days prior to the first day of competition. Each sport has a specific age requirement. No professional athlete is allowed to compete in the sport of his or her profession within one year of active professional competition, except in the sports categories of alpine skiing and figure skating.

Each year, the games host more than 22,000 athletes at some of Wisconsin's finest sports facilities, such as Granite Peak Ski Area at Rib Mountain in Wausau. Some Wisconsin athletes have used the Badger State Winter Games as a means to progress to the next level in their sport. Olympic speed skater Casey FitzRandolph, for example, grew up competing in the Badger State Games.

The Badger State Winter Games competitive sports include:

Alpine Skiing	Indoor Archery
Billiards (added in 2006)	Nordic Skiing
Bowling	Quadrathlon (run, mountain bike,
Curling	snowshoe, and cross-country ski)
Figure Skating	Ski Jumping
Freestyle Skiing	Snowboarding
Hockey (Adult)	Snowshoe Racing
Hockey (Youth)	Speed Skating

Woods. On a snowmobile trail and 10 minutes from Granite Peak Ski Area at Rib Mountain, your base of operations at The Lodge at Cedar Creek will be convenient and provide you with two queen beds, a microwave, refrigerator, coffee machine, gas fireplace, and separated bedroom and living-room areas.

Take a quick trip through the 50,000-square-foot water park to familiarize yourself with the slides and pools, and make plans for which ones you'll be trying out tonight.

EVENING

For a sophisticated dinner, try the **Back When Café**. Lamb, duck, and seafood are among the specialties, all prepared with fresh herbs. The café features live jazz on Fridays.

After dinner, stop at the **Fourth Street Ice Rink** at Fourth Street Square for some nighttime **ice-skating** under the lights. Don't worry if you forgot your ice skates—rentals are available at **Shepherd and Schaller Sporting Goods** on Scott Street. You may want to watch the **Wausau Curling Club** play at Marathon Park on Stewart Avenue or go back to the lodge for some watery thrills.

AN OLD SPORT: CURLING

Both the Scots and continental Europeans claim to be the origina-
tors of the sport of curling. Europeans point to the fact that in 1565,
Holland's Peter Breugel painted *Hunters in the Snow* and *Winter
Landscape with Skaters and a Birdtrap* that depict the game. The first
handwritten record, however, of what could be called an early curling
game is dated February 1540, when John McQuhin of Scotland wrote down, in Latin, a
challenge to a game on ice between a monk named John Sclater and a man named Gavin
Hamilton. Added to that, a curling stone, bearing the date of 1511, was unearthed near
Stirling, Scotland. Whatever the case, the Scots are generally recognized as the developers
of the modern game. By the mid-1800s, the Scottish Royal Caledonian Curling Club had
established curling's rules of play.

The game is played on sheets of ice 146 feet long and 14 feet wide, much like a bowling
alley. At either end are four concentric circles ranging from four feet to 12 feet in diameter,
which serve as targets called "houses." The object of the game is to position your stones
closest to a target's bulls-eye. Only those pieces nearer than any of your opponents' pieces
score points. Good curlers are adept at blocking their opponents' shots with their own
pieces, or knocking the other players' pieces out of scoring position.

The playing pieces are 16 stones, machine-flattened into thick, rounded disks about one
foot wide, four inches high, and weighing 42 pounds. A handle is bolted to the top of each,
which the player uses to spin the stone on release, either "inside" (counterclockwise) or
"outside" (clockwise), causing it to bend or "curl" in that direction.

The "skip," or captain, of each four-person team decides the order of play, calls for
inside or outside spin, depending on the position of the opponents' stones, and analyzes
the condition of the ice on each release. Machine-made rinks are "pebbled" with small
bumps to give the stone traction for curling.

When the curler throws his stone, his two teammates race ahead of it with brooms,
brushing the ice slightly in front of it, according to the skip's shouted instructions. If the
stone starts to lose velocity and begins to curl too early, the skip calls for furious sweeping
to maintain its pace; if a stone moves too fast to catch the pebbling, the skip calls the sweep-
ers off.

The Kay Bonspiel Company in Scotland manufactures all the granite stones used in the
sport. The granite used is virtually fault-free—minimizing the chance that the stones will
fracture if hit by another stone.

The United States Curling Association (USCA) was founded in 1958 and governs curling in this country. It has 131 member clubs in 11 regions. Curling debuted as a medal
sport in the 1998 Winter Olympic Games in Sapporo, Japan. About 1.5 million people in
more than 33 countries curl.

Day Two
MORNING AND AFTERNOON

Energy is what you'll need today as you choose from a wide variety of winter activities. Get
the morning started with breakfast in Schofield at the **Log Cabin Restaurant.** As the name
implies, everything about this eatery is log cabin-ish. Canoes decorate the walls, iron acorns

BIG AIR IN THE TERRAIN PARK

Considered somewhat of an "outlaw sport" just two decades ago, snowboarding has now gone mainstream. Once the exclusive domain of young men, snowboarding has become popular among women, children, and even grandparents. At some downhill ski areas, snowboarders have even begun to outnumber skiers.

A snowboard is a cross between an alpine ski and a surfboard. Like a ski, the tip and tail of a snowboard are wider than its middle, a design feature known as a "sidecut."

A snowboard works like an edged ski. When tilting the board to make a turn, you press the weight of your body against the board's center, and the board bends like a bow. The bending causes the board to carve an arced turn, as the steel edges of the board cut into the snow like a knife.

Snowboarding looks daunting at first, but usually after two or three runs, the single board will start to feel comfortable to classic skiers. The simplicity of the sport—no poles and less rigid boots—is addictive. And let's face it, snowboarders just look and sound cool, especially when the board swiftly cuts through the snow with a loud *swish*.

Here's a brief glossary of terms you'll need to know as a "noob" (new snowboarder):

❄ **TERRAIN PARK:** A place on the mountain where obstacles have been built to help snowboarders perform tricks. Terrain parks usually have jumps, pipes, and tabletops.

❄ **HALF-PIPE:** A channel built in the snow that resembles a pipe cut longitudinally. Half-pipes or pipes have consistent walls on both sides and are 100 to 400 feet long, with walls up to 20 feet high.

❄ **QUARTER-PIPE:** A channel with only one wall.

❄ **TABLETOP:** A mound of snow with the top sheared off, providing a flat surface for snowboarders to jump over.

❄ **BIG AIR:** When a snowboarder rides up the side of a pipe or jump, and goes airborne.

❄ **SHRED:** To tear up the terrain.

❄ **PLANK:** An older snowboard.

❄ **CORDUROY:** A freshly groomed trail with a finely ridged surface after a machine passes over it; an excellent condition for clean turns.

❄ **OLLIE:** The act of lifting the nose and tail of your board into the air at the same time.

---

adorn the hanging lamps, and a tall, faux-fieldstone fireplace dominates the dining room under a beamed ceiling. A fantastic, seven-foot, wood-and-brass clock festoons the mantle.

If you happen to be in Wausau during the **Badger State Winter Games** (late January and early February), don't miss the events taking place at several sites. Wisconsin's finest athletes compete in "the nation's largest Olympic-style winter sports festival" *[see "The Badger State Winter Games" sidebar]*. The games include **opening ceremonies, downhill and cross-country skiing, snowshoeing, snowboarding, ice hockey, curling** *[see "An Old Sport: Curling" sidebar]*, **ski jumping,** and **speed and figure skating.**

Four skiers begin their downhill run at Granite Peak Ski Area at Rib Mountain.

If you're a **downhill ski** enthusiast, spend the day at **Granite Peak Ski Area at Rib Mountain**. Formerly called Rib Mountain, Granite Peak is the closest thing to true mountain skiing in Wisconsin and the Midwest. It features 72 ski runs, some with 60- to 70-degree grades. Ski down **the highest skiable peak in Wisconsin and Michigan** (700-foot vertical drop) and enjoy freestyle runs. The area features state-of-the-art snow-making—with 500 snow guns—and a six-seat "Comet Express" lift, the longest and highest high-speed chairlift in the Midwest.

Granite Peak is also a popular spot for **snowboarders** *[see "Big Air in the Terrain Park" sidebar]*, with half-pipes, jumps, and various terrain features. This is the weekend for high energy: rent a board and give it a shot!

At the base of the mountain is the restored historic **10th Mountain Chalet**, named after a famous World War II elite army alpine division. Inside, you'll find two massive, two-story stone fireplaces, the Stone Hearth Eatery, Reindeer Coffee Bar, and the Bear's Den Saloon and Tavern, with microbrews, wine, and appetizers. Sit on the deck equipped with infrared heaters. At the Alpine Learning Center, you can arrange to take a ski lesson, and at the Mountain Rental Shop, you'll find 1,500 Salomon and Rossignol skis and snowboards. At the Peak Performance Demo and Tuning Center, you can try out the latest equipment or get your own skis tuned or sharpened. At the Granite Ski and Sports shop, you can purchase Salomon and Volkl skis.

Grab lunch at Granite Peak's **Sundance Chalet and Grill**. Claim your place next to one of the two large fireplaces or near the large floor-to-ceiling windows facing the slopes. Hot chocolate always tastes better when you can see a snowy scene outside.

If instead of downhill skiing or snowboarding you'd prefer to **winter hike, cross-country ski**, or **snowshoe, Rib Mountain State Park** will fit the bill for this afternoon—or for the whole day! The park covers 1,528 acres with a well-maintained network of trails, including the beautiful **White Birch Nature Trail** for winter hiking or snowshoeing. The steep and twisting **Yellow Trail** is also popular with snowshoers, where you lose and gain more than 500 feet of elevation. In fact, Rib Mountain State Park is one of the few in Wisconsin to provide trails—five miles of them—specifically for snowshoeing. During the Badger State Games, Rib Mountain is the site of the **Mountaineer Five-Mile Run/Tour**, one of the snowshoe events. In the early afternoon hours, the sun shines through the ice crystals on the trees, making your snowshoeing trek a journey through a magical winter landscape. Ice-covered rocks give off a silvery glaze at this time of day. Watch for animal tracks in the snow, and enjoy your closeness to nature.

The **Red, Blue, Green, and Gray winter hiking trails** all wind around the top of Rib Mountain and feature several overlooks. Don't forget to climb the 60-foot observation tower on the top of the mountain for one of the most spectacular and highest views in the state.

Part of the fun at the Merrill Ice Drags is arriving early and checking out the different vehicles and classes.

A don't-miss area event is held on every Saturday in January. Billed as the showcase for "The World's Best Drag Strip On Ice," the **Merrill Ice Drags**, a short 15 miles north of Wausau, pack a lot of excitement into one narrow patch of ice. A 1/8-mile lane is cleared of snow on frozen Lake Alexander at the boat landing in **Council Grounds State Park**. Stock car racers get a grip on the ice by starting from a dead stop at the beginning of the lane. The drivers rev their engines and they're off, sometimes reaching more than 100 miles per hour in seven seconds. Speeds of up to 135 miles per hour have been clocked. The Merrill Ice Draggers, Inc., is the only organized club in the world devoted strictly to ice dragging, and thousands of dollars in cash and prizes have been awarded over the years. Miss Wisconsin has even been known to show up for the excitement.

Even if you're not in Wausau during ice drags weekends, the 509-acre **Council Grounds State Park** is worth the trip. **Cross-country ski** on 7.2 miles of groomed trails in a heavily wooded area along the Wisconsin River. The density of pines gives you a sense of isolation. The two-mile **River Run Trail** leads along the 21-acre **Krueger Pines State Natural Area**, where old-growth white pines reach 125 feet tall. Watch steam rise off the water near the dam and circle around frozen pockets. Deer, foxes, badgers, and an occasional black bear are fellow woodsmen. **Ski-skating** is accommodated.

If you like motorized adventure, check out the **Burma Road Unit of Marathon County Forest** with 11 miles of logging roads that can be used for **ATVing**. Many of the snowmobile trails are open to ATV use as long as the temperature is below 29 degrees Fahrenheit and snow conditions are favorable. ATV trail information is included in the **Marathon County Snowmobile Trail Map**. More than 800 miles of **snowmobile** trails are found in Marathon County with some of the most scenic vistas in the state. The adventurous **Mountain Loop** goes 110 miles in and around Rib Mountain. **Ice fishing** is recommended on Lake Wausau, Half Moon Lake, Lake Du Bay, or the Eau Pleine Flowage.

EVENING

If you like grilling your own meat over open fires, **Hereford & Hops Steakhouse & Brew Pub** can accommodate you and provide you with lots of locally brewed beer as you cook. The pub was recently voted the "Best Place for a Good Time" and the "Best Place for Impressing Out-of-Town Guests" in a city survey. Or dine at the **Wagon Wheel,** a 50-year-old, rustic eatery known for its dry-aged steaks, barbecue ribs, and butterball tenderloin. They also serve bison and New Zealand venison. For dessert, indulge in the house specialty, flaming Irish coffee. Or relax with a glass of wine; *Wine Spectator* has favorably acknowledged the Wagon Wheel's wine cellar.

If all of your energy hasn't been expended yet today, go back to **Granite Peak Ski Area**

JOHN T. ANDREWS

A line of snow tubers are towed up Sylvan Hill, near downtown Wausau.

at Rib Mountain for **nighttime downhill skiing**—open until 9:00 p.m.—or **Nine-Mile County Forest Recreation Area** for **lighted cross-country skiing**.

Day Three
MORNING

Sleep late and savor a breakfast at your bed and breakfast or get in a last hour of play at the water park. Catch breakfast at the **Saw Mill Grill** in The Lodge at Cedar Creek. Settle in at a table in front of the large stone fireplace and take part in the brunch buffet. The photographs on the walls here will take you back to Wausau's early logging days.

Make sure you hit **Sylvan Hill Park** by noon for some serious **snow tubing**. Just north of downtown Wausau off Sixth Street, Sylvan Hill provides tubes for use in the park. Don't be frightened at the sight of the high hill—you'll be laughing all the way down. If Granite Peak proved a little too much for your particular alpine skills this weekend, Sylvan Hill has three runs, with a rope tow, for beginning **downhill skiers**. You can **cross-country ski** classically or skate-ski on four miles of groomed trails.

For more cross-country venues, choose from the hidden-away, classic-style, 3.7-mile **Ringle Trail** in the **Ringle Marsh County Forest Unit**, located on Poplar Lane off Highway 29 and County Road Q. Or try the remote **Big Eau Pleine County Park Trail**, 9.3 miles along a peninsula that juts into the Big Eau Pleine Reservoir. The trail is on a gently rolling moraine and is rife with wildlife. For **snowshoeing**, try the **Dells of the Eau Claire County Park**, about 15 miles northeast of Wausau on Highway Y. The Eau Claire River twists through the jagged rock formations here, and natural ice sculptures make spectacular scenes on the river's edge. A narrow, rocky gorge leads you through woodlands of hemlock, sugar maple, yellow birch, and mountain maple, making for one of the most scenic snowshoeing treks you'll find in the state.

There's one more stop you should make before leaving Wausau. Visit the **Leigh Yawkey Woodson Art Museum**, housed in a 1931 English Tudor mansion at Franklin and 12th Streets in

JOHN T. ANDREWS

At 1,924 feet, Rib Mountain is Wisconsin's fourth highest peak. The park's observation tower adds another 60 feet and some terrific views of the surrounding area.

Wausau. Admission is free. Probably best known for the fall "Birds in Art" juried exhibition—an international event—the museum's permanent collection celebrates nature with historic and contemporary artworks that focus on birds and art-in-nature and nature-in-art themes. Stroll through the galleries of wildlife oil paintings, watercolors, photographs, sculptures, and lithographs produced by naturalists such as John James Audubon, and John and Elizabeth Gould. It's almost like getting a bird's-eye view of the "place from which you can see far."

FOR MORE INFORMATION

WAUSAU/CENTRAL WISCONSIN CONVENTION & VISITORS BUREAU
10204 Park Plaza, Suite B , Mosinee, WI 54455
(715) 355-8788 or (888) WI-VISIT (948-4748)
www.visitwausau.com

WINTER ATTRACTIONS

BIG EAU PLEINE COUNTY PARK
3301 Eau Pleine Park Rd., Mosinee, WI 54455
(715) 261-1580
www.dnr.state.wi.us/org/land/er/sna/sna235.htm

BURMA ROAD UNIT OF MARATHON COUNTY FOREST
County Forestry Department, Courthouse
500 Forest St., Wausau, WI 54403
(715) 261-1583

COUNCIL GROUNDS STATE PARK
N1895 Council Grounds Dr., Merrill, WI 54452
(715) 536-8773, www.wiparks.net

DELLS OF THE EAU CLAIRE COUNTY PARK
P2150 Highway Y, Aniwa, WI 54408
(715) 261-1580
www.dnr.state.wi.us/org/land/er/sna/sna109.htm

FOURTH STREET ICE RINK
Located between Scott St. and Jefferson St.
(715) 355-8788 or (888) WI-VISIT (948-4748)

GRANITE PEAK SKI AREA AT RIB MOUNTAIN
3605 N. Mountain Rd., Wausau, WI 54402
(715) 845-2846, www.skigranitepeak.com

ICE-SKATING (INDOORS):
Greenheck Fieldhouse, 6400 Alderson St.,
  Schofield, WI 54476, (715) 359-6563
Marathon Park, 1201 Stewart Ave.,
  Wausau, WI 54401, (715) 261-1550
Mosinee Recreation Center, 701 11th St.,
  Mosinee 54455, (715) 693-3095

KRUEGER PINES STATE NATURAL AREA
Council Grounds State Park
N1895 Council Grounds Dr., Merrill, WI 54452
(715) 536-8773
www.dnr.state.wi.us/org/land/er/sna/sna20.htm

LEIGH YAWKEY WOODSON ART MUSEUM
700 N. 12th St., Wausau, WI 54403-5007
(715) 845-7010, www.lywam.org

MARATHON COUNTY SNOWMOBILE TRAILS INFORMATION
(715) 355-8788 or (888) 948-4748

NINE-MILE COUNTY FOREST RECREATION AREA
500 Forest St., Wausau, WI 54403
(715) 261-1550, www.co.marathon.wi.us

RIB MOUNTAIN STATE PARK
4200 Park Rd., Wausau, WI 54401
(888) 847-2527 or (715) 842-2522
www.wiparks.net

RINGLE MARSH COUNTY FOREST UNIT
Wausau and Marathon County Parks,
Recreation, and Forestry Department
212 River Dr., Suite 2, Wausau, WI 54403
(715) 261-1550, www.co.marathon.wi.us

SHEPHERD AND SCHALLER SPORTING GOODS
(snowshoe and ice skate rentals)
324 Scott St., Wausau, WI 54403, (715) 845-5432

SLEDDING HILLS (open as soon as snow cover permits; sunrise to 11:00 p.m. daily):
Pleasant View Park, 1221 Sumner St.
  Wausau, WI 54403, (715) 261-1550 (lighted hill)
Riverside Park, 100 Sherman St.
  Wausau, WI 54401, (715) 261-1550
Scholfield Park, 606 E. Randolph St.
  Wausau, WI 54401, (715) 261-1550
Schulenburg Park, 1533 Summit Dr.
  Wausau, WI 54401, (715) 261-1550 (lighted hill)
Three "M" Park, 405 Park Blvd.
  Wausau, WI 54401, (715) 261-1550 (lighted hill)

SYLVAN HILL PARK
1329 Sylvan St., Wausau, WI 54403
(715) 842-5411, www.co.marathon.wi.us

WAUSAU CURLING CLUB
1201 Stewart Ave., Wausau, WI 54401
(715) 842-3614

WINTER FESTIVALS

HMONG NEW YEAR CELEBRATION—early November. Folk music, traditional dance, ethnic foods, and displays. Greenheck Fieldhouse, 6400 Alderson St., Schofield, WI 54476. (715) 842-8390.

MERRILL HOLIDAY PARADE—early December. Sixty holiday floats, with Santa as the final guest. More than 50,000 lights will illuminate Merrill, a display that can be seen more than a mile away. (877) 907-2757 or www.merrillchamber.com.

WAUSAU HOLIDAY PARADE AND TREE LIGHTING—early December. More than 100 floats glide past downtown Wausau, with Santa in attendance. (715) 843-0748 or www.wausau area events.org.

COUNCIL GROUNDS STATE PARK CANDLE-LIGHT WALKS—late December. Walk a route lit with 400 candles, beginning at dusk. (715) 536-8773 or www.merrillchamber.com.

SNEKKEVIK CLASSIC—first Saturday in January. A classic cross-country ski race that is one of the oldest in the Midwest. Wausau Nordic Ski Club. (715) 355-8080.

MERRILL ICE DRAGS—every Saturday in January. Council Grounds State Park at noon. Dragsters, muscle cars, and trucks race on a 1/8-mile strip of ice on Lake Alexander. Speeds up to 135 mph are reached in under seven seconds. (877) 907-2757 or www.merrillicedrags.com.

PINE RIVER RUN SLED DOG RACES—mid-January. Merrill. More than 100 teams compete for cash prizes in these International Sled Dog Racing Association-sanctioned races. The weekend includes skijoring. (877) 907-2757.

CANDLELIGHT SNOWSHOE HIKES—mid-January and mid-February. Rib Mountain State Park. 6:00–8:30 p.m. (715) 842-2522.

BADGER STATE WINTER GAMES—late January and early February. Wausau area. Open to Wisconsin residents, this is the largest Olympic-style winter sports festival in the nation. (608) 226-4780 or www.badgerstategames.org.

SPECIAL OLYMPICS WISCONSIN WINTER GAMES—mid-February. This state championship competition challenges eligible Special Olympic athletes in cross-country skiing, alpine skiing, speed skating, snowboarding, and snowshoeing. (800) 552-1324 or (608) 222-1324.

RESTAURANTS

BACK WHEN CAFÉ (Friday and Saturday, lunch and dinner)
606 S. Third Ave., Wausau, WI 54401
(715) 848-5668

CARMELO'S ITALIAN RESTAURANT (dinner)
3607 N. Mountain Dr., Wausau, WI 54401
(715) 845-5570, www.foodspot.com/carmelos

GULLIVER'S LANDING (lunch and dinner)
1701 Mallard Ln., Wausau, WI 54401
(715) 849-8409
www.gulliverslanding.com

HEREFORD & HOPS STEAKHOUSE & BREW PUB (lunch and dinner)
2305 Sherman St., Wausau, WI 54401
(715) 849-3700

LOG CABIN RESTAURANT (breakfast, lunch, and dinner)
1522 Metro Dr., Schofield, WI 54476
(715) 359-3669

SAW MILL GRILL (breakfast, lunch, and dinner)
The Lodge at Cedar Creek Resort and Waterpark
805 Creske Ave., Mosinee, WI 54455
(715) 241-6300 or (888) 365-6343
www.lodgeatcedarcreek.com

THE STAGE STOP (breakfast, lunch, and dinner)
450 Orbiting Dr., Mosinee, WI 54455
(715) 693-1661

SUNDANCE CHALET AND GRILL (lunch and dinner)
Granite Peak Ski Area at Rib Mountain
3605 N. Mountain Rd., Wausau, WI 54402
(715) 845-2846, www.skigranitepeak.com

WAGON WHEEL (Friday and Saturday dinner)
3901 N. Sixth St., Wausau, WI 54403
(715) 675-2263

WAUSAU MINE CO. (lunch and dinner)
3904 Stewart Ave., Wausau, WI 54401
(715) 845-7304

LODGING

EVEREST INN BED AND BREAKFAST
601 McIndoe St., Wausau, WI 54403
(715) 848-5651 or (888) 848-5651
www.everestinn.com

THE LODGE AT CEDAR CREEK RESORT AND WATERPARK
805 Creske Ave., Mosinee, WI 54455
(715) 241-6300 or (888) 365-6343
www.lodgeatcedarcreek.com

RIB MOUNTAIN INN
2900 Rib Mountain Way, Wausau, WI 54401
(715) 848-2802 or (877) 960-8900
www.ribmtninn.com

ROSENBERRY INN BED AND BREAKFAST
511 Franklin St., Wausau, WI 54403
(715) 842-5733 or (800) 336-3799
www.rosenberryinn.com

STEWART INN BED AND BREAKFAST
521 Grant St., Wausau, WI 54403
(715) 849-5858, www.stewartinn.com

STONY CREEK INN
1100 Imperial Ave., Mosinee, WI 54455
(715) 355-6858 or (800) 659-2220
www.stonycreekinn.com

INDOOR WATER PARKS AND
FLAKE OUT FESTIVALS
Wisconsin Dells

F AT MAN'S MISERY, Witches' Gulch, and the Wonder Spot. Wisconsin Dells is widely known as the place with funny names attached to breathtaking natural phenomena. Many of those unusual names were assigned more than 150 years ago by sightseeing boat tour companies for the purpose of attracting visitors. Attract visitors they did: By the 1850s, rowboats were taking wealthy passengers up and down the river for a fee. By the 1870s, the first riverboats and steamships began carrying customers on the waters. Today, more than 2.5 million visitors come to the Dells each year, making it the Midwest's number-one family vacation destination. That has led to the building of more tourist attractions, and the end result is a town that blends spectacular Cambrian sandstone cliffs with amazing manmade wonders.

Recognized as the "Water Park Capital of the World," Wisconsin Dells is home to the largest indoor water parks in America. Thrill-ride slides, "lazy rivers," fountains, and "tipping buckets" have kept summer and winter tourists here happily occupied. But in the winter, the noisy arcades and frenetic businesses and shops quiet down, and the narrow Highway 12 business strip is navigable and small-town pleasant.

The biggest festival of the year in the Dells is held in the winter: January's Flake Out Festival. This three-day event features the state's only sanctioned snow-sculpting competition. Watching a large block of snow transform over a three-day period into an intricate and beautiful work of art is an experience in Wisconsin pride. Artists come from all over the state to compete. The festival is also host to a long list of celebratory winter activities, including "The Perfect Snow Slide," ice-carving demonstrations, mitten football, and more.

The area is also a rich source of pride for its Wisconsin Native American history. Indians of the Ho-Chunk (formerly Winnebago) Nation were the first inhabitants in this region, and the area is still flavored with that past in its lore, landmarks, and businesses. Attractions such as Parsons Indian Trading Post, with its Native American arts museum, reflect that past.

In the winter, a softer, gentler side of the Dells can be appreciated. You can still enjoy the

THE FATHER OF THE INDOOR WATER PARK
Provided by the Wisconsin Dells Visitor & Convention Bureau

Wisconsin Dells used to be a one-season destination: packed in the summer, barren in the winter. The indoor water park changed all that.

The roots of the indoor water park craze in the United States can be traced back to 1994 and a casual observation made by Stan Anderson, co-owner of the Polynesian Resort Hotel in Wisconsin Dells. Anderson was on a scouting trip to a Texas resort looking for ideas for new water attractions, accompanied by two other business partners, Tom Lucke and David Kaminski. Each owned additional properties with indoor swimming pools but felt the pool thing was getting to be ho-hum.

Anderson commented that one of the featured attractions at the Texas resort, called The Water Factory, might be a good fit for his resort, particularly with young families. It was an outdoor feature, but Anderson wondered whether he could put a roof over it as a way to extend the Dells' tourism season which, at that time, ran from Memorial Day to Labor Day. Not long after, construction began at the Polynesian for the first indoor water park, with The Water Factory as the main attraction. As Anderson notes, "It was successful beyond our dreams." The Polynesian was packed, even in the off-season. One year later, both the Wilderness Resort and Treasure Island water parks opened. A few years after that, Great Wolf Lodge expanded its offerings. In 2000, the Kalahari Resort opened and then quickly expanded its indoor water park. There was no turning back.

To put it all in perspective, in 1993 the local visitor bureau listed 1.6 million visitors. Today, that number is nearly double. The money spent by those visitors in what had been considered the off-season of September to May quadrupled. The Water Factory still stands in the Polynesian, and little ones still giggle when the sprays turn on. While it may seem tame by today's standards, it has a prominent place in local lore as the attraction that helped transform Wisconsin Dells into the "Water Park Capital of the World."

---

fun and boisterous indoor water parks, while having the relative solitude to take in its natural areas and participate in its best art festival. There are a lot of natural wonders and manmade beauties to be found, just under the watery kitsch and behind the funny names.

Day One
MØRNING

If you grew up anywhere in southern Wisconsin, you have memories of your younger self going to Wisconsin Dells every summer. Your parents probably started your family's visit downtown, hitting all of the touristy shops, and chances are you still have some childhood token with "Wisconsin Dells" written on it in gold lettering. One Wisconsin Dells shop that is worth rediscovering as an adult is **Parsons Indian Trading Post and Museum**.

This store/museum/artifact gallery is divided into two halves—the first is the "trading post" part where souvenirs, T-shirts, shoes, knickknacks, pottery, jewelry, and baskets line the walls. But behind some of the typical Dells merchandise, there are great finds, including

A tipping bucket drops almost 1,000 gallons of water on happy guests at the Great Wolf Lodge.

SUNDARA INN & SPA

Sundara Inn & Spa offers a heated outdoor pool that makes winter swimming possible.

wool Pendleton blankets. In the "museum" part of the store, Native American–made items are displayed in overflowing, antique-looking glass cases. Take time to let your eyes wander over the items from past and present.

The afternoon will require physical stamina (waterslides ahead!), so stop for lunch at **Moose Jaw Pizza & Brewing Company**. This locally owned and operated restaurant is Wisconsin Dells' only microbrewery. Amid the rustic North Woods decor under antler chandeliers, you can customize your own pizza or fill up on elk burgers. There are at least 10 microbrews, such as pale and raspberry ales, stouts, and pilsners. The dining room's huge, stone fireplace and framed reprints of covers of *Field & Stream* and *Outdoor Life* will get you ready for an afternoon on the slopes and down the slides!

AFTERNOON

Just four miles from downtown Wisconsin Dells is **Christmas Mountain Village**. At this year-round resort, you'll be able to **ski** down 11 runs and take one of two high-speed chairlifts, a rope tow, or handle tow back up. A new **snow-tubing** area has four tube chutes with a handle tow. Learn to **snowboard** with first-timer lessons, **ice-skate** on the pond, or **cross-country ski** on 6.2 miles of groomed trails. The rest area even includes a campfire.

After an active afternoon of downhill runs on snow, get ready for some downhill excitement on water. Wisconsin Dells has many indoor water park hotels; choose one and plan to spend the rest of your day all wet *[see "The Father of the Indoor Water Park" sidebar]*.

The **Great Wolf Lodge** has been a water park and hotel favorite since 1997. Popular with parents of young children for its ongoing, kids-only activities, it has the thrills to keep grownups delighted, as well.

Just about everything you see as you enter the Great Wolf lobby was handcrafted by Amish and Mennonite artisans from 10 different states. Look up: An artist from northern Wisconsin created the large elk and moose chandelier above you.

Wide and open hallways have room for four-top tables with chairs, where families and friends can play board games and cards while looking out the windows at the snow-covered, log-timber exterior. A 1998 certificate from Wolf Haven International hung near the massive fireplace in the lobby declares that "Great Wolf Lodge is helping to protect this wolf, *canis lupus,* known as Moose and is helping to protect the wolf in the wild."

All of the resort's 309 guestrooms, arranged on four floors, are suites. Various floor plans include a loft sleeping area, gas fireplace, bunk beds, or even a "wolf den" built into a

AN ARTIST'S TOOLS

When sculptor Jeffrey Olson wants to work big, he doesn't go for a block of bronze or terra cotta. He simply waits for cold temperatures and walks outside.

As a student at the University of Wisconsin-Superior in the 1960s, Jeff began competing in snow-sculpting contests for his fraternity during winter carnivals. After earning his master's degree in sculpting and painting, he was employed as an art teacher in the Oak Creek School District, where he remained for 35 years. He now runs the Hytte (Norwegian for "cabin") Art Gallery in Egg Harbor. But every year, he still looks forward to snow-sculpting season and working with one of his favorite mediums.

Olson and his teammates, Jim Malkowski and Dave Gass, have placed first in the Wisconsin Dells state snow-sculpting contest twice, have won first place in the National Snow Sculpting Competition in Lake Geneva, and were named the alternate demonstration team for the 1998 Winter Olympics in Japan. He's competed in states as far away as Maine.

"I keep a sketchbook all year," says Olson. "As I get ideas, I draw them out. When a competition comes up, I go through my designs, decide which one would best fit and submit that sketch with the entry form." From there, Olson makes a small model of the design in wax and casts it in pewter. "You can put a small model in your pocket; and while you're sculpting, you can reach in and get it, turn it around in your hand, and see all the different positions. When we would use larger models, we'd have to climb down from our ladders, walk around the model and climb back up. You can lose perspective that way," he says.

While most competitions provide snow sculptors with three hand tools—

Snow sculptors at the Flake Out Festival can get an amazing amount of detail in their creations with the simplest of tools.

an ice scrapper, a machete, and an axe—Olson says he's come to rely on five tools. "Primarily, we like to use a roofing shovel for roughing in. We've found that a roofing shovel (used for taking shingles off a roof) really cuts the snow with its jagged edges and roughs in fast. The second tool we started using on snow is an ice pick. We replace the handles on the picks with long poles, and they work great on getting down to the final finish. When we want to articulate details, the third tool we use is a wood chisel," he says.

During the final stage of sanding down, Olson uses truss fasteners and a damp drywall sponge. "You can bend the fasteners into different shapes, and they work nicely for rough sanding down. We used to use sandpaper, but the grit can get the piece dirty. I then wring out a damp drywall sponge, wipe the sculpture down, and the result is a very fine, smooth finish without soaking the snow and discoloring it."

Lately, Olson and his team have been trying to push the snow's limits by creating optical illusions. One recent artwork that he created in Chicago drew lots of attention. "We made a jungle gym, and snow children were hanging and climbing the bars," Olson explains. "People asked, 'How in the world can these thin ribbons of snow hold up all these kids?' Actually, it was the kids holding up the snow! One of the figures was hanging from the bars with her hands and hair hitting the ground, which was actually the column of snow that was supporting the bars."

Olson says his next step is to challenge himself to see how thin he can actually sculpt snow. "I've got an idea for a transparent piece," he says, which he'll debut next winter. "Snow sculpting is a fantastic sport; it's fun, it's an art. You don't get to work on such a large scale that often as an artist. If you were working in bronze or clay at this size, the cost of the materials would be horrendous. I get the fun of working monumentally—without having to shovel all that snow."

"cave." All have microwaves and refrigerators.

In the water park area, young children can play in an eight-inch pool surrounding a volcano that erupts every three to five minutes. A two-speed slide with an on-duty lifeguard, water-basketball pool, hair-braiding, and temporary tattoo stands keep older kids busy—along with a full snack bar serving pizza and subs. At Fort McKenzie, an overhead scaffolding, almost 1,000 gallons of water roar down from a tipping bucket every few minutes, drenching happy patrons waiting below.

The *pièce-de-résistance*, however, may be the Great Wolf's Howlin' Tornado, a six-story, extreme water-tubing ride with a 53-foot vertical drop. It is the first enclosed ride of its type in the world. Too big to fit inside the 64,000-square-foot indoor entertainment area, the Howlin' Tornado leads you up a heated, enclosed stairwell to the top of the giant funnel. On four-person rubber tubes, you'll swirl and twist back and forth across a 65-foot funnel, dropping 30 feet every second at 25 miles per hour. You'll eventually fall into a plunge pool back inside the indoor water park. Combine the Howlin' Tornado with 10 water slides, a 110,000-gallon indoor wave pool, the world's longest indoor lazy river, a family mat-race ride, and a four-story treehouse water fort, and you've got the evening covered.

Reserve accommodations at the Great Wolf Lodge in December, and you'll find the winter spirit has come indoors. The North Woods–style Grand Lobby is decorated from floor to ceiling with larger-than-life snowflakes, icicles, lights, wreaths, and Christmas trees in a month-long celebration called **Snowland**. It even "snows" indoors!

The Great Wolf also has a 65-game arcade with redemption tickets for prizes. In **Wiley's Woods**, you can play a two-hour, live video adventure in a 20,000-square-foot, four-story landscape. Lest you think this is just for the kids, corporations have even reserved Wiley's Woods for some team-building workshops.

JOHN T. ANDREWS

A snow sculpture begins to take shape as it rises into the January sky.

BUILDING A SNOWMAN

Okay, so maybe you're not ready for the Flake Out Festival snow-sculpting competition. But anyone can build a snowman—or snow-woman—with a little snow, time, and willingness to have some winter fun. Here's a step-by-step guide to get you started:

❉ **Make sure you have the right snow for the job.** Fresh, wet, packable snow works best. Wetter snow clumps together and sticks; firmer snow, although older, is a little easier to sculpt.

❉ **Scoop up a double handful of snow and make a ball.** Continue adding snow until the ball is too big to hold. Place it on the ground and slowly roll it away from you into more snow. As the snow accumulates on the ball, continue to pack it around the ball with your mittened hands. Keep rolling and packing until it's the size you want for the bottom third of the snowman's body.

❉ **Make two more balls for the snowman's midsection and head.** The second ball should be slightly smaller than the first. Place it on top of the first ball. Make the third ball smaller than the second ball, and place it on top of the second ball. Pack in handfuls of snow where the balls meet to cement them together.

❉ **Create the snowman's face.** The traditional carrot nose works well, or try using a banana. Anything round and dark will work for eyes: coal, rocks, pine cones. A horizontal or curved twig makes an expressive mouth.

❉ **Give your snowman a hat or hairdo that says something about his personality.** A knit hat, a scarf, a beret, an old plant, a carrot "Mohawk," pine boughs—you get the picture.

❉ **Add his arms and fashion accessories.** Push sticks into the sides of the midsection for arms. Hang mittens, gloves or boxing gloves on the ends. Pine cone buttons down his front will give him a well-dressed look.

Then be sure to take your winter visitor's photo, because he probably won't stay long.

EVENING

When your skin starts to turn prune-like from the water activities, make an appointment at the **Cameo Aveda Concept Spa/Salon** located inside the hotel, with six treatment rooms and more than a dozen massage selections.

If you'd like to stay inside the hotel tonight, there are several eating venues from which to choose. In the **Bear Claw Café**, find homemade pastries and a wide variety of sandwiches. In the **Loose Moose Bar & Grill**, try the "Slab-O-Ribs" or "Loose Moose Burger." Off premises, located on the Wisconsin Dells Parkway main strip, is the **Del-Bar** restaurant. In a Frank Lloyd Wright–influenced, prairie-style dining room, you'll learn why the Del-Bar has a reputation for excellent char-broiled steaks and delectable seafood.

MORNING

After breakfast at your water park hotel, plan to attend a festival of contemporary—and temporary—art!

The annual **Flake Out Festival** held at the La Crosse Street parking lot is the state's only

252

sanctioned snow-sculpting competition. The winner goes on to compete in the national competition in Lake Geneva, Wisconsin [see Chapter 13: The Resort Life, Winter Style (Lake Geneva/Delavan/Williams Bay)]. The contest usually garners national attention and has been covered on television news shows, such as *Good Morning America*.

On the festival grounds, you'll be able to stroll among the sculptors as they work [see *"An Artist's Tools" sidebar*] and take advantage of some unusual winter fun: mitten football—where you sit in an armchair rocker and throw a foam football through a cutout target—pony rides, hay-wagon rides, ice-sculpting demonstrations, snow tubing, hockey for kids, blacksmith demonstrations, Eskimo pie-eating contest, and kite flying. There is a heated warming tent, and food is available. The competition draws 30,000 visitors from around the Midwest, and everyone is eligible to vote for his or her favorite sculpture in the People's Choice award category [see *"Building a Snowman" sidebar*].

AFTERNOON

A few blocks down from the La Crosse Street parking lot is **Mexicali Rose** restaurant. Watch **ice fishermen** on the Wisconsin River from large dining room windows as you sip margaritas and enjoy a variety of authentic Mexican dishes.

This afternoon, you'll rediscover as an adult yet another facet to the Wisconsin Dells. From Broadway Street downtown, follow River Road north for two miles, where you'll find the **Dells of the Wisconsin River State Natural Area**. This is the quiet, natural side of Wisconsin Dells that is often misplaced in the summertime. Here on 1,300 acres, you can **snowshoe** through oak savannas and forests of hemlock, red oak, and white pine. You'll make new discoveries in this spectacular gorge, with tributary canyons, cliffs, and stellar Cambrian sandstone formations.

Snowshoers in the Dells aren't the only ones who have the opportunity to use winter modes of travel to access incredibly picturesque spots. There are 80 miles of well-groomed, scenic tails for **snowmobilers**. Horseback riders, too, can get to some hidden-away places. On Highway 82 just 15 minutes north of the Dells, **Red Ridge Ranch Riding Stable** offers one-hour, guided trail rides through 250 acres of farmlands and wooded hills along the Lemonweir River. Reservations are required, though, so call ahead. Closer to town, located between the Great Wolf Lodge and the Wilderness Resort on Hillman Road is **Canyon Creek Riding Stable,** which offers one-hour trail rides to Lost Canyon.

EVENING

Pecan-crusted walleye, king crab legs, and pork ribs hickory-smoked in a custom-designed smokehouse are on your menu tonight at the intimate and romantic **Wally's House of Embers** restaurant in Lake Delton. Don't leave without a helping of homemade dessert.

After dinner, head back downtown to enjoy **live music and fireworks at the Flake Out Festival**. Or, if you're sure your dinner has settled, take a spin on the Howlin' Tornado.

Day Three
MORNING

Co-workers on Monday will wonder why you look so good after your weekend in the Dells. The answer is: today's relaxed pace.

Start the day with a long, last look at the beautiful Wisconsin River. Have brunch at the **River Walk Pub & Restaurant** located on River Road. The pub serves homemade soups and sandwiches, along with Wollersheim wines *[see Chapter 2: A Natural WInter (Baraboo/ Prairie du Sac)]]*. Afterward, take the **Dells RiverWalk**, accessed outside the pub, and stop to photograph the pristine banks of snow along the Wisconsin River's edge.

There might not be a more picturesque spot in the state to ice fish than below the dam near downtown Wisconsin Dells.

AFTERNOON

Sundara Inn & Spa is one of the Dells' manmade wonders that manages to keep its focus on the natural world. Spending your last hours at Sundara is an excellent contrast to the active water park hotels and brings a nice balance to your weekend. And swimming outdoors in winter? It's an experience just too good to pass up.

The long, winding road that leads you to the main building of the spa was designed to set the tone for your visit here before you even enter the cork-lined lobby—meant to quiet loud sounds. Sundara was built with a commitment to the environment; in fact, it was recently named one of the Top 10 eco-spas by *USA Today*. In the last two years, the spa has been featured in magazines such as *National Geographic Traveler*, *Smart Money*, and *Midwest Living*.

Native plants have been placed strategically along the walk up to the red and earth-toned building, so that the only sound you hear is the swishing grasses blowing in the winter winds. Sundara also accommodates overnight guests, who can choose from a variety of suites designed by a *feng shui* consultant. The spa has no obvious restaurant or kitchen, which would cause too much clanging noise. Instead, guests can dine on organic food in their suites, by the pool, or in the rotunda. Buying just one service, such as a massage, will allow you to spend the whole day there.

Silent sports are encouraged at Sundara, such as **cross-country skiing** on the golf course next door, and **winter hiking** or **snowshoeing** on the grounds' forested 26 acres. You might even run into the wild turkeys that took up residence on top of the hill behind the spa or an occasional red fox.

One of most exquisite winter pleasures at Sundara is the outdoor pool. The stone deck has radiant heat, and the water is kept at 85 degrees. The smaller, hot pool is kept at 100 degrees. Steam rises from the hot waters into the cold air, creating a mystical environment. Even when the temperature drops to 20 below or in a light snowfall, you'll be warm.

Sundara in Sanskrit means "beautiful," and ending your Wisconsin Dells weekend here will make you feel that way and put you in a calm and relaxed state of mind. The spa is another side of the Dells you probably didn't know existed from your childhood memories. There's no kitsch here; just, perhaps, a funny-sounding name.

FOR MORE INFORMATION

WISCONSIN DELLS VISITOR & CONVENTION BUREAU
701 Superior St., Wisconsin Dells, WI 53965
(800) 223-3557, www.wisdells.com

WINTER ATTRACTIONS

CAMEO AVEDA CONCEPT SPA/SALON
Great Wolf Lodge, 1400 Great Wolf Dr.,
Wisconsin Dells, WI 53965, (800) 559-9653
www.greatwolflodge.com

CANYON CREEK RIDING STABLE
60 Hillman Rd., Wisconsin Dells, WI 53965
(608) 253-6942, www.dells.com/horses.html

CHRISTMAS MOUNTAIN VILLAGE
S944 Christmas Mountain Rd., Wisconsin Dells,
WI 53965, (608) 254-3971
www.christmasmountainvillage.com

DELLS OF THE WISCONSIN RIVER STATE NATURAL AREA
Wisconsin Department of Natural Resources
101 S. Webster St., Madison, WI 53703
(608) 266-2621, www.dnr.state.wi.us/org/land/
er/sna/sna283.htm

PARSONS INDIAN TRADING POST AND MUSEUM
370 Wisconsin Dells Pkwy.
Wisconsin Dells, WI 53965, (608) 254-8533

RED RIDGE RANCH RIDING STABLE
W4881 State Road 82, Mauston, WI 53948
(608) 847-2273 or (888) 847-2272
www.redridgeranch.com

SUNDARA INN & SPA
920 Canyon Rd., Wisconsin Dells, WI 53965
(608) 253-9200 or (888) 735-8181
www.sundaraspa.com

WILEY'S WOODS
1400 Great Wolf Dr., Wisconsin Dells, WI 53965,
(800) 559-9653, www.wileyswoods.com

WINTER FESTIVALS

SNOWLAND—month of December. Great Wolf Lodge. A family celebration with holiday carol sing-alongs in the lobby, door-decorating contest, Writing Depot where children can write, decorate, and send letters directly to Santa, and Secret Santa Station where kids can make gifts. On December 31, you can ring in the New Year at the Snowball, with dancing, children's activities, a grand buffet, and final countdown with party favors and streamers. (800) 559-9653 or www.greatwolf lodge.com.

FLAKE OUT FESTIVAL—mid-January. Annual winter festival that includes Wisconsin's only state-sanctioned snow-sculpting competition. Ice-carving demonstrations, kite flying, mitten football, sledding hill, Eskimo pie-eating contest, fireworks, food, music, wagon rides, and pony rides. La Crosse Street parking lot downtown. (800) 223-3557 or www.wisdells.com.

CHRISTMAS MOUNTAIN VILLAGE WINTER CARNIVAL—early February. This annual winter carnival has the nation's largest sanctioned sled dog weight-pull. Dogsled races, chili cook-off, wood-splitting contest, live entertainment, fireworks, and more. (608) 254-3971 or www. christmasmountainvillage.com

RESTAURANTS

THE CHEESE FACTORY RESTAURANT *(lunch and dinner)*
521 Wisconsin Dells Pkwy.
Wisconsin Dells, WI 53965, (608) 253-6065
www.cookingvegetarian.com

DEL-BAR *(dinner)*
800 Wisconsin Dells Pkwy.
Wisconsin Dells, WI 53965, (608) 253-1861
or (866) 888-1861, www.del-bar.com

MEXICALI ROSE *(lunch on weekends; dinner daily)*
195 Highway 13 *(corner of Highways 12 and 13)*
Wisconsin Dells, WI 53965
(608) 254-6036

MOOSE JAW PIZZA & BREWING COMPANY
(lunch and dinner)
110 Wisconsin Dells Pkwy. South, Wisconsin Dells,
WI 53965, (608) 254-1122
www.moosejawbrewpub.com

PEDRO'S MEXICAN RESTAURANT
(lunch and dinner)
951 Stand Rock Rd., Wisconsin Dells, WI 53965
(608) 253-7233, www.pedrosmexican.com

RIVER WALK PUB & RESTAURANT *(lunch
and dinner; Sunday brunch)*
911 River Rd., Wisconsin Dells, WI 53965
(608) 254-8215

SARENTO'S ITALIAN RESTAURANT *(dinner)*
The Wilderness Hotel & Golf Resort
441 Wisconsin Dells Pkwy. (Highway 12) Wisconsin
Dells, WI 53965
(608) 253-3300, www.sarentosrestaurant.com

WALLY'S HOUSE OF EMBERS *(dinner)*
935 Wisconsin Dells Pkwy.
Lake Delton, WI 53940, (608) 253-6411
www.houseofembers.com

LODGING

BENNETT HOUSE BED & BREAKFAST
825 Oak St., Wisconsin Dells, WI 53965
(608) 254-2500, www.historicbennetthouse.com

GREAT WOLF LODGE
1400 Great Wolf Dr., Wisconsin Dells, WI 53965
(800) 559-9653, www.greatwolflodge.com

KALAHARI RESORT–WISCONSIN DELLS
1305 Kalahari Dr., Wisconsin Dells, WI 53965
(608) 254-5466 or (877) 525-2427
www.kalahariresort.com

POLYNESIAN RESORT HOTEL
857 N. Frontage Rd.
Wisconsin Dells, WI 54965, (608) 254-2883
or (800) 272-5642, www.dellspolynesian.com

TREASURE ISLAND WATER PARK RESORT
1701 Wisconsin Dells Pkwy.
Lake Delton, WI 53940, (608) 254-8560
or (800) 800-4997
www.wisdellstreasureisland.com

THE WHITE ROSE BED & BREAKFAST
910 River Rd., Wisconsin Dells, WI 53965
(608) 254-4724 or (800) 482-4724
www.thewhiterose.com

WILDERNESS HOTEL & GOLF RESORT
511 E. Adams St., Wisconsin Dells, WI 53965
(800) 867-9453, www.wildernessresort.com

**WINTERGREEN RESORT &
CONFERENCE CENTER**
60 Gasser Rd., Wisconsin Dells, WI 53965
(608) 254-2285 or (800) 648-4765
www.wintergreen-resort.com

APPENDIX

ACTIVITIES BY LOCATION	X-CTY SKIING	DH SKIING	SNOWSHOE	WINTER HIKE	SNOWBOARD	SLEIGH RIDE	SLEDDING	ICE SKATING	ICE FISHING	SNOWMOBILE	WINTER CAMP	DOG SLED
Appleton (Chapter 1)	X		X	X			X	X	X			
Baileys Harbor (Chapter 6)	X		X	X					X			
Baraboo (Chapter 2)	X		X	X			X	X	X	X	X	
Bayfield (Chapter 3)	X	X	X	X	X			X	X	X		X
Belgium (Chapter 4)	X									X		
Brule (Chapter 19)	X		X							X		
Cable (Chapter 10)	X		X		X	X	X	X		X		
Campbellsport (Chapter 11)	X			X			X			X	X	
Cedarburg (Chapter 4)	X			X				X				
Chippewa Falls (Chapter 8)	X		X	X				X	X	X	X	
Coon Valley (Chapter 12)	X											
Delafield (Chapter 16)	X		X	X			X	X			X	X
Delavan (Chapter 13)	X			X		X				X		
Dodgeville (Chapter 5)	X		X	X			X	X	X	X	X	
Door County (Chapter 6)	X		X	X			X	X	X	X	X	
Eagle River (Chapter 7)	X		X							X		
East Troy (Chapter 13)		X			X							
Eau Claire (Chapter 8)			X	X		X						
Ellison Bay (Chapter 6)	X		X	X							X	

ACTIVITIES BY LOCATION

	X-CTY SKIING	DH SKIING	SNOWSHOE	WINTER HIKE	SNOWBOARD	SLEIGH RIDE	SLEDDING	ICE SKATING	ICE FISHING	SNOWMOBILE	WINTER CAMP	DOG SLED
Fall Creek (Chapter 8)	X		X	X							X	
Fish Creek (Chapter 6)	X		X	X			X		X	X	X	
Green Bay (Chapter 6)	X		X	X								
Green Lake (Chapter 9)	X		X	X			X	X	X	X		
Hales Corners (Chapter 16)	X			X			X	X				
Hayward (Chapter 10)	X		X									
Kaukauna (Chapter 1)	X		X	X								
Kohler (Chapter 11)	X		X	X		X						
La Crosse (Chapter 12)	X	X	X	X	X	X		X	X	X		
Lake Geneva (Chapter 13)	X	X	X	X	X	X	X	X	X	X		
Madeline Island (Chapter 3)	X		X	X							X	
Madison (Chapter 14)	X		X	X			X	X	X	X		
Manitowoc (Chapter 15)	X			X			X	X		X		
Menasha (Chapter 1)			X	X								
Menomonie (Chapter 8)	X											
Merrill (Chapter 20)	X											
Merrimac (Chapter 2)	X	X		X	X		X	X				
Milwaukee (Chapter 16)	X		X				X	X	X			
Minocqua (Chapter 17)	X		X					X		X		

Location	1	2	3	4	5	6	7	8	9	10	11
Mount Horeb (Chapter 14)	X	X						X		X	X
Mt. Morris (Chapter 9)	X	X						X		X	
Neenah (Chapter 1)						X					
New Glarus (Chapter 5)	X	X						X		X	
Newburg (Chapter 4)	X							X			
Port Washington (Chapter 4)								X			
Portage (Chapter 2)		X	X					X			
Prairie du Chien (Chapter 18)	X	X				X		X		X	X
Princeton (Chapter 9)	X	X		X		X				X	
Sayner (Chapter 7)	X	X				X					
Sheboygan (Chapter 11)	X	X					X	X		X	X
Sister Bay (Chapter 6)						X				X	
Sonlon Springs (Chapter 19)	X	X								X	
Sturgeon Bay (Chapter 6)	X	X					X	X		X	X
Superior (Chapter 19)	X	X	X					X		X	X
Two Rivers (Chapter 15)	X	X						X		X	X
Washburn (Chapter 3)	X	X						X		X	
Wausau (Chapter 20)	X	X					X	X		X	X
Westby (Chapter 12)						X		X		X	
Williams Bay (Chapter 13)		X									
Wisconsin Dells (Chapter 21)	X	X				X		X		X	X
Woodruff (Chapter 17)	X	X				X		X		X	X

259

INDEX